P9-DNU-676

Equal Protection

EQUAL PROTECTION

*Rights and Liberties
under the Law*

FRANCIS GRAHAM LEE

ABC ⬥ CLIO

Santa Barbara, California • Denver, Colorado • Oxford, England

Library of Congress Cataloging-in-Publication Data
Lee, Francis Graham.
   Equal protection : rights and liberties under the law / Francis Graham
Lee.
      p.   cm. — (America's freedoms)
Includes bibliographical references and index.
   ISBN 1-57607-850-7 (hardcover : alk. paper) ISBN 1-57607-851-5 (e-book)
   1. Discrimination—Law and legislation—United States. 2. Equality
before the law—United States. 3. Discrimination—Law and
legislation—United States—Cases. 4. Equality before the law—United
States—Cases.   I. Title. II. Series.
KF4755.L438 2003
342.7308'5—dc22

                                                                        2003020751

07 06 05 04 03 10 9 8 7 6 5 4 3 2 1

ABC-CLIO, Inc.
130 Cremona Drive, P.O. Box 1911
Santa Barbara, California 93116-1911
This book is printed on acid-free paper.
Manufactured in the United States of America

*To the memory of
Frank X. Gerrity,
who taught by example the value of
being a good colleague and friend*

Contents

SERIES FOREWORD

America's Freedoms promises a series of books that address the origin, development, meaning, and future of the nation's fundamental liberties, as well as the individuals, circumstances, and events that have shaped them. These freedoms are chiefly enshrined explicitly or implicitly in the Bill of Rights and other amendments to the Constitution of the United States and have much to do with the quality of life Americans enjoy. Without them, America would be a far different place in which to live. Oddly enough, however, the Constitution was drafted and signed in Philadelphia in 1787 without a bill of rights. That was an afterthought, emerging only after a debate among the foremost political minds of the day.

At the time, Thomas Jefferson was in France on a diplomatic mission. Upon receiving a copy of the proposed Constitution from his friend James Madison, who had helped write the document, Jefferson let him know as fast as the slow sailing-ship mails of the day allowed that the new plan of government suffered one major defect—it lacked a bill of rights. This, Jefferson argued, "is what the people are entitled to against every government on earth." Madison should not have been surprised at Jefferson's reaction. The Declaration of Independence of 1776 had largely been Jefferson's handiwork, including its core statement of principle:

We hold these truths to be self-evident, that all men are created equal, that they are endowed by their Creator with certain unalienable Rights, that among these are Life, Liberty, and the pursuit of Happiness. That to secure these rights, Governments are instituted among Men, deriving their just powers from the consent of the governed.

Jefferson rejected the conclusion of many of the framers that the Constitution's design—a system of both separation of powers among the legislative, executive, and judicial branches, and a federal division of powers between national and state governments—would safeguard liberty. Even when combined with elections, he believed strongly that such structural checks would fall short.

Jefferson and other critics of the proposed Constitution ultimately had their way. In one of the first items of business in the First Congress in 1789, Madison, as a member of the House of Representatives from Virginia, introduced amendments to protect liberty. Ten were ratified by 1791 and have become known as the Bill of Rights.

America's Bill of Rights reflects the founding generation's understanding of the necessary link between personal freedom and representative government, as well as their experience with threats to liberty. The First Amendment protects expression—in speech, press, assembly, petition, and religion—and guards against a union of church and state. The Second Amendment secures liberty against national tyranny by affirming the self-defense of the states. Members of state-authorized local militia—citizens primarily, soldiers occasionally—retained a right to bear arms. The ban in the Third Amendment on forcibly quartering troops in houses reflects the emphasis the framers placed on the integrity and sanctity of the home.

Other provisions in the Fourth, Fifth, Sixth, Seventh, and Eighth Amendments safeguard freedom by setting forth standards that government must follow in administering the law, especially regarding persons accused of crimes. The framers knew firsthand the dangers that government-as-prosecutor could pose to liberty. Even today, authoritarian regimes in other lands routinely use the tools of law enforcement—arrests, searches, detentions, as well as trials—to squelch peaceful political opposition. Limits in the Bill of Rights on crime-fighting powers thus help maintain democracy by demanding a high level of legal scrutiny of the government's practices.

In addition, one clause in the Fifth Amendment forbids the taking of private property for public use without paying the owner just compensation and thereby limits the power of eminent domain, the authority to seize a person's property. Along with taxation and conscription, eminent domain is one of the most awesome powers any government can possess.

The Ninth Amendment makes sure that the listing of some rights does not imply that others necessarily have been abandoned. If the Ninth Amendment offered reassurances to the people, the Tenth Amendment was designed to reassure the states that they or the people retained those powers not delegated to the national government. Today, the Tenth Amendment is a reminder of the integral role states play in the federal plan of union that the Constitution ordained.

Despite this legacy of freedom, however, we Americans today sometimes wonder about the origin, development, meaning, and future of our liberties. This concern is entirely understandable, because liberty is central to the idea of what it means *to be American.* In this way, the United States stands apart from virtually every other nation on earth. Other countries typically define their national identities through a common ethnicity, origin, ancestral bond, religion, or history. But none of these accounts for the American identity. In terms of ethnicity, ancestry, and religion, the United States is the most diverse place on earth. From the beginning, America has been a land of immigrants. Neither is there a single historical experience to which all current citizens can directly relate: someone who arrived a decade ago from, say, Southeast Asia and was naturalized as a citizen only last year is just as much an American as someone whose forebears served in General George Washington's army at Valley Forge during the American War of Independence (1776–1783). In religious as in political affairs, the United States has been a beacon to those suffering oppression abroad: "the last, best hope of earth," Abraham Lincoln said. So, the American identity is ideological. It consists of faith in the value and importance of liberty for each individual.

Nonetheless, a long-standing consensus among Americans on the *principle* that individual liberty is essential, highly prized, and widely shared hardly assures agreement about liberty *in practice*. This is because the concept of liberty, as it has developed in the United States, has several dimensions.

First, there is an unavoidable tension between liberty and restraint. Liberty means freedom: we say that a person has a "right" to do this or that. But that *right* is meaningless unless there is a corresponding *duty* on the part of others (such as police officers and elected officials) not to interfere. Thus, protection of the liberty of one person necessarily involves restraints imposed on someone else. This is why we speak of a *civil* right or a *civil* liberty: it is a claim on the behavior of another that is enforceable through the legal process. Moreover, some degree of order (restrictions on the behavior of all) is necessary if everyone's liberties are to be protected. Just as too much order crushes freedom, too little invites social chaos that also threatens freedom. Determining the proper balance between freedom and order, however, is more easily sought than found. "To make a government requires no great prudence," declared English statesman and political philosopher Edmund Burke in 1790. "Settle the seat of power; teach obedience; and the work is done. To give freedom is still more easy. It is not necessary to guide; it only requires to let go the rein. But to form a *free government;*

that is, to temper together these opposite elements of liberty and restraint in one consistent work, requires much thought; deep reflection; a sagacious, powerful, and combining mind."

Second, the Constitution does not define the freedoms that it protects. Chief Justice John Marshall once acknowledged that the Constitution was a document "of enumeration, and not of definition." There are, for example, lists of the powers of Congress in Article I, or the rights of individuals in the Bill of Rights, but those powers and limitations are not explained. What is the "freedom of speech" that the First Amendment guarantees? What are "unreasonable searches and seizures" that are proscribed by the Fourth Amendment? What is the "due process of law" secured by both the Fifth and Fourteenth Amendments? Reasonable people, all of whom favor individual liberty, can arrive at very different answers to these questions.

A third dimension—breadth—is closely related to the second. How widely shared is a particular freedom? Consider voting, for example. One could write a political history of the United States by cataloging the efforts to extend the vote or franchise to groups such as women and nonwhites that had been previously excluded. Or consider the First Amendment's freedom of speech. Does it include the expression of *all* points of view or merely *some?* Does the same amendment's protection of the "free exercise of religion" include all faiths, even obscure ones that may seem weird or even irritating? At different times questions like these have yielded different answers.

Similarly, the historical record contains notorious lapses. Despite all the safeguards that are supposed to shore up freedom's foundations, constitutional protections have sometimes been worth the least when they have been desperately needed. In our history the most frequent and often the most serious threats to freedom have come not from people intent on throwing the Bill of Rights away outright but from well-meaning people who find the Bill of Rights a temporary bother, standing in the way of some objective they want to reach.

There is also a question that dates to the very beginning of American government under the Constitution. Does the Constitution protect rights not spelled out in, or fairly implied by, the words of the document? The answer to that question largely depends on what a person concludes about the source of rights. One tradition, reflected in the Declaration of Independence, asserts that rights predate government and that government's chief duty is to protect the rights that everyone naturally possesses. Thus, if the Constitution is read as a document designed, among other things, to protect liberty, then protected liberties are not limited to those in the text of the Constitution but may also be derived from experience, for example, or from one's assessment of the requirements of a free society. This tradition places a lot of discretion in the hands of judges, because in the American political system, it is largely the judiciary that decides what the Constitution means. Partly due to this dynamic, a competing tradition looks to the text of the Constitution, as well as to statutes passed consistent with the Constitution, as a *complete* code of law containing *all* the liberties that Americans possess. Judges, therefore, are not free to go outside the text to "discover" rights that the people, through the process of lawmaking and constitutional amendment, have not declared. Doing so is undemocratic because it bypasses "rule by the people." The tension between these two ways of thinking explains the ongoing debate about a right to privacy, itself nowhere mentioned in the words of the Constitution. "I like my privacy as well as the next one," once admitted Justice Hugo Black, "but I am nevertheless compelled to admit that government has a right to invade it unless prohibited by some specific constitutional provision." Otherwise, he said, judges are forced "to determine what is or is not constitutional on the basis of their own appraisal of what laws are unwise or unnecessary." Black thought that was the job of elected legislators who would answer to the people.

Fifth, it is often forgotten that at the outset, and for many years afterward, the Bill of Rights applied only to the national government, not to the states. Except for a very few restrictions, such as those in section 10 of Article I in the main body of the Constitution, which expressly limited state power, states were restrained only by their individual constitutions and state laws, not by the U.S. Bill of Rights. So, Pennsylvania or any other state, for example, could shut down a newspaper or barricade the doors of a church without violating the First Amendment. For many in the founding generation, the new central government loomed as a colossus that might threaten liberty. Few at that time thought that individual freedom needed *national* protection against *state* invasions of the rights of the people.

The first step in removing this double standard came with ratification of the Fourteenth Amendment after the Civil War in 1868. Section 1 contained majestic, but undefined, checks on states: "*No State* shall make or enforce any law which shall abridge the privileges or immunities of citizens of the United States; nor shall any *State* deprive any person of life, liberty, or property, without due process of law; nor deny to any person with in its jurisdiction the equal protections of the laws" (emphasis added). Such vague language begged for interpretation. In a series of cases mainly between 1920 and 1968, the Supreme Court construed the Fourteenth Amendment to include within its meaning almost every provision of the Bill of Rights. This process of "incorporation" (applying the Bill of Rights to the states by way of the Fourteenth Amendment) was the second step in eliminating the double standard of 1791. State and local governments became bound by the same restrictions that had applied all along to the national government. The consequences of this development scarcely can be exaggerated because most governmental action in the United States is the work of state and local governments. For instance, ordinary citizens are far more likely to encounter a local police officer than an agent of the Federal Bureau of Investigation or the Secret Service.

A sixth dimension reflects an irony. A society premised on individual freedom assumes not only the worth of each person but citizens capable of rational thought, considered judgment, and measured actions. Otherwise democratic government would be futile. Yet, we lodge the most important freedoms in the Constitution precisely because we want to give those freedoms extra protection. "The very purpose of a Bill of Rights was to . . . place [certain subjects] beyond the reach of majorities and officials and to establish them as legal principles to be applied by the courts," explained Justice Robert H. Jackson. "One's right to life, liberty, and property, to free speech, a free press, freedom of worship and assembly, and other fundamental rights may not be submitted to vote; they depend on the outcome of no elections." Jackson referred to a hard lesson learned from experience: basic rights require extra protection because they are fragile. On occasion, people have been willing to violate the freedoms of others. That reality demanded a written constitution.

This irony reflects the changing nature of a bill of rights in history. Americans did not invent the idea of a bill of rights in 1791. Instead it drew from and was inspired by colonial documents such as the Pennsylvania colony's Charter of Liberties (1701) and the English Bill of Rights (1689), Petition of Right (1628), and Magna Carta (1215). However, these early and often unsuccessful attempts to limit government power were devices to protect the many (the people) from the few (the English Crown). With the emergence of democratic political systems in the eighteenth century, however, political power shifted from the few to the many. The right to rule belonged to the person who received the most votes in an election, not necessarily to the firstborn, the wealthiest, or the most physically powerful. So the focus of a bill of rights had to shift too. No longer was it designed to shelter the majority from the minority, but to shelter the minority from the majority. "Wherever the real power in a Government lies, there is the danger of oppression," commented Madison in his exchange of letters with Jefferson in 1788. "In our Government, the real power lies in the majority of the Community, and the invasion of private rights is *chiefly* to be apprehended, not from acts of government contrary to the sense of its constituents, but from acts in which the Government is the mere instrument of the major number of the Constituents."

Americans, however, do deserve credit for having discovered a way to enforce a bill of rights. Without an enforcement mechanism, a bill of rights is no more than a list of aspirations: standards to aim for, but with no redress other than violent protest or revolution. Indeed this had been the experience in England with which the framers were thoroughly familiar. Thanks to judicial review—the authority courts in the United States possess to invalidate actions taken by the other branches of government that, in the judges' view, conflict with the Constitution—the provisions in the Bill of Rights and other constitutionally protected liberties became judicially enforceable.

Judicial review was a tradition that was beginning to emerge in the states on a small scale in the 1780s and 1790s and that would blossom in the U.S. Supreme Court in the nineteenth and twentieth centuries. "In the arguments in favor of a declaration of rights," Jefferson presciently told Madison in the late winter of 1789 after the Constitution had been ratified, "you omit one which has great weight with me, the legal check which it puts into the hands of the judiciary." This is the reason why each of the volumes in this series focuses extensively on judicial decisions. Liberties have largely been defined by judges in the context of deciding cases in situations where individuals thought the power of government extended too far.

Designed to help democracy protect itself, the Constitution ultimately needs the support of those—the majority—who endure its restraints. Without sufficient support among the people, its freedoms rest on a weak foundation. The earnest hope of *America's Freedoms* is that this series will offer Americans a renewed appreciation and understanding of their heritage of liberty.

Yet there would be no series on America's freedoms without the interest and support of Alicia Merritt at ABC-CLIO. The series was her idea. She approached me originally about the series and was very adept at overcoming my initial hesitations as series editor. She not only helped me shape the particular topics that the series would include but also guided me toward prospective authors. As a result, the topic of each book has been matched with the most appropriate person as author. The goal in each instance as been to pair topics with authors who are recognized teachers and scholars in their field. The results have been gratifying. A series editor could hardly wish for authors who have been more cooperative, helpful, and accommodating.

Donald Grier Stephenson, Jr.

PREFACE

Justice Felix Frankfurter once observed that many of our liberties had been won as a result of cases brought by "not very nice people." Certainly this was true in many of the Warren Court's criminal procedure decisions. Ernesto Miranda surely was not one of his community's outstanding citizens. The plaintiffs in many of the Court's First Amendment cases have also frequently been either unsavory characters, such as some of the merchants of obscenity or the loud-mouthed racists whose hate-filled sermons bring condemnation on them more than any court could ever do. However, the same generally cannot be said of the individuals who have brought suit claiming violations of their guarantee under the Fourteenth Amendment to the equal protection of the laws.

Linda Brown and Alan Bakke surely fall into the category of "nice people." Linda was the oldest of three daughters of Oliver Brown. Brown worked for the railroad as a welder, and the family was relatively comfortable by the standards of the day. Linda's school, the Monroe School, was located about a mile from the Brown home. Brown walked to and from school, and on the way she passed the Sumner School, which by law was reserved for white children, just as the Monroe School was reserved for blacks.

Before the start of the school year, the Topeka school authorities sent a registration form to the Brown house for enrollment of students into the Sumner School. Oliver Brown filled it out for Linda, who would be entering the third grade. When her registration was refused, Oliver Brown went to the local office of the National Association for the Advancement of Colored People (NAACP) to complain. Brown was the perfect plaintiff. "Thirty-two years old in 1951, he was a lifelong resident of Topeka and a World War II veteran. . . . [In addition to his job with] the Santa Fe Railroad . . . [he] served as an assistant pastor and sexton of a local Methodist church. . . . There was no way that segregationists could paint Oliver Brown as a dangerous radical" (Patterson 2001, 34). The NAACP had decided in 1930 that the only way to bring change in a heavily segregated society was to turn to the courts. By the late 1930s, under the leadership of former Howard University Law School Dean Charles Hamilton Houston and one of his former students, Thurgood Marshall, this approach had become a carefully crafted strategy that was beginning to bring results. The United States Supreme Court and even the occasional state court in a border state were beginning to look more skeptically at practices that had been in place since the "separate but equal" decision in *Plessy v. Ferguson* in 1896.

Oliver Brown had come to the Topeka office at the right time. Two 1950 Supreme Court decisions involving postgraduate education had emboldened Marshall and his colleagues at the NAACP's Legal Defense Fund to try to convert the victories in graduate and law school cases into a triumph that would end all segregation in education. Early on they had concluded that if the equality promised to all by the Declaration of Independence, if the equality for blacks in particular that the freedom amendments were supposed to have secured, if the glaring inequalities between blacks and whites in America were to be erased, education was the key.

As the Supreme Court has interpreted it, the Constitution's grant of jurisdiction in Article III to "cases or controversies" requires, among other things, that there be an actual claimant who alleges that he or she has suffered some injury. The Court declared early on that it would not issue advisory opinions, a practice many contemporary state courts routinely engage in. Therefore, to challenge the various ways in which blacks were discriminated against in educational opportunities, the NAACP had to have people who had actually felt the bite of segregation. In those areas where segregation was seen as part of the culture and a means to enforce the superiority of whites, challenging such laws was an act of great courage. The fact that Congress had never passed an antilynching law was not because the practice had ended in the South. Blacks who did not know their place were routinely subjected to a variety of vigilante actions, ranging from killings and beatings to having their homes burned, their credit at local stores stopped, and being fired from their jobs.

At the 1951 trial challenging Topeka's refusal to admit Linda Brown to the Sumner School, only Oliver Brown from the Brown house testified. In fact, Linda did not even attend. Her father wanted to protect her as much possible from the limelight that he feared the case would draw.

Jack Greenburg, who would later head up the NAACP's Legal Defense Fund, was in charge of the case. With a sympathetic court, Greenburg was able to introduce evidence that emphasized not the differences in the facilities—in fact, the NAACP's strategy entailed emphasizing how equal they were—but rather how segregation adversely affected the ability of the black children to learn. Although the judge ruled against Brown, the decision made clear that he agreed with the facts presented by the witnesses Greenburg and the other NAACP lawyers had called. Much of his opinion would be quoted by Chief Justice Earl Warren when he delivered the Court's opinion in 1954. For the lower court judge, the precedent of *Plessy* could be set aside only by the institution that had saddled the American courts with it in the first place, the U.S. Supreme Court.

As a result of the suit, Linda Brown was admitted to the Sumner School, although she never attended. In the fall of 1954, she entered the junior high school, which had not been segregated (Patterson 2001, 242, n. 16). Resistance to the Court's decision was much less in a border state such as Kansas than it would prove to be in those states that had seceded from the Union and formed the Confederate States of America. By the 1970s, Brown had two daughters who attended schools that were two-thirds white. Most blacks who went to public schools in Topeka, however, attended schools that were overwhelmingly black, and in the 1990s a suit was filed charging that the Topeka schools were segregated.

Alan Bakke grew up in Minnesota. His father was a mailman and his mother a teacher. He attended the University of Minnesota and received a degree in engineering, graduating with an average slightly under an A. In order to finance his education, he had joined the Navy Reserve Officers' Training Corps (ROTC). After graduation, he moved to California, where he worked as an engineer and earned a master's degree at Stanford. He was married and the father of three children.

Although these facts would seem to point to a person whose career and lifestyle were pretty well set, Bakke was not sure. He had a dream, which was to attend medical school and become a physician. He set about taking the prerequisite courses for medical school that he had not taken as an undergraduate. He also did volunteer work in a hospital. In 1973, at age thirty-three, he applied to twelve medical schools. He was rejected by all of them. He applied again the following year (Sindler 1978, 63–78).

He applied both times to the medical school at the University of California at Davis. Bakke found out that Davis had a special program that allocated sixteen seats at the medical school to minorities and that none of the minority students admitted had undergraduate grades or scores on the Medical College Admission Test (MCAT) as high as his. Bakke sued. Five years after he initiated his suit in the state courts of California, the U.S. Supreme Court ruled that the Davis admissions system contravened the guarantee of equal protection. At age thirty-eight, in 1978, Alan Bakke finally began medical school.

More than one author has called race the "American dilemma" (Myrdal 1944). A better description, perhaps, is that race is America's "tar baby." Like the tar baby in the story of Uncle Remus, race is something from which neither America nor Americans can seem to extricate themselves. No sooner do they deal with one aspect of the "American dilemma" than they find themselves stuck on another part of it. Having come to a consensus that state-mandated segregation is unacceptable, for example, they found themselves again divided, this time on the question of whether equal protection mandates integration, and, more specifically, court-ordered busing to achieve racial balance in public schools. When the busing controversy subsided, America found itself stuck on another limb of the racial "tar baby," the contemporary and, at least for now, apparently intractable issue of affirmative action, which first entered the Court's docket with the *Bakke* case. Very likely when affirmative action moves from the scene, another race-related issue—reparations for slavery, perhaps—is apt to enmesh Americans.

Obviously, the dreadful legacy of slavery is the major factor in making race the "American dilemma." It is unlikely, however, that it is the only cause of the failure of the American people to put the issue of race behind them. The great value Americans place on equality may very well be a complicating factor. The frequently forgotten subtitle of Gunnar Myrdal's 1944 classic *An American Dilemma* is *The Negro Problem and Modern Democracy*. Both the United Kingdom and Canada, each long-standing democratic polities, generally could not, at least until very recently, be categorized as democracies that placed great emphasis on the value of equality. Possibly as a result, both countries appear to have had fewer problems than America in dealing with race or ethnicity. For instance, no matter how heated the debate over Québec's role in the Canadian confederation becomes, the dramatic strides the federal government has taken to increase the numbers of francophones in the federal bureaucracy has not become nearly the significant and divisive political issue that race frequently has been in the United States. The differences in voting patterns that sharply distinguish black and white Americans are greater than those between French- and English-speaking Canadians.

Is it possible that the emphasis American society places on equality makes it even more difficult for Americans to deal with the legacy of slavery? The contradiction between Thomas Jefferson's proclamation in the Declaration of Independence that "all men are created equal" and the existence of slavery may typify the tension American society faces in its attempts to deal with race.

Jefferson's proclamation of equality has sounded through the decades as a first principle of American politics. Although the Constitution of 1787 and the amendments added to it in 1791, the Bill of Rights, make no mention of the concept, equality as an underlying value of the American political culture has had a powerful life of its own. From the Jeffersonian Democratic-Republican Party's infatuation with the French Revolution's proclamation of *"liberté, égalité, et fraternité"* to the Jacksonian era's expansion of the right to vote and development of the now familiar American long ballot, to the current debates on education and health care, equality has been seen as the fundamental value of American society.

Abraham Lincoln's Gettysburg Address, delivered in 1863 in the midst of the country's bloodiest war, reconsecrated the nation to the principles of the Declaration by dating America's founding not to the first Continental Congress in 1774, nor to the government under the ill-fated Articles of Confederation of 1781, nor even to the Constitution of 1789, but rather "four score and seven years ago," establishing forever the 1776 Declaration of Independence as the beginning. The Constitution, what one New England participant at the Philadelphia convention in 1787 had called a "pact with the devil" because of its silent condoning of slavery, was hardly a popular document in the 1860s, at least among those who supported Abraham Lincoln's vision of America. Chief Justice Roger Taney's decision in *Dred Scott v. Sandford* (1857), struck down the Missouri Compromise as an unconstitutional limitation on the right of "a citizen from holding and owning property" and held that African Americans were "a subordinate and inferior class of beings . . . and, whether emancipated or not . . . had no rights or privileges but such as those who held the power and the Government might choose to grant them." The decision quickly erased whatever prestige the federal judiciary had earned under the leadership of Chief Justice John Marshall and under Taney's own leadership during the previous two decades. The Court's efforts under Taney to rein in what it saw as unconstitutional exercise of power by Lincoln during the Civil War added to the diminution of respect for both the Court and the Constitution among those who sought to hold the Union together.

Although the abolition of slavery had not originally been the driving force for Lincoln's prosecution of the war, the cost in property and especially in lives almost required the evocation of some goal nobler than simply the preservation of the Union. The Emancipation Proclamation of 1863 did that even though it had little if any effect on the condition of slaves, since it applied only to states or areas still in rebellion, areas over which, by definition, the government of the United States exercised no power.

The Union victory led to a spate of measures that were designed to deal with the condition of the slave class. The Thirteenth Amendment, which abolished slavery, was quickly adopted in December 1865, just over eight months after Robert E. Lee's surrender at the Appomattox Courthouse. Its adoption mooted any continuing concern about the legality of the Emancipation Proclamation. The remaining two post–Civil War amendments, sometimes referred to as the "freedom amendments," attempted to improve further the status of the newly freed slaves. Like the Thirteenth, the Fourteenth and Fifteenth Amendments also expanded the power of the federal government by providing that Congress had the power to enforce the provisions of the amendment through appropriate legislation, thereby helping place the postwar Reconstruction legislation on firmer constitutional footing. Whereas the Fifteenth Amendment was phrased specifically in terms of protecting the newly freed slaves' right to vote, the language of the Fourteenth Amendment, which provides to persons the guarantees of due process and equal protection of the laws, is not as clear in its purpose. Does it protect only rights denied "on account of race, color, or previous condition of servitude," as the Fifteenth Amendment is phrased, or do its protections extend to other classes of persons subject to classification by government?

Even today, a person who reads the Thirteenth or the Fifteenth Amendment would realize from their words that they applied particularly to the race that had been enslaved. The language of the Fourteenth, however, is different. The sections of the Amendment that deal with how the former rebels are to be treated is clear, but these sections have little relevance to contemporary America. Probing the meaning of the Fourteenth Amendment's due process guarantee is beyond the scope of this book. What equal protection of the laws means, however, is central to this volume.

It was not a coincidence that as Congress was drafting and proposing the Thirteenth, Fourteenth, and Fifteenth Amendments, others outside Congress were pushing to expand the suffrage—the right to vote—to women. Just as Jefferson's language in the Declaration must have stirred some unease among slaveholders and, perhaps, lit small fires of hope in the breasts of some slaves, before the Civil War the abolitionist movement marched somewhat in tandem with the movement for women's rights. The fact that the Fourteenth Amendment introduced into the Constitution, for the first time, what contemporary Americans would describe as gender-specific language—Section 2 of the Fourteenth Amendment provides that "when the right to vote . . . is denied to any of the male inhabitants . . . the basis of representation therein shall be reduced in the proportion which the number of such male citizens shall bear to the whole number of male citizens twenty-one years of age in such State"—was to draw a wedge between the two groups that formerly had seemed to work together, abolitionists and suffragettes.

The adoption of the Nineteenth Amendment in 1920, which guaranteed women the right to vote, occurred during the third great period of constitutional amendments. The first period saw the adoption of the Bill of Rights and the Eleventh and Twelfth Amendments, the latter clearing up functional problems in the system not foreseen by the framers of the Constitution. The second period produced the three postwar amendments just discussed. It also may be argued that the second period included the failed Blaine Amendment, which would have specifically denied states the power to fund religious schools while at the same time guaranteeing the constitutionality of Bible reading in the public schools. The Nineteenth Amendment was part of the Progressive Era, which also saw passage of the amendments allowing the federal income tax (the Sixteenth) and direct election of senators (the Seventeenth), both in 1913, and the 1920 Prohibition Amendment (the Eighteenth). A failed amendment during this period, one of only three amendments proposed by Congress not to be ratified by the states, was the Child Labor Amendment. The most recent spate of amendment activity produced the Twenty-third Amendment in 1961, giving the vote for presidential electors to residents of the District of Columbia, the Twenty-fourth, which abolished poll taxes (1964), the Twenty-fifth, which provided for a declaration of presidential disability and the ability to fill the office of vice president were it to become vacant (1967), and the Twenty-sixth, which extended the vote to eighteen-year-olds (1971). This period also witnessed Congress's proposing to the states an Equal Rights Amendment (ERA), which failed to gain the necessary ratifications from three-quarters of the states despite Congress's controversial extension of the time period during which states could ratify.

The civil rights movement of the 1960s and the women's movement of the 1970s succeeded not only in achieving many of these groups' objectives but also triggered demands for equality and for equal protection by other segments of American society that saw themselves as the recipients of less than their just slice of the American pie. The poor, those born outside marriage (illegitimates), the handicapped, and homosexuals all have seized on the concept of equality and the Constitution's guarantees of equal protection to advance their particular agendas, agendas that they claim are as rightfully theirs as any of the rights that other American enjoy.

Chapter 1 of this book examines the issue of segregation and how the Supreme Court and society addressed this particular "badge of slavery." Chapter 2 focuses on two of the more troublesome issues involving the "American dilemma," busing and affirmative action. Chapter 3 looks at the issue of gender and the myriad of other claims for equal protection advanced in the courts by other groups that believe they have been discriminated against.

Although the quest for equality clearly provides the theme for this book, another theme runs through these pages to which the reader should be attentive, namely, the role the Court plays in American society. From the time of the framing of the Constitution to the present day, what should be the proper role of the federal judiciary has been debated. Also controversial has been the issue of how the Constitution is to be interpreted by the judges who staff these courts. Advocates of different positions have invoked concepts such as judicial activism and judicial self-restraint, interpretism, noninterpretism, and literalism as well as original intent and the need to ensure that the Constitution reflects the values of contemporary society. As we begin the twenty-first century, my own conclusion is that it is time to realize that the Court is as much a political institution as the other two branches of government. The politicization of the nomination and confirmation process, I believe, will only serve to make judges less likely to play what some once thought was their proper role, "disembodied spirits."

In accepting that judges have political agendas that color their reading of the Constitution, I am not suggesting that such a role dooms democracy in America. As the authors of *The Federalist* realized, the Court is the weakest of the three branches of government. Its success in wielding power and in increasing its power depends more than either of the other two branches of government on its ability to persuade. A simple grab for "raw judicial power" will not long serve the Court well. Chief Justice Earl Warren, who came to the Court after a long and successful career in politics, understood this better than most. Those who bring less of what Warren had much of need to be careful as they exercise judicial power.

In this vein, the cases discussed in the following three chapters will frequently be examined not only in terms of how they reflect the values or the text of the Constitution but also how they represent the success or failure of their authors to win support from the public and the other two branches of government for what the Court has announced as the "law of the land."

Francis Graham Lee

REFERENCES

Myrdal, Gunnar. 1944. *An American Dilemma: The Negro Problem and Modern Democracy*. New York: Harper.

Patterson, James T. 2001. Brown v. Board of Education: *A Civil Rights Milestone and Its Troubled Legacy.* New York: Oxford University Press.

Sindler, Allan P. 1978. Bakke, DeFunis, *and Minority Admissions.* New York: Longman.

1

INTRODUCTION

THE LONG ROAD FROM
SLAVERY TO INTEGRATION

No case has better captured for the American public the role of the Supreme Court of the United States than *Brown v. Board of Education of Topeka, Kansas* (1954). Not only does *Brown* easily rank among the Court's most recognized opinions—*Miranda v. Arizona* (1966), given the plethora of cops-and-robbers shows on television today, may be as well known—but *Brown* served to alter the image the Court held in American life, particularly among the group of Americans who can be styled opinion makers.

Brown transformed the Court. Almost overnight, Chief Justice Earl Warren's opinion laid to rest the ghosts that had haunted the Court in the 1940s and had hobbled its role in reviewing the actions of other government actors, at both the national and the state level. Almost at once, the Court shed its image of an institution that acted to block change. The Court was now recognized instead as the institution that could prod the other branches of government and the broader public to make or at least to consider change. That this change came in a case that involved race is more than a little ironic.

The irony arises from the fact that it was the Supreme Court that had used its power of judicial review—the power Chief Justice John Marshall had originally asserted in *Marbury v. Madison* (1803)—both to solidify the inferior status generally accorded to members of the African race in America and to strike down those efforts by the other branches of government, most often the Congress, to improve the lot of African Americans.

Compromising with the Devil

Richard Kluger, in his monumental study of the *Brown* decision, has characterized slavery as it existed in the United States as a crueler and more severe form of the institution than in any other country. It was America's "original sin" (Kluger 1975, 32). Although Africans were brought as slaves to other countries in the Western Hemisphere—to Latin America and especially to Brazil—slavery never had the hold on those lands in the particular way that it did in what were first the southern colonies and then the southern states. In the Latin countries, the plantation class never had the power that it achieved in what would become the United States, both before and after the Declaration of Independence. In the Portuguese and Spanish colonies, the power of the plantation owners was checked at times by that of the interests of the Crown or of the Church. In contrast to the "open system" that existed in societies in which people could and did move from the slave sector to the free sector, America developed what Stanley Elkins has characterized as a "closed system" from which slaves could not escape (Elkins 1976, 81–82). The Court for much of its history helped preserve this closed system, not only during the period in which slavery was legal but also after its abolition by the Thirteenth Amendment.

The power of the slave-owning class was exercised in the drafting of two key political documents of eighteenth-century America, the Declaration of Independence and the Constitution. Commentators regularly note the paradox between the Declaration's proud commitment to the principle that "all men are created equal" and the fact that its chief author, Thomas Jefferson, was a slave owner who, despite apparent misgivings about slavery throughout his life, never freed or manumitted his slaves. Less often do they note that Jefferson's original draft of the Declaration had listed the role of the British government in the slave trade as yet another item in the litany of charges laid against King George III in the Declaration of Independence. The Crown's alleged role in the slave trade was, in Jefferson's original version, part of "a History of repeated Injuries and Usurpations, all having in direct Object the Establishment of an Absolute Tyranny. . . ." Southern opposition forced Jefferson to delete it from the final version that we celebrate every Fourth of July.

The issue of slavery loomed even larger over the Constitutional Convention that convened in Philadelphia in the summer of 1787. As every student knows, two issues threatened to frustrate those who had come to Philadelphia "to form a more perfect Union." The matter of representation was the first issue that threatened to derail James Madison's carefully crafted plan to establish a stronger federal government. The demand by the small states for equal representation in the proposed Congress produced the "Great Compromise," the deal by which representation in the House of Representatives would be based on population, whereas in the Senate each state, regardless of population, would have equal representation in the form of two senators.

The issue of slavery was the other matter that endangered the success of the convention of 1787. The compromise on slavery paradoxically produced no mention of what Abraham Lincoln would later dub "the peculiar institution" itself but resulted in no fewer than five clauses in the Constitution that were designed to protect slavery. Abolitionists of the 1850s were generally united in their conclusion that far from representing a compromise, it was a sellout to the "slavocracy," an "agreement with Hell," according to William Lloyd Garrison.

Article I, Section 2 of the Constitution contains the famous Three-Fifths Clause. This section represented a compromise between, on the one hand, the demands of the delegates from the slave-holding states that slaves be counted the same as free persons in determining the number of representatives in the House and, on the other hand, the position of northerners that slaves should not be counted at all. The result was language that provided that "representation . . . shall be determined by adding to the whole Number of free Persons, including those bound in Service for a Term of Years [indentured servants], and excluding Indians not taxed, three fifths of all other Persons." The phrase "other persons" referred, of course, to slaves.

Section 9 of Article I contains two more provisions on slavery that also avoided any mention of the term. The better-known one dealt with Congress's potential power under the Commerce Clause in Article I, Section 8 to prohibit the slave trade. As with the previous matter of representation, the language is wonderfully oblique: "The Migration or Importation of such Persons as any of the States now existing shall think proper to admit, shall not be prohibited by Congress prior to the Year one thousand eight hundred and eight. . . ." The fourth clause of Section 9 also limited the taxes that could be levied on slaves.

Article V deals generally with the procedures by which the Constitution can be amended. As part of these procedures, however, Article V stipulated that no constitutional amendment could be adopted prior to 1808 that would either speed up the date at which time Congress could end the slave trade or alter the Three-Fifths Clause. Article V's provision that the Constitution could be amended only by a two-thirds vote of both houses of Congress and that ratification entailed approval by three-quarters of the states can also be seen as a further guarantee that the status quo relative to slavery could not be easily changed.

Finally, Section 2 of Article IV, which guarantees that "the Citizens of each State shall be entitled to all Privileges and Immunities of Citizens of the several States," also contained a clause mandating that "No Person held to Service or Labour in one State, under the Laws thereof, escaping into another, shall, in Consequence of any Law or Regulation therein, be discharged from such Service or Labour, but shall be delivered up on Claim of the Party to whom such Service or Labour may be due."

Charles Cotesworth Pinckney, a delegate from South Carolina and the leader of the proslavery forces at the Constitutional Convention, advocating South Carolina's ratification of the Constitution, assured the members of the state's legislature that "we have a security that the general government can never emancipate them, for no such authority is granted, and it is admitted on all hands, that the general government has no powers but what are expressly granted by the constitution; and that all rights not expressed were reserved by the several states" (Finkelman 1992, 792). A delegate from New England, coming to a similar conclusion about the effects of the Constitution, ruefully admitted that by signing the Constitution he had made "a pact with the devil."

The division between states with large populations and those with small populations ended with the convention. Delaware, one of the smallest states, was the first to ratify the Constitution, and the schism seems never again to have been a factor in American politics. By contrast, the issue of slavery continued to bedevil the American political scene until the end of the Civil War. Its abolition, however, seems only to have resulted in the substitution of race as a dividing and troubling force in American politics for the older issue of slavery. Its impact on American political behavior has proved more durable than any of the other fault lines that have appeared over the years in American society. Neither religion nor social class, for example, has affected American society as long or as deeply as race has.

The second of the compromises made in Philadelphia in 1787 ensured the convention's success. However, the careful omission of the words slave or slavery from the Constitution did nothing to keep slavery from reemerging repeatedly as a prime political issue in the years after the ratification of the Constitution. The battle over slavery and its extension into areas encompassed first by the Northwest Territory and then by the Louisiana Purchase continued to enmesh American politics in the struggle between abolitionists and slaveholders, between free states and slave states. Indeed, increasingly it threatened to tear apart the Union that the Constitution had created. The compromises that were worked out by Congress in the first half of the eighteenth century were no more successful in stilling the controversy than the compromises the framers had incorporated into the Constitution.

For a while after the adoption of the Constitution it seemed possible that slavery might disappear as a result of a growing moral unease with the institution, which extended even into the South and in particular into Virginia, as well as for economic reasons. The slave economy was experiencing problems as the eighteenth century drew to a close. The states that were admitted to the Union in the first decade of the nineteenth century did not upset the delicate balance between slave and free states. Nor was there much controversy over their admission. The Northwest Ordinance, enacted under the Articles of Confederation and reenacted by the First Congress, had outlawed slavery in the territory north of the Ohio River, a region that was not thought to be conducive to the development of a plantation system.

The invention of the cotton gin and the growing importance of cotton to the South's economy changed matters considerably and swiftly. The admission of new states now posed a growing threat to what had increasingly become a very fragile peace. The Louisiana Purchase vastly expanded the boundaries of the United States. The westward expansion of both northerner and southerner populations and the realization that the new territory would soon spawn new states heightened the tension. In 1820 further strain was avoided by an arrangement by which Missouri, a slave state, was admitted to the Union paired with the admission of a free state, Maine, which had until that point been part of Massachusetts.

As part of the bill authorizing the admission of these two states, Senator Jesse Thomas of Illinois attached an amendment that would "forever" prohibit slavery in the part of the Louisiana Purchase that lay above latitude 36'30". This arrangement is what became known as the Missouri Compromise. Like the compromises worked out in the Constitutional Convention, it defused the controversy for a while, but it did not resolve the underlying problem, which Abraham Lincoln would capture best in his question of whether "a nation half free and half slave" could survive.

In the years after the adoption of the Missouri Compromise and up to the secession of the eleven southern states and the outbreak of the Civil War, various other compromises were attempted with varying success. These were offered in the belief that Congress was the ultimate arbiter of the constitutionality as well as the legality of slavery.

During this period, the Supreme Court played but a minor role. Despite *Marbury*, the Marshall Court had never again declared another act of Congress void. The Marshall Court did succeed in extending its assertion of judicial review to review of state court decisions as well as state laws—not an uncontroversial subject at that time in the United States. The Marshall Court also succeeded in giving a broad interpretation to the congressional power over "Commerce . . . among the several States" as well as finding that "the necessary and proper" clause, also found in Article I, could be used by the federal government to legislate in areas not explicitly enumerated in the Constitution.

THE COURT AND SLAVERY

For almost the entire period leading up to Lincoln's election to the presidency in 1860, the Court was dominated by southerners, who, along with certain northerners (referred to as "doughfaces" for their willingness to be molded by their southern brethren), supported slavery. The Court's decisions during this time involving issues such as the African slave trade and the fugitive slave laws largely supported the southern "slavocracy."

Several attempts were made before *Dred Scott v. Sandford* (1857) (the correct spelling of the respondent's name is Sanford, but a clerical error resulted in its being recorded as Sandford) to have the Supreme Court determine whether the fact that a slave entered territory made free by congressional action, by either the Northwest Ordinance or the Missouri Compromise, resulted in the slave's gaining freedom. The Supreme Court refused to take any of these cases prior to *Dred Scott,* and as a result the various state court decisions became the final word within those particular states. The same could have occurred in the case of Dred Scott.

Roger Brooke Taney had served both as attorney general and as secretary of the treasury under President Andrew Jackson. Jackson nominated him as an associate justice in 1835, but the Senate refused to act on the nomination, and so nothing came of it. Jackson, angered by the Senate's refusal to act on the nomination of his close ally, whom the Senate had also rejected earlier for a permanent appointment as treasury secretary, refused to submit another name. In the interim, Chief Justice Marshall died. Jackson now nominated Taney again, this time as Marshall's successor as chief justice. The Senate confirmed Taney, and he would occupy the Court's center chair from 1836 to 1864.

Unfortunately, Taney is best known for his decision in *Dred Scott,* the Court's "self-inflicted wound," according to later Chief Justice Charles Evans Hughes. Despite the notoriety surrounding that decision, Taney is still regularly identified as one of the great justices, ranked alongside Chief Justices Marshall and Warren in the highest porticos of the judicial pantheon.

Dred Scott was a slave, the property of an army doctor, John Emerson. Emerson moved around, living both in slave states and in the free states of Illinois and Wisconsin. In 1846, Scott brought suit in a Missouri court for his and his wife's freedom. In 1850, Scott won his suit, with a state court following the long-standing Missouri precedent that "once free, always free." However, in 1852, the Missouri Supreme Court reversed the lower court's decision and the Missouri precedents on which it had been based. The court seems to have been acting somewhat in pique in response to the growing cries of abolitionists. Scott appealed to the U.S. Supreme Court, which then twice held oral argument on the case.

The Taney Court generally has been characterized as carefully avoiding unnecessary controversies. Those such as Daniel Webster, who had opposed the Taney nomination because they feared that the new chief justice would undo the achievements of the Marshall Court, had been comforted by the Taney Court's adoption of much of the Marshall Court's legacy. *Dred Scott* could have easily been decided similarly to other cases, in which the Court had determined that it should defer to the judgment of the appropriate state court. Why Taney and the Court failed to do so remains a matter of controversy.

Some argue that Taney's opinion in *Dred Scott* reflected the partisan views of a southern chief justice determined to defend the rights of slavery, that he was an ideologue who allowed his prejudices to overwhelm his duties as a justice. Others argue that Taney's tone was largely a reaction to the opinions framed by the two dissenters in *Dred Scott* and that like the country as a whole he was reacting to their less than moderate tone. Still others argue that Taney's atypical activism was the result of his conclusion that neither Congress nor the president could deal with the growing crisis and that it was up to the Court to act so as to save the Union. The era of Clay and Webster was past. The Court alone could interpret the Constitution; the Court alone could save the nation from disaster.

Chief Justice Taney began his opinion (all nine justices wrote opinions in *Dred Scott*, almost reverting to the practice prior to Marshall of the Court delivering opinions *seriatim*) by posing a question: "The question is simply this: Can a negro, whose ancestors were imported into this country and sold as slaves, become a member of the political community formed and brought into existence by the Constitution of the United States?"

The answer was simple for Taney: "They were not included. . . . On the contrary, they were . . . considered as a subordinate and inferior class of beings, who had been subjugated by the dominant race, and, whether emancipated or not, yet remained subject to their authority. . . . They had no rights which the white man was bound to respect." Even the Declaration of Independence, claimed Taney, supported this conclusion. Speaking of "the men who framed this declaration," Taney concluded "they perfectly understood the meaning of the language they used . . . and they knew it would not in any part of the civilized world be supposed to embrace the negro race." Based on this reasoning, Taney announced that "Scott was not a citizen of Missouri within the meaning of the Constitution . . . and not entitled to sue in its courts; and consequently, that the Circuit Court had no jurisdiction of the case." That said, Taney could have been done with the case. No jurisdiction normally would mean no decision. That was not the result obviously that Chief Justice Taney wanted. Instead of dismissing the case for want of jurisdiction, Taney proceeded to examine the power of Congress to legislate for the territories as well as the power of Congress to adopt the Missouri Compromise.

According to Taney, the power delegated by Article IV to Congress authorizing it to "make all needful Rules and Regulations respecting the Territory . . . belonging to the United States" was not without limit. The Congress could not violate the prohibitions of the Bill of Rights. That was a conclusion with which no one could take issue. Taney went well beyond that to interpret very narrowly the power of the federal government to use its police powers, its power to make rules to protect the welfare of inhabitants of the territories. Specifically, Taney found that Congress could not use its police powers under Article IV to abolish slavery, since this was not among the enumerated powers of Congress. In addition, Taney, writing a year after a New York court had invalidated a state law banning liquor sales as a violation of due process (*Wynehamer v. New York* [1856]), invoked what was then a novel doctrine, namely, that of substantive due process. The New York court had found the state's prohibition act void not because of a violation of some procedure but because of the substance of the law. No matter how many procedural niceties were included in it, it involved a realm of activity that government simply could not regulate.

For Taney, slavery was off limits for the federal government. The Missouri Compromise was void for depriving Sanford—the brother of Dr. Emerson's widow and eventually Dred Scott's legal owner—of his property without due process of law, a violation of the Fifth Amendment. If Taney and the other six justices who agreed generally with his opinion thought that by putting the Court's hard-won prestige on the line they could end the increasingly divisive debate over slavery, they were greatly mistaken. Far from tamping down the flames, *Dred Scott* exacerbated the growing schism within the nation. The response issued by Horace Greeley's *New York Tribune* was typical of many of the newspapers outside the South when it thundered that *Dred Scott* deserved "just so much weight as would be [accorded] the judgment of a majority of those congregated in any Washington bar-room" (Burner et al. 1991, 416). Abolitionists, extrapolating from the Taney opinion, warned that the logic behind it could be used to bar any state from prohibiting slavery within its boundaries. The Court's opinion had elevated the ownership of another human being to the status of a constitutionally protected right.

THE CIVIL WAR AND
THE RECONSTRUCTION-ERA AMENDMENTS

Although the Civil War was not launched to end slavery, it did have that result. Lincoln's September 1863 Emancipation Proclamation, which granted freedom to all slaves in areas that were still in rebellion, was issued by the president using his constitutional power as commander in chief of the armed forces. It was largely symbolic, since by its very terms it did not apply to the border states that had not seceded and where slavery still existed, nor to those portions of the confederacy controlled by Union forces.

The victory of the Union forces raised the question of what to do with the states that had left the Union as well as that of how to deal with the slaves. Both questions raised issues involving the power of the federal government. The plaintive plea sounded by many northern Democrats during the Civil War of "the Constitution as it was and the Union as it is" clearly was unacceptable. The South's bid for secession had failed and the Constitution had changed.

The change in the Constitution was not only in terms of the broad assertions of executive power made by Lincoln, assertions that Taney unsuccessfully sought to limit, but also in terms of an amendment. The Thirteenth Amendment, which abolished slavery, was introduced in Congress in April 1864, while the Civil War was still being fought. In the Senate it secured the necessary two-thirds majority, but it initially failed to garner the necessary votes in the House. The vote on June 15, 1864, was 93 in favor, 65 opposed. Lincoln's reelection in November—Lincoln secured 55 percent of the popular votes—may have convinced some of the House members to change their positions on the amendment. The House voted again on January 31, 1865. This time 110 votes were recorded in favor and 56 opposed. The amendment was sent to the states for ratification (Fairman 1971, 1136–1138). On December 6, the necessary three-quarters of the states had ratified the amendment. Included in this number were all but two of the states that had made up the Confederacy.

Like the other two post–Civil War amendments, or as they are sometimes called, the "Freedom Amendments," the Thirteenth Amendment represented a radical change in the nature of the federal system. For the first time, the federal government was given the power to pass legislation directly affecting the behavior of citizens of the states. Each of these amendments—the Thirteenth, Fourteenth, and Fifteenth—ended with a clause that specifically gave Congress the power to enforce the amendment's provisions "by appropriate legislation." This was a truly revolutionary change from the division of powers provided for by the Constitution of 1787. Although the debate over states' rights would continue—indeed continues in a fashion even today—the post–Civil War amendments shifted the boundaries of the division, or the balance of power, inexorably in favor of the federal government as opposed to the state governments.

Whether the process of reincorporation of the South into the Union would have proceeded better had Lincoln not been assassinated is one of the great "what ifs" of American history. President Andrew Johnson's appeals to restore the southern states to the Union on fairly generous terms found little support in Congress. Increasingly, power in Congress shifted to the faction within the Republican Party that was styled the "Radical Republicans." Among their goals was the "reconstruction" of the South and the elevation of the former slaves to full citizenship. Just as their goals were mixed—political advancement and financial gain were hardly absent in the minds of many of their leaders—so too was their definition of what full citizenship entailed and of what equality meant.

The legislative record of the Congresses that proposed the Freedom Amendments and the numerous civil rights and freedman acts, however, can leave no doubt as to their desire to improve in some significant measure the status of the former slaves.

The speed with which they enacted their program sometimes raised questions about the constitutionality of the measures they enacted. Definitely the adoption of the Fourteenth and Fifteenth Amendments, and possibly that of the Thirteenth as well, was motivated in part by a concern to put particular pieces of congressional legislation on a firmer constitutional basis.

During this period, the suspicion of the Court as not being fully in line with the agenda of the Radical Republicans continued. The Court still carried the baleful legacy of *Dred Scott*. This legacy of distrust was compounded by the efforts of Taney to rein in what he and certain other Supreme Court justices saw as excessive and unconstitutional uses of executive power in the prosecution of the Civil War. Edward Corwin, commenting on the disaster that was *Dred Scott*, opined that as a result, "during neither the Civil War nor the period of Reconstruction did the Supreme Court play anything like its due role of supervision," leading in his opinion to the exercise of excessive power first by the president and then by Congress (Lewis 1965, 423). As the public became concerned a century later with the use of executive power in waging the war in Vietnam, Taney's opinions in *Ex parte Merryman* (1861) and *The Prize Cases* (1863) helped a bit to refurbish Taney's tarnished reputation in the public mind. Despite persistent hopes by his opponents that the aged chief justice would die, Taney held on to his post until 1864. His death allowed Lincoln to make his fifth appointment to the Court, nominating his treasury secretary, Salmon Portland Chase.

Despite the fact that Lincoln had made more appointments to the Supreme Court than any president since Andrew Jackson (Jackson had seven appointments; President George Washington still has the record with eleven appointments), the Congress still viewed the Court as an unreliable ally in its drive to reconstruct the states of the former Confederacy. They were equally concerned lest President Andrew Johnson make any appointments to the Court. Two seats became vacant during Johnson's time in the White House, and the Senate took no action on his one nominee.

Not only did it refuse to vote on the president's nomination of Attorney General Henry Stanbery—Henry Abraham has observed that "it is doubtful that the Senate would have approved God himself had he been nominated by Andrew Johnson" (Abraham 1974, 115)—but it abolished his seat and provided that the Court be reduced in size from ten to eight if another vacancy occurred. Still, the fear on the part of many members of Congress was that the Court was still not a reliable ally for its programs. The unanimous decision in the case of *Ex parte Milligan* (1866), which held that trials of civilians before military courts-martial without legislative action was unconstitutional, more than confirmed these fears.

The fast-developing case of William McCardle aggravated these fears further. McCardle was an ex-Confederate who attacked the Reconstruction government in his state in his newspaper and urged noncooperation with the government. He was arrested and was tried before a military court-martial. He invoked an act adopted by Congress in 1867 as providing the basis upon which he should be released. Jeremiah Black, who had successfully argued the case for Milligan before the Supreme Court, argued for McCardle as well before the high court.

To ensure that the Court would not block congressional efforts to root out the societal system in the South that had led to secession and to reconstruct the South, Congress moved speedily on two fronts to counter the threat posed by McCardle's suit. First, Congress repealed the 1867 statute; second, it took from the Court its appellate jurisdiction to hear cases arising from the act.

Article III distinguishes between the Court's original jurisdiction—those cases the Court hears in the "first instance"—and those that have already been decided by another court and come on appeal before the Supreme Court—its appellate jurisdiction. The original jurisdiction, as Chief Justice Marshall had held in *Marbury v. Madison* (1803), is set by the Constitution and cannot be changed by ordinary legislation but only by amendment. Using its power under Article III to fix the appellate jurisdiction, Congress proceeded to strip the Court of its power to hear cases under the now repealed 1867 statute.

Both these congressional actions took place after the Court had heard oral argument by Black on behalf of McCardle. The Court, in turn, "very much aware of the Radicals' mood," delayed its decision (Murphy et al. 2003, 490). Finally in 1869 in the case of *Ex parte McCardle*, the Court sanctioned the congressional action as constitutional. Chief Justice Chase, noting that the Court was "not at liberty to inquire into the motives of the legislature" and could "only examine its power under the Constitution," concluded, "Without jurisdiction the court cannot proceed at all in any cause."

Although commentators continue to debate what *McCardle* means in terms of the power of Congress to limit the Court by restricting its appellate jurisdiction, there is no doubt that the Court in the 1860s and 1870s had entered a period in which its room to exercise power had been seriously circumscribed. The *Dred Scott* decision and subsequent efforts on the part of the Court to rein in presidential power during the Civil War had already gravely damaged the Court's prestige in the eyes of those who supported the Union cause. The Court was further limited by its realization that Congress clearly intended to brook no opposition to its Reconstruction program, either from the presidency or from the judiciary.

The Court that had so disgraced itself in the eyes of abolitionists by its language on the "inferiority" of blacks returned only obliquely to the issue of race in the *Slaughterhouse Cases* (1873). These cases, arising from an action by a thoroughly corrupt Louisiana legislature that had, in return for stock certificates in the company, bestowed a monopoly on the Crescent City Slaughtering Company in New Orleans, gave the Court its first opportunity to interpret the Fourteenth Amendment.

The butchers, through the Butchers' Benevolent Society, protested the monopoly, invoking the guarantees of both the Thirteenth and Fourteenth Amendments in their briefs. Their attorneys contended that the power the Crescent City Company exercised as a result of the actions of the Louisiana government reduced the butchers' condition to that of the servitude proscribed by the Thirteenth Amendment. Most of the brief's constitutional arguments, however, involved the act's alleged violations of the protections offered by the more recently ratified Fourteenth Amendment (1868). The challenged legislation was said to deny the butchers their "privileges or immunities" as "citizens of the United States." These "privileges" clearly included the right to pursue the legitimate calling of slaughtering and preparing meat for sale. In addition, they claimed that it deprived them of their liberty and property without due process of law. This was the same argument that Taney had embraced sixteen years earlier in *Dred Scott.* Finally, they asserted that by treating them unequally the law denied them "the equal protection of the laws" that the Fourteenth Amendment protected against state abridgment.

In a 5–4 decision, the Butchers' Benevolent Society lost the case. The Supreme Court majority, speaking through Justice Samuel Miller, rejected all four lines of argument. The bulk of the Miller opinion for the Court and of the dissents dealt with the Privileges or Immunities Clause (often referred to as the "p or i clause"). The other constitutional claims were dismissed with little comment. Miller, however, in rejecting claims of the Butchers' Benevolent Society, made it very clear that he believed that "the freedom of the slave race, the security and firm establishment of that freedom, and the protection of the newly-made freedman and citizen from the oppression of those who had formerly exercised unlimited dominion over him" were at the core of each of the post–Civil War amendments. This was particularly true of the guarantee of equal protection found in the first section of the Fourteenth Amendment.

In light of the history of these amendments, and the pervading purpose of them . . . it is not difficult to give meaning to this clause. The existence of laws in the States where the newly emancipated negroes resided, which discriminated with gross injustice and hardship against them as a class, was the evil to be remedied. . . . We doubt very much whether any action of a State not directed by way of discrimination against the negroes as a class, or on account of their race, will ever be held to come within the purview of this provision. It is so clearly a provision for that race and that emergency, that a strong case would be necessary for its application to any other.

Miller's characterization of the amendments and, in particular, of the Equal Protection Clause continues to be significant, particularly as the latter clause, dismissed by Justice Oliver Wendell Holmes as the last resort of every lawyer's failing argument, becomes one of the most litigated and controversial sections of the Constitution.

Seven years after Miller's opinion in the *Slaughterhouse Cases*, the Court was faced with a practice common in the South—the exclusion of blacks from juries. In the most famous of the four cases, *Strauder v. West Virginia* (1880), Justice William Strong struck down a state statute limiting jury service to "all white male persons who are twenty-one years of age and who are citizens of this State." Strauder, a black man, had been convicted of murder. Strong's opinion took up the theme first developed by Miller. Departing from Miller's stance on the potential scope of the Equal Protection Clause, Strong saw the clause as offering a guarantee to other groups against class-based discrimination.

Nor would it be [constitutional] if the persons excluded by [law] were white men. If in those States where the colored people constitute a majority of the entire population a law should be enacted excluding all white men from jury service, [we] apprehend no one would be heard to claim that it would not be a denial to white men of [equal protection]. Nor if a law should be passed excluding all naturalized Celtic Irishmen, would there be any doubt of its inconsistency with the spirit of the amendment. The very fact that colored people are singled out and expressly denied by a statute all right to participate in the administration of the law, as jurors, because of their color, [is] practically a brand upon them, affixed by the law, an assertion of their inferiority, and a stimulant to that race prejudice which is an impediment to securing to individuals of the race that [equal justice guaranteed by the Fourteenth Amendment].

In *Ex parte Virginia*, decided the same year, the Court found that although the state of Virginia did not have a law excluding blacks from jury service, the actions of a Virginia judge that denied blacks the right to serve on juries had the same effect and was also prohibited by the Equal Protection Clause. In another case, *Virginia v. Rives*, decided in 1880, the Court concluded, however, that the absence of black jurors on its own was not enough to justify a finding of a constitutional violation.

Strong's opinion in *Strauder* still resonates today as the Court continues to wrestle with questions involving the application of the Equal Protection Clause. Although the Court would not formally establish the classification of "suspect categories" until 1944 in the case of *Korematsu v. United States*, the outlines of this distinction are apparent in Strong's opinion. Strong's opinion also made it clear that despite the fact that the Freedom Amendments were designed especially to protect the rights of the newly freed slaves, they could be used to protect the rights of nonblacks as well. Distinctions based on nationality were also covered. Strong's argument evoking laws that might deprive whites of the right to serve on juries is also interesting for the contemporary Court. Interesting as well is the question of what degree of discrimination prompts a finding of an equal protection violation. For example, must the class of persons be totally deprived of a right for the law to be found constitutionally defective? Finally, Strong's decision established the need to show "state action" in order to raise an equal protection claim.

Although it is common today to refer to a violation of civil rights, many argue that the members of Congress who framed, debated, and proposed the post–Civil War amendments understood distinctions between political rights—the right to enter into judicially enforceable contracts, to give testimony, and to serve on juries, for instance—voting rights, and civil rights. The latter involved the right to engage in social relations with other people, and more specifically to move about freely as an equal among whites.

No one would deny that the authors of the three amendments wanted to abolish slavery and to guarantee political equality and the right to vote to the newly freed. Nor would they deny that Congress by those same amendments was delegated appropriate power to enforce such rights and to sweep away any state law or practice that interfered with them. However, aside from prohibiting private individuals from holding another human being in bondage, it was an open question—or, at least, a debatable question—whether private action that discriminated could be acted on by the federal government.

The Civil Rights Act of 1875 was the last gasp of the fast-failing Radical Republicans. The brainchild of Massachusetts Senator Charles Sumner, it provided that

> all persons within the jurisdiction of the United States shall be entitled to the full and equal enjoyment of all accommodations, advantages, facilities, and privileges of inns, public conveyances . . . , theatres, and other places of public amusement; subject only to the conditions and limitations established by law, and applicable alike to citizens of every race and color, regardless of any previous condition of servitude.

Violation of the law was a misdemeanor, and the person who had been deprived of his or her civil rights could sue for damages of $500 "for every such offense." Unlike earlier legislation, this act was directed at changing the behavior of individuals. Private acts of discrimination were now proscribed. The act's authors assumed that as a result of the adoption of the Thirteenth and Fourteenth

Amendments, the federal government now had the power to enact legislation that directly affected the ways in which private individuals conducted their businesses in order to protect the newly freed slaves in their enjoyment of basic civil rights.

THE END OF RECONSTRUCTION

By 1883, when the Court ruled on the constitutionality of the Civil Rights Act of 1875 in a series of cases collectively cited as the *Civil Rights Cases,* much had changed, and the spirit behind the act had largely vanished as a major force on the national political scene. Support for the reconstruction agenda of the Radical Republicans was waning in the 1870s. As it declined, the notion of reaching out to the former Confederates became more and more popular. The Democratic Party continued to rise from the ashes of the Civil War, and nearly captured the presidency in 1876. Democrats had gained control of the House of Representatives in 1874 and also closed the gap with the Republicans in the Senate. The disputed election of 1876, which many saw as having been stolen by the Republicans, prompted the new Republican president, Rutherford B. Hayes, to remove the remaining federal troops from the South. With that, any serious effort to change the South and to root out the old plantation system effectively came to a close. The death of Chief Justice Chase, an ardent abolitionist who had become known initially for his defense of persons accused of violating the fugitive slave laws, and his replacement by Morrison Waite in 1873 also had an effect. By 1883, the nation had changed and the Court had changed, and, sensing this, the Court may have followed "the eliction retoorns" as Finley Peter Dunne's Mister Dooley would note regarding another later shift by the Supreme Court.

However much Justice Joseph Bradley's opinion is criticized today, it was hardly unpopular when it was delivered. Many agreed with the idea that the time had come to restore some balance between a too-powerful federal government and the weakened states. The *New York Times* editorialized, "The fact is, that so long as we have State governments, within their field of action we cannot by National authority prevent the consequences of misgovernment. The people of the State are dependent on their own civilized ideas and habits for the benefits of a civilized administration of laws" (Mason and Stephenson 1999, 619).

With only the former Kentucky slaveholder John Marshall Harlan in dissent, the Supreme Court found no basis in either the Thirteenth or the Fourteenth Amendment for a congressional power to regulate behavior that had traditionally been considered reserved to the states. Accordingly, it found those sections that did not involve state action—the Civil Rights Act did prohibit the exclusion of blacks from juries—null and void.

Justice Joseph Bradley, in language that continues to be the "law of the land," handed down the Court's opinion. Writing in bold strokes, he proclaimed that it

> is state action of a particular character that is prohibited. . . . Individual invasion of individual rights is not the subject-matter of the amendment. . . . [The Fourteenth Amendment] does not invest Congress with power to legislate upon subjects which are within the domain of State legislation. . . . The power to remedy these wrongs rests where it has always rested: with the states. An individual cannot deprive a man of his right to vote, to hold property, to buy and sell, to sue in the courts, or to be a witness or a juror; he may, by force or fraud, interfere with the enjoyment of the right in a particular case . . . but unless protected in these wrongful acts by some shield of state law . . . he cannot destroy or injure the right; he will only render himself amenable to satisfaction or punishment; and amenable therefor to the laws of the State where the wrongful acts are committed.

Frequently overlooked in the opinion is Bradley's somewhat prescient observation that whether "Congress, in the exercise of its power to regulate commerce amongst the several States, might or might not pass a law regulating rights in public conveyances passing from one state to another, [is] a question which is not now before us." When Congress adopted the Civil Rights Act of 1964, the first significant federal rights legislation enacted since the 1875 act, it chose to base the legislation on its power under the Commerce Clause in Article I, Section 8 of the Constitution.

The second constitutional basis argued in support of the constitutionality of the Civil Rights Act of 1875 was the Thirteenth Amendment. Discrimination was a "badge of slavery." The enforcement section of the Thirteenth Amendment combined with the "necessary and proper" language of Article I gave Congress the right to legislate. This argument also failed to convince the Court's majority.

> It would be running the slavery argument into the ground to make it to apply to every act of discrimination which a person may see fit to make as to the guests he will entertain, or as to the people he will take into his coach or cab or car, or admit to his concert or theatre. . . . When a man has emerged from slavery, and by the aid of beneficent legislation has shaken off the inseparable concomitants of that state, there must be some stage in the progress of his elevation when he takes the rank of a mere citizen and ceases to be the special favorite of the [laws].

Justice Harlan, the sole dissenter, rejected every point made by Bradley in his opinion. Whereas Bradley argued that the Fourteenth Amendment only marginally increased federal power, Harlan claimed that it dramatically altered the balance of power between the federal government and the states. Whereas Bradley dismissed the "badge of slavery" argument, Harlan saw the Thirteenth Amendment as empowering the federal government to act against any discrimination based on race. "Congress . . . [may] enact laws to protect that people against the deprivation, *because of their race,* of any civil rights granted to other freeman in the same State; and such legislation may be of a direct and primary nature operating . . . upon, at least such individuals and corporations as exercise public functions and wield power and authority under the [state]."

Finally, Harlan argued that the distinction the majority made between state and private action was irrelevant in this particular case. Innkeepers, theater owners, and those who offered transport were "agents or instrumentalities of the State, because they are charged with duties to the public, and are amenable . . . to governmental regulation."

Although the *Civil Rights Cases* were a severe blow to the hopes of those who sought, in the memorable words of Harlan's dissent, to include blacks as "part of the people for whose welfare and happiness government is ordained," it was not as severe as the blows that would be struck in quick succession soon afterward. The most serious of these was the disfranchisement of most blacks in the South. Literacy tests, poll taxes, and raw intimidation purged most blacks from the voting rolls. When such practices were challenged as violations of the Fifteenth Amendment, the Court regularly upheld such restrictions as not being based on race. Justice Joseph McKenna wrote for the Court in *Williams v. Mississippi* in 1898, "They do not on their face discriminate between the races, and it has not been shown that their actual administration was evil; only that evil was possible under them."

In addition to moving to disfranchise blacks, the southern states now took action to separate the races by law. Like disfranchisement, a good deal of the impetus for segregation came as a result of the battle for power between white southern conservatives and their poorer white compatriots who were increasingly attracted to causes like that of the Populists. Both had vied for the support of black voters. Both then concluded that to give blacks such a key role in deciding who won elections would be dangerous. Whites must come together at least to deny blacks such unwarranted power.

State-mandated segregation would seem to fly in the face of Justice Bradley's reasoning in the *Civil Rights Cases.* Here was a clear case of state action. Both Mississippi and Florida adopted laws requiring that railroad cars be racially segregated. In 1890 Louisiana followed suit. Louisiana—or at least southern Louisiana, and New Orleans in particular—were quite different from the rest of the South. French, Spanish, and Catholic influences had many effects, not the least of which was a significant number of persons of mixed race. Homer Plessy was seven-eighths white. He was chosen by opponents of the legislation to test the new Louisiana statute. Many have suggested that his action was encouraged by railroad owners, who saw the state requiring "equal but separate" carriages as increasing their costs of doing business (Kluger 1975, 90). Plessy was arrested for sitting in a car reserved for whites and convicted in a Louisiana court. His appeal to the state supreme court was rejected, and he appealed to the U.S. Supreme Court.

Plessy's argument alleged violations of both the Thirteenth and Fourteenth Amendments. Justice Henry Brown made short work of the "badges of slavery" argument. It had not worked in the *Civil Rights Cases;* there was no more reason for it to work here. "Slavery involves involuntary servitude—a state of bondage . . . and the absence of a legal right to the disposal of his own person, property and services" and nothing more. "A distinction between the white and colored races . . . has no tendency to destroy the legal equality of the two races, or reestablish a state of involuntary servitude."

The Fourteenth Amendment argument posed more of a hurdle for Brown. A native of Massachusetts, Brown cited a decision of that state's supreme court in the case of *Roberts v. Boston* (1849) in which Chief Justice Lemuel Shaw had upheld Boston's segregation of its public schools. Brown also made much of the fact that the same Congress that had proposed the Fourteenth Amendment has segregated the schools of the District of Columbia. Brown's invocation of school segregation may have been designed in order to rally more support for his position. "Education was a bugbear for anyone who suggested legislation mandating racial equality" (Pratt 1992, 638).

Such distinctions as these were reasonable. "Every exercise of the police power [of a state] must be reasonable, and extend only to such laws as are enacted in good faith for the promotion of the public good, and not for the annoyance or oppression of a particular class." Bradley's distinction in the *Civil Rights Cases* between state action and private action seemed to have been ignored entirely. Brown then penned the most famous passage of his opinion: "We consider the underlying fallacy of the plaintiff's argument to consist in the assumption that the enforced separation of the two races stamps the colored race with a badge of inferiority. If this is so, it is not by reason of anything found in the act, but solely because the colored race chooses to put that construction on it."

Harlan was, as he had been in the *Civil Rights Cases,* the sole dissenter. With Justice David Brewer not participating—Brewer very likely would have voted with the majority—Harlan issued a dissent that fused the guarantees of the Thirteenth and Fourteenth Amendments with Article IV's guarantee of "a Republican form of Government." In what might be the best known lines of any Supreme Court decision, Harlan thundered:

> In view of the Constitution, in the eye of the law, there is in this country no superior, dominant, ruling class of citizens. There is no caste here. Our Constitution is color-blind, and neither knows nor tolerates classes among citizens. . . .
>
> In my opinion, the judgment this day rendered will, in time, prove to be quite as pernicious as the decision . . . in the *Dred Scott* case. . . .
>
> The arbitrary separation of citizens, on the basis of race, while they are on the public highway, is a badge of servitude wholly inconsistent with the civil freedom and the equality before the law established by the Constitution. . . .

Such a system is inconsistent with the guarantee given by the Constitution to each State of a republican form of government, and may be stricken down by Congressional action, or by the courts in the discharge of their solemn duty to maintain the supreme law of the land, anything in the constitution or laws of any State to the contrary notwithstanding.

Harlan's appeal for congressional action went unanswered, and it would be almost a half century before federal courts would reexamine segregation as a violation of the Fourteenth Amendment's guarantee of equal protection. Instead, *Plessy* gave the green light to the imposition of state-mandated segregation in almost all aspects of public life, both in the states of the old Confederacy and in the border states, which extended from Delaware in the East to Kansas in the Midwest.

As Harlan had predicted, *Plessy* planted the "seeds of race hate" that would lead to a legacy of lynchings and other forms of physical and financial intimidation designed to keep blacks "in their place."

THE COURT REENTERS THE FRAY

The Taft Court (1920–1930) marked a turning point that is often not recognized as much as it should be in terms of the Court's concern with individual rights and, specifically, its willingness to use the Fourteenth Amendment to rein in state action that interfered with noneconomic rights. Although the Court under Chief Justice William Howard Taft continued along the course developed in the late nineteenth century of using the Fourteenth Amendment as a means of protecting businesses from state regulations it deemed unreasonable, it also saw the Fourteenth Amendment as protecting certain individual rights. This was a position that Justice Harlan had advanced, but with no more success than in the cases involving race. Justice Oliver Wendell Holmes,

Jr., writing in *Moore v. Dempsey* (1923), found that the murder
trial of two blacks accused of killing a white sheriff was so defective that it should be reviewed in federal court. In *Gitlow v. New
York* (1925), the Court found that among the liberties protected
by the Fourteenth Amendment was the guarantee of freedom of
speech. At the same time it should be noted of the Taft Court that
it upheld restrictive covenants—contracts that prohibited the sale
of property to nonwhites—and a Mississippi law that required
Chinese students to attend schools reserved for "colored" children. The Hughes Court (1930–1941) proceeded even further
along this course.

Two of these cases had particular relevance for African Americans. Southern blacks were not only segregated from whites, but
they were denied equal treatment in many other ways. Perhaps
the most notorious aspect of this discrimination was in the area of
criminal justice. *Powell v. Alabama* (1932) and *Brown v. Mississippi* (1936) forced the Court to take a close look at what southern
justice meant for blacks. The 1932 case is generally referred to as
the *Scottsboro Cases.* Powell and the other defendants were young
black males who were accused of raping a white girl who had
shared a railroad boxcar with them. The trials were separated. In
all, three separate trials took place; each ended in a day, and each
resulted in the jury finding the defendants guilty and recommend-
ing the death penalty. By a vote of 7–2, with Chief Justice Charles
Evans Hughes writing for the majority, the Court overturned the
convictions. Hughes found that the state action violated due process. Specifically, Hughes held that due process required that persons accused of capital offenses be provided legal counsel for their
defense at state expense if they could not afford it. In *Brown*, the
Court, with Hughes again writing the opinion, reversed the convictions for murder of two blacks. Again the Hughes opinion
rested on the Fourteenth Amendment's due process guarantee.
Although the defendants had confessed to the murder, the evidence clearly showed that they had suffered repeated beatings;

one had actually been hanged for a few seconds. At the trial, a deputy admitted that he had beaten the defendants, but added, "'Not too much for a negro; not as much as I would have done if it were left to me.'" Hughes reversed, observing that while "the State may abolish trial by jury ... it does not follow that it may substitute trial by ordeal. The rack and torture chamber may not be substituted for the witness stand."

All of this occurred before the dawn of what is generally styled the "modern Court." Until 1937, the Court demonstrated little interest in what is generally called today individual rights or liberties. The lack of concern or indeed prejudice that it exhibited to African Americans was not much different from its attitudes toward religious or political minorities. Justice Henry Brown, the author of the *Plessy* decision, was characterized by one biographer as "a privileged son of the Yankee merchant class, . . . a reflexive social elitist whose opinions of women, African-Americans, Jews and immigrants now seem odious" (Helminski 1992, 93).

THE NAACP AND ITS LEGAL STRATEGY

The Court's transformation after 1937 came as a result of changes in the Court's personnel—President Franklin Roosevelt had been the first president in history to have served a full four-year term without any opportunity to make appointments to the Court— and as a result of the political realities of the day. The Court's traditional defense of the rights of property and, more specifically, the economic doctrine of laissez-faire, the theory that government should let business alone, was no longer tolerable in the America of the 1930s and in a country mired in the Great Depression. Either the Court would be radically altered, or it had to get out of the way of the New Deal and its legislative program. The Court opted for the latter course.

As will be discussed in more detail in chapter 3, one result of this change by the Court was its gradual emergence as a defender of the rights and liberties of minority groups, including the rights of African Americans. At the same time that the Court was changing, there were also rumblings of change in America's African American community. The division between those who saw in the words and works of Booker T. Washington the path to full acceptance and those who followed the philosophy of W.E.B. DuBois had faded. Economic prosperity and the development of a larger professional class in the African American community provided a basis out of which developed an ability to take up the challenge put forth in Harlan's *Plessy* dissent.

The political route offered little promise of success, however. In the South, few African Americans retained the franchise. Although the Republican Party still was seen as the party of Lincoln and continued to draw the loyalty of many African Americans throughout the 1930s, the party had done little for them in the twentieth century and after 1932 was in no position politically to deliver. Those African Americans who had become Democrats found themselves in a party that nationally was still in the thrall of the South. Even in the state party organizations in the North, African Americans found that the Irish American political bosses were not willing to give them much for their votes. The courts, as a result, were their only hope.

The National Association for the Advancement of Colored People (NAACP), accordingly, set about developing a strategy to achieve what it saw as the yet unfulfilled promise of the Freedom Amendments. In 1939, as part of this legal thrust, the NAACP established its Legal Defense Fund. The organization's lawyers, eventually including future Supreme Court Justice Thurgood Marshall (the first head of the Legal Defense Fund), realized at once that the *Plessy* opinion would not fall easily. As John W. Davis would eventually argue in *Brown v. Board of Education*, "controlling precedents preclude a construction which would abolish segregation in the public schools. . . . [I]t has been so often announced, so confidently relied upon, so long continued, that it passes the limits of judicial discretion and disturbance" (Friedman 1969, 214–215). They also realized that no matter how controversial the issue was, segregation in the realm of education was the battle that needed to be fought. Education was the path that both followers of Washington and of DuBois recognized as necessary for African Americans to achieve equality.

The first move was to ensure that "separate but equal" was in fact provided. Chief Justice Taft, speaking for a unanimous Court in *Gong Lum v. Rice* (1927), while ordering a Chinese girl to attend the school reserved for "colored," had allowed that had there been "no colored school in Martha Lum's neighborhood, a different question would have been presented." Taft's observation opened up lines of attack for the NAACP to pursue. The first was to ensure that schools were actually available; the second was to test whether the facilities offered were equal, as required by *Plessy.*

The NAACP lawyers also realized that their strategy could prove disastrous if it led to yet another decision that sustained segregation. Consequently, they were careful to pick cases that they believed that they could win. With that in mind, they decided to focus on the border states—states where segregation existed but where they believed public opinion was not as strong in its support as it was in the Deep South—and on graduate or professional education. Admitting African Americans to law schools or graduate schools would definitely not produce the emotional shock waves that would occur were blacks to enter formerly all-white elementary schools. Justice Brown likely understood this when he introduced somewhat incongruously the issue of school segregation into his opinion in *Plessy.*

Accordingly, the refusal by the law school of the University of Maryland to admit a black applicant despite the fact that there was no law school in the state for blacks proved an excellent opportunity to begin the process of dismantling the structure of apartheid that had been imposed after the Court's *Plessy* ruling. The case was tried before a sympathetic judge in the city of Baltimore. The state's defense appears to have been either incompetent or half-hearted. The trial judge ordered the law school applicant admitted. The state appealed, but the state's highest court upheld the lower court's decision. Other states were better prepared. Some instituted programs that made scholarships available to black applicants who wanted to attend professional or graduate schools. They could not attend the state's all-white schools but could attend schools that accepted blacks. The fact that these schools might not necessarily be in their state was an added bonus for segregationists. The applicant to the law school of the University of Maryland had been told to apply to Howard University in Washington, D.C. Another alternative, although more expensive, was to establish separate colleges and even law schools for African Americans.

THE SUPREME COURT REEXAMINES "SEPARATE BUT EQUAL"

Lloyd L. Gaines had applied for admission to the University of Missouri Law School. Quite predictably, he was rejected on racial grounds. That decision was sustained by the state courts. Missouri officials, though, did offer to pay Gaines's tuition at an out-of-state law school. The NAACP succeeded in convincing the U.S. Supreme Court to review the case. The Court found Missouri in violation of the Equal Protection Clause of the Fourteenth Amendment. Chief Justice Charles Evans Hughes found neither the offer of tuition to an out-of-state law school nor the promise that the state would establish a law school at all-black Lincoln University sufficient to meet the Fourteenth Amendment's demands on the state. The success secured by the NAACP in *Missouri ex rel. Gaines v. Canada* (1938) would be repeated in two cases decided by the Vinson Court (1946–1953).

These victories further validated the wisdom of the plan the NAACP adopted in 1930 and paved the way to the ultimate triumph, *Brown v. Board of Education.* Both were decided in 1950 and both were decided by unanimous Courts. (In the earlier *Gaines* case, Justices Pierce Butler and James McReynolds had dissented.) *Sweatt v. Painter* (1950) arose out of Texas's action in establishing a law school for blacks. Herman Sweatt had applied for admission to the University of Texas Law School at Austin. A state judge gave the state six months to provide a facility for black students. After a series of false starts, the Texas legislature authorized a school located eight blocks from the University of Texas Law School. At the same time, the NAACP pushed a case involving an applicant to the University of Oklahoma's graduate program in education. Oklahoma had already been the focus of a suit as a result of its refusal to admit an African American woman to its law school. When the woman, Ada Lois Sipuel, was finally admitted as a result of a *per curiam* opinion, she was forced to sit behind a cordon rope that separated her from her classmates. George W. McLaurin was a sixty-eight-year-old African American who had a master's degree and wanted to pursue a doctorate in education at the University of Oklahoma. McLaurin was treated slightly better by Oklahoma authorities than the law school applicant in *Sipuel v. Board of Regents* (1948). He sat in an anteroom next to the regular classroom and had a table reserved for him in both the library and the cafeteria.

Both the *Sweatt* and *McLaurin* cases were accepted for argument by the Supreme Court. In the law school case, Marshall argued that there was no way that the facilities offered Sweatt were in any sense equal to those offered to white students at the nearby University of Texas School of Law. *McLaurin* gave him the opportunity to take a step even closer to overturning *Plessy.* In *Sweatt,* the NAACP argument was based on the fact that the two law schools were simply not equal. In the Oklahoma graduate case, however, McLaurin was being offered an equal education. He sat in the same classes and studied in the same library, but he was separated from his classmates. Was this a violation of equal protection?

Chief Justice Fred Vinson had assigned himself the task of writing both opinions. It was not hard on the facts for Vinson and his fellow justices to conclude that Texas was not offering its African American citizens a legal education comparable to that available to whites. All the numbers showed the great chasm in quality between the University of Texas School of Law and its new neighbor. Vinson did not stop there. As the NAACP attorneys had hoped in their strategy of bringing *Sweatt* and two other cases involving law schools to the Court, the judges' personal knowledge of how law schools worked and what a legal education entailed might make them more willing to reach decisions—and articulate reasoning for those decisions—that would provide a better foundation for the NAACP to launch its eventual attack on segregation in public elementary and secondary schools.

Although the law is a highly learned profession, we are well aware that it is an intensely practical one. The law school, the proving ground for legal learning and practice, cannot be effective in isolation from the individuals and institutions with which the law interacts. Few students and no one who has practiced law would choose to study in an academic vacuum, removed from the interplay of ideas and the exchange of views with which the law is concerned. The [separate] law school to which Texas is willing to admit petitioner excludes from its student body members of the racial groups which number 85 percent of the population of the State and include most of the lawyers, witnesses, jurors, judges and other officials with whom petitioner will inevitably be dealing.... With such a substantial and significant segment of society excluded, we cannot conclude that the education offered petitioner is substantially equal to that which he would receive if admitted to the University of Texas Law School.

Having ordered Sweatt's admission to the University of Texas Law School, the Court proceeded to order the University of Oklahoma to end the segregation of McLaurin. In a brief opinion,

Vinson held that Oklahoma, by separating him from his fellow graduate students, denied McLaurin "his personal and present rights to the equal protection of the laws. . . . [He] must receive the same treatment . . . as students of other races." Failure to do so will adversely affect his education. This in turn will result in his students not receiving an adequate education. "Their own education will necessarily suffer to the extent that his training is unequal to that of his classmates. State-imposed restrictions which produce such inequalities cannot be sustained."

SCHOOL SEGREGATION BEFORE THE COURT

These two victories gave Thurgood Marshall and the NAACP confidence finally to make the move that had been their ultimate goal since the decision of 1930 to use litigation as the means by which to attack *Plessy* and to end segregation in public education. In addition to the victories in these two cases and triumphs in other court cases involving transportation and restrictive covenants—the Court in *Shelley v. Kraemer* (1948), with the U.S. Department of Justice filing an amicus curiae brief in support of the NAACP's argument, had reversed *Corrigan,* finding that judicial enforcement of such agreements constituted forbidden state action—the NAACP was buoyed by changes in society. The Democratic Party, despite protests and then a walkout from the party's 1948 national convention of many southerners led by then South Carolina Governor Strom Thurmond, had adopted a strong plank on civil rights. Despite the loss of the Deep South to Thurmond's Dixiecrat candidacy and the candidacy of former Vice President Henry Wallace siphoning away the votes of left-wing Democrats, Democrat Harry Truman won the election over his Republican rival. Truman used his power as commander in chief to issue an executive order that ended segregation in the military. The growing rivalry between the Soviet Union and the United States and the growing pro-independence stirrings among the

black- and yellow-skinned inhabitants of Britain and France's
African and Asian colonies also put pressure on America for internal change. How could the United States argue that it was the
defender of freedom against Soviet and then Chinese Communist
oppression so long as Jim Crow laws ruled the lives of most
African Americans? The struggle for the hearts and minds of
those leaders who were advocating independence from the United
Kingdom and the other European colonial rulers could be lost to
the Soviets and their then Chinese allies if nothing changed in
America in terms of race relations.

Despite all this, the NAACP knew that the victory they would
seek in the five cases that would come to be known simply as
Brown v. Board (1954) was by no means assured. Although the
Court's decisions in *Shelley v. Kraemer, Sweatt,* and *McLaurin*
had all been unanimous, the Vinson Court was not necessarily a
liberal bench. The sudden deaths of Justices Frank Murphy and
Wiley Rutledge had removed two liberal stalwarts. The Truman-
nominated replacements, Tom Clark and Sherman Minton, like
Truman's other two Supreme Court appointees, were much more
conservative than the men they replaced.

Another concern for the NAACP was the manner in which the
Vinson Court wielded its power of judicial review. A secondary
question was how much power the Court actually commanded as
the decade of the 1950s opened. The Court's battle over the New
Deal had cost the judiciary dearly. "The nine old men"—Roosevelt had described them as unable to deal with the new problems
facing American society, "little by little, new facts become blurred
through old glasses fitted, as it were, for the needs of another generation" (Kelly, Harbison, and Belz 1991, 483)—had escaped the
disaster that would have ensued had President Roosevelt's "court-
packing" bill been adopted. The stratagem devised by Chief Justice Charles Evans Hughes that led to his unprecedented appearance along with Associate Justice Louis D. Brandeis before the
Senate's Judiciary Committee was brilliant and showed again

Hughes's superb political and leadership skills. The Roosevelt "court reform" bill was defeated, but both the president and the Court would pay for the defeat. For Roosevelt, it was his first legislative defeat, and it brought together an alliance between Republicans and southern Democrats that would dominate the Congress until the 1960s. As for the Court, the defeat meant that it had to abandon its traditional role within the American system of government as the defender of property rights. The so-called "switch in time that saved nine"—the Roosevelt bill sought to increase the size of the Court from nine to a maximum of fifteen, the president being given the right to appoint one justice for every current member of the Court who was over seventy years of age—saw the Court that had only a few years earlier gutted the New Deal voting now to uphold legislation that differed, in many cases, only a little from the laws it had earlier struck down.

In the wake of this battle, the Court also adopted a more limited definition of its role. Judicial self-restraint, the passive virtues that justices such as Oliver Wendell Holmes Jr. had preached while conservative judges had used their power to strike down legislation that they felt violated property rights, was now the prevailing religion of the Court and of Justice Felix Frankfurter, its self-appointed high priest. Judges should only void legislation that clearly violated the Constitution. The Vinson Court seemed to subscribe fully to this view of the Court's role. In fact, some commentators have noted that it embraced self-restraint with a fervor that even Holmes would not have endorsed. "The strong legislature–weak judiciary formula which Holmes developed for the . . . purpose of controlling judicial review over state economic legislation" was extended by the Vinson Court to apply even to specific guarantees of individual rights found in the Bill of Rights (Pritchett 1954, 240).

Would a Court that was weakened from the struggles of the 1930s, that was weakened by its own limited view of judicial review, and, finally, that was weakened by sharp personal and political divisions among its members, be up to the task with which

Marshall and his colleagues at the NAACP Legal Defense Fund
were preparing to present it?

It was not an accident that what would become the lead case,
Brown v. Board of Education of Topeka, Kansas, came from a border state, nor that another case, *Briggs v. Elliott,* originated in South
Carolina. Segregation in the border states was generally less severe
than in the Deep South, particularly in the "black belt" counties of
that region in which blacks outnumbered whites. South Carolina
was a state that, under the leadership of former Supreme Court Justice and now Governor Jimmy Byrnes (Byrnes served as an almost
de facto deputy president during the war years of the Roosevelt
presidency and later, for two years, as secretary of state under Truman) had taken significant steps finally to achieve *Plessy*'s mandate
of "equal" facilities. Byrnes had warned the legislature and the citizens of South Carolina that the nation and, in particular, the Court
would no longer tolerate the gross disparities in educational opportunities that the South provided to the children of the two races.
New schools for blacks were built and more money was directed to
teacher training and for the staffing of segregated schools.

Byrnes also sought the legal services of John W. Davis to meet
the challenge of Marshall and his team. Davis was a former solicitor general of the United States. At least twice he had been offered
appointments to the Supreme Court. The Democratic Party's unsuccessful nominee for president in 1924, Davis was a highly successful attorney and argued more cases before the Supreme Court
than any other lawyer during the twentieth century. At age sev-
enty-nine, Davis was still in his prime. His most recent victory
had come in the case of *Youngstown Sheet and Tube Company v.
Sawyer* (1952), in which he successfully argued that President
Truman's seizure of the steel mills of the United States exceeded
his power as commander in chief.

Only in the Delaware case did the NAACP come close to victory, but even there the state court refused to set aside the "separate but equal" standard even as it ordered black students admit-

ted to schools formerly reserved for whites. In Virginia, South Carolina, Kansas, and the District of Colombia, courts upheld the precedent Justice Henry Brown had set more than a half century earlier. The Supreme Court took all five cases, combining them for the purposes of oral argument.

The precise reaction of the justices to this first set of arguments, delivered in December 1952, remains a matter of dispute. John W. Davis, leaving the Court after oral argument, allowed that he thought, "We've got it won, five-to-four—or maybe six-to-three" (Kluger 1975, 736). For the NAACP, Frankfurter was seen as key, not because they feared he would vote to uphold segregation, but rather that only he could lead what had been called a "passive" Court (Pritchett 1954, 2) to take what was admittedly a very bold, activist stance. Their concern centered in particular on the two Kentuckians, Chief Justice Vinson and Associate Justice Stanley Reed. Reed had voted to strike down the white primary (the Democratic Party in certain southern states claimed that as a private organization it could determine who its members were and, accordingly, could exclude nonwhites from the party). Vinson, as noted earlier, had authored the opinions in *Sweatt* and *McLaurin*. Still, would these two self-restraint-oriented judges feel that the Court, "the weakest of the three branches," should involve itself in the passions that would naturally be aroused if segregation were struck down? More recent speculation has focused on the vote of Justice Robert Jackson as a result of the discovery of a draft opinion written by his clerk at the time, William Rehnquist, that concluded that the Court should not overturn the "separate but equal" doctrine as it applied to secondary and elementary education. Did this draft opinion reflect the views of the justice or the clerk who wrote it, or was it simply an academic exercise? Even the way that the normally activist and liberal Justice Hugo Black would vote has been questioned.

Whatever the actual disposition of the justices was, they were not in any great hurry to proceed with a decision. Instead, they took the unusual step of ordering a second round of oral arguments, which they scheduled for October 12, 1953. In ordering reargument, the Court directed opposing counsel to concentrate on five questions. These largely were the result of a proposal authored by Justice Frankfurter and one of his clerks, Alexander Bickel. "The general purpose of the questions . . . was to determine whether the Congress . . . and the state legislatures . . . regarded the Amendment as abolishing separation of the races in the public schools" and whether, if they did, that power rested with the judiciary or with Congress (Reams and Wilson 1975, v–vi).

The task for the attorneys defending segregation seemed easier. The same Congress that had proposed the Fourteenth Amendment had segregated the schools of the District of Columbia. Southern and border states had early on segregated their public schools. For the NAACP, the only hope was that something could be culled from the congressional debates. They found some support in the speeches of Thad Stevens and of John Bingham; the latter had been the floor manager of the amendment in the House of Representatives.

More significant, probably, than all of the historical research in determining the final decision, however, was the sudden death of Chief Justice Vinson on September 8, 1953. Vinson's death prompted the sharp-tongued Frankfurter to remark, "This is the first indication I have ever had that there is a God" (Kluger 1975, 829).

Vinson's passing provoked immediate speculation both on and off the Court as to whom the new president, Dwight Eisenhower, would appoint to the Court's center chair. Vacancies for the post of chief justice inevitably prompt debate as to whether the new chief should be selected from among the current justices or from outside. The tensions that had led President Truman to select Vinson, an outsider, as chief in 1946 had not been eased in the intervening years. The fact that there was only one Republican on the

Court, Harold Burton, also may have led Eisenhower to discount seriously looking at an in-Court candidate. Although several prominent names surfaced, including former GOP presidential candidate Thomas Dewey as well as Secretary of State John Foster Dulles, it was California Governor Earl Warren on whom Eisenhower's favor finally fell. Warren had played a key role in delivering the crucial California delegation to Eisenhower at the party's 1952 convention and appears to have been promised the first opening on the Court. Neither Eisenhower nor Warren could have anticipated that the first vacancy would be the sixty-three-year-old chief justice's seat. Eisenhower was reluctant at first to give such a "plum" appointment to Warren, but Warren was quite clear as to how he understood the earlier promise and the president quickly acquiesced. With the Senate in recess, Eisenhower made a recess appointment on October 2. Warren was now the fourteenth chief justice. The Senate confirmed Warren on March 1, 1954. *Brown* was decided by a unanimous Court on May 17, 1954.

Frankfurter immediately offered his services to the chief. As would be the case in so many similar situations, both before and after, Frankfurter would eventually overstay his welcome as the helpful professor. Frankfurter had been a professor at Harvard Law School before he was appointed to the Court in 1939, and, at least according to his critics, he never ceased playing the role of the imperious professor during his twenty-three years on the bench. By all accounts, however, Frankfurter's role in guiding newcomer Warren and steering him clear of the bitter personal differences among the Court's members was invaluable in allowing the new chief justice to lead the Court to the eventual decisions in *Brown* and *Bolling v. Sharpe* (1954). *Bolling* involved the segregation of the public schools of the District of Columbia and involved the Court's use of the Fifth Amendment's guarantee of due process. Still, it is Warren, the "superchief," who must be accorded the greatest praise for the Court's final product in *Brown*.

Warren's opinion displayed none of Frankfurter's hesitation about the proper role the Court should play in interpreting the Constitution. When Frankfurter finally realized that the new chief justice's view of the Court's role was totally at odds with his own is not entirely clear, but it was inevitable that Warren, who had been an activist governor of California for three terms, was not apt to subscribe to Frankfurter's sermons on judicial abstinence. Warren was part of what was dubbed the "modern Republican Party." This was not the party of Coolidge, Hoover, or even "Mr. Republican," Senator Robert Taft of Ohio, the son of the former president and chief justice. An activist governor would in turn become an activist justice.

Judicial activism, in contrast to judicial self-restraint in the style of Holmes and Frankfurter, does not dwell on the weakness or undemocratic character of the Court but rather stresses its role as a coordinate branch of government charged with the duty and responsibility of interpreting the laws and the Constitution of the United States. The Court does not need to fret unduly about exercising judicial review, the power to review laws to determine whether they are in accord with the basic document and to declare void those that contravene the Constitution. As Chief Justice John Marshall had pronounced in *Marbury v. Madison* (1803), judges, by swearing to uphold the Constitution, are bound to declare null any law that violates the Constitution. "This is of the very essence of judicial duty."

Marshall continued his argument for the Court's power to determine the constitutionality of legislation:

The framers of the Constitution contemplated that instrument as a rule for the government of courts, as well as of the legislature.

Why otherwise does it direct the judges to take an oath to support it? This oath certainly applies in an especial manner, to their conduct in their official character. How immoral to impose it on them, if they were to be used as the instruments, and the knowing instruments, for violating what they swear to support!

Warren's opinion was brief and was likely directed more to the general media and to the general public than to lawyers or other students of the law. Despite the pages of historical research presented by the opposing sides (the response of the defenders of segregation exceeds 700 pages in book form [Reams and Wilson 1975]), Warren observed of their documents that, "[a]t best, they are inconclusive."

Instead, Warren focused on the role education played in people's lives today, a role far different from the one it served in the 1860s and 1870s. "Today, education is perhaps the most important function of state and local governments. . . . Such an opportunity, where the state has undertaken to provide it, is a right which must be made available to all on equal terms." Warren then turned to the issue that Marshall and the NAACP most wanted addressed: Could separate schools ever be equal? *Sweatt* had concluded that Texas could not establish a law school for blacks that would be equal to the whites-only University of Texas Law School; but law schools were not elementary schools. The cost of replicating a law school such as that of the University of Texas would be significant. In addition, as Vinson had noted, there was the issue of reputation. How could a new law school ever be able to equal an established and well-regarded school such as the law school of the University of Texas? The same could scarcely be said of elementary and secondary schools. South Carolina was trying to equalize the schools in terms of facilities and staff. No one could argue that the reputation for excellence of a particular elementary school could not be quickly achieved with the right infusion of talented teachers and the proper resources to assist them in educating their pupils.

Warren posed and answered the question unhesitatingly: "We come then to the question presented: Does segregation of children in public schools solely on the basis of race, even though the physical facilities and other 'tangible' factors may be equal, deprive the children of the minority group of equal educational opportunities? We believe that it does."

Warren argued that the decisions in *Sweatt* and *McLaurin* had turned on the "intangible" factors. In *Brown,* however, the "intangible" factors were different.

> To separate them from others of similar age and qualifications solely because of their race generates a feeling of inferiority as to their status in the community that may affect their hearts and minds in a way unlikely ever to be undone. . . . "Segregation of white and colored children in public schools has a detrimental effect upon the colored children. The impact is greater when it has the sanction of law. . . ." [Warren is quoting from the lower court decision in *Brown.*]
>
> We conclude that in the field of public education the doctrine of "separate but equal" has no place. Separate educational facilities are inherently unequal. Therefore, we hold that the plaintiffs and others similarly situated . . . are, by reason of the segregation complained of deprived of [the guarantee of equal protection under the Fourteenth Amendment].

Brown not only represented a triumph for Marshall and the NAACP and returned the nation to the commitment of the Declaration of Independence and to the ideals that drove the authors of the Freedom Amendments, but it also restored the Court to its proper role as a coordinate branch of government. It is more than a little ironic that it was race and feelings about race that caused the Court through its *Dred Scott* decision to squander overnight the legacy of respect and power that the Taney Court and its predecessor, the Marshall Court, had earned. It is ironic that it was *Brown* that won for the Court and the federal judiciary the respect and power that the Court had lost in the 1930s in its clash with President Roosevelt and Congress. Yet another irony can be discerned in the fact that it was the doctrine of substantive due process, which had in part supported Taney's conclusion in *Dred Scott,* that would serve in part also to undo the Court in the 1930s.

Despite all the praise that *Brown* has received, the very real fact is that it had almost as little effect on conditions for blacks as Lincoln's Emancipation Proclamation had on the condition of slaves. The Court hesitated in deciding how it would be implemented. It asked for further argument, and the result of this is the less well known and certainly less hailed ruling of *Brown v. Board of Education* (1955), or, as it is sometimes entitled, *Brown II*. Also sometimes ignored is that *Brown* neither overturned *Plessy*—"'separate but equal' has no place" in public education—nor adopted Justice Harlan's idea of a "color-blind Constitution." *Brown II*, however, introduced Americans to a phrase borrowed from a nineteenth-century poem by Francis Thompson, "The Hound of Heaven." The phrase was "with all deliberate speed." This was the standard by which federal courts were to carry out the mandate of *Brown I*.

Just as commentators speculate on whether the Constitution's framers needed to make the compromises they did with the South, so commentators speculate today as to whether the Court could have ordered segregation to end immediately. To use the words of Marshall in *Marbury,* is it not "worse than solemn mockery" to allow judges who have taken an oath to uphold the Constitution to continue to countenance, even for a day, continued violations of the Constitution. Like all of the "what-if" questions of history, no one knows exactly what the reaction would have been had the Court ordered immediate compliance by southern and border state school districts. What is known is that meaningful desegregation began to occur only in the 1960s, far more as a result of action by the president and Congress than as a result of federal courts.

The *Cooper v. Aaron* and *Green v. County School Board* Decisions

Two additional Warren Court decisions on race and equal protection must be examined. Like *Brown*, both added greatly to the power of the Court in American life, and both continue to be the subject of debate. For those who speculate as to what would have occurred had the Court ordered immediate compliance with *Brown*, the situation that developed in 1957 in Little Rock, Arkansas, may be useful for their musings. Arkansas, and Little Rock in particular, had never produced the race-baiting politicians who had populated southern state houses and state legislatures before and after *Brown*. The governor of Arkansas, Orval Faubus, was seen by many as a moderate on matters of race. Little Rock and Faubus, however, entered America's history books in a very different way as a result of events in 1957. What started out in Little Rock as what appeared as a serious effort by the local school board to comply with *Brown* quickly spun out of control, leading first to a state takeover of the local schools, then the federalization of the state's national guard, and, finally, the introduction of federal troops to guard the black students entering Little Rock High School.

In justifying his defiance of federal authorities, Governor Faubus claimed that although he was bound by his oath of office to uphold the Constitution, he was not bound to bow to decisions of the Supreme Court. To defenders of the Court and to members of the Court, this was perceived as a blatant attempt to undo more than a century of American constitutional history.

The Court's response came in the case of *Cooper v. Aaron* (1958). The unanimous opinion was issued by the Court in the name of all nine justices, a step taken to show the seriousness that all felt was required in rejecting Faubus's claim. The Court wrote that the oath Faubus and other state officials take imposes on them the duty to support not only the language and commands of the Constitution but also the decisions of the Supreme Court interpreting the Constitution. At the time, few outside the South saw anything particularly unusual or significant about the Court's decision in *Cooper*. The grandstanding by Faubus, who wanted to win an unprecedented third term as governor, the sight of armed federal troops and angry white crowds shouting at the few black students who dared to enter the high school, generally eclipsed the full implication of what the Court was saying in *Cooper*. Can an elected official, without violating the oath of office, oppose a decision of the Supreme Court? Current conservative critics argue that *Cooper* renewed the debate that Abraham Lincoln and Stephen Douglas had over the implications of Taney's infamous *Dred Scott* decision. Douglas had essentially claimed that it was the law of the land and that, accordingly, the issue was settled. Lincoln demurred, saying that he was obliged only to support the particular decision as it applied to the particular parties to the case.

The final word the Warren Court spoke on the issue of segregation was voiced in an opinion announced on May 27, 1968, just weeks before Chief Justice Warren would inform President Johnson of his intention to retire at the end of the term. *Green v. County School Board of New Kent County* (1968) announced the end of the Court's patience with "all deliberate speed," which one wag had long before suggested involved endless deliberation and no speed. Justice Brennan announced the Court's unanimous opinion. Just as important as bringing to an end the endless delays that had been put in the way of ending segregation, indeed perhaps more important was the Court's reinterpretation in *Green* of what *Brown I* entailed.

Virginia had adopted freedom of choice plans for ending segregation. In theory, it might be argued that such plans could work. Students in formerly all-black schools could opt to attend the schools previously reserved for whites, and whites could do the same. New Kent County had two high schools. In fact, no whites chose to transfer to the formerly all-black school, and only 115 blacks moved to the formerly all-white high school. As a result, 85 percent of the county's black students still attended an all-black school.

Justice Brennan proceeded to reinterpret *Brown*, holding that "school boards operating state-compelled dual systems [were] clearly charged with the affirmative duty to take whatever steps might be necessary to convert to a unitary system in which racial discrimination would be eliminated root and branch." The only constitutionally acceptable plan a school board could pursue was one that "promise[d] realistically to convert promptly to a system without a 'white' school, and a 'Negro' school, but just schools."

No longer was it sufficient for formerly segregated schools to dismantle the system that had resulted in black students' being bused past white schools and into black schools. Now it was the duty of school boards, in order to comply with the guarantee of equal protection, to take affirmative steps to achieve integration. Ending segregation was no longer sufficient. Integration was the goal that formerly segregated schools, dual systems, must pursue.

CONCLUSION

Green lowered the curtain on the era of the Warren Court, which had begun with *Brown.* In turn, *Brown, Cooper v. Aaron,* and *Green* had established the Warren Court's image as an activist Court bent on giving the guarantees of the Constitution the broadest definition possible to achieve a fairer, more democratic society.

By wielding the sword of judicial review on behalf of those who were powerless and those who had been discriminated against, the Court renewed itself and reestablished itself as a major player in American politics. In the election of 1952 neither of the presidential candidates, Dwight Eisenhower and Adlai Stevenson, mentioned the Court. Warren was a recess appointment who was only later confirmed by a Senate that raised no questions about what his judicial philosophy was, much less how he would vote on certain issues.

In 1968, the Court was one of the issues that Richard Nixon used to win the presidency. Earlier that year, President Johnson thought he could easily secure Warren's spot for his former attorney and longtime confidante, Abe Fortas. Instead, the president was forced to withdraw the nomination and to allow the choice of the next chief justice to fall into the hands of the victor in the 1968 presidential race, Richard Nixon.

As the Federalists had predicted, ambition could be harnessed to counter ambition. The Court's ambition had brought it power; it had also allowed it to transform American society, and generally these changes were for the better. Now, the Court's ambition had been met by the ambition of other political actors.

REFERENCES AND FURTHER READING

Abraham, Henry J. 1974. *Justices and Presidents: A Political History of Appointments to the Supreme Court.* New York: Oxford University Press.

Burner, David, et al. 1991. *A College History of the United States.* St. James, NY: Brandywine Press.

Elkins, Stanley. 1976. *Slavery: A Problem in American Institutional and Intellectual Life,* 3rd ed. Chicago: University of Chicago Press.

Fairman, Charles. 1971. *Reconstruction and Reunion, 1864–88, Part One.* New York: Macmillan.

Finkelman, Paul. 1992. "Slavery." In Kermit Hall, ed., *The Oxford Companion to the Supreme Court of the United States.* New York: Oxford University Press.

Friedman, Leon. 1969. *Argument: The Oral Argument before the Supreme Court in* Brown v. Board of Education of Topeka, *1952–55.* New York: Chelsea House.

Helminski, Francis. 1992. "Henry Billings Brown." In Kermit Hall, ed., *The Oxford Companion to the Supreme Court of the United States.* New York: Oxford University Press.

Kelly, Alfred H., Winfred A. Harbison, and Herman Belz. 1991. *The American Constitution: Its Origins and Development,* vol. 2., 7th ed. New York: W. W. Norton.

Kluger, Richard. 1975. *Simple Justice: The History of* Brown v. Board of Education *and Black America's Struggle for Equality.* New York: Alfred A. Knopf.

Lewis, Walker. 1965. *Without Fear or Favor: A Biography of Roger Brooke Taney.* Boston: Houghton Mifflin.

Mason, Alpheus Thomas, and Donald Grier Stephenson Jr. 1999. *American Constitutional Law: Introductory Essays and Selected Cases,* 12th ed. Upper Saddle River, NJ: Prentice-Hall.

Murphy, Walter F., James E. Fleming, Sotirios A. Barber, and Stephen Macedo. 2003. *American Constitutional Interpretation.* 3rd ed. Mineola, NY: Foundation Press.

Pratt, Walter F., Jr. 1992. *"Plessy v. Ferguson."* In Kermit Hall, ed., *The Oxford Companion to the Supreme Court of the United States.* New York: Oxford University Press.

Pritchett, C. Herman. 1954. *Civil Liberties and the Vinson Court.* Chicago: University of Chicago Press.

Reams, Bernard D., Jr., and Paul E. Wilson. 1975. *Segregation and the Fourteenth Amendment in the States.* Buffalo: William S. Hein.

2

ORIGINS AND
DEVELOPMENT

In describing the powers of the three branches of government under the newly drafted Constitution, Alexander Hamilton, writing in "Federalist Paper 78," spoke of the judiciary as possessing "neither force nor will, but merely judgment." Congress, Hamilton wrote, held the purse, and the president the sword. As *Brown* and subsequent desegregation cases amply demonstrate, those two powers—exemplified by the use of federal troops by both Presidents Dwight Eisenhower (in Little Rock) and John F. Kennedy (at the University of Mississippi) and President Lyndon Johnson's success in securing a federal role in funding elementary and secondary education—were crucial in transforming American society. Only positive action by the president and Congress helped America to realize at least some of the promise of the Court's landmark decision in *Brown v. Board of Education* (1954). As Hamilton had predicted, the judiciary "must ultimately depend upon the aid of the executive arm even for the efficacy of its judgments."

Still, these events in no way diminish the importance of Chief Justice Earl Warren's opinion in *Brown* in bringing about change in American society. Although some constitutional historians have not been totally enamored of his somewhat perfunctory dismissal of the importance of history in ascertaining the meaning of the Fourteenth Amendment's equal protection guarantee and others have debated his failure to frame a "neutral principle" that could be applied to other cases involving race, both probably miss the real point of Warren's opinion (Patterson 2001, 68–69). Warren was not writing for legal scholars or even for lawyers but rather seeking to influence a broader audience. His likely goal was to persuade the American people that even if school facilities, funding, and teaching staff were in every other respect equal, segregation still ran counter to bedrock American values. Segregation simply was not fair. That judgment, no matter how often it may be scrutinized by legal Monday-morning quarterbacks, resonated with most Americans. By the 1960s, and all the more so by the 1970s, even those who had protested and pledged eternal resistance—persons like former Dixiecrat presidential candidate Strom Thurmond—had finally accepted the legitimacy of *Brown*. They had either to accept it or reject the American dream and the American creed "that all men are created equal . . . [and] are endowed by their Creator with certain unalienable Rights."

Warren's *Brown* opinion succeeded by persuading. Richard Neustadt, in his classic study *Presidential Power and the Modern Presidents,* concluded that presidential power is ultimately also based on the ability to persuade. Persuasion also seems to be at the core of Hamilton's observation that the judiciary's power was one of "merely judgment." Indeed, the power to persuade can be said to be the foundation of all political power in a democracy.

Although *Brown* had little immediate effect on the number of African American students attending formerly all-white southern schools, eventually it did change the views and values of Americans. These developments were necessary for the success of the civil rights movement of the 1960s as well as for the many advances won by African Americans and other minorities in the years that followed.

Possessed of neither the sword nor the purse—in other words, without the power to enforce its decisions—the Court is probably the most dependent of the three branches on the power to persuade. If it fails in that endeavor, its decisions, although not likely to be entirely ignored, run a great chance of provoking lengthy and sometimes endless resistance on the part of lower courts, the other two branches of government, and state governments. Such resistance in turn would tend to erode the Court's prestige among the general public, and consequently its power in turn to persuade the relevant actors and publics that its decisions are right.

Whereas Warren's opinion in *Brown* did prove to be persuasive, Chief Justice Warren Burger's opinion in the first of the Court's busing cases, *Swann v. Charlotte-Mecklenburg Board of Education* and Associate Justice Lewis Powell's opinion on affirmative action in *Regents of the University of California v. Bakke*, have largely failed to change opinions. Three decades after *Swann* was handed down, it has still failed to gain widespread acceptance, particularly from those who disagree with either the opinion's results or its authors' reasoning. However, in 2003, *Bakke* was reaffirmed in *Grutter v. Bollinger*. Although these cases certainly do not rise to a level worthy of the memorable phrase Chief Justice Charles Evans Hughes applied to *Dred Scott*—"self-inflicted wounds"—they have not entirely redounded to the Court's credit. It can also be argued that they have provided much less benefit to society than decisions that produced different results or that were based on different lines of reasoning. Indeed, in many respects they may have caused other problems that might otherwise never have arisen. In the case of busing, Court decisions may have done more damage than good even to those individuals or groups that the Court found to have been the victims of discrimination. The fact that American public schools are more segregated now than they were in the 1970s says something about the success of busing, for instance. A recent report in the *New York Times*, for example, found that the proportions of African American and Latino students who now attend schools with large numbers of whites had declined since 1970. This decline has been precipitous since the mid-1980s, with the result that African American students "now typically go to schools where fewer than 31 percent of their classmates are white" (Winter 2003, A14). As for affirmative action, it continues to trigger debate in American society.

The line that the Burger Court drew between de jure segregation—segregation that results from government action—and de facto segregation—segregation that occurs as a result of behavior that government has not directed, such as residential housing patterns—is one that few Americans have ever understood. Similarly, the distinction between quotas and goals might have been as confusing to Lewis Carroll's Alice as Wonderland itself was.

J. Harvie Wilkinson III, a member and former chief judge of the Fourth Circuit's Court of Appeals who is widely considered to be on the short list for nomination to the Supreme Court by the George W. Bush administration, drew what may be an important distinction between the *Brown* decision and the Court's later rulings on affirmative action and busing. Wilkinson, who clerked for Justice Lewis Powell and taught as a law professor, argued that the later opinions "were neither morally assertive nor empirically grounded. Instead, the Court saw the matter legalistically, as one of 'violation and remedy.' This framework lent the Court's actions a legal veneer, even as it masked subjective judgments and avoided frank exploration of the issues over which the larger American society was deeply divided" (Wilkinson 1979, 133).

Busing as a remedy for segregation was, like affirmative action, a product of the Burger Court. Ironically, the Burger Court was supposedly designed by its principal architect, Richard Nixon, to avoid the activism and controversies of the Warren Court—indeed, to reverse many of the Warren Court's liberal decisions. Instead, the Burger Court proved to be far more activist than the Warren Court. In cases involving race, the Court reignited racial politics. In fact, its decisions triggered political consequences much greater than any produced by *Brown*. The latter did lead to the "Southern Manifesto," drawn up and signed by almost every single representative from the old Confederacy protesting the Court's decision in *Brown*, but the Deep South nevertheless continued to vote Democratic in national and local elections. Republican presidential candidates Dwight Eisenhower and Nixon, at least publicly, expressed no differences on *Brown* with their Democratic opposites, Adlai Stevenson and John Kennedy.

Things would be quite different with busing and affirmative action. Both profoundly affected voter behavior and altered regional voting trends that had persisted for more than a century. It may be that they helped realize for the Republican Party, more than anything Nixon himself did, the benefits of Nixon's "southern strategy" by transforming the formerly solidly Democratic South into the solid GOP stronghold on which recent Republican victories in presidential and congressional campaigns have been built.

THE BURGER COURT

The Supreme Court first approved of busing as an appropriate remedy with which to deal with segregation in public schools in a unanimous 1971 decision in *Swann v. Charlotte-Mecklenburg Board of Education*. *Swann* was in many respects a logical consequence of the Warren Court's final decision on segregation, *Green v. County School Board of New Kent County* (1968). In that case, Justice William Brennan had proclaimed the end of the Court's patience with southern school boards' intransigence, which was sometimes masked under the guise of proceeding with "all deliberative speed." The *Green* opinion required that previously segregated school districts take immediate measures or be directed to take such steps that would result in their becoming fully unitary systems. No longer would it suffice for the laws, regulations, and practices that produced segregation simply to be dismantled or jettisoned. That still had to happen, but in addition, it was now necessary for these school districts to take positive steps to ensure equality. "Equal protection of the laws" meant integration and not simply the ending of segregation.

The Court that carried out this mandate, however, was dramatically different from the Court that had produced the *Green* edict. Warren E. Burger had replaced Earl Warren in the Court's center chair as chief justice. Harry Blackmun sat in place of Justice Abe Fortas. Some would also claim that Justice Hugo Black, the Court's senior member, had himself changed. Black, the first of the Roosevelt appointees to the Court (confirmed in 1937) had long been the leader of the Court's liberal bloc. Toward the end of his thirty-four years on the bench, however, many saw Black as pulling away from his longtime liberal activist moorings and adopting much more conservative stances on issues of individual rights than would have been expected of him during the course of most of his career. To these observers, therefore, it was a different Black who sat for oral argument in the *Swann* case than the justice who had heard *Brown* seventeen years earlier or even *Green* three years before.

The Court would soon undergo even more changes. In 1972, President Nixon replaced Justice John Marshall Harlan Jr., often a swing vote on the Warren Court, with Assistant Attorney General William Rehnquist, a conservative who had cut his political teeth on Barry Goldwater's 1964 presidential campaign. Black was succeeded by former American Bar Association President Lewis Powell. Like Black, Powell was a southerner, but otherwise they were poles apart. Black was a former United States senator, a Populist, and an avid New Deal supporter who had started his career representing workers in the steel mills of Birmingham and had risen up the Alabama political ladder rung by rung. Powell, in contrast, was a member of the First Families of Virginia. He had served as president of the American Bar Association and chaired the Richmond School Board.

In 1975 Justice William O. Douglas retired from the Court and was replaced by John Paul Stevens. Indeed, by the end of the 1970s only two members of the Court had been appointed by Democratic presidents: Justice Byron White, a Kennedy appointee, and Justice Thurgood Marshall, the NAACP's lead attorney in *Brown*, the Court's first African American justice, and a Johnson nominee. More important still, only Justices Marshall and Brennan remained of the six-member majority that had dominated the Warren Court during the 1960s, the Court's period of greatest activism, when it truly seemed to be remaking the fabric of American life.

Court personnel and changes in the overall national political climate do not fully explain the differences between *Brown* and the later busing and affirmative action decisions. Outside of the South, few voices had been heard defending segregation as good. Even within the South, some of the debate centered more on how *Brown* was to be implemented than on whether the decision was mandated by the Constitution or violated state sovereignty. Apart from the most blatant of racists—and the 1950s and 1960s produced many—some who argued against *Brown* used the arguments of excessive judicial power or states' rights to give their arguments at least a veneer of respectability.

No such disguises were necessary in the affirmative action and busing debates. They too produced more than their fair share of racists. Yet in these debates, it can also be argued that there is a degree of right on both sides. Obviously, depending on one's perspective, one will claim that one side has more right than the other, that society is better served by one outcome rather than another, but it is hard to paint the opposing viewpoint as having no basis in justice.

Accordingly, the task facing the Burger Court was every bit as great as the one that had confronted Earl Warren when he succeeded Chief Justice Fred Vinson and presided over the second round of arguments in *Brown*. Burger did have the advantage of the prestige that the Warren Court had accumulated, particularly in the media and within the academic community. The scars of the 1930s Court, which were still somewhat tender in 1953, were long gone by 1969. What Burger did not have was the political skill that Warren had brought to his role as chief justice. Warren understood public opinion. He had been enormously popular in California, winning reelection as governor after winning the nomination of both the Republican and Democratic parties. He was equally effective in marshaling the justices to unanimous decisions. Burger, on the other hand, lacked all the great political skills of his predecessor. He proved generally unable to win votes from the Warren Court remnant and, more surprisingly, was frequently unable even to keep his fellow Nixon appointees in line. Even worse, perhaps, he did not seem able to sense what the public's reactions would be to the Court's decisions. Notably, he did not appreciate the powder-keg potential of busing in cities outside of the South.

The *Swann* decision and the subsequent affirmative action decision in *Bakke* are examples of how Warren Burger, again because of a lack of political skills, failed as chief justice. Unlike those among his predecessors who have been labeled "great," Burger seemed unable as chief to establish himself either as social or task leader of the Court (Danelski 2002, 662–670). A task leader, such as Charles Evans Hughes, is able to lead the Court by dint of his intellect and his command of the Court's work. A social leader, such as William Howard Taft, is able to ensure a degree of harmony among nine independent individuals—"nine scorpions in a bottle" to use one of the many memorable phrases coined by Justice Oliver Wendell Holmes Jr. (Lerner 1994, book jacket).

In *Swann*, Burger, at least on the surface, appeared able to hold the Court together. Warren had considered unanimity in the race cases to be essential. When the chief justice is in the majority, he has the traditional responsibility of determining who will write the opinion of the Court. Burger elected to write the *Swann* opinion himself. Later events, however, would demonstrate that the Burger opinion masked serious divisions on race among the justices. By 1978 and the *Bakke* case, these fissures had become chasms and Burger, then obviously in the minority, found himself without the votes to control the assignment of the opinion.

Unlike *Brown*, upon which the eyes of most of the nation were directed in 1954, *Swann* attracted little attention before the Court announced its decision on April 20, 1971. Politically, though, the issue of busing had already caused some political stirrings. Certain members of Congress understood the possible implications of *Green* and had begun pushing for legislative restrictions on busing. These efforts would continue throughout the 1970s, with varying degrees of success. Perhaps because some members of Congress also understood that however politically charged the busing question was, it was not an issue that, like segregation, clearly pitted the forces of good against those of evil, legislation that emerged was strangely ambivalent on the subject. "[I]t invariably included a provision that allowed the courts to set aside the law or to interpret it in line with past Supreme Court precedents" (Wasby et al. 1977, 409). As a result, the legislation's actual effect was only "symbolic."

Although critics of the Court's busing decisions never succeeded in getting the most radical legislation adopted, busing ended up polarizing many urban communities along racial and ideological lines. Many big-city Democrats, sometimes styled "hard-hat" Democrats, began to see Republican President Nixon as more sympathetic to their plight than were many of the leaders of the national Democratic Party. Nixon, in turn, saw them as part of the "silent majority" that he hoped to mobilize behind his banner, if not that of the Republican Party.

By the 1980s, busing had largely vanished as a national political issue. In fact, by the 1990s, the Court itself seemed bent on putting the whole issue behind it. Decisions now came down permitting school systems previously under court orders to take steps to achieve a unitary system to be removed from court supervision and, if they chose to do so, to discontinue the positive steps that had been previously seen as necessary for achieving an integrated or "racially balanced" system. School systems thus could cease busing for racial integration and return to neighborhood schools so long as the new school boundaries did not evidence a desire to segregate.

Affirmative action, by contrast, remains highly controversial. Ironically, the dispute seems more active within the walls of the nation's universities than in the supposedly more conservative private sector of the economy. Many of the nation's largest corporations are among its greatest supporters. The Bush administration's decision in early 2003 to file a brief in opposition to the affirmative action plans in operation at the University of Michigan prompted an opposing brief by a corporate group that included such giants as General Motors and Exxon-Mobil. Within the government, affirmative action seems more generally accepted in the military than it does among the white- and pink-collar bureaucracies.

THE BUSING CONTROVERSY

The yellow school bus has long been part of the modern American education scene. Until the 1970s any mention of "busing" likely referred to the issue of whether students attending private schools, particularly private religious schools, were eligible for free, state-funded transportation to such schools. The Court in 1947, in its first case (*Everson v. Board of Education*) interpreting the Establishment Clause of the First Amendment—"Congress shall make no law respecting an establishment of religion"—had found that providing free bus transportation to students attending Catholic schools was constitutional. Justice Black's opinion, though, did not require states to provide such transportation. Some states chose to do so, some demurred, and, in some, state courts found that such aid violated their own state constitutions. This issue of busing and the thousands of little controversies local school boards faced involving who should be bused would pale in comparison with the controversy produced by court-ordered busing designed to achieve racial integration.

The adoption in 1964 of the Civil Rights Act both allowed and prompted the federal government to take a more active role in instigating actions to force compliance with *Brown*. The Supreme Court had reentered the fray in 1963. Increasingly, it made it clear that the time for "all deliberate speed," a phrase that Chief Justice Warren had included in the second *Brown* (1955) decision, the decision that set the parameters for how federal courts would implement *Brown I*, was rapidly coming to a close. In *Green v. County School Board of Kent County* (1968), the Court finally rejected what had become a typical remedy offered by southern school boards: freedom of choice. Although the Court, speaking through Justice Brennan, did not hold that freedom of choice plans could never work, it did acknowledge that political and social realities made them unlikely solutions at best. Interestingly, in oral argument, counsel for the NAACP "conceded ... that the new remedy [of busing] paradoxically required the states and the Court to sanction what *Brown* notionally condemned—racially based pupil assignments" (Hutchinson 1992, 347). Given Brennan's careful language, and coming as it did at the end of the Warren Court (1953–1969), *Green*, at the time, attracted little attention, although it did, as noted earlier, prompt some legislative activity designed to limit busing. *Green's* full implications, however, would be made clear by the Burger Court's (1969–1986) first major case involving race, *Swann v. Charlotte-Mecklenburg Board of Education* (1971).

The Charlotte-Mecklenburg school district, which encompassed 550 square miles, was already under court supervision to ensure that it complied with the mandate of *Brown*. In light of the Supreme Court's 1968 decision in *Green*, the federal district court judge ordered busing as a further remedy. *Swann* thus offered the Burger Court an opportunity to demonstrate whether what was then often referred to as the "Nixon Court" would honor this particular part of the Warren Court legacy, given that it was expected or hoped, depending on the individual's political ideology, that it would scuttle much of the Warren Court's work in the realm of civil liberties.

One important part of the Warren Court's legacy on race was the Court's unanimity. Much has been written on Warren's masterful "massing" of the Court in the 1954 *Brown* decision. In the later and highly publicized showdown in Little Rock, which resulted in *Cooper v. Aaron* (1958), the Court had taken the unprecedented step of issuing an opinion signed by each of the nine justices. In light of these and other Warren Court decisions, Burger realized that a decision that was not unanimous would reflect poorly on his leadership and prejudice his place in the Court's history.

Unlike Earl Warren, Chief Justice Burger was rarely effective in winning over doubting colleagues. Worse still, Burger found himself in *Swann*, as he would two years later in the abortion decision, *Roe v. Wade* (1973), in the minority when the Court first voted on the case. In both cases, if Burger wanted to establish himself as more than *primus inter pares* (first among equals), and if he wanted to influence what the Court ultimately held, he needed to join the majority—which he did in both cases.

By voting with the majority, Burger was able to exercise the traditional function of the chief and assign the task of writing the opinion of the Court. In *Roe*, he would give this duty to Justice Harry Blackmun, then known either as "hip pocket Harry" or the "Minnesota twin" as a result of the influence Burger appeared to exercise over him. In *Swann*, Burger, having changed his vote, gave himself the assignment of writing the opinion. When his first draft was circulated, it was immediately apparent that Burger's own views and that of most of the Court greatly differed. Justice Douglas claimed that "most of the justices were 'astounded' by Burger's rationale" (Epstein and Knight 1998, 106). Burger faced the choice of either compromising or writing a dissenting opinion. Burger chose the former tack.

Typical of compromises that seek to incorporate a variety of ideas and opinions, the *Swann* opinion, at thirty pages, set a record in length for an opinion on civil rights. In contrast to Warren's succinct and eloquent opinion in *Brown*, which was designed more for the media, for school boards, and for the general public than for lawyers and law professors, Burger's opinion produced no memorable quotations and enough shifts of focus to confuse even the most skilled of attorneys. Its only merit was that it kept the Court unanimous. Despite all of its backpedaling, it also put the Supreme Court's imprimatur on the use of busing to achieve a unitary—that is, an integrated—school system.

The basis of the Burger opinion was that busing was necessary to "dismantle the dual system." As pointed out by one of busing's most vociferous legal critics, Lino A. Graglia,

> although the school board lost in each [of the three] court[s] it came before, it lost each time on the basis of a different theory. . . . Racial balance was . . . required by the district court [on the theory that it was necessary] to improve the academic performance of blacks and by the Fourth Circuit [on the basis that it was needed] to counteract the effects of racial residential patterns thought to be the result of official racial discrimination. (Graglia 1976, 116–117)

Despite the protests it triggered and the criticism of the Court—Graglia's book is entitled *Disaster by Decree*—the *Swann* decision itself might have been swiftly relegated to a minor place in the American civil rights history. It was, after all, a case in a southern school district. The district was also an atypical one, because of its huge size, its general use of busing to transport students, and the relatively small proportion (29 percent) of African Americans it contained. Ironically, the district that was to produce a case that would help change the face of American politics proceeded with relatively little fuss to implement the Court's decision.

The Court's next foray into the busing issue would produce very different results. The Denver, Colorado, school district had never maintained a dual system in the sense that the term had been applied to school districts in the County of Charlotte-Mecklenburg, in Little Rock, or in Topeka. In the latter communities, government action—whether at the state level or at the level of the school board—had formally prescribed separate systems or separate schools solely on the basis of race. This had never been true of Denver. Despite that, suit was brought against the district alleging that the school district had redrawn school boundary lines so as to preserve overwhelmingly white schools. In addition, its construction program was faulted. The charge was that the Denver district had built school buildings and added mobile classrooms in a manner designed again to ensure that whites went to certain schools and blacks to other schools.

Seventeen months after rendering its *Swann* opinion, the Court heard oral argument in the case of *Keyes v. Denver School District No. 1* (1973). The issues raised by *Keyes* shattered the fragile unity that characterized the *Swann* decision. Brennan wrote the opinion. Burger concurred without opinion. Douglas authored a separate concurring opinion. Powell, while concurring in the judgment, dissented from some of the remedies ordered. Justice Rehnquist, for his part, issued an outright dissent, the first dissent in a case involving race during the Court's so-called modern era. The Court was now as divided as the nation would soon be on the issues of busing and of integration.

The Brennan opinion, while finding that the school district's segregative acts affected only a small portion of the Denver school district, ordered busing throughout the district. Only this promised to achieve racial balance. Brennan's opinion rested on the premise that for there to be an equal protection violation there had to be an instance of specific government action that caused segregation—this was the essence of de jure segregation. As mentioned earlier, Burger concurred without an opinion. Justices Douglas, Blackmun, and Powell each took issue with the belief expressed in the Court's opinion that a clear distinction could be made between de jure and de facto segregation. With Justice White having recused himself for knowing individuals involved in the lawsuit, and Rehnquist in dissent, it can be concluded that the opinion of the Court in *Keyes* really enjoyed the full support of only three judges: Justices Brennan, Marshall, and Stewart.

The Watergate controversy and other news stories of the day momentarily distracted attention from what the Court had done. For those who were dissatisfied with the state of education in the big cities, and especially for those who felt that minorities were not receiving appropriate education, *Keyes* was welcomed as a means by which radical change could be brought to bureaucratized urban educational systems that appeared either unaware or unresponsive to the needs of their African American students.

Keyes offered no quick remedies, however. The Brennan opinion required plaintiffs in such suits to marshal evidence that demonstrated an intent to discriminate on the part of a school board. Although the plaintiffs in the famous Boston case did not have to look hard, the Massachusetts legislature had previously passed a law calling for steps to be taken to racially balance public schools, a measure that was quickly met with public defiance by the members of the Boston School Committee, who seemed bent in outdoing one another in voicing their defiance of the state statute. In contrast, in most cities the bias was much more carefully disguised. Nevertheless, gradually cases were made in most of the old cities of the Northeast and the Midwest and in the cities of the West. These cases exposed governmental steps that had been taken to preserve white schools in the face of growing numbers of minorities in public schools.

Busing opponents in many of these cities—notably at Charleston and South Boston High Schools—at times made the protests seen in Little Rock look mild by comparison. The massive resistance seen in the South was matched by massive truancy of white students in many cities. Buses were bombed; police overtime soared; state national guards were mobilized; and politicians reaped a rich harvest of political hay for denouncing busing and embracing the newly canonized "neighborhood school."

Of all the opinions in *Keyes*, Justice Powell's is possibly the most interesting. Powell argued that no bright-line distinction was possible between de jure and de facto segregation. In many places, residential segregation was a product of past government action, including the enforcement of racially exclusionary covenants that courts prior to the decision in *Shelley v. Kraemer* (1948) had upheld. Residential segregation resulted in part from the desire of white families to move to housing located in areas that fed students into all-white or overwhelmingly white schools. According to Powell,

> the familiar root cause of segregated schools in *all* the biracial metropolitan areas of our country is essentially the same: one of segregated residential and migratory patterns the impact of which on the racial composition of the schools was often perpetuated and rarely ameliorated by action of public school authorities. This is a national, not a southern, phenomenon. And it is largely unrelated to whether a particular State had or did not have segregative school laws.

Powell also demonstrated in *Keyes* and in subsequent cases a reluctance to issue busing mandates that were as far reaching as those favored by the majority. Powell explained his hesitation as growing out of his realization that massive court-ordered busing would in most cities lead to white flight, either to existing private schools or to neighboring suburbs. In others words, busing would lead to more segregation rather than to less. As an attorney representing the Richmond Board of Education, Powell had made very much the same argument in a case that had been tried in the federal courts.

The very same Court that had triggered the battles over busing subsequently acted in a way that dramatically reduced the issue's importance in national politics. As important as anything in tamping down the fires set by court-ordered busing was the 1974 case of *Milliken v. Bradley.* As Powell, Douglas, and Blackmun had noted in *Swann,* what constituted de jure segregation and what could be dismissed as simply the results of de facto segregation clearly depended on the eyes of the beholder. Justice Potter Stewart, who joined in opinions that held that such a distinction could be made, perhaps should have urged on his colleagues a variation of his famous definition of obscenity, "I know it when I see it," in *Jacobellis v. Ohio* (1964).

A district court in Michigan "saw it" in the case that was known as *Milliken v. Bradley.* Finding numerous examples of the Detroit School Board's engaging in practices that resulted in racial segregation and concluding that the district lines that separated the Detroit school district from the suburban school districts were "simply matters of political convenience and may not be used to deny constitutional rights," the district court ordered cross-district busing that included the city of Detroit and fifty-three suburban districts. Despite there being no personnel changes on the Court since *Keyes,* Burger was now able to reassert control and muster a majority to reverse the district court. By a vote of 5–4, with Brennan, Marshall, Douglas, and White in dissent, Burger was able finally to muster the votes of all three other Nixon appointees and that of Justice Stewart for an opinion that loudly sung the praises of local control of education. The opinion also emphasized the need for plaintiffs to establish a constitutional violation on the part of each of the individual school boards before they could hope that a judicial remedy could be imposed on those districts.

Although the controversy did not die away totally after *Milliken*, the Burger opinion immunized most suburban school districts from successful suits to integrate. By effectively limiting the issue to districts with significant numbers of minorities, the Court restricted such suits to the older urban core cities. It also set the stage for the busing cases that would come before the Rehnquist Court (1986–present), cases in which the justices were asked to decide when busing and other forms of affirmative steps, ordered to create unitary systems, could be brought to a close.

An example of such a case—and an indication of how much the Court has changed as a result of the justices appointed during the Reagan and George H. W. Bush administrations—is the Court's 1992 decision in a case involving the DeKalb County, Georgia, school system. The county's school system had been under court supervision since 1969, and in 1986 it went back to the district court to ask to be relieved of the supervision. The district court found that the school system had achieved unitary status in four of the six categories—student assignments, transportation, physical facilities, and extracurricular activities—but still fell short of the standards in faculty assignments and in the allocation of resources. Nevertheless, the court reduced the level of judicial oversight over the school system. This decision was appealed by parents of black children attending the DeKalb County schools and reversed by the court of appeals, which found that until full compliance was achieved, there could be no diminution of court supervision. The appeals court's decision in turn was reversed by a unanimous Supreme Court.

Speaking through Justice Anthony Kennedy, the Court held that "in the course of supervising desegregation plans, federal courts have the authority to relinquish supervision and control of school districts in incremental stages, before full compliance has been achieved in every area of school operations" (*Freeman v. Pitts*, 1992).

Freeman signaled the beginning of an end of an era. For some, it is an example of how the best of intentions can lead to "disaster by decree" and of judicial usurpation of democratic rights of self-government at the local level as well as an example of the numerous urban school districts that have become impossible to integrate because so few nonminorities are left in their schools. For others, there remains hope that the courts can remedy school segregation, as demonstrated by districts such as Charlotte-Mecklenburg, where the degree of integration hoped for by the plaintiffs was largely achieved. Subsequent population shifts of whites out of the county, however, have had the adverse effect of reducing the percentage of nonminorities currently enrolled in the county's schools.

Busing, for better or worse, seems permanently off the political radar screen. Few new busing orders are issued today, and in communities where busing continues, it has come to be accepted as routine, although *Freeman* signals that some of these communities will be able to end the use of busing when they can demonstrate that they have largely complied with court orders to integrate. Affirmative action, by contrast, presents a quite different situation.

AFFIRMATIVE ACTION

Few quotations from Supreme Court opinions are as recognizable as the elder Justice John Marshall Harlan's proclamation that "our Constitution is color-blind, and neither knows nor tolerates classes among citizens" (*Plessy v. Ferguson,* 1896). Many who would nod in acknowledgment when they hear these words are likely to think either that it reflects the clear language of the Constitution or that it was vindicated by the Court's 1954 decision in *Brown.* As is the case with those who believe the Constitution contains a clear reference to a right of privacy or that the phrase "life, liberty, and the pursuit of happiness" is included in the same document, Harlan's memorable phrase is not in the Constitution.

As important is the fact that it has never been accepted by a majority of the Court to be a principle commanded by the Fourteenth Amendment's guarantee of "equal protection of the laws."

Debate in Congress on the implications of Title VII of the Civil Rights Act of 1964 adds to the confusion. The Civil Rights Act prohibits discrimination in employment on the basis of, among other things, race. Opponents of the measure argued that, if adopted, it would lead to the use of quotas. The most famous rejoinder to this view was uttered by one of the great pioneers of the civil rights movement, the senior senator from Minnesota, Democrat Hubert H. Humphrey. Replying to one of the bill's opponents, Senator Willis Robertson (a Democrat from Virginia), Humphrey confidently claimed that "if the Senator can find in Title VII . . . any language which provides that an employer will have to hire on the basis of percentage or quota related to color, race, religion, or national origin, I will start eating the pages one after another, because it is not there" (Robinson 2001, 100).

An executive order issued by President Lyndon Johnson a year later contained somewhat different language requiring that "the head of each executive department shall establish and maintain a positive program of equal opportunity employment for all civilian employees and applicants within his jurisdiction" (Robinson 2001, 108). With the adoption of the so-called "Philadelphia Plan," which implemented an executive order of President Richard Nixon in 1970, the language changed again: Now government contractors were required to develop an affirmative action program that included the establishment of "goals and timetables." "Goals may not be rigid and inflexible quotas . . . but must be targets reasonably attainable by . . . every good faith effort" (Robinson 2001, 134–135).

The Court was quickly presented with an opportunity to enter into the growing debate on affirmative action. In *Griggs v. Duke Power Company* (1971), a unanimous Court found that job tests that were not clearly related to job requirements and that resulted in screening out African Americans from job positions violated Title VII of the Civil Rights Act of 1964. A subsequent suit by an applicant for admission to the University of Washington Law School attempted to force the Court to address whether there was in fact a difference between goals, percentages, and quotas.

DeFunis v. Odegaard (1974) was brought by a disappointed law school applicant who argued that minorities had been admitted to the law school with lower grades and lower scores on the Law School Admission Test (LSAT) than his. By the time the case reached the Supreme Court, DeFunis, who had been ordered admitted to the law school by a state court, was in his third year of studies. Accordingly, a five-member majority found that there was no longer a justiciable controversy: The case was moot. Of the four justices who would have taken the case, one, William O. Douglas, insisted—as was not atypical for him—on writing an opinion that went to the merits of the case.

Douglas, who was without question the modern Court's most activist and liberal member, penned an opinion that came close to embracing the elder Harlan's famous words from his *Plessy* dissent. Surprisingly, it is an opinion that even in the 1970s was rarely included at any great length in constitutional law casebooks. In addition to ordering the University of Washington Law School to render admissions decisions *"in a racially neutral way"* and proclaiming that "[t]here is no constitutional right for any race to be preferred," the always iconoclastic Douglas went on to suggest that law schools should abandon their numbers-driven admissions procedures entirely, an idea that seems prescient given developments in the 1990s that led most law schools to rely more than ever on numbers in making their admissions decisions.

Although the Court had avoided for the moment entering the fray, no knowledgeable observer could expect that the Court would not eventually be drawn into the dispute. As Alexis de Tocqueville noted in the early 1800s, there is not a political issue in America that does not eventually become a legal issue. Four years after *DeFunis,* the Court finally addressed the issue of quotas in the famous 1978 *Regents of the University of California v. Bakke* case. In hindsight, it is not surprising that the controversy created by the *DeFunis* case had not disappeared. However, few observers could have predicted how much the controversy would grow between the Court's finding that the original controversy in *DeFunis* was moot and its decision to grant *certiorari* in *Bakke.* The number of amicus curiae briefs (literally, friend of the court; such briefs are legal arguments submitted, with permission of the Court, by groups interested in the outcome of a case but not directly involved in the particular litigation) filed in the case, fifty-seven, set what was at the time a record (Sindler 1978, 242). One of the briefs, not a little ironically, filed on behalf of the conservative Young Americans for Freedom, was authored by a young attorney by the name of Marco DeFunis, the same DeFunis who had brought suit in the 1974 case that the Court had refused to decide.

Just as with the busing cases, the Court that heard *Bakke* was quite different from the Court that had decided *Duke Power Company.* The 1970s had been hard times both economically and socially for Americans, and the Court was not unaffected. The Nixon Court was now the Burger Court, but neither the views of its creator nor those of its titular leader dominated an increasingly divided bench. The four Nixon appointees not only were voting together less and less, but they seemed to be going in very different directions. Rehnquist was dubbed "the Lone Ranger," not just for his penchant for wearing cowboy boots with his judicial robes, but for his tendency to stake out what then seemed radical judicial positions, ones that failed to attract even a single vote from his fellow justices. Blackmun, possibly stung by the personal invective his abortion decision had incurred, possibly disturbed by his fellow Minnesotan's (Burger) sometimes cavalier attitude toward him, possibly wooed successfully by overtures from the Court's preeminent playmaker, William Brennan, increasingly voted in a

more liberal way. Finally, the patrician Powell more and more occupied the catbird seat in an increasing number of 5–4 decisions.
All of this left Burger to fume and to devote more and more of his
time to working on getting the Supreme Court Building reno-
vated and championing, unsuccessfully, his far-reaching agenda
for reforms in the federal judicial system.

As a result of and despite all the attention the Court's decision
in *Bakke* attracted, the message it produced pleased few of the advocacy groups that had busily filed the record number of amicus
curiae briefs. Four justices (Burger, Rehnquist, Stewart, and
Stevens) found, in a relatively short opinion authored by Justice
John Paul Stevens, the lone appointee to the Court of President
Gerald Ford, that the program violated Title VI the Civil Rights
Act of 1964, which prohibits "discrimination under any program
or activity receiving Federal financial assistance."

The opinions written by Justices Brennan, Blackmun, White,
and Marshall take up the bulk of the pages in the *United States
Reports* (the official reporter of Supreme Court decisions) devoted
to the *Bakke* case. Their opinions argued that neither the Civil
Rights Act nor the Fourteenth Amendment limits government
from using race as a factor in making decisions. What they prohibit is using race in order to stigmatize a group.

Between these polar positions, Justice Lewis Powell was able to
stake out his own position. Powell, who retired in 1987, considered his opinion in *Bakke* to have been his most important during
his fifteen years on the Court (Abraham and Perry 2003, 488).
Whether that judgment was wise, indeed whether Powell's *Bakke*
opinion remained good law, more and more was seen as an open
question, at least until Chief Justice William Rehnquist agreed in
Gratz v. Bollinger (2003) that "diversity in education" could be "a
compelling state interest."

In short, Powell, joined by Burger, Stevens, Stewart, and Rehnquist, found that the admissions system operated by the medical
school of the University of California's Davis campus constituted

a quota and thus violated the Fourteenth Amendment. Unlike the four justices joining him in this opinion, however, Powell argued that race could be used as a factor in making admissions decisions. With this, he garnered the votes of Justices Brennan, Blackmun, Marshall, and White.

Among the problems left by Powell's *Bakke* opinion, however, was how it applied to the more run-of-the-mill admissions cases. Powell spent much time praising the undergraduate admissions program at Harvard College as a model for diversity in an under-graduate student body. Harvard, though, is hardly typical of American education in general. The overall quality of its applicants gives it a luxury that even competitive undergraduate schools and law schools do not have in shaping a student population that is both highly talented academically and highly diverse. It certainly is not typical of the majority of American undergraduate schools. These schools are far more apt to place much more emphasis on standard-ized test scores and school grades. As a result, their admissions pro-grams are likely to be much more mechanical, that is, to use a for-mula that employs these factors to make both admissions decisions and decisions on the awarding of financial aid or scholarships.

In *Bakke,* Powell argued that "achieving a diverse student body [may be] sufficiently compelling to justify consideration of race in admissions decisions." This claim echoed Chief Justice Vinson's conclusion in *Sweatt v. Painter* that excluding African Americans from the all-white University of Texas School of Law and limiting them to an all-black law school was constitutionally flawed be-cause it meant that they would not have the benefit of studying with students and professors of the white race, the race that would dominate the courts in which they would later practice. Whatever merit this argument has in the field of education, it seems difficult to apply it to the work setting. Diversity may have an educational value, but does it result in buildings being built quicker and better or in more sales being made? These were the questions that *Bakke* left unanswered.

As in the scenario that developed with busing, the personnel changes on the Court that occurred in the 1980s during the Reagan-Bush administrations, along with subsequent decisions the Court handed down on affirmative action, brought the vitality of Powell's *Bakke* opinion into question.

In the Court's decisions on busing, where race is clearly a factor as to who gets on the bus and where that person gets off, the Court has made clear that busing requires proof of governmental violation of civil rights—in other words, proof of de jure segregation. Under the leadership of Chief Justice Rehnquist (who was elevated to the chief justiceship by President Reagan in 1986), the Court has proceeded to make it clear that the use of race in programs conferring benefits must also be confined to those situations for which there is evidence of past governmental discrimination. Just because a system was segregated or just because there was discrimination by government in the past, however, does not mean that a remedy can be ordered today that employs race to classify persons. There must be either evidence that there is still discrimination or evidence that shows that past government actions continue to have a discriminatory impact on today's outcomes. Only then, apparently, would the Court permit legislators or lower court judges to fashion remedies that use race for purposes of "affirmative action."

Three decisions of the Rehnquist Court highlight this doctrinal development. They show as well how personnel changes have affected the Court's stance and how Rehnquist has displayed leadership skills that have allowed him to move in directions that he had plotted out in his dissents during the Burger Court, when he was popularly known as the "Lone Ranger."

Richmond v. J. A. Croson Co. (1989) sent a clear signal to supporters of affirmative action that the Rehnquist Court might well break away from the Burger Court's precedential moorings. Richmond had been the capital of the old Confederacy. The Virginia legislature, meeting in the capital at Richmond, had used its various powers to attempt to hold back the effects of *Brown* in the state that styled itself the Old Dominion. Future Justice Powell had served as chairman of the city's school board during desegregation and had written a brief for the district that made arguments that he would later urge on the justices in *Keyes* and *Milliken*. The city had changed dramatically over the years, however. It now had a black majority, which was reflected in the composition of its city council. The new Richmond adopted a program that attempted to increase the number of minority contractors doing business with the city and the amount of business they received through city-awarded contracts. Richmond's attorney concluded that under the Burger Court's *Fullilove v. Klutznick* (1980) ruling, set-asides for minorities were constitutional. In that case, Burger had sustained a federal program that required 10 percent of federal funds used for local public works programs be used to employ minority-controlled contractors. Justices Rehnquist, Stevens, and Stewart had dissented. *Croson,* like *Fullilove,* was decided in a 6–3 vote, but the result was exactly opposite.

This reversal was the result of an atypical vote by Justice Byron White, a Kennedy appointee, and the votes of the three Reagan appointees. Until *Croson,* White had regularly voted in a way that reflected his previous work as a deputy attorney general in the Kennedy administration who had the responsibility of fighting southern officials who sought to thwart all efforts directed at them to comply with *Brown.*

The six judges who voted to strike down Richmond's 30 percent set-aside for minority contractors agreed only on the fact that it violated the Constitution. They were far from agreement on the reasons that led them to this conclusion. Their opinions reveal three different approaches. Justice Sandra Day O'Connor's judgment of the Court (a judgment of the Court is issued instead of the normal opinion of the Court when there is not a majority that agrees with both the results and the reasoning) stressed the difference between the powers of the federal government and those of the states in remedying disparities between blacks and whites. O'Connor concluded as a result that Richmond's program, unlike the federal program examined in *Fullilove*, required the reviewing courts to apply "strict scrutiny." The fact that "Congress may identify and redress the effects of society-wide discrimination does not mean that, *a fortiori*, the States and their political subdivisions are free to decide that such remedies are appropriate." The post–Civil War amendments were designed both to give additional power to the federal government and to limit that of the states. Accordingly, although "strict scrutiny" was not appropriate in reviewing federal legislation, it was required to deal with "race-based measures" adopted by other levels of government. "Indeed, the purpose of strict scrutiny," continued O'Connor,

> is to "smoke out" illegitimate uses of race by assuring that the legislative body is pursuing a goal important enough to warrant use of a highly suspect tool. The test also ensures that the means chosen "fit" this compelling goal so closely that there is little or no possibility that the motive for the classification was illegitimate racial prejudice or stereotype.

Justice Stevens, who dissented in *Fullilove* and was one of the four justices in *Bakke* who saw the use of race as a violation of the Civil Rights Act, wrote a separate concurring opinion. He disagreed "with the premise that seems to underlie today's decision . . . that a governmental decision that rests on a racial classification is never permissible except as a remedy for a past wrong." Stevens expanded on this idea in a footnote in which he allowed that programs using racial classifications "that may produce tangible and fully justified future benefits" might be constitutional.

Justice Antonin Scalia propounded a third approach that clearly was the most restrictive in terms of the room it left for government to act. According to Scalia, the only justification for race-based remedies was to make whole those minorities who themselves had suffered discrimination as a result of positive government action. Government could not engage in social engineering that involved the use of racial classifications.

The views of the *Croson* dissenters were most eloquently rendered by Justice Marshall. Marshall characterized the classification produced by the Richmond ordinance as benign. It was not based on stereotypes of inferiority or superiority of a particular racial group, as was the case of the old Jim Crow laws. As a result, it need not be subjected to the highest level of judicial scrutiny, as the O'Connor opinion seemed to suggest, but demanded a lesser level of scrutiny. "[My] view," he wrote, "has long been that race-conscious classifications designed to further remedial goals 'must serve important governmental objectives and must be substantially related to achievement of those objectives.'" This intermediate standard had been developed by the Court earlier in order to determine whether legislation that distinguished on the basis of gender was constitutional. As will be discussed in chapter 3, the Court has refused to consider sex to be equivalent to classifications based on race, nationality, or alienage. It is instead seen as a semisuspect category. Marshall wanted to use this test for legislation that used race for benign reasons.

Croson was quickly hailed by many of those who had supported the elections of Presidents Reagan and Bush in the 1980s as a sign that the Court had finally returned to what they saw as the "original intent" of the authors of the Fourteenth Amendment. For these organizations and individuals, the elder Justice Harlan's invocation of the concept of a "color-blind Constitution" seemed finally within reach.

Metro Broadcasting Inc. v. FCC (1990) thus was for these groups a rude shock. It was also further evidence of Justice Brennan's effectiveness in putting together judicial majorities. Twenty-two years after the close of the Warren Court, Brennan was still demonstrating an almost uncanny and inexplicable talent for coming up with five votes to support positions that seemed hopeless given the fact that the judicial appointments made during this period were made by presidents bent on reversing many of the liberal precedents of the Warren and Burger Courts.

The Federal Communications Commission, the body that controls the awarding of television and radio broadcast licenses, had adopted "minority preference policies." Unlike *Croson,* these policies involved federal action. Perhaps this is what brought Justice White back into the fold. Minority broadcasters also served "the public interest in broadcast diversity." For Justice Stevens, this was, "like the interest in an integrated police force, diversity in the composition of a public school faculty or diversity in the student body of a professional school," "unquestionably legitimate."

O'Connor wrote a dissenting opinion in which Chief Justice Rehnquist and Associate Justices Scalia and Kennedy joined. Her dissent appears to indicate a shift from the position she took in *Croson.* There, O'Connor seemed to distinguish between the type of review to which state acts were to be subjected and that which would be applied in cases of federal action. Her dissent now firmly rejected that distinction, concluding that all government action required "strict scrutiny."

The lines that divided the two camps of judges in *Metro Broadcasting* continued largely to hold despite the personnel changes that occurred on the Court in the early 1990s. The two Clinton appointees, Justices Ruth Bader Ginsburg, who replaced Justice White, and Stephen Breyer, who succeeded Justice Blackmun, vote pretty much as the judges they replaced would have voted on issues involving race. Justice David Souter, the so-called "stealth" nominee of President George H. W. Bush, seems, despite the hopes of the Bush administration, to have metamorphosed into what appears in many ways to be a carbon copy of the man he succeeded, Justice William Brennan.

The same cannot be said of the other Bush appointee: Clarence Thomas's voting record on the high bench is almost in direct opposition to that of the man he replaced, Thurgood Marshall. A former chairman of the Equal Employment Opportunity Commission, Thomas has established a voting pattern that seems as closely tied to that of the Court's previously leading conservative, Antonin Scalia, as Marshall had been to Brennan. Thomas, whose silence during oral argument is a source of frequent media comment that generally makes no mention of the fact that the late Justice Brennan was almost equally quiet, is hardly reticent about his attitudes on affirmative action. A case involving a federal program that gave contractors a financial bonus if they hired minority subcontractors gave Thomas an opportunity to voice his views from the bench on the subject. Thomas's vote also transformed the *Metro Broadcasting* minority into a majority bloc highly skeptical of affirmative action.

As the sole African American on the Court, Thomas opted to write a concurring opinion that took aim at the dissent's defense of affirmative action programs. He characterized it as an example of "racial paternalism."

Government cannot make us equal; it can only recognize, respect, and protect us as equal before the law. That these programs may have been motivated, in part, by good intentions cannot provide refuge from the principle that under our Constitution, the government may not make distinctions on the basis of race. As far as the Constitution is concerned, it is irrelevant whether a government's racial classifications are drawn by those who wish to oppose a race or by those who have a sincere desire to help those thought to be disadvantaged. . . .

These programs not only raise grave constitutional questions, they also undermine the moral basis of the equal protection principle. Purchased at the price of immeasurable human suffering, the equal protection principle reflects the Nation's understanding that such classifications ultimately have a destructive impact on the individual and our society.

Chief Justice Rehnquist assigned Justice O'Connor the task of writing the Court's opinion in *Adarand Constructors v. Pena* (1995). Although Thomas's vote provided the majority, O'Connor's vote on affirmative action remains the key vote, because on this issue, as with so many other controversial matters—for example, abortion and church-state issues—she has shown an ability to remain independent of the Court's two competing voting blocs. O'Connor's champions hail this independence as a product of her open-mindedness and her unwillingness to become the slave of a particular ideological outlook. Her detractors conclude that her independence really clothes her indecision and her inadequacy to rise to the level appropriate for a member of the nation's highest court.

More than any of her colleagues, O'Connor seems to be affected more by the particular facts of a case, finding distinctions that frequently elude the rest of the Court. If Souter has taken on the mantle of the judge he succeeded, Brennan, if Stevens sometimes seems as idiosyncratic as his predecessor, Douglas, O'Connor may exhibit many of the characteristics of Potter Stewart, the justice she succeeded. Stewart was often styled as a "lawyer's judge" for his reluctance to postulate broad theories of the law, content instead to decide each case "on its own merits." This also seems to be the tradition into which O'Connor falls.

O'Connor's opinion in *Adarand* demonstrated how fragile, however, the Rehnquist, Scalia, Thomas, Kennedy, and O'Connor majority may be. Although all five judges believe that any use of racial classifications by government requires courts to apply "strict scrutiny," what constitutes a "compelling state interest" still appears to divide them. For O'Connor and Kennedy, "strict scrutiny" should not be "strict in theory, but fatal in fact." "The unhappy persistence of both the practice and the lingering effects of racial discrimination against minority groups in this country is an unfortunate reality," argued O'Connor in a portion of her opinion in which only Justice Kennedy joined, "and government is not disqualified from acting in response to it."

Justice Scalia reiterated his earlier stance that "government can never have a 'compelling interest' in discriminating on the basis of race." Government, according to Scalia, can only act to make whole those particular individuals against whom discrimination has been found. It cannot use its power to improve the social or economic conditions of a particular race, however much that race has previously suffered from discrimination.

The four dissenters (Stevens, Souter, Ginsburg, and Breyer) challenged both the Court's decision to use one standard for both invidious (e.g., segregation in schools) and benign (e.g., affirmative action programs) classifications and the majority's refusal to acknowledge that the federal government, because of the Fourteenth Amendment, had more power than the states to pass remedial legislation. Perhaps in order to drive a wedge among members of the *Adarand* majority, they noted that O'Connor in her opinion seemed to be at pains to suggest that "strict scrutiny" might not always mean that the Court would strike down legislation that used race as a basis for governmental action.

The result of the Court's decision in *Adarand* was that it was sent back to the lower court for further review under the standards spelled out in the O'Connor opinion. It also prompted the Clinton administration in May 1996 to issue "Proposed Reforms to Affirmative Action in Procurement." The Clinton administration's famous policy of "triangulation," the brainchild of Clinton adviser Dick Morris, quickly became evident in the matter of affirmative action.

"Triangulation" called for Clinton to stake out positions that put him between the hard right of the Republican Party, as represented by the likes of House Speaker Newt Gingrich, and the left wing of his own party, made up of people such as Massachusetts Senator Edward M. Kennedy. Although "triangulation" is usually seen in terms of policy decisions such as welfare reform, where the President pledged to "end welfare as we know it," it seems to have cropped up more quietly on the judicial front as well.

Clinton's two Court nominees, Ginsburg and Breyer, although much more liberal than the justices appointed by Presidents Reagan and Bush, are not the liberal firebrands that might have been expected from a Democratic president. According to one Court observer, neither "represent the 'homerun' that President Clinton claimed he wished to hit" (Silverstein 1994, 174). Both nominees, however, were positioned between a Robert Bork (the unsuccessful Reagan nominee) and a Lawrence Tribe, liberal Democrats' dream appointment to the bench. Both were easily confirmed, unlike the Reagan and Bush nominees who followed O'Connor.

Speaking on affirmative action, the president showed the same finesse in appearing to respond to the critics of affirmative action while at the same time assuring the other side that he would not abandon affirmative action, but rather fix it.

> When affirmative action is done right, it is flexible, it is fair, and it works.... I know there are times when employers don't use it in the right way.... They may ... allow a different type of discrimination. When that happens, it is also wrong. But it isn't affirmative action, and it is not legal. (Robinson 2001, 329)

Cynics might suggest that Clinton's definition of affirmative action was similar to his subsequent parsing of the word sex.

In addition to revamping federal affirmative action rules, the administration filed an amicus curiae brief in a case that affirmative action opponents saw as the case that would finally lead to the end of all affirmative action programs except for the narrow category that would be permitted under Scalia's theory.

The Piscataway, New Jersey, school board, facing financial difficulties, was required to lay off a teacher from its business department to balance its budget. Traditionally layoffs were made by reverse seniority. In this case, two women on the faculty—one black, the other white—who had been hired on the same day had the least seniority and equal qualifications in all other respects.

The board laid off the white woman, who promptly sued. Her case immediately attracted support from the increasing number of conservative legal advocacy groups and of senior members of the Bush administration, which charged the board with violating Title VII of the Civil Rights Act. The dismissed teacher, Sharon Taxman, prevailed both in the district court and in the United States Court of Appeals. The Piscataway school board continued its appeal, and the Supreme Court agreed to hear the case.

The Clinton administration originally urged the Court not to take the case. When the Court failed to follow this tack—the Court usually agrees with the Solicitor General's Office in terms of the cases it does take—the Clinton administration filed a brief that, while supporting affirmative action, argued that it was rarely justified when it resulted in layoffs. Before the Court heard the case, however, Taxman and the board reached an out-of-court settlement, which rendered the issue moot.

Like *Taxman v. Board of Education of Piscataway*, *Adarand*, which had been remanded to the district court, failed, despite several attempts to bring it back to the Supreme Court, to provide a final answer to the debate on affirmative action. With that, the battle over affirmative action shifted back to the earlier and highly charged terrain of university admissions.

Despite Justice Douglas's plea to law schools in *DeFunis* to abandon what he saw as their overreliance on numerical factors, the emphasis on numbers in admissions has, if anything, increased in the years since. The *U.S. News and World Report* annual editions ranking undergraduate schools and professional schools have led many schools, and in particular law schools, to become even more attentive to the need for attracting a student class with the right numerical profile so that their schools continue to receive a high ranking.

In addition, many admissions directors were as confused as many employers about the precise difference between goals and quotas. If year after year a school reaches its goal of minority admissions, does that mean that it in fact has a quota, or is it simply the result of good recruiting? Three cases involving admissions have been decided in recent years by federal appeals courts (established by Congress in 1891, the thirteen United States Courts of Appeals sit between the district courts and the Supreme Court of the United States). Two have found the challenged programs unconstitutional; one court has upheld an affirmative action program.

The first case involved the admissions program at the University of Texas School of Law. Almost inexplicably, the law school had put in place a program that seemed totally contrary to what Justice Powell had established as a model in *Bakke*. It operated with two separate admissions committees, one dealing with minority students and the other with white students. When this program was challenged, the school's administration immediately replaced it. The revised system, too, was challenged, and a three-judge panel of the Fifth Circuit Court of Appeals found it to be constitutionally deficient. Two of the judges, however, went further and concluded that according to their reading of recent Supreme Court decisions, *Bakke* and Justice Powell's "lonely opinion" were no longer good law and that "diversity" no longer served to meet the standard of "a compelling state interest." A concurring opinion in the case refused to take this step and left open the possibility that a more "narrowly tailored" program could be found constitutional, one that would achieve the goal of diversity in the classroom without the great emphasis on race that the program at the University of Texas School of Law exhibited. The decision, *Hopwood v. Texas* (1996), sent shock waves throughout American higher education.

Since the provisions of the Civil Rights Act of 1964 impose the same restrictions on private actors as the Fourteenth Amendment's Equal Protection Clause does on states, the *Hopwood* decision could prompt challenges to the admissions practices at private colleges and universities as well as state schools such as the

University of Texas. An attempt was made later to appeal the case
to the Supreme Court, but the Court refused to hear the case. As
a result, *Hopwood* was binding only on Texas, Louisiana, and
Mississippi, the states that compose the Fifth Circuit.

In the case of *Johnson v. Board of Regents* in 2001, the Eleventh
Circuit found that the admissions policies of the University of
Georgia failed the test of being "narrowly tailored." In reaching
this conclusion the circuit court assumed that "strict scrutiny"
must be applied to racial classifications. In doing this it avoided
determining whether or not "student body diversity ... [is] a
compelling state interest for purposes of strict scrutiny under the
Equal Protection Clause of the Fourteenth Amendment," finding
it unnecessary to do so given that "the Supreme Court has placed
as much importance on the requirement that any race-conscious
program be narrowly tailored." The appeals court found that the
Georgia program, although it avoided the blatant defects found in
Bakke and *Hopwood,* nevertheless failed, because a

> race-conscious admissions policy still must ensure that, even when us-
> ing race as a factor, the weight accorded that factor is not subject to
> rigid or mechanical application, and remains flexible enough to ensure
> that each applicant is evaluated as an individual and not in a way that
> looks to her membership in a favored or disfavored racial group as a
> defining feature of her candidacy.

The fact that the Georgia program awarded bonus points on the
basis of race in calculating what it called the total student index,
which was otherwise composed of academic and extracurricular
accomplishments, was not a permissible way of achieving diversity. The University of Georgia opted to change its admissions
process and not to appeal to the Supreme Court.

Such a division within the circuits on affirmative action—one
appeals court found that *Bakke* was no longer good law; another
saw *Bakke* and affirmative action as still possible, but found the

total student index constitutionally flawed; and, yet another in *Smith v. University of Washington Law School* found diversity to be a "compelling state interest"—is one of the better predictors of whether or not the Supreme Court will take a case. Thus, it was not a great surprise when the Supreme Court voted to docket two cases involving admissions practices at the University of Michigan for the October 2002 term. After much speculation as to what it would do, the Bush administration announced that it would file amicus curiae briefs in support of the unsuccessful white applicants to the university's law school and undergraduate programs. The administration, however, opted not to make the argument that all types of affirmative action were unconstitutional. Affirmative action was finally back on the political and judicial front burners.

Unlike the Texas and Georgia cases, the rejected white applicants in Michigan had lost in the lower federal courts. The Sixth Circuit Court of Appeals had upheld the University of Michigan's law school admissions practices, reversing a contrary result reached by the trial court. A district court reached a similar conclusion and sustained the undergraduate admissions process as meeting the requirements of *Bakke.* For reasons that have never been fully explained, the appeals court did not render a decision in the undergraduate admissions case even though it did hear arguments on the issue.

In the law school case, *Grutter v. Bollinger,* a majority of the judges of the Sixth Circuit found that it was not necessary to show past discrimination in order to use race. The court then proceeded to see whether the two criteria for affirmative action programs required by the Supreme Court were met. Diversity in a student body, they concluded, was "a compelling state interest." Based on the testimony of the law school's admissions staff and other administrators, the court concluded that the program was also "narrowly tailored" since there was evidence that "the law school considered and ultimately rejected various race-neutral alternatives." None would have produced the degree of diversity desired by the school. In an atypically bitter dissent to Chief Judge Boyce Martin's opinion, Judge Danny Boggs charged that the program characterized as an attempt to achieve a "critical mass" was in fact a quota.

Boggs argued that there were alternative means available to the law school. It could, he argued, "consider experiential diversity in a race-neutral manner." Boggs also floated an idea that was first suggested by leaders of the critical legal studies movement, widely viewed as a left-wing group within law school faculties. "[C]onduct . . . a lottery for all students above certain threshold figures for their GPA [grade point average] and LSAT [Law School Admission Test]."

Boggs's dissent along with the attorneys' arguments on behalf of Grutter failed to convince a majority of the Supreme Court to abandon Powell's *Bakke* opinion. In fact, far from rejecting *Bakke,* Justice O'Connor's opinion in *Grutter* puts the Powell position on firmer judicial ground. It now has the explicit endorsement of five justices. The fact that O'Connor was selected to write the opinion (since Chief Justice Rehnquist was in the minority, Justice John Paul Stevens, as the senior justice in the majority, designated O'Connor to write the opinion) was widely expected, given her decisive role on this sharply divided Court. Far from jettisoning Powell's reasoning as had the lower court in the University of Texas Law School case (*Hopwood*), O'Connor clearly sought to reaffirm the arguments Powell had made in 1978. As she had done in 1992 in *Planned Parenthood v. Casey,* O'Connor seemed concerned that a standard that had "served as a touchstone for constitutional analysis of race-conscious admissions policies [and one that had been relied upon by p]ublic and private universities across the Nation . . ." could be dropped given the uproar it would cause in those same colleges and universities. O'Connor may also have been influenced by the briefs filed in support of affirmative action by many of leading U.S. corporations and service academies.

O'Connor's opinion examined whether the law school's use of race in admissions could meet the requirement of "strict scrutiny" or, in other words, whether it was sufficiently "narrowly-tailored to further compelling governmental interests." Citing Powell, O'Connor found "that the Law School has a compelling interest in a diverse student body. . . . Attaining a diverse student body [indeed] is at the heart of the Law School's proper institutional mission." Breaking from her usual allies on the Court's right wing—Rehnquist, Scalia, Thomas, and Kennedy—O'Connor also announced that the Court has "never held that the only governmental use of race that can survive strict scrutiny is remedying past discrimination." Proceeding then to determine whether or not the program was "narrowly-tailored," O'Connor concluded that there was the necessary "highly individualized, holistic review of each applicant's file" that Powell in *Bakke* had identified in Harvard's admissions procedures as distinguishing it from the mechanical quota used by California-Davis's medical school. O'Connor did add one important caveat on the subject of affirmative action, pursuant to an issue she had raised at oral arguments on April 1: a sunset provision.

> It has been 25 years since Justice Powell first approved the use of race to further an interest in student body diversity in the context of public higher education. Since that time, the number of minority applicants with high grades and test scores has indeed increased. . . . We expect that 25 years from now, the use of racial preferences will no longer be necessary to further the interest approved today.

In the companion undergraduate admissions case from Michigan, *Gratz v. Bollinger* (2003), a six-member majority found the program constitutionally flawed because it did not give the "highly individualized" scrutiny that the justices in *Grutter* interpreted *Bakke* to require. The crux of the issue in the undergraduate program was that underrepresented minorities automatically received a twenty-point bonus in computing their index for admission. Chief Justice Rehnquist wrote the opinion for a majority composed of the dissenters from *Grutter* (Scalia, Kennedy, Thomas, and Rehnquist) and Justices O'Connor and Breyer.

Although the Rehnquist and O'Connor opinions relied heavily on Powell's *Bakke* opinion, the Thomas and Ginsburg dissents sought to take the Court down very different paths. The Thomas opinion, even more than his earlier opinions on affirmative action, appears to represent a true *cri de coeur*. It begins with a lengthy quote from Frederick Douglass in which the former slave "delivered a message" that, according to Thomas, was "lost on today's majority." The message was "Do nothing with us! If the apples will not remain on the tree of their own strength, if they are worm-eaten at the core, if they are early ripe and disposed to fall, let them fall! . . . And if the negro cannot stand on his own legs, let him fall also."

Thomas rejected the claim that Michigan showed "a compelling state interest," pointing out that the state was under no compulsion to maintain a highly selective elite law school that produced only a small number of graduates who practiced law in Michigan. This did not rise to the level of "compelling state interest" unless that term was watered down to mean something it had never meant before, Thomas argued. More central to Thomas, however, was the impact that the use of race has on African American students. It stigmatizes those who meet the regular admissions practices because they are viewed as unqualified; it gives no impetus to the less well-prepared as they know they will be accepted even with lower grades. Thus, according to Thomas, they do not seek to improve themselves.

Justice Ginsburg's dissent in *Grutter* took up all of seven pages in the Court's slip opinion and is dwarfed by the other opinions, particularly those of O'Connor and Thomas. Still, she makes two very important points that were generally ignored by the other justices. First, Ginsburg reminds us that "we are not far distant from an overtly discriminatory past, and the effects of centuries of law-sanctioned inequality remain painfully evident in our community and schools." Secondly, Ginsburg, a former law professor, seems somewhat skeptical of the distinction that the majority drew between the undergraduate and law school admissions practices. "If honesty is the best policy, surely Michigan's accurately described, fully disclosed college affirmative action program is preferable to achieving similar numbers through winks, nods, and disguises." One wonders whether Justice Ginsburg thought the latter characterization was appropriate to how Michigan's law school put together its diverse class of students.

The debate over affirmative action has produced significant stirrings at the state level as well. The voters of California in 1996 passed Proposition 209, which became part of the state's constitution. It prohibited "preferential treatment . . . on the basis of race." In contrast, the legislature of Georgia refused in 1998 to ban affirmative action. Three years later, the U.S. Court of Appeals held that the University of Georgia's affirmative action policy was unconstitutional.

Texas and Florida (under the leadership of then Governor George W. Bush and his brother, Governor Jeb Bush) have adopted measures that guarantee acceptance to state universities to students in the top of their high school classes regardless of other factors and, in particular, regardless of scores on standardized admissions tests such as the SAT or ACT. The Florida plan guarantees admissions to students in the top 20 percent of their graduating class. Florida also authorized the establishment of two new state law schools on campuses with large percentages of Hispanic and African American students. In traditionally liberal San Francisco, the public school system is now considering economic status as opposed to race in trying to bring diversity to its schools (Fletcher 2002, 30).

CONCLUSION

The busing and affirmative action issues should not be dismissed simply as "full of sound and fury signifying nothing." The 2003 Michigan decisions (*Grutter* and *Gratz*) are unlikely to end the

debate, as Justice Scalia pointed out in his dissent. One can imagine a host of new cases brought by rejected applicants, who will
claim that they have not received the constitutionally mandated
"individualized, holistic" review from admissions committees or
admissions offices. The Center for Individual Rights, the group
that financed the Michigan challenges, announced the day after
the decisions that it would monitor academia's responses to the
Supreme Court rulings. Indeed, the Michigan decisions may only
serve to throw more gas onto the fire that surely will be lit when
the next Supreme Court vacancy occurs. Justice Thomas's questions also cannot be ignored. Is it possible in fact that affirmative
action stigmatizes those it is designed to help and that it discour-
ages certain minority students from seeking to improve themselves?

But perhaps the Michigan decisions will finally settle the issue,
as their proponents claim. Polls consistently show broad support
for the concept of affirmative action. Justice O'Connor's pro-
nouncement indicating that the use of race should be subject to
what could almost be called a "sunset provision," ending its use
twenty-five years hence, is also interesting. Is it a bow to those
who argue that African Americans deserve reparations for the
legacy of slavery and past discrimination?

The devil in affirmative action, however, has been the details
from the beginning. By failing to take a more courageous stand—
the Ginsburg and Thomas dissents in the Michigan cases are an
example—the Court has failed to accept the challenge that Chief
Justice Warren met in *Brown*.

In a more positive vein, all indices show that African Americans
have made great strides in catching up with white America in the
years since the earlier rulings. Even though the progress has been
for many exasperatingly slow, the *Hopwood* appeals court, for example, did note that the gap in LSAT scores between whites and
minorities had become noticeably smaller and that there has been
undeniable progress. The momentum in the private sector will

likely continue regardless of government policy. Only the most bigoted executive is apt to risk alienating a growing minority market by risking a charge that the company discriminates in the ways in which it conducts its business. Consumer boycotts may bring justice more quickly than hearings before the Equal Employment Opportunity Commission.

That said, the Court in addressing the busing and affirmative action problems could have been more effective. The Powell opinion in *Bakke,* despite the praise heaped on it by Justice O'Connor, seems in hindsight more clever than wise. As the appeals court majority in *Grutter* noted, Powell's praise for Harvard's admissions policies for undergraduates did not specify the degree to which race could tip the admissions scales. Both opponents and supporters of current affirmative action practices in university admissions can claim to champion *Bakke.* The reality, however, is that, as some commentators noted in the 1970s, Harvard is, if not unique, unusual. Few schools have the luxury that a Harvard or Amherst has in selecting among very qualified students. The problem at the level of professional schools is even greater, particularly at law schools where numerical indices based on grades and standardized test scores reign supreme.

As Judge Wilkinson wrote in his book on the subject of school integration, *From* Brown *to* Bakke (1979), a less legalistic approach may have been better advised. Chief Justice Earl Warren surely grasped the importance of this in his *Brown* opinion. Although in the short run it had much less effect than either *Swann* or *Duke Power* or *Bakke,* in the long run its influence on developments in the 1960s and even the twenty-first century cannot be overestimated. Could Chief Justice Burger have done better? Could he have cast the issue as one that called upon society to provide more resources to urban schools? Justice Ginsburg's dissent in *Gratz* takes this approach. Would the Court have been better advised to have followed the urging of certain of its members and discarded efforts to distinguish between de jure and de facto segregation and simply called for society to realize that the disadvantages faced by African Americans are a part of the legacy of slavery? Are reparations owed by all of society and not just the white applicant or job seeker or the parent of the white student at an already substandard, though lily-white, South Boston High School? To have viewed affirmative action this way would have involved greater political risk. At the same time, it would have offered the possibility of more political gain both for society and for the Court.

The Court, in one sense, seems to have survived the onslaught. After being at issue in presidential campaigns from 1968 through 1988, the Court seemed to have disappeared from the nation's political radar screen until the elections of 2000. The current controversy over affirmative action and looming openings on the Court obviously may bring the Court back into the public eye, particularly as the presidential election of 2004 looms more closely on the political horizon. Much more than his predecessor in the White House, George W. Bush seems willing to use judicial nominations to advance his agenda and to secure the votes of the conservative base of the Republican Party. The confirmations of Ruth Bader Ginsburg and Stephen Breyer, Clinton's two nominees, bore little resemblance to the political theater of the 1980s that characterized the Bork, Thomas, and Souter hearings. In contrast, the next vacancy on the high bench has been predicted as likely to trigger "the mother of all confirmation battles."

The Court's foray into other issues of equal protection, including gender and fundamental rights, offers another viewpoint from which to judge the Court's current work. In these areas, the Court has drawn much less attention and, consequently, less criticism. Even in those areas that have been contested, the Court's decisions seem to rest on much firmer foundations than its busing and affirmative action rulings. Chapter 3 will take up this part of the equal protection narrative.

References and Further Reading

Abraham, Henry J., and Barbara Perry. 2003. *Freedom and the Court: Civil Rights and Liberties in the United States,* 7th ed. Lawrence: University Press of Kansas.

Browne, Kingsley R. 2001–2002. "'Race-Neutral' Schemes for Diversity." *Academic Questions* 15: 33–38.

Danelski, David J. 2002. "The Influence of the Chief Justice in the Decisional Process." In Walter F. Murphy, C. Herman Pritchett, and Lee Epstein, eds., *Courts, Judges, and Politics: An Introduction to the Judicial Process,* 5th ed. Boston: McGraw-Hill.

Epstein, Lee, and Jack Knight. 1998. *Choices Justices Make.* Washington, DC: Congressional Quarterly Press.

Fletcher, Michael A. 2002. "Desegregation, but Not by Race." *Washington Post National Weekly Edition,* March 25, 30.

Graglia, Lino A. 1976. *Disaster by Decree: The Supreme Court Decisions on Race and the Schools.* Ithaca, NY: Cornell University Press.

Graham, Hugh Davis. 1992. *Civil Rights and the Presidency.* New York: Oxford University Press.

Hutchinson, Dennis J. 1992. "*Green v. County School Board of New Kent County.*" In Kermit L. Hall, ed., *The Oxford Companion to the Supreme Court of the United States.* New York: Oxford University Press.

Jeffries, John C., Jr. 1994. *Justice Lewis F. Powell, Jr.: A Biography.* New York: Charles Scribner's Sons.

Lawrence, Charles R., III, and Mari J. Matsuda. 1997. *We Won't Go Back: Making the Case for Affirmative Action.* Boston: Houghton Mifflin.

Lerner, Max. 1994. *Nine Scorpions in a Bottle: Great Judges and Cases of the Supreme Court.* New York: Arcade.

Patterson, James T. 2001. Brown v. Board of Education: *A Civil Rights Milestone and Its Troubled Legacy.* New York: Oxford University Press.

Robinson, Jo Ann Ooiman, ed. 2001. *Affirmative Action: A Documentary History.* Westport, CT: Greenwood Press.

Silverstein, Mark. 1994. *Judicious Choices: The New Politics of Supreme Court Confirmations.* New York: W. W. Norton.

Simon, James F. 1973. *In His Own Image: The Supreme Court in Richard Nixon's America.* New York: David McKay.

Sindler, Allan P. 1978. Bakke, DeFunis, *and Minority Admissions: The Quest for Equal Opportunity.* New York: Longman.

Wasby, Stephen L., et al. 1977. *Desegregation from* Brown *to* Alexander. Carbondale: Southern Illinois University Press.

White, G. Edward. 1982. *Earl Warren: A Public Life.* New York: Oxford University Press.

Wilkinson, J. Harvie. 1979. *From* Brown *to* Bakke: *The Supreme Court and School Integration, 1954–1978.* New York: Oxford University Press.

Winter, Greg. 2003. "Schools Resegregate, Study Finds." *New York Times,* January 21, A14.

3

THE TWENTIETH CENTURY

EQUAL PROTECTION AND
NON–RACE-BASED LEGISLATION

Among the possible questions that applicants for U.S. citizenship must be prepared to answer on the citizenship test administered by the Immigration and Naturalization Service (INS) is one that asks what the role of the Supreme Court of the United States is. The credited answer, according to the INS, is that the Supreme Court interprets the Constitution. Like a good number of the citizenship test's other questions, this is one that might easily elicit a very different response from many native-born citizens. Quite a few would be surprised to discover that protecting individual rights and liberties is not the correct answer.

However common such an answer might be today, the view of the Court as defender of civil liberties and civil rights—that is, the rights enumerated in the Bill of Rights and the rights of minorities—is a conception of the Court's role that has emerged only since the World War II. Certainly it was not the view of the framers of the Constitution. Even after the adoption of the Bill of Rights, a concession the Federalists made only reluctantly. Madison described his work in drafting the Bill of Rights as "a nauseous project." Few, if any, of the framers, or of their opponents, the Anti-Federalists, would have envisioned the Court as the defender of what we today understand as civil rights and liberties. The same would have been true of the members of the Congress that drafted the Fourteenth Amendment. For them, protection of individual rights was primarily the business of Congress, an idea that only a few today might espouse (Fisher 2002).

In fact, until 1937 and the famous "switch in time that saved nine," the Supreme Court's role was generally acknowledged by both supporters and detractors as the protector of property rights. The framers, men such as Alexander Hamilton and James Madison, had foreseen the federal judiciary as providing a necessary check against the natural tendency of the popularly elected legislature to favor the have-nots against the haves. The famous precedents of the pre–Civil War Court, the decisions of the Marshall and Taney Courts, more than bore out this expectation. *Marbury v. Madison* (1803), *McCulloch v. Maryland* (1819), *Dartmouth College v. Woodward* (1819), *Gibbons v. Ogden* (1824), *Charles River Bridge v. Warren Bridge* (1837), and *Dred Scott v. Sandford* (1857) each evidenced the Court's strong interest in either defending vested property rights or fostering the development of the United States as "a commercial republic." The judiciary's interest in property rights continued throughout the nineteenth century. Indeed, well into the first third of the twentieth century, federal courts used their powers to check what they viewed as violations of property rights, whether on the part of the federal government or as a result of state action.

Although every high school student is familiar with the phrase "clear and present danger" and probably also with Justice Oliver Wendell Holmes's caution that "the most stringent protection of free speech would not protect a man in falsely shouting fire in a theatre ..." (*Schenck v. United States,* 1919), many, if asked, would assume that Holmes's memorable rhetoric must have resulted in overturning Schenck's conviction. Unfortunately for Schenck, as well as for defendants in the other famous First Amendment cases that the Court handled in the 1920s, this was not the result. Not only were cases involving civil liberties and civil rights few prior to the Court's 1937 about-face, but when they were decided, they generally were decided in favor of government and against the individual.

THE DEMISE OF "THE OLD COURT" AND THE RISE OF "THE MODERN COURT"

This was to change radically in 1937. The Hughes Court's showdown with President Roosevelt ended when, in the view of many scholars, the Court blinked. Having been reelected in 1936 by a record margin of both electoral and popular votes, Roosevelt vowed to move against a Court that had already gutted most of the legislation adopted in what has been dubbed the first New Deal. Roosevelt's solution was to have his attorney general draft a bill expanding the size of the Supreme Court. The number of justices on the Court is not set in the Constitution but rather is determined by legislation, and the Court's size was altered several times in the nineteenth century. As finally drafted, the so-called Court-packing bill—a term attached to it by its opponents—would have resulted in a Court of thirteen members, giving the president the opportunity to fill four new positions (one for every justice then over seventy years of age). The additional four justices would have just tipped the balance on the Court, their addition ensuring that any future challenges to New Deal legislation would fail.

The resulting "switch in time that saved nine," that is, the preservation of a nine-member Supreme Court but one that now regularly upheld government's power to regulate the economy, witnessed the Court's overturning of many of the "Old Court's" precedents protecting property rights. The Roosevelt administration and subsequent presidents were now free to take whatever measures they and Congress saw as necessary to deal with the economy and with working conditions. The era of the Old Court, the Court that had been concerned almost exclusively with protecting property rights from the excesses of popular majorities, was finally at an end.

No sooner, however, had the Court abandoned its traditional role as protector of property rights than it staked out a new role, the one that we generally associate with the Court today. This new focus was famously announced in perhaps the most notable footnote in Court history, footnote 4 from the case of *United States v. Carolene Products* (1938).

In what was by 1938 an unremarkable case—the Court upheld the right of the federal government to prohibit the shipment of "filled milk" against a challenge that it both violated the Fifth Amendment's guarantee of due process and exceeded Congress's power to regulate "commerce among the states"—Justice Harlan Fiske Stone spelled out how the "Modern Court" would in the future wield its power of judicial review. Stone announced that the degree of scrutiny the Court would exercise in cases involving individual rights and liberties would be quite different from its review of legislation challenged as interfering merely with the rights of property.

The three paragraphs of footnote 4 specify the two levels of scrutiny that the Court committed itself to observing. For legislation involving property, there would be minimal scrutiny. Indeed, there would gradually develop a presumption of constitutionality for government's right to adopt such legislation. On the other hand, legislation that touched on civil rights or liberties would be subject to a much higher level of scrutiny, with the government frequently seeming to have the burden of justifying its actions. The result is a sort of judicial double standard.

There may be narrower scope for operation of the presumption of constitutionality when legislation appears on its face to be within a specific prohibition of the Constitution, such as those of the first ten amendments, which are deemed equally specific when held to be embraced within the Fourteenth. . . .

It is unnecessary to consider now whether legislation which restricts those political processes which can ordinarily be expected to bring about repeal of undesirable legislation is to be subjected to more exacting judicial scrutiny under the general prohibitions of the Fourteenth Amendment than are most other types of legislation. . . .

Nor need we enquire whether similar considerations enter into the review of statutes directed at particular religions, . . . or national, . . . or racial minorities . . ., whether prejudice against discrete and insular minorities may be a special condition, which tends seriously to curtail the operation of those political processes ordinarily to be relied upon to protect minorities, and which may call for a correspondingly more searching judicial inquiry.

Footnote 4 provided a road map for the cases and issues the Court would deal with in the 1940s and later. In addition to spelling out a judicial double standard, it led in turn to the development of the concept of "preferred freedoms," which is the idea that certain of the guarantees of the Bill of Rights, specifically those contained in the First Amendment (freedoms of speech, press, association, and religion), were superior to other rights and deserved the greatest level of judicial protection against government. Perhaps even more important, footnote 4 claimed for the Court the role of protector of the rights of "discrete and insular minorities."

THE NEW EQUAL PROTECTION

Although the ideas sketched out in footnote 4 influenced the Court in the 1940s, they started to come to true fruition during the era of the Warren Court (1953–1968), particularly during the 1960s. During this latter period, the Court's activist liberal bloc, eventually composed of the Chief Justice and Justices Hugo Black, William O. Douglas, William Brennan, and Arthur Goldberg (and later Abe Fortas), succeeded in leading a judicial revolution that, among other things, resulted in the incorporation or carrying over of almost all of the guarantees of the Bill of Rights to the states (those "of the first ten amendments, which are deemed equally specific when held to be embraced within the Fourteenth . . .," paragraph 1 of footnote 4).

In addition to its work in "nationalizing" the Bill of Rights, the Court increasingly turned its attention to ideas found in the second paragraph of footnote 4, "legislation which restricts those political processes," and to paragraph 3's concern with minorities, and in particular nonracial minorities. Both of these developments involved the Court's dramatic expansion of the traditional role of the Fourteenth Amendment's guarantee of equal protection. In turn, they ushered in changes that affected American society almost as profoundly as the Warren Court's earlier decisions involving racial equality (discussed in chapter 1).

These non–race-related uses of the Equal Protection Clause may be better understood by dividing them into three categories, though this division is hardly watertight—the Court's decisions, unfortunately, are not formulated to please the needs of the Court' students.

The first category consists of cases involving legislative apportionment. The second focuses on the concept of "fundamental rights" or what some would label "substantive equal protection." The third addresses the question of whether the Court's concern with "discrete and insular minorities" calls for the Court to examine legislation that classifies on bases other than those of race or ethnicity, the traditional "suspect categories."

Almost all scholars acknowledge that the Fourteenth Amendment's guarantee of equal protection arose out of its authors' concern with the rights of the newly freed slaves (Gunther and Sullivan 1997, 628). Still, its general language did not seem to preclude entirely its use in preventing states from engaging in other types of classifications that denied equal protection. Despite Justice Samuel Miller's observation in the *Slaughterhouse Cases* (1873) that "the existence of laws in the States where the newly emancipated negroes resided, which discriminated with gross injustice and hardship against them as a class, was the evil to be remedied," in fact, later nineteenth-century cases such as *Strauder v. West Virginia* (1880)—"naturalized Celtic Irishmen" as well as African Americans enjoy the protection of the Fourteenth Amendment—and *Yick Wo v. Hopkins* (1886)—discrimination against Chinese laundries violated equal protection—found justices, who were contemporaries of the authors of the Fourteenth Amendment, who believed that its prohibitions extended also to citizens other than African Americans.

Ironically, as seen in chapter 1, this same Court interpreted the Fourteenth Amendment in the *Civil Rights Cases* (1883) and *Plessy v. Ferguson* (1896) in a way that rendered the amendment almost a nullity in terms of protecting the civil rights of African Americans. Subsequent decisions involving voting, such as the literacy tests and the "grandfather" clause that allowed illiterate whites to vote, would also deny to African Americans political rights that the Fifteenth Amendment clearly had been framed to guarantee.

The Modern (post-1937) Court's first invocation of the guarantee of equal protection demonstrated the clause's remarkable capability to expand to meet problems unlikely to have been foreseen by its nineteenth-century authors. *Skinner v. Oklahoma* (1942) involved the Oklahoma Criminal Sterilization Act, a statute that directed that persons who were convicted for the third time of "felonies involving moral turpitude" were to "be rendered sexually sterile," by vasectomy for men and by salpingectomy for women. The state's power to do so seemed solidly grounded on the earlier, high-visibility case of *Buck v. Bell* (1927), in which Justice Holmes had uttered the famous—or infamous—line, "three generations of imbeciles are enough."

Holmes had based his decision on his conclusion that Virginia's actions leading up to Carrie Buck's sterilization were in accord with the Fourteenth Amendment's guarantee of due process. Simply put, the state had the right to sterilize a person if doing so was in the public interest and would not affect the person's general health—it was, after all a "lesser sacrifice" than the state had asked of its "best citizens" during war. Moreover, the procedures that Virginia had in place gave Buck adequate protection before she could be sterilized. Thus, Carrie had received all the process due to her. Holmes also had been presented with an equal protection argument, but, typical of the Old Court, he had dismissed it as an essentially frivolous claim, quipping that claims of a denial of equal protection are "the usual last resort of constitutional arguments."

Justice William O. Douglas, however, saw the Oklahoma issue quite differently. In his eyes, it definitely raised equal protection issues with which the Court was obligated to deal. For Douglas, there were two primary equal protection matters raised by *Skinner*. The first was that the statute exempted persons from a compelled sterilization who had been convicted for either embezzlement or political corruption. The second was that sterilization involved deprivation of a fundamental right, the right to procreate. For whatever reason, neither the unanimous Court that ruled in favor of the three-time offender in *Skinner* nor the 1973 Court that struck down state antiabortion statutes in *Roe v. Wade* challenged Holmes's holding in *Buck*. In fact, Justice Harry Blackmun explicitly noted in his *Roe* opinion that nothing the Court held in the least undermined *Buck*'s vitality as precedent.

Perhaps even more important for later developments on the issue of equal protection was the 1944 Japanese exclusion case, *Korematsu v. United States*. In upholding the power of the president to order all persons of Japanese ancestry to federal detention camps, Justice Hugo Black sketched out what would later become known as the "compelling state interest" test or simply "strict scrutiny." This is the test that subsequent courts would use to test whether legislation that employs race as the standard was or was not constitutional.

> All legal restrictions which curtail the civil rights of a single racial group are immediately suspect. That is not to say that all such restrictions are unconstitutional. It is to say that the courts must subject them to the most rigid scrutiny. . . . Citizenship has its responsibilities as well as its privileges, and in time of war the burden is always heavier.

The Court and Legislative Apportionment

Douglas's excursion into the realm of the Equal Protection Clause in a non–race-related case, however, proved generally to be an exception both in the 1940s and throughout the 1950s. In 1962, however, the Court returned to the clause in what Chief Justice Warren termed the most important case decided during his chief justiceship, *Baker v. Carr.* Until then, the Court had refused to interfere with controversies arising out of legislative apportionment. They were identified as "political questions" from which the Court was barred. There was one exception. The Court had intervened in what was essentially a racial gerrymander (*Gomillion v. Lightfoot* [1960]), but this was certainly seen, at least by the author of the opinion of the Court, Justice Felix Frankfurter, as an exception to the long-standing rule against intervening in controversies involving legislative apportionment. Such controversies were "political questions"—issues best left either to the two political branches (the president and Congress) to handle or to the people through the electoral process. They were not for the judiciary to dispose of; they were, in other words, nonjusticiable.

The most famous ruling to this effect had been written by Justice Frankfurter in the case of *Colegrove v. Green* (1946). In the

Colegrove opinion, Frankfurter had flatly rejected an invitation to involve the Court in an Illinois controversy arising from the state's apportionment of its seats in the U.S. House of Representatives. The lines drawn by the state legislature had produced what was then the nation's largest (based on population) congressional district. Located in Chicago, it had a population almost nine times larger than that of a downstate rural district. In refusing to rule on the case, Frankfurter issued his famous admonition against judges getting themselves and their judicial ermine caught in what he labeled the "political thicket" of legislative apportionment.

Frankfurter's position held sway until 1962. Then in *Baker v. Carr,* by a vote of 6–2, the Court, led by Justice William Brennan, entered Frankfurter's forbidden "thicket," finding Tennessee's legislative apportionment not to be a political question and, accordingly, justiciable. For the majority, the Fourteenth Amendment's guarantee of equal protection offered the justices a more than adequate standard by which judges could monitor the constitutionality of legislative apportionment. (In order to stay faithful to his *Colegrove* opinion, Frankfurter had relied in *Gomillion* on the Fifteenth Amendment. The latter, unlike the Fourteenth, is clearly limited to discrimination based on "race, color, or previous condition of servitude.")

The Tennessee case was a particularly good test for those who wanted the Court to abandon its earlier reluctance to get involved in redistricting disputes. In Tennessee, despite the state constitution's mandate that reapportionment take place every ten years, there had been no revision since 1901. Even the 1901 apportionment had created districts with drastic population differences that overrepresented rural voters at the expense of urban voters. By 1959, when the case was first filed in the state courts, the disparities had grown even greater, with urban and suburban areas even more seriously underrepresented than they had been at the time of the 1901 districting. Twice argued before the Supreme Court—a total of six hours was set aside for oral argument—the decision was finally announced on March 26, 1962.

Justice Brennan made quick work of Frankfurter's *Colegrove* opinion. He characterized his former professor's opinion as a minority decision—Frankfurter had secured the votes of only three of the seven justices who participated—and thus not as binding on subsequent Courts as opinions that represented the views of a majority of the justices.

Brennan's opinion opened the floodgates for suits challenging the manner in which states apportioned legislative districts. For his part, Frankfurter penned a lengthy dissent (sixty-four pages) that warned of the perils the Court was facing by entering the "political thicket." It was to be his judicial swan song. He retired from the Court in 1962. His leaving provided President John F. Kennedy an opportunity to make his second appointment. Kennedy nominated Labor Secretary Arthur Goldberg to fill what was then styled "the Jewish seat." Goldberg would give the Court's activist liberal bloc a solid majority, making possible the subsequent decisions that have come largely to be associated in the public's mind with the record of the Warren Court. Within a year of Brennan's *Baker* opinion, thirty-six legislative plans were under attack in federal courts.

Although Brennan had characterized the Tennessee scheme as arbitrary and capricious, subsequent decisions emphasized that malapportionment of any kind and for any purpose infringed on the fundamental right to vote and that no reason existed that could justify dilution or debasement of this fundamental right. This included the so-called federal analogy, which Chief Justice Earl Warren flatly rejected in the landmark 1964 case of *Reynolds v. Sims*. The fact that representation in the U.S. Senate is based on geography—each state has two senators—and not population was irrelevant, said Warren. Counties, cities, or towns were not analogous in any way to states. Before the ratification of the federal Constitution in 1789, the states had been independent. Counties and other units of local government had never been independent.

Indeed, they were the creatures of the states. Thus, there was no parallel at the state level to the "Great Compromise" and no basis for allowing government units to be "represented" in legislatures if such representation led to disparities in the numbers of voters.

According to Warren, his *Reynolds* opinion was the most important of his sixteen-year career as chief justice—more important, apparently in his view, than even his *Brown* opinion. Although most observers would differ in this assessment, there is no doubt that *Reynolds* is among the Court's most important decisions and that Warren was as persuasive in his language in *Reynolds* as he had been a decade earlier in the desegregation case.

> Legislators represent people, not trees or acres. Legislators are elected by voters, not farms or cities or economic interests. As long as ours is a representative form of government, [the] right to elect legislators in a free and unimpaired fashion is a bedrock of our political system. . . . We are cautioned about the dangers of entering into political thickets and mathematical quagmires. Our answer is this: a denial of constitutionally protected rights demands judicial protection; our oath and our office require no less of us. [To] the extent that a citizen's right to vote is debased, he is that much less a citizen.

As the Court proceeded ever deeper into the "thicket," it consecrated the now familiar standard of "one person, one vote," first announced in an opinion by Justice William O. Douglas in the case of *Gray v. Sanders* (1963), as its sacred talisman. In justifying its entrance into the "political thicket" and its rejection of practices of apportionment that dated back to the founding and were in place at the time the state legislatures had ratified the Fourteenth Amendment, the Court contended that such involvement was based not on the particular view of the Court's majority, but that decisions were required if the nation wished to remain true to the democratic principles on which it was founded. In this regard, Justice Douglas, in *Gray,* had concluded: "The conception of political equality from the Declaration of Independence to Lincoln's Gettysburg Address, to the Fifteenth, Seventeenth, and Nineteenth Amendments can mean only one such thing—one person, one vote."

In *Brown,* Chief Justice Warren had settled the question of whether the authors of the Fourteenth Amendment had intended to outlaw school segregation—counsel for the school districts had tellingly pointed out in their briefs that the same Congress that proposed the Fourteenth Amendment had voted to segregate the schools in the District of Columbia—by concluding that a study of that history was "inconclusive." Whatever the merits of Warren's reading of history, there was no way he could square the history in this case with the results the majority of the Court had reached. Surely, it was inconceivable to anyone that the legislators who ratified the Fourteenth Amendment, legislators who sat in forums apportioned in ways Warren and the *Reynolds* Court held were unconstitutional, would have approved an amendment whose language would lead to the results that *Reynolds* required. As a result, the only alternative for the majority was to ignore history entirely, which they did over the protests of the dissenters and of critics who either represented the interests hurt by the reapportionment decisions or saw the Court's apportionment decisions as involving judicial activism gone wild.

To say that the reapportionment decisions were not met with universal applause would be a gross understatement. The rulings produced howls of protest from those, to use Governor Alfred E. Smith's picturesque phrase, who had had their oxen severely gored. How much the decisions actually altered the political calculus in the states and in the U.S. House of Representatives continues to be debated and studied. Nevertheless, whatever the consequences in terms of legislation adopted or not adopted, the rulings definitely meant that many rural legislators were likely to find their districts merged, with the result that many would be turned out of office after the required redistricting took effect.

Obviously, no legislator likes to give up or lose his or her seat. Harrisburg or Sacramento might not be Paris, but they offered many things that are not found "back on the farm."

Protests of the decision came from all over the nation. Whereas public opposition to *Brown* had been confined almost entirely to the eleven states that had formed the Confederate States of America and to the so-called border states, opposition to the reapportionment decisions was geographically much more broadly based. As a result, at least initially, opponents seemed confident that they could do something to reverse at least some of the effect of these rulings. By the mid-1960s also, a great number of people thought that the Warren Court had gone too far in exercising its powers. Opponents of *Reynolds* could, for example, expect to enlist the support of those who had axes to grind against the Court as a result of the *Brown* decision or of the Court's controversial decisions on freedom of speech. To the displeasure of many legislators, for example, the Warren Court had considerably narrowed the definition of obscenity and had regularly jousted with legislation aimed at limiting the Communist Party.

The reapportionment decisions provided an opportunity for all these critics of Court decisions to join forces. More than 130 bills were introduced in Congress after *Reynolds* that sought to void the decision or to restrict the federal courts' power in matters of legislative apportionment. One bill, sponsored by Representative William V. Tuck (a Democrat from Virginia), passed in the U.S. House of Representatives by a vote of 218–175 on August 18, 1964. It would have taken away from federal courts their right to hear any apportionment cases. Luckily for the Court, the Senate never acted on the proposal.

The failure of the Senate to act on the Tuck proposal, however, by no means meant that the majority of senators supported what the Court had done, nor did it end efforts to reverse the Court. Indeed, the Senate fired the next major volley in the battle. Republican Minority Leader Everett Dirksen, of Illinois, introduced an amendment that would have allowed the states, provided the voters gave their approval in a referendum, to apportion one branch of the state legislature on a basis other than population. It was put to a vote on August 4, 1965. Fifty-seven senators were recorded in favor and thirty-nine opposed. A subsequent vote the following January also failed to gain the necessary two-thirds vote, as required by Article V of the Constitution.

Article V provides an alternative means of amending the Constitution, however. "On the application of the Legislatures of two thirds of the several States, [Congress] shall call a Convention for proposing Amendments." By 1967, thirty-two state legislatures had called for a convention to deal with the issue of apportionment—two states short of the required two-thirds. The drive for additional states stalled, however.

The fact that the call for a convention fizzled only two states short of success and that the battle over apportionment soon died down stands in contrast with the situation after *Brown*. That reapportionment was accepted more quickly than desegregation can be explained in part by the speed with which the former was implemented. There was no need in this case for a call for implementation to proceed "with all deliberate speed."

The ability and willingness of the federal courts to carry out the *Reynolds v. Sims* mandate and to do so speedily stand in obvious contrast with the foot-dragging that followed *Brown*. It also explains why opposition to *Reynolds,* although much more broadly based than that to *Brown,* dissipated much more rapidly. Despite the fears of Justice Frankfurter and his judicial soul-mate, Justice John Marshall Harlan Jr., about "political thickets" and "mathematical quagmires," federal courts were able to "persuade" legislatures to go along, although often after threats of court-ordered reapportionment. In those cases where states failed to do so, judges drew the district lines. Legislators soon learned that no matter how politically difficult it was, they were well advised to do it themselves rather than allow federal judges to determine their political futures or, possibly worse still, to allow them to bring in outside experts from universities to draw legislative boundaries.

As the mandate of "one person, one vote" was implemented, support for a constitutional amendment that would have returned boundaries, and with them political power to the status quo ante, not surprisingly, became less and less popular. Those whose political oxen had been gored the worst by the decisions were no longer in power or even, in many cases, in office, and incumbents were loath to change the new status quo that had brought them to office and to power.

Although the Court would continue to be drawn repeatedly back into the "thicket" of legislative apportionment—being asked, for example, to determine what other types of legislative bodies, such as school boards, needed to comply with the mandate of "one person, one vote" and how close to mathematical equality districts had to be—the major public controversy and criticism that had been stirred by the reapportionment cases had largely vanished by the 1970s. That is not to say that there are not periodic flare-ups that require judicial intervention, but these controversies are not about whether the principle of "one person, one vote" should be the standard followed in reapportionment but rather how it is to be implemented in a particular situation.

The Court's reapportionment decisions clearly added to the judiciary's prestige. Whatever the Court's critics said, it was hard, in both the short run and the long run, to argue against the logic of the Court's opinions.

The now regularized process of reapportionment, occurring after the release of the U.S. census data every ten years, did exacerbate an old issue, gerrymandering. The growing importance of partisan gerrymandering was one of the unanticipated consequences of the "one person, one vote" rule. The drawing of political boundaries for partisan purposes was not a new practice. It existed long before a Massachusetts political cartoonist in 1811 had seized upon the similarity between a newly drawn legislative district in that state and a salamander. The cartoonist gave the district legs and eyes and christened it a gerrymander after the state's governor, Elbridge Gerry.

In the pre-*Baker* era, gerrymandering existed, but it was not nearly as prevalent as it would become after *Baker*, for the simple reason that before 1962 legislative boundaries were not regularly adjusted. In *Baker*, the controversy was less over how district lines were drawn than over the issue of there having been no redrawing of lines for almost six decades. The same was true in *Reynolds v. Sims*. There, the districts mirrored county or town lines with no regard for population or for the partisan composition of the electorate in the district.

Legislatures now redraw lines every ten years. Immediately after the completion of the decennial U.S. census, state legislatures must adjust district lines to ensure that they meet the Supreme Court's mandate of population equality. Computer technology and old-fashioned political acumen together allow legislative majorities both to comply with court requirements on population and to increase the number of seats their party holds in the legislature. They do this by creating districts that distribute their putative supporters across the largest number of districts possible, but in a way that ensures that their members constitute a majority in as many of these districts as possible. In contrast, the members of the minority party are concentrated in the smallest number of districts. Like the New England missionaries who went to Hawaii in the nineteenth century to bring the Christian message to the natives, state legislative leaders have learned that by doing good (following the Court's order to create equal districts), they can do well (by increasing their majorities in state legislatures).

In the 1980s there was speculation that the Supreme Court might intervene in the issue of gerrymandering. Although gerrymandering is not as obviously undemocratic as the malapportionment that existed prior to the 1960s—in those days it was not at all uncommon for a quarter or less of the electorate effectively to control at least one branch of a state legislature—situations regularly occur where the majority party wins more than its "fair share" of seats. The Court's major gerrymandering case, decided in 1986, probably raised more questions than it answered. Like many of the decisions handed down in the later days of the Burger Court (1969–1986), the case produced a plethora of opinions, none of which secured the support of a majority of the justices.

Davis v. Bandemer arose from a challenge to a Republican-controlled apportionment in Indiana. "In elections held under the plan in 1982, the Democrats received 51.9 percent of the total [state] House [of Representatives] vote and 53.1 percent of the total [state] Senate vote, yet won only forty-three of 100 House seats and only thirteen of twenty-five Senate seats." Chief Justice Warren Burger, along with Associate Justices William Rehnquist and Sandra Day O'Connor, would have dismissed the suit as a nonjusticiable political question. They could conceive of no judicially manageable standard by which judges could determine when legislators, in their desire to draw lines to advantage the party in power, had gone too far. The only possible standard would be one that would require proportional representation. For Burger, Rehnquist, and O'Connor, a Court that would do this would be truly an example of judicial activism gone amok. If voters want proportional representation, it is up to the voters or their representatives to adopt such a system. Judges should not impose such a standard.

In contrast, the remaining six Court members concluded that challenges to gerrymandering were not a political question, although they disagreed on when courts should intervene. Justice Byron White wrote the judgment of the Court (a judgment of the Court, rather than an opinion of the Court, is issued when less than a majority of the justices agree with the reasoning upon which the decision was based). White held that judicial intervention was warranted only when it could be shown that "the electoral system substantially disadvantages certain voters in their opportunity to influence the political process." White emphasized that the operative word was "substantial" and that obviously any reapportionment by politicians would result in some diminution of certain groups' level of influence. A single disproportionate result, as in the present Indiana case, was not enough for White to justify judicial intervention. Justices Lewis Powell and John Paul Stevens refused to accept White's standard. They argued that it was necessary to adopt a more neutral standard, one that different judges could apply and be confident that they were reaching similar results. According to Powell,

> the merits of a gerrymandering claim must be determined by reference to the configurations of the districts, the observance of political subdivision lines and other criteria that have independent relevance to the fairness of [redistricting]. The most important are the shapes of voting districts and adherence to established political subdivision boundaries. Other relevant considerations include the nature of the legislative procedures by which the apportionment law was adopted and [the] legislative history.

The Supreme Court has not revisited the issue of gerrymandering since this 1986 case, but lower courts have tried to impose some restraint on overly partisan gerrymanders with varying levels of success. The issue, however, will return in the 2003–2004 term. The Supreme Court agreed to hear a case challenging a Republican gerrymander of Pennsylvania's congressional districts. What the Court will do remains to be seen. Short of mandating proportional representation, there does not seem to be a standard the Court could devise that would not guarantee the federal judiciary's being involved regularly with what is a highly partisan process. Even the most partisan of gerrymanders does not result in the degree of voter dilution prevalent until the 1960s. The Court's recent involvement with what have been dubbed racial gerrymanders may be a cautionary tale on the merits of continued Court abstention from this issue.

This more recent controversy brings together the issue of apportionment with that of race in a highly combustible mixture. Its occurrence is somewhat ironic since it was the racial gerrymander in *Gomillion v. Lightfoot* that persuaded the Court to look for the first time at constitutional issues arising from the drawing of governmental boundaries. In that case, Justice Felix Frankfurter, writing for a unanimous Court, found that the Alabama legislature's redrawing of the boundary lines of the city of Tuskegee—transforming it from its previous square configuration to a figure that had twenty-eight sides and, in the process, excluding almost all blacks from the city—violated the Fifteenth Amendment.

More recent cases arise from legislative acts whose purposes are directly contrary to those that drove the Alabama legislature in the late 1950s. In contrast to the efforts of that period to exclude blacks from representation, more recent legislative efforts are designed to increase black representation. Under the Voting Rights Act of 1965, the U.S. Department of Justice must approve redistricting in states that had a record of denying blacks the vote or where there was previously a significantly low level of voter participation.

In the past, the Justice Department has used this power to prod legislatures to create more districts likely to elect black representatives. To do this, legislatures clearly have to take race into consideration since majority white districts will rarely elect a black candidate. Complicating the process in the South is that southern blacks, particularly in rural areas, are not always concentrated in certain areas. The resulting districts at times have made the twenty-eight-sided district created by the Alabama legislature in Tuskegee look "compact and contiguous" by comparison.

Advocates of such districts, writing in the 1980s, argued that evidence demonstrated that in order for African Americans to win election, they needed districts with overwhelming majorities of minority voters. Districts that were simply a majority black largely elected or reelected whites to legislatures. The reason for this was that voting rates among blacks were significantly lower than among whites, and whites were unlikely to vote for a black candidate (recent research finds that this may no longer be as true).

Certain Republican leaders seized upon these findings to serve another interest: increasing the number of Republican legislators. By creating "max-black" districts in the South, districts that would elect blacks to Congress, they drained the remaining districts of their most reliable Democratic voters, African Americans, and thereby created more districts that would elect Republicans. This may have helped Republicans keep control of the House of Representatives during the 107th Congress (2001–2003), when their majority was one of the smallest in the history of the House.

The fact that such districts helped Republicans in legislatures has, however, had no effect on the voting patterns of the Court's most conservative justices. In *Shaw v. Hunt* (1996), the Court by a vote of 5–4, with Chief Justice Rehnquist writing for the majority, found that a North Carolina congressional district approved by the Justice Department and upheld by a three-judge district court as narrowly tailored to meet the state's compelling interest in meeting the requirements of Sections 2 and 5 of the Voting Rights Act, nevertheless violated the Equal Protection Clause. Rehnquist found that the use of race in drawing the district—a district whose design would have made Governor Gerry blush—failed because it did not meet the requirement of "a compelling state interest," since its goal was merely "an effort to alleviate the effects of societal discrimination." As in the affirmative action cases discussed in Chapter 2, Rehnquist found that although discrimination on the part of government had existed, it had long ceased. As a result, it no longer had an effect on the current processes and, accordingly, could not be used to meet the "compelling state interest" requirement necessary to use race as a basis for government action.

The issue of North Carolina's congressional redistricting returned to the Court three more times after *Shaw*. As a result of the litigation, North Carolina legislators continued to tinker with the contours of the disputed district. The 1998 revision of North Carolina's twelfth congressional district produced a district that, although by no means compact, had fattened up considerably so that at its longest it was now only half as long as the 1992 effort. This iteration apparently was enough to win the vote of Justice O'Connor, whose vote since the 1990s frequently tips the balance in the Court's increasing number of 5–4 decisions.

In *Hunt v. Cromartie* (2001), Justice David Souter, writing for a five-member majority that included O'Connor, found the new boundary lines constitutional. According to Souter, while the legislature had considered race in drawing the district's boundaries, it had done so because race was a better indicator of actual voting behavior than party identification.

> [T]his is because white voters registered as Democrats "cross over" to vote for a Republican candidate more often than do African Americans, who register and vote Democratic between 95 percent and 97 percent of the time. A legislature trying to secure a safe Democratic seat is interested in Democratic voting behavior. Hence, a legislature may, by placing reliable Democratic precincts within a district without regard to race, end up with a district containing more heavily African American precincts, but the reasons would be political rather than racial [and, therefore, would not violate the Fourteenth Amendment's guarantee of equal protection].

Justice Clarence Thomas wrote the dissenting opinion in which Chief Justice Rehnquist and Associate Justices Antonin Scalia and Anthony Kennedy concurred. For Thomas, "racial gerrymandering offends the Constitution whether the motivation is malicious or [as in *Hunt*] benign." The voting breakdown in *Hunt* not surprisingly paralleled exactly the vote pattern in *Grutter v. Bollinger*

(2003), the affirmative action case involving the University of Michigan Law School.

In the Court's most recent decision on race and legislative districting, *Georgia v. Ashcroft* (2003), O'Connor rejoined her conservative allies in a decision that gave state legislatures more discretion in reapportioning districts even if the result was to reduce the number of seats "safe" for minority candidates. The suit, brought under the terms of Voting Rights Act of 1965, challenged a reapportionment of Georgia's legislature supported overwhelmingly by the legislature's African American members (all of whom are Democrats). O'Connor spoke for the same justices who decided *Bush v. Gore*. The difference was that this time Republicans were the losers.

SUBSTANTIVE EQUAL PROTECTION

Critics of the Old Court, and in particular critics of the Court's decisions that eviscerated New Deal legislation, argue that what the Court was doing in those cases was substituting its judgment for that of Congress. These critics scoffed at the Court's claim that it was merely applying the Constitution, as Justice Owen Roberts so famously claimed in striking down the New Deal's first effort in adopting the Agriculture Adjustment Act:

> [When] an act of Congress is appropriately challenged in the courts as not conforming to the constitutional mandate the judicial branch of the Government has only one duty,—to lay the article of the Constitution which is invoked beside the statute which is challenged and to decide whether the latter squares with the former. [This] court neither approves nor condemns any legislative policy. (*United States v. Butler,* 1936)

The broad charge that the Court's detractors during the 1930s brought against the Court was that it was engaging in "substantive due process." Although many scholars have tried to define it, in very different ways, any definition should begin with the dissent Justice Oliver Wendell Holmes Jr. penned in the case of *Lochner v. New York* (1905):

> [This] case is decided upon an economic theory which a large part of the country does not entertain. If it were a question whether I agreed with that theory, I should desire to study it further and long before making up my mind. But I do not conceive that to be my duty, because I strongly believe that my agreement or disagreement has nothing to do with the right of a majority to embody their opinions in law. It is settled by various decisions of this court that [state laws] may regulate life in many ways which we as legislators might think as injudicious or if you like as tyrannical as this, and which equally with this interfere with the liberty to contract.... The Fourteenth Amendment does not enact Mr. Herbert Spencer's Social Statics.... [A] constitution is not intended to embody a particular economic theory, whether of paternalism ... or laissez faire. It is made for people of fundamentally differing views, and the accident of our finding certain opinions natural and familiar or novel and even shocking ought not to conclude our judgment upon the question whether statutes embodying them conflict with the [Constitution]....
>
> I think that the word liberty in the Fourteenth Amendment is perverted when it is held to prevent the natural outcome of a dominant opinion, unless it can be said that a rational and fair man necessarily would admit that the statute proposed would infringe fundamental principles as they have been understood by the traditions of our people and our law.

From Holmes's dissent, two key concepts can be drawn. The first is that under the guarantees of due process, legislation that is irrational can be struck down as unconstitutional. However, rational cannot be understood to be the equivalent of wise or just. Holmes indicates that legislation that might be viewed as "tyrannical" by some can nevertheless be constitutional. Rational means simply that there is some link between the proposed goal of the legislation and the legislative means adopted to achieve that goal. It does not require that the means be the best means or the wisest means or even the fairest means.

The second concept that can be extracted from Holmes's comment concerns "fundamental principles as they have been understood by the traditions of our people and our law." Generally, this has been interpreted to mean those rights that are either explicit in the Constitution, such as the guarantees of the Bill of Rights, or that can be argued to be implicit in the Constitution, such as the idea that a freedom of association arises naturally from the other specific guarantees of the First Amendment.

In contrast, substantive due process involves judges' substituting their views, such as Justice Rufus Peckham's preference in *Lochner* for an unfettered marketplace, or laissez-faire, for the will of the people as expressed in legislation. To strike down the challenged legislation, a New York public health law that regulated the working conditions and the number of hours bakers could be made to work, Peckham found that the law interfered with the bakers' "liberty of contract." The bakers' liberty gave them the right to work as many hours as they chose and under whatever conditions they were willing to accept.

Peckham's opinion coined the verb "to lochnerize," which is defined as the judiciary's imposing its will, its prejudices, over and against the will of the people as expressed by their legislators. "Liberty of contract" was one of the concepts that was buried with the emergence in 1937 of the Modern Court. Substantive due process seemingly was relegated along with it into "the dustbin of history." In its place, the Court proclaimed a new credo, best captured by Justice Stone's footnote 4 from *Carolene Products*.

Like the mythical vampires of the Middle Ages, substantive due process proved difficult to kill entirely. Stone and "the switch in time" apparently failed to spike its heart, although it did enter a lengthy period of somnolence from which it began to stir only in the 1960s.

The Warren Court in the 1960s truly transformed constitutional law. Even with Frankfurter on the bench, the Court was well advanced in the process of applying almost all the guarantees of the Bill of Rights to the states. With Frankfurter's 1962 replacement by Arthur Goldberg, the process sped up, and by the end of the Warren Court in 1968 almost all of the guarantees of the Bill of Rights and all of its important provisions had been carried over to or "incorporated" onto the states. As a result, the textual constitutional interdiction, "Congress shall make no law . . ." now was understood to read "Neither Congress nor the states nor any level of government may make any law. . . ." The Bill of Rights, the product of anti-Federalist agitation, designed to limit what critics saw as too powerful a federal government, now existed to limit the states as well. The Court did this—the process actually began in the 1925 case of *Gitlow v. New York*—by interpreting the incorporated provisions of the Bill of Rights as constituting liberties that states, pursuant to the Fourteenth Amendment, could not abridge ("nor shall any state deprive any person of life, liberty, or property, without due process of law").

If one accepts the criticism of the day, such decisions by the Warren Court represented the height of judicial activism. The Court's detractors claimed that they were analogous to *Lochner* and, worse still, *Dred Scott* (1857). In short, they were evidence of a Court hell-bent on reaching judicial supremacy. The Court, said the detractors, needed to return to the virtues of self-restraint as preached by Justices Holmes and Benjamin Cardozo and later by Frankfurter.

The Frankfurtian philosophy of judicial self-restraint is based on the twin premises that the Court is the least democratic and least powerful branch of government. Accordingly, the Court in exercising its power of judicial review should wield this sword only when legislation is clearly unconstitutional. Any doubt as to constitutionality needs to be decided in favor of the legislatures, since this is a democracy and they are the vox populi (the voice of the people).

In contrast, judicial activism argues that it is not only the right of the Court to determine matters of constitutionality, but, when presented with a case, it is the justices' duty to decide, in their judgment, whether a statute is or is not constitutional. Justice Hugo Black, Frankfurter's nemesis on the Court, was identified by many as the exemplar of activism on the Warren Court; later critics of the Court, however, would find this judgment inaccurate. In his dissent in the so-called birth control case, *Griswold v. Connecticut* (1965), Black surprised not a few observers in voting to uphold the constitutionality of a Connecticut statute prohibiting the use of contraceptives. Said Black: "I like my privacy as well as the next one . . . I am nevertheless compelled to admit that government has a right to invade it unless prohibited by some specific constitutional [provision]."

The height of judicial activism in the eyes of many of the Warren Court critics came with *Griswold,* when the Court struck down Connecticut's law prohibiting the use of contraceptives. By a vote of 7–2, the Court, in a sometimes diffuse opinion by Justice William O. Douglas, justified voiding the statute on the grounds that it violated a right of privacy. According to Douglas, this right of privacy existed in the Bill of Rights within the "emanations" of several of the explicit guarantees of that document. This, alleged Court detractors, was nothing less than a return by the Court to the discredited doctrine of "substantive due process." The right of privacy sprang from the same undemocratic soil as Peckham's liberty of contract.

Whether because of the fear that the Court's work would be tarred by association with *Lochner* or for some other reason, the Warren Court discovered no other new rights, after that of privacy, lurking either in constitutional "emanations" or "penumbras." Instead, the Court turned to the Equal Protection Clause in its quest to make American society fairer.

For observers of Earl Warren, it was obvious that fairness was the ultimate value to be pursued. Regularly, Warren in oral argument would ask government attorneys making the case that a challenged government action conformed to long-standing Court precedents, "'But was it fair?' (Sometimes personalizing the question, he would ask a government lawyer who had first heard of the case when it reached the Supreme Court, 'Why did you treat him that way?')" (Lewis 1968, 6). Certainly, that concern about fairness ran throughout the fabric of the chief's opinion in *Reynolds v. Sims.* It provided a foundation for the Warren Court's concern with the rights of those accused of crime, such as in *Miranda v. Arizona* (1966). It would surface also in other cases, particularly those in which the Court pushed the boundaries of the Fourteenth Amendment's Equal Protection Clause to remedy what it saw as violations of the people's fundamental rights.

University of Virginia Law Professor G. Edward White sums up Warren's judicial philosophy as follows:

> Warren repeatedly emphasized that he had a "duty" under the Constitution to see that his understanding of its imperatives were implemented, and he saw the Constitution's imperatives as ethical imperatives.... If a branch of government had engaged in or tolerated a practice that Warren found inconsistent with his conception of American citizenship under the Constitution, the power of that branch was thereby undermined. Warren's perception of constitutional values overwhelmed institutional values in his decision making calculus. (White 1982, 218)

Warren's concern with fairness and decency, with his and the Constitution's ethical imperatives, might explain why this "knight-errant" turned increasingly in the 1960s to the Equal Protection Clause in his drive for a fairer, more decent, more egalitarian society. If he shared the view of his colleague, William Douglas, that "the Bill of Rights is not enough," the Equal Protection

Clause offered a less controversial means of advancing this agenda than a return to substantive due process even if the latter concept was now being used to protect rights other than property rights, as it had been in *Griswold.*

The Warren Court began to discuss "fundamental rights" in the context of the Equal Protection Clause. This course of action was prepared in part by the Court's reapportionment cases. The fundamental right in those cases was the right to vote. Like the right of privacy that lay at the heart of *Griswold,* the right to vote is a right that most people would assume is found in the Constitution or at least in one of its amendments, but which is not. One could argue, as John Hart Ely does, that the right to vote is found in a juncture of the Fourteenth Amendment's Equal Protection Clause and Article IV's provision that "the United States shall guarantee to every State . . . a Republican Form of Government." For Ely, this is the only basis upon which *Reynolds* can be rendered "intelligible" (Ely 1980, 122). If Warren believed this, he did not make it part of his opinion, possibly out of reluctance to overturn such a long-standing precedent as that of *Luther v. Borden* (1849), in which Chief Justice Taney had opined that questions concerning the guarantee of a "republican form of government" were nonjusticiable political questions.

The Warren Court's discovery of other "fundamental" rights, however, had much less of a claim to have a basis in the Constitution's text. Obviously this had not stopped Justice Douglas in the pre-Warren Court case of *Skinner* from positing a fundamental right to procreate. The Warren Court would consider the rights to marry and to travel as well. It would also examine whether or not wealth was a classification that required heightened scrutiny under the terms of the Equal Protection Clause.

Poll taxes were used as a revenue-raising device in colonial times and were continued after independence and after the adoption of the Constitution. Poll taxes involve the payment of a fee to be eligible to vote. Defenders argued that they were analogous to other fees that governments impose on people who wish to drive, hunt, or fish. As the franchise expanded during the nineteenth century, many states abolished the poll tax, but southern states continued to levy it. Its imposition maintained low voting rates among both blacks and poor whites. In 1964 the Twenty-fourth Amendment was adopted, abolishing poll taxes for federal elections but leaving states free to impose them for state elections. As a result, Virginia kept in place its dollar and a half poll tax. Acknowledging that "the right to vote in state elections is nowhere expressly mentioned," Justice Douglas, writing the Court's opinion in *Harper v. Virginia State Board of Elections* (1966), found that Virginia "violates the Equal Protection Clause . . . whenever it makes the affluence of the voter or payment of any fee an electoral standard. Voter qualifications have no relation to wealth. . . ." Legislation that limits this right "must be closely scrutinized."

A year later, in *Loving v. Virginia* (1967), Chief Justice Warren found that "marriage is one of the 'basic civil rights of man,' fundamental to our very existence and survival. . . . The Fourteenth Amendment requires that the freedom of choice to marry not be restricted by invidious racial discriminations." Accordingly, Virginia's antimiscegenation law, although applied against both blacks and whites, had to be struck down. Like the poll tax in *Harper*, it was a form of "invidious discrimination" that required "the 'most rigid scrutiny.'"

In 1968, the Court addressed governmental regulations that treated children born outside of marriage—illegitimate children—differently from those born to couples who were married. A Louisiana law denied unacknowledged illegitimate children the right to sue in cases involving the wrongful death of their mother. Writing in *Levy v. Louisiana* (1968), Justice Douglas, while admitting that the law was rational, saw the distinction as an example of "an invidious classification even though it has history and tradition on its side. . . . [It] is invidious to discriminate against [the illegitimate] when no action, conduct, or demeanor of theirs is possibly relevant to the harm that was done to their mother."

Residency requirements for eligibility for welfare benefits provided the Warren Court with its final exposure to fundamental rights. Suit was brought against the District of Columbia and the states of Connecticut and Pennsylvania for requiring persons to reside in those jurisdictions for a minimum of one year before being eligible to collect state welfare benefits. This classification between those who resided in the state less than a year and those who lived there for a year or longer posed equal protection concerns for six of the Court's members. As in the two previous cases, the Court found the regulation rational. "We do not doubt that the one-year waiting-period device is well suited to discourage the influx of poor families in need of assistance." That, however, was not enough for Justice William Brennan and the five other justices that joined his opinion in *Shapiro v. Thompson* (1969). There was a "fundamental right of interstate movement," and the residence requirement impaired this fundamental right. To survive, the law had to promote "compelling state interests," a standard the majority found the statute fell far short of.

Justices Harlan and Black and Chief Justice Warren dissented. The chief justice, a former California governor, possibly saw the implications that this decision might have on his and other states that provided welfare benefits well above the national average.

In *Harper, Loving, Levy,* and *Shapiro,* attorneys for the states could and did argue that their programs were rational. Under non–race-based analysis, that should have been sufficient to pass constitutional muster. As seen in chapters 1 and 2, in cases involving race, a so-called suspect category, government not only must convince the Court that the classification has a relationship to the achievement of the legislation's purported goal, but also the classification must meet a "compelling state interest" and be as "narrowly tailored" as possible to achieve that goal. In cases not involving race, rationality was sufficient to enable a statute to pass constitutional muster.

Obviously, however, this was not enough for the Warren Court where voting, marriage, wealth, or illegitimacy were involved. As much as race, such classifications raised red flags for the Court, triggering the "heightened scrutiny" which Justice Stone had discussed in his *Carolene Products* footnote.

Warren's retirement and replacement by President Nixon's nominee, the supposedly strict constructionist Warren E. Burger, raised many questions concerning the durability of a whole array of Warren Court precedents. Although the Court's First Amendment and criminal procedure rulings took center stage, close Court watchers speculated on what would be the fate of the Court's so-called substantive equal protection decisions. Was there a fundamental right to welfare, for example, or to a job? Was education a fundamental right? Given the Warren Court's decisions, those who wanted a more activist government and who realized that major social reforms were unlikely to emanate from Congress and especially from a White House occupied by their nemesis, Richard Nixon, could only look to the federal courts for solace. Yet, if the Court were to fulfill Nixon's wishes and strictly interpret the Constitution, the finding of new "fundamental rights" should cease.

THE BURGER COURT AND
FUNDAMENTAL RIGHTS

There was no doubt that Richard Nixon intended to be much more careful in vetting potential nominees to the federal bench and, in particular, to the Supreme Court, than administrations dating back at least to Roosevelt's. In his successful 1968 campaign against Democrat Hubert H. Humphrey, Nixon had made a major political issue of the Warren Court's decisions in a way that was unprecedented.

Nixon's criticism of the Court was probably summed up best by his charge that the *Miranda* and *Escobedo* decisions, which dealt with restraints imposed on police in their questioning of criminal suspects, "have had the effect of seriously hamstringing the peace forces in our society and strengthening the criminal forces" (Simon 1973, 6–7).

As discussed earlier, Nixon was able early in his first term to begin reshaping the Court. A 1970 decision seemed to indicate that Nixon's efforts to change the Court would be successful. *Dandridge v. Williams* (1970) involved an effort by Maryland to limit the amount of welfare payments individuals could receive. The state had established a sliding scale of benefits with a maximum of $250 a month. Linda Williams sued, arguing that the program penalized her for having a large family. Justice Potter Stewart, an Eisenhower appointee whom Nixon had considered for chief justice before nominating appeals court Judge Warren Burger to succeed Chief Justice Warren, wrote a very self-restraint-oriented opinion that seemed to ignore totally the equal protection decisions of the 1960s Warren Court:

In the area of economics and social welfare, a State does not violate the Equal Protection Clause merely because the classifications made by its law are imperfect. If the classification has some "reasonable basis," it does not offend the Constitution simply because the classification "is not made with mathematical nicety or because in practice it results in some inequality." . . .

We do not decide today that the Maryland regulation is wise, that it best fulfills the relevant social and economic objectives that Maryland might ideally espouse. . . . The Constitution may impose certain procedural safeguards upon systems of welfare administration. . . . But [it] does not empower this Court to second-guess state officials charged with the difficult responsibility of allocating limited public welfare funds among the myriad of potential recipients.

Justices Douglas, Brennan, and Marshall dissented. They found the distinction between large and small families to be arbitrary. Stewart's use of a low level of scrutiny might be permissible for economic regulations that affected businesses, but not one that affected welfare recipients. Wrote Marshall:

> Appellees are not a gas company or an optical dispenser; they are needy dependent children and families who are discriminated against by the State. The basis of the discrimination—the classification of individuals into large and small families—is too arbitrary and too unconnected to the asserted rationale, the impact on those discriminated against—the denial of even a subsistence existence—too great, and the supposed interests served too contrived and attenuated to meet the requirements of the Constitution.

Marshall used his dissent in *Dandridge* to sketch out a theme that he would develop in much greater detail later in *San Antonio School District v. Rodriguez* (1973). As equal protection analysis had developed during the Warren Court, there appeared to be two standards available to the Court. In dealing with nonsuspect categories and rights not deemed fundamental, the Court used a highly deferential rationality test that almost invariably saw the challenged legislation upheld. In contrast, the determination that legislation impacted on a suspect category or affected a fundamental right required government to show a compelling state interest. This regularly resulted in the legislation being struck down. Marshall argued that it was unwise to create such an either-or situation. There should be a different approach, one that would allow different levels of scrutiny in cases that did not neatly fall into one or the other of the Court's two traditional categories.

Two years later, the Burger Court dealt a further blow to the hopes that grew out of *Shapiro* and the other Warren Court decisions. By a vote of 5–2, the Court in *Lindsey v. Normet* (1972) rejected a claim that "decent shelter" was a fundamental right. The final blow to hopes for expansion of what Gerald Gunther has dubbed the "new equal protection" (Gunther 1972, 468) came in the case of *San Antonio Independent School District v. Rodriguez* (1973).

Of all the possible candidates for elevation to the status of a new fundamental right protected under the Equal Protection Clause of the Fourteenth Amendment, none seemed as promising as education. Like the right to vote, it could be argued that a right to education, though not explicit in the U.S. Constitution—it is specified in some form in almost all state constitutions—was so closely linked to the freedoms protected by the First Amendment that it, too, was fundamental. An uneducated population cannot truly enjoy any of the "preferred freedoms" of the Bill of Rights. Adding to the expectation that the Court would embrace right to education were state court decisions that had found the use of the property tax for school funding constitutionally defective. The California Supreme Court's decision in *Serrano v. Priest* (1971) was seen by many as a precursor of what the U.S. Supreme Court was likely to do. Adding to the momentum was a series of studies that pointed out the inefficiency and unfairness of the property tax for raising revenue for public schools.

Although those who favored a more self-restraint-oriented or "strict constructionist" judiciary would be frequently disappointed by the Burger Court—the issues of busing and affirmative action, discussed in chapter 2, are only two among many instances that might have justified one of President Nixon's now-famous excursions into profanities—they would not be disappointed with what the Nixon appointees would accomplish in *San Antonio*. The four Nixon justices—Burger, Blackmun, Powell, and Rehnquist—voted with Stewart to turn back what seemed at the time to have become an inevitable march toward finding education a fundamental right and to disallowing the use of property tax for school funding.

The plaintiffs in the *San Antonio* case advanced two equal protection arguments. They claimed not only that education was a fundamental right, but also that the funding of schools primarily at the local level and the use of the property tax to do so resulted in an unconstitutional classification, because it distinguished between the wealthy and the poor. Texas had further exacerbated the differences between wealthy districts and poor districts by putting caps on property tax rates that made it impossible for poor districts, even if they wished to, to raise the same amount of money per student that wealthy districts could raise.

Justice Lewis Powell wrote the opinion for a 5–4 Court. Powell, during much of his fifteen years on the Court, held the crucial vote in such close cases, as we saw in chapter 2 in the case of *Bakke*. Powell painted the Court's task in *San Antonio* as a very clear one:

> [We] must decide, first, whether the Texas system of financing public education operates to the disadvantage of some suspect class or impinges upon a fundamental right explicitly or implicitly protected by the Constitution, thereby requiring strict judicial scrutiny. If so, the judgment of the District Court [which had ruled in favor of Rodriguez's claim on the basis that wealth was a "suspect" category and education, a "fundamental interest"] should be affirmed. If not, the Texas scheme must still be examined to determine whether it rationally furthers some legitimate, articulated state purpose and therefore does not constitute an invidious discrimination in violation of [the Equal Protection Clause].

Powell proceeded to set forth "the traditional indicia of suspectness" as well as what was necessary for a determination of what was a fundamental right or interest. To qualify as a suspect class, similar to race, ethnicity, or alienage, according to Powell, "the class [must be] . . . saddled with such disabilities, or subjected to such a history of purposeful unequal treatment, or relegated to such a position of political powerlessness as to command extraordinary protection from the majoritarian political processes." Concluding that the classification challenged in *San Antonio* was between wealthy school districts and poor school districts, not between poor people and wealthy people, and that there was no absolute deprivation of education, Powell found that this distinction failed to rise to the level of a suspect category.

Powell was equally unmoved by the claim that education was a fundamental right. "[T]he importance of a service performed by a State does not determine whether it must be regarded as fundamental. . . . Rather the answer lies in assessing whether there is a right to education explicitly or implicitly guaranteed by the Constitution." To those who argued that education is "a fundamental personal right because it is essential to the effective exercise of First Amendment freedoms and to intelligent utilization of the right to vote," Powell replied that such an argument proved too much, because the same could be said also of "the significant personal interests in the basics of decent food and shelter" as well as clothing.

Not only did Powell and the *San Antonio School District* majority appear to shut the door on any further expansion of fundamental rights under the Equal Protection Clause, but the Powell opinion seemed finally to bring a modicum of intellectual coherence to what the Warren Court had been doing in the 1960s.

Powell's argument did not convince Thurgood Marshall. Justice Marshall had his own ideas about equal protection and had broached the possibility of a "sliding scale" of scrutiny in *Dandridge*. In *San Antonio School District*, he further expanded the idea. Marshall's dissent in *San Antonio* is arguably the most important opinion of his twenty-four years on the Court. Given later developments, Marshall's analysis of the Equal Protection Clause may more accurately describe what the Court has done than the one advanced by Powell.

In reviewing the relevant precedents, Marshall concluded, "It seems to me inescapably clear that the Court has consistently ad-

justed the care with which it will review state discrimination in
light of the constitutional significance of the interests affected and
the invidiousness of the particular classification."

Marshall termed Powell's and the majority's distinction between classifications that demanded "heightened scrutiny" and
those that required only a showing of "rationality" evidence of a
"rigidified approach." He further charged that Powell's analysis of
the precedents and his fitting them neatly into two categories was
totally unconvincing when one examined the cases.

Eschewing either "strict scrutiny" or rationality in this particular situation, Marshall argued that what was needed in this case
was "careful scrutiny." Under this standard, Marshall found the
funding scheme to fall short of the requirements of equal protection, since "it is apparent that the State's purported concern with
local control is offered primarily as an excuse rather than as a justification for interdistrict inequality. [Districts] cannot [by state
law] choose to have the best education in the State by imposing
the highest tax rate."

That Marshall had the better part of the argument would be
borne out by the Court's revolutionary holdings in cases involving classification based on gender. In fact, two years before *San
Antonio*, the Court in *Reed v. Reed* (1971) had handed down a decision that was at odds with what Powell claimed in his *San Antonio* opinion to be the appropriate standard.

THE BURGER COURT AND
SEX DISCRIMINATION

The adoption of the Fourteenth Amendment ranks as one of the
most important political events in the development of the American nation. Its importance for constitutional law cannot be exaggerated. Even the most cursory examination of what the modern
Court does would reveal that the provisions of the Fourteenth
Amendment are involved in more cases than any other part of the

Constitution. The Fourteenth Amendment is the basis for most of the Court's decisions on civil liberties as well as on civil rights. The Fourteenth Amendment and the two other post–Civil War amendments transformed the nature of federalism, shifting the calculus of power finally and irretrievably away from the states and to the federal or national government.

The Fourteenth Amendment is also notable in that it introduced for the first time gender-specific language into the Constitution (Article II, in referring to the president, does use the pronoun "he," but otherwise avoids distinctions based on sex). The same is not true of the Fifteenth Amendment. Although Section 1 mentions "persons," Section 2, in discussing the matter of the apportionment of representatives, refers to "male inhabitants." This language and the fact that the Radical Republicans, the former abolitionists, proposed to do nothing for the cause of women's rights caused many of the early suffragettes, despite their long record of support for the cause of abolition, to part company with the Radical Republicans and, in many cases, even to join those who opposed the amendment's ratification. As Congress was beginning to draft the language that would eventually become the Fourteenth Amendment, Elizabeth Cady Stanton, Susan B. Anthony, and others urged Congress, while "placing new safeguards round the individual rights of four million emancipated slaves," to "extend the right of suffrage to women, the only remaining class of disenfranchised citizens, and thus fulfill your constitutional obligation 'to guaranty to every State in the Union a republican form of government.'" These women were keeping watch in the congressional galleries (Fairman 1971, 1263).

The amendment's drafters ignored their pleas. Similar to what would happen with the Civil Rights Act of 1964 when the conservative chairman of the House Rules Committee, Representative Howard Smith, inserted sex as one of the categories of prohibited discrimination (Fisher and Devins 2001, 307), opponents of civil rights for blacks appeared to take up the cause of women's rights, claiming that they preferred "the white women of my country to the negro" (Fairman 1971, 1264). In debate, Congressman Thad Stevens, a leader of the Radical Republicans, pointed out that equal protection would not mean that the law could not continue to distinguish between married women, whose rights in law were subordinate to those of their husband, and unmarried women (Fairman 1971, 1278).

Advocates of women's rights would also be ignored when it came time for Congress to draft the Fifteenth Amendment, designed to give protection to black voters. Taney's observation in *Dred Scott* (1857), "Women and minors who form part of the political community cannot vote," was to be left undisturbed.

The nineteenth-century Court was as unsympathetic to the cause of women's rights as it was to the rights of the former slaves. Women, for example, had no right to practice law. Regardless of their education, they could be barred from admission to the profession (*Bradwell v. Illinois*, 1873). The Court also rejected a claim that a woman's right to vote was a "privilege or immunity of citizenship" (*Minor v. Happersett*, 1875). Justice Joseph Bradley's concurrence in *Bradwell* summed up the Court's thinking on the subject pretty well. "Natural and proper timidity and delicacy which belongs to the female sex evidently unfits it for many of the occupations of civil life. . . . The paramount destiny and mission of women are to fulfill the noble and benign offices of wife and mother. This is the law of the Creator."

Unlike the situation involving race, the twentieth century did not witness any quick change in the Court's position vis-à-vis women's rights. Indeed, the old stereotypes were reinforced well into the twentieth century, even after the 1954 *Brown* decision.

The Court that decided the case of *Muller v. Oregon* (1908) was little changed from the one that two years earlier, in *Lochner*, had struck down a New York law aimed at protecting the health of bakers. As noted earlier, Justice Peckham claimed that such a law interfered with the bakers' "liberty of contract." Despite that, the

Court upheld what was in many ways a similar Oregon statute protecting women. Obviously, women were different. "Woman's physical structure and the performance of maternal functions place her at a disadvantage in the struggle for subsistence."

Although the Taft Court (1920–1930) refused in *Adkins v. Children's Hospital* (1923) to sustain a minimum wage law that applied to women, the margin in *Adkins* was closer (5–3, Justice Louis Brandeis did not participate because his daughter and son-in-law had helped draft the challenged law) than for similar legislation that applied to men. Among the three dissenters was Chief Justice William Howard Taft, despite his well-known distaste for judicial dissents.

Even the post-switch-in-time Modern Court regularly upheld legislation that treated women differently than men. In *Goesaert v. Cleary* (1948), the Court upheld a law that limited women working behind the bar in taprooms to the wives and daughters of bar owners and, in *Hoyt v. Florida* (1961), the Warren Court unanimously upheld a law that routinely resulted in all-male juries. Women served only if they requested to serve.

The Burger Court's unanimous decision in *Reed v. Reed* (1971) thus represented a major shift by the Court. Judges who supposedly were strict constructionists would, while claiming to adhere to the dichotomy posited by Justice Powell in *San Antonio School District,* achieve by judicial means what advocates of women's rights had been seeking through political means, and largely without success, for almost a century and a half.

Reed was the product of a seven-member Court. The seats that would subsequently be filled by Justices Powell and Rehnquist were vacant. At issue was an Idaho law providing that when a person died intestate—that is, without a will—and where the two closest relatives were a male and a female, the male was to be chosen automatically as executor of the estate. Under rationality analysis, an argument could be made that this process, designed to speed up the settlement of estates, was rational. At the time, men could generally

be expected to have considerably more experience in handling
money and paying taxes than women. Despite this, the Court,
speaking through Chief Justice Warren Burger, found the statute
not to be rational, although Burger did allow that it was "not without some legitimacy." Two years later, with Powell and Rehnquist
on the bench, the Court handed down a ruling that attracted much
greater public attention than *Reed*, which had caused hardly any
stir. This was the case of *Frontiero v. Richardson* (1973).

The U.S. Air Force provided that a married male officer who
claimed a dependent spouse would automatically receive an increase in his living quarters allowance and medical and dental benefits for his spouse. A married female officer, by contrast, had first
to prove that her spouse was in fact dependent on her for more
than half of his support before she could receive these benefits.
The Air Force was able, far more than the state government had
been in *Reed*, to make a case that the regulation was rational.
Overwhelmingly, female officers who were married were married
to other Air Force personnel, which was not the case for male officers. Moreover, married women were much less likely to work
outside the house in the 1970s, and the remote location of many
Air Force bases made it very difficult for those who wished to
find work to do so. Thus most wives of male Air Force officers
could be assumed to be dependent on their husbands.

The Court that heard argument in *Frontiero* not only included
two new judges who had not been on the bench for *Reed*, but also
took place in a social and political environment that was significantly different from that of two years earlier. In the interim,
Congress had overwhelmingly and with little debate passed an
Equal Rights Amendment (ERA) after having pried the proposed
amendment from a reluctant House Judiciary Committee. With
this and the Nineteenth Amendment (1920) guaranteeing the right
to vote to women, the program of women's rights that Stanton
and Anthony had sought unsuccessfully from the Reconstruction-era Congress would be achieved.

Proposed Equal Rights Amendment (1972)

Section 1. Equality of rights under law shall not be denied or abridged by the United States or by any State on account of sex.

Section 2. The Congress shall have the power to enforce, by appropriate legislation, the provisions of this article.

Section 3. This amendment shall take effect two years after the date of ratification.

Once the hurdle of Congress had been jumped, ratification by the states seemed a foregone conclusion. Within three months after its submission, almost half the number of states necessary for ratification had approved the amendment. As the Court heard argument in *Frontiero* and as the justices went about their business of writing opinions in the case, the Court's members probably shared the sense that ratification was inevitable. Little did anyone realize how effective the ERA's opponents would prove to be. Congress was forced to extend the time of ratification beyond the original seven years. When the second deadline expired in 1982, ratification by three more states was still needed in order to make the ERA part of the U.S. Constitution. By then, however, ratification would only have been symbolic. The Court, by its interpretation of the Equal Protection Clause, had accomplished much, if not all, that would have resulted from the adoption of the ERA. The Rehnquist Court would go even further in this regard.

In the landmark *Frontiero* case, only Justice William Rehnquist, the "Lone Ranger" of the Burger Court, voted to uphold the Air Force regulation. The eight-justice majority, however, broke into two camps as to the basis for overturning the regulation. The judgment of the Court was authored by Justice Brennan and joined by Justices Douglas, Marshall, and White.

By the 1970s, Brennan was emerging from the shadows of Warren and Black, with whom he had served for much of the time since his appointment in 1956. Increasingly, commentators were noting the breadth and importance of Brennan's contributions to the Court. By the time he retired in 1990, Brennan was frequently identified as the most influential twentieth-century jurist.

His *Frontiero* opinion certainly evidences the boldness with which he wielded the Court's power of judicial review. The fact that the Air Force regulation was designed for "administrative convenience," he wrote, was not sufficient. A higher level of scrutiny was necessary, since Brennan and his three colleagues found "that classifications based on sex, like classifications based upon race, alienage, and national origin, are inherently suspect and must therefore be subjected to close judicial scrutiny." Brennan claimed that his conclusion that sex was a suspect category was but an inevitable outgrowth of the Court's previous ruling in *Reed.* In addition, sex shared many characteristics with the commonly accepted suspect categories, which included a history of discrimination. Brennan quoted Bradley's concurring opinion from *Bradwell* as partial evidence for this conclusion. In addition, he wrote, sex "is an immutable characteristic determined solely by the accident of birth"; it "invidiously [relegates] the entire class of females to inferior legal status without regard to the actual capabilities of its individual members." To buttress further his conclusion that a higher level of scrutiny was needed, Brennan cited a series of federal statutes, beginning with the Civil Rights Act of 1964, that demonstrated a congressional intent to undo past discrimination against women.

Justice Powell, having just written his *San Antonio School District* opinion, rejected Brennan's efforts to elevate sex to suspect category status. Powell saw no reason to do so; the rationality test as employed in *Reed* was sufficient to allow Powell to vote to strike down the regulation. Powell then proceeded to feign deference to Congress and the political processes. The Brennan stance, argued Powell (with whom Chief Justice Burger and Associate Justice Blackmun concurred), was an example of "reaching out to preempt by judicial action a major political decision which is currently in process of resolution [and] does not reflect appropriate respect for duly prescribed legislative processes." Whether in using the word "resolution" Powell was suggesting that he, like most other Americans at the time, assumed that the adoption of the ERA was inevitable is an interesting question.

For Justice Stewart, it was enough to classify the regulation as an example of "invidious discrimination." Justice Rehnquist, the lone dissenter, was even more succinct than Stewart, simply stating that he "dissents for the reasons stated by Judge Rives in his opinion for the District Court" (deference to the needs of the military).

By 1976, with ratification of the ERA apparently stalled, the Court again addressed the issue of sex discrimination. This time, however, most of the fractious majority from *Frontiero* had found a basis on which at least five of them could agree (Justice Blackmun had crossed over to join the four justices who had voted in *Frontiero* to make sex a suspect category).

Craig v. Boren (1976) arose from an Oklahoma statute that allowed females to consume beer with an alcohol content of 3.2 percent (widely referred to as near-beer) at age eighteen while restricting its consumption by males until their twenty-first birthday. Among the reasons the state advanced for the distinction was the statistically significant difference between men and women in arrest rates for drunken driving.

Brennan did not have five votes to use *Craig* as a vehicle to elevate gender to suspect category status. He did, however, have the votes to move sex to an intermediate status, somewhere between suspect categories, such as race, and nonsuspect categories, such as general economic regulations. From the previous cases of *Reed* and *Frontiero*, Brennan claimed to be able to tease out a test for what would later be called semisuspect categories. These "previous cases establish that classifications by gender must serve important governmental objectives and must be substantially related to achievement of these objectives."

Stewart again concurred, finding that the distinction "amounts to total irrationality" and "invidious discrimination." Powell, for his part, continued to try to keep alive the two-tiered approach he had championed in *San Antonio School District.* In a footnote, Powell allowed that although he "would not welcome a further subdividing of equal protection analysis, candor compels the recognition that the relatively deferential 'rational basis' standard of review normally applied takes on a sharper focus when we address a gender-based [classification]." Justice John Paul Stevens, who had succeeded Justice Douglas, and would soon earn the reputation, like his predecessor, of staking out positions that left him isolated, confessed his dissatisfaction with the two-tiered approach. However, rather than create a third or an intermediate standard as Brennan had done or adopt Marshall's sliding-scale approach, Stevens concluded that since "there is only one Equal Protection Clause," the Court should accept the need to decide cases on an individual basis and not seek to establish prematurely a general standard.

Rehnquist dissented, observing that Brennan's new test came "out of thin air." Chief Justice Burger recorded himself as being "in general agreement" with the Rehnquist opinion.

Whether the test came "out of thin air" or was a logical development of the Court's precedents, the Burger Court's decisions on gender discrimination provoked nothing like the opposition triggered by the Warren Court's decisions on segregation and legislative apportionment. *Reed, Frontiero,* and *Craig* also generated little of the protest that greeted the Burger Court's busing and affirmative action rulings. They did, however, put the final nail in the coffin of the Equal Rights Amendment. Why should anyone push for renewal of an amendment that had failed, despite Congress's extension of the time for ratification, and that now would largely have only symbolic value?

THE REHNQUIST COURT AND THE NEW EQUAL PROTECTION

Few if any of the critics of the Warren Court found the Burger Court much of an improvement. In fact, many concluded that the

Burger Court had been more freewheeling in its exercise of "raw judicial power" than its predecessor. Students of the Court and its opinions now more often than not spoke of interpretist as opposed to noninterpretist approaches to constitutional decision making. The terms self-restraint and activism no longer seem apt descriptions of the process.

Interpretism calls for justices in making their decisions to stay within the "four corners of the Constitution." Justice Black's literalism (for example, the First Amendment's command of "no law" means just that, no law), which had led his 1950s critics to charge that he would transform the Constitution into a "suicide pact," now was embraced by those who sought to restrain the Court. Advocates of noninterpretism, in contrast, argue that judges could, and indeed should, in making their decisions take into consideration contemporary community values.

If there actually was a litmus test for judicial nominees during the presidencies of Ronald Reagan and George H. W. Bush, as liberal commentators repeatedly charged, part of this test would have consisted on where a potential nominee came down on the distinction between interpretism and noninterpretism.

Although by no means totally successful, these two Republican administrations seem to have had more luck in picking individuals, both for the Supreme Court and for the lower federal courts, who have lived up to their expectations than their two Republican predecessors, Richard Nixon and Gerald Ford. Reagan, early on in his presidency, was able to make good on a campaign promise to appoint a woman to the Court by nominating Sandra Day O'Connor in 1981 to fill the vacancy created by the retirement of Potter Stewart (1958–1981). The subsequent retirements of Chief Justice Burger (1969–1986) and Associate Justice Powell (1972–1987) resulted in Rehnquist's elevation to the chief's chair and the addition of Justices Antonin Scalia (1986) and Anthony Kennedy (1988) to the bench. President Bush was able to replace the two remaining Warren Court stalwarts, William Brennan (1956–1990) and Thurgood Marshall (1967–1991), with David Souter (1990) and Clarence Thomas (1991). Although these appointees did not make good on the entire judicial agenda of the appointing presidents—the right to an abortion, for instance, although cut back a bit in *Planned Parenthood v. Casey* (1992), has survived—in the main, they have provided fewer surprises than the Nixon appointees.

This is certainly true in the realm of equal protection. The Reagan-Bush appointees have not "discovered" any further fundamental rights, and, as we saw in chapter 2, they have called into question what the limits are for affirmative action programs and have sanctioned the end of court supervision of school districts that had been found to have engaged in the past in de jure segregation. At the same time, they have not cut back on fundamental rights and have left in place the sometimes less-than-clear distinctions between strict scrutiny, intermediate scrutiny, and rationality. As seen in Chapter 2, they also stopped short of proclaiming a "color-blind" Constitution and reaffirmed *Bakke.*

Whether this summary would have held true had the elder President Bush been reelected in 1992 is an interesting question. The string of appointees to the Supreme Court by Republican presidents was broken with the election of Bill Clinton. President Clinton's nomination of Ruth Bader Ginsburg in 1993 to succeed Byron White (1962–1993) represented for the Democrats the end of a thirty-six-year drought in making appointments to the nation's high court. A year later, Clinton named Stephen Breyer to succeed Harry Blackmun (1970–1994). Since then, there have been no further vacancies on the Supreme Court. The Republicans' recapturing the Senate in 2002 increased speculation that one or more of the justices might retire at the end of the 2002–2003 term in order to allow Republican President George W. Bush to fill the resulting vacancies. The reason for this is that with the two branches under control of the same party, the confirmation process might be easier. In addition, the general feeling is that the nomination process, which became increasingly politicized in the 1980s, might be a little calmer in a nonelection year than in 2004, when the presidency, a third of the Senate, and all of the House is up for election. Despite this, there were no retirements after the end of the 2002–2003 term.

The two most significant changes not involving race made by the Rehnquist Court in the area of equal protection are the Court's announcement of a new test for classifications involving gender and its rulings involving homosexuality.

After much backing and filling, the Burger Court acknowledged in *Craig* that legislation that categorizes individuals by gender was to be scrutinized by a standard more demanding than rationality. The so-called "intermediate scrutiny" test was born in *Craig,* and gender and illegitimacy were established as "semisuspect" categories. The Rehnquist Court left this legacy undisturbed. Indeed, in the area of gender discrimination, the Court went further by refining the intermediate scrutiny test to move it much closer to the "compelling state interest" test used in cases of suspect categories such as race.

The case that provided the Court with the opportunity to do this was *United States v. Virginia* (1996). The Clinton administration had concluded that the state of Virginia, by excluding women from the state-supported Virginia Military Institute (VMI) while providing a similar program at Mary Baldwin College, a private women's college, violated the Equal Protection Clause. With only Justice Scalia dissenting (Justice Thomas, who regularly votes in tandem with Scalia, recused himself because of his son's attendance at VMI), the Court agreed with the government. Clinton appointee Justice Ruth Bader Ginsburg, who had argued many of the landmark women's rights cases before the Court, including *Frontiero,* before her appointment to the U.S. Court of Appeals by President Jimmy Carter, was assigned the task of writing the opinion of the Court:

> Parties who seek to defend gender-based government action must demonstrate an "exceedingly persuasive justification" for that action.

Today's *skeptical scrutiny* [emphasis added] of official action denying rights or opportunities based on sex responds to volumes of history. . . . Without equating gender classifications . . . to classifications based on race or national origin, the Court, in post-*Reed* decisions, has carefully inspected official action that closes a door or denies opportunity to women (or to men).

According to "the Court's current directions for cases of official classification based on gender," she wrote, "the proffered justification [must be] 'exceedingly persuasive.'" Ginsburg stressed in her opinion that this new standard did not mean that gender was to be considered a suspect category.

Chief Justice Rehnquist concurred, arguing that there was no need to alter the *Craig* test. Some commentators, however, argue that the diversity argument raised by Virginia (the value of single-sex schools), reminiscent of a similar argument made by Justice Powell in *Bakke*, required Ginsburg to raise the hurdle presented to state action. The solitary dissenter, Justice Scalia, certainly saw the diversity argument advanced by Virginia as meeting the *Craig* requirement of being "substantially related to an important governmental objective."

Although the Court did uphold the exclusion of women from the requirement that males between the ages of eighteen and twenty-six must register for the draft (*Rostker v. Goldberg* [1981], by a 6–3 vote), the Court very likely would have reached the same result, given its traditional deference to the government in matters related to the military and to national security, even if the ERA had been adopted. With the Court's decision in the VMI case, the Court has erected a standard that seems to be as demanding as would have been the case had the ERA been ratified.

In contrast to the widespread acceptance of its decisions involving sex discrimination, it is obvious that the issue of homosexuality might prove to be highly explosive for the Court. Clearly, public opinion has changed dramatically and swiftly with regard to homosexuals. American attitudes are clearly more liberal today than they were only a decade earlier. Somewhat the same comment, however, could have been made prior to the Court's decisions in the 1973 cases involving abortion rights, *Roe v. Wade* and *Doe v. Bolton*. Prior to the Court's ruling, changed attitudes resulted in state after state liberalizing previously existing restrictions on access to abortion.

In *Bowers v. Hardwick* (1986), the Court upheld, by the narrowest of margins, a Georgia statute that criminalized consensual sodomy. The right of privacy discovered in *Griswold* (1965) and applied in *Roe* (1973) to strike down state antiabortion statutes did not provide a basis for overturning Hardwick's conviction. Chief Justice Burger and Justice Powell joined *Roe* dissenters Justices White and Rehnquist and newly appointed Justice O'Connor to uphold the law. The dissenting opinion, written by Justice Blackmun, emphasized the importance of the right of privacy, the right to be left alone, and the majority's failure to confront issues the minority saw as required by the Ninth Amendment. That amendment has been viewed by noninterpretists as inviting justices to find additional, nonenumerated rights. Neither opinion looked at the Equal Protection Clause as possibly offering a better lens for judicial analysis.

Equal protection did play a role in the Court's second case involving homosexuals, *Romer v. Evans* (1996). A referendum in Colorado had resulted in the amendment of the state's constitution so as to deprive government of any power to protect homosexuals from discrimination. The amendment read as follows:

No Protected Status Based on Homosexual, Lesbian, or Bisexual Orientation. Neither the State of Colorado, through any of its branches or departments, nor any of its agencies, political subdivisions, municipalities or school districts, shall enact, adopt or enforce any statute, regulation, ordinance, or policy whereby homosexual, lesbian or bisexual orientation, conduct, practices or relationships shall constitute or otherwise be the basis of or entitle any person or class of persons to have or claim any minority status, quota, preferences, protected status or claim of discrimination. This Section of the Constitution shall be in all respects self-executing.

The amendment was challenged by the governor of Colorado and struck down by the Colorado Supreme Court on the grounds that it failed to meet the test of "strict scrutiny" required of laws that violate fundamental rights. In this case, the fundamental right was that of homosexuals to participate in the political process.

The U.S. Supreme Court upheld the Colorado Supreme Court's decision but rejected the court's use of the "strict scrutiny" test. Justice Kennedy wrote the opinion for the majority (the same majority that would decide *Lawrence v. Texas* in 2003) in a 6–3 decision that infuriated social conservatives who had hoped that the recent appointments would ensure not only that *Roe* would be reversed but also that the federal courts would never again intervene so as to overturn laws that protected what they saw as the basic moral fabric of American society. Kennedy argued that the amendment must be struck down because of the "animus" it demonstrated to a particular class of citizens and because "it lacks a rational relationship to legitimate state interests." Disadvantaging persons on the basis of their sexual orientation was not a legitimate state interest.

Kennedy's opinion drew a scathing dissent from Justice Scalia, who characterized it as having

no foundation in American constitutional law. . . . The people of Colorado have adopted an entirely reasonable provision which does not even disfavor homosexuals in any substantive sense, but merely denies them preferential treatment. Amendment 2 is designed to prevent piecemeal deterioration of the sexual morality favored by a majority of Coloradans, and is not only an appropriate means to that legitimate end, but a means Americans have employed before. Striking it down is an act, not of judicial judgment, but of political will.

Despite the scorn Justice Scalia's dissent heaped on the Kennedy opinion, the result of *Romer* was to maintain the status quo ante of Colorado state and local regulations dealing with homosexuals. There was no stability, however, with respect to the types of laws that had been challenged unsuccessfully in *Bowers*. At the time the *Bowers* decision was handed down, twenty-five states had criminal statutes prohibiting sodomy. By 2003, that number had fallen to thirteen states (in 1961, every state had such a law), and four, including Texas, limited the proscription to same-sex couples.

At the same time, the issue of same-sex marriage was more and more openly discussed. Although some states have toyed with the idea, no state has adopted laws permitting homosexuals to marry. Given changing attitudes, however, it would seem only a matter of time when one state does adopt such a law. Vermont has gone the furthest in this direction by allowing civil unions between homosexuals. The Vermont legislature's adoption of this measure was in part prompted by a decision by that state's supreme court (*Baker v. Vermont* [1999]). Not surprisingly, the legislature's action fueled a predictable backlash by social conservatives in the next election, who rallied behind the slogan of "taking back Vermont."

The possibility that some state will go further and legalize marriage of same-sex couples, or that someone might ask a court to require other states to recognize Vermont's civil unions, has prompted opponents of same-sex unions to take action on a couple of fronts. For example, Congress quickly and with little debate or opposition adopted the Defense of Marriage Act (DOMA). This law seeks to insure that if any one state legalized same-sex marriage, other states would not, under Article IV's Full Faith and Credit Clause, be required to accept such unions as the equivalent of heterosexual marriage. Some members of Congress, such as Colorado's Representative Marilyn Musgrave, fearing that the act alone will not suffice, have even suggested that a constitutional amendment defining marriage as limited to persons of the opposite sex is necessary to ward off homosexual marriage. Even before the Court's recent decision in *Lawrence v. Texas* (2003), several Canadian courts had found that country's Charter of Rights guaranteed homosexuals the right to marry. Combined with the *Lawrence* decision, these actions are likely to stir a reaction among social conservatives. What they will do, particularly after *Lawrence*, will be interesting to those who enjoy political theater, American style.

Lawrence v. Texas involved facts identical to *Bowers*. Unlike the Georgia statute examined in the former case, the Texas statute only criminalized sodomy involving persons of the same sex. This difference prompted attorneys for Lawrence and his codefendant, Garner, to raise an equal protection claim. This ploy failed to secure victory in the Texas courts. Other than Justice O'Connor, it also failed to make an impression on the Supreme Court justices who voted to strike down the Texas law.

Justice Anthony Kennedy wrote the opinion of the Court. Had he followed the equal protection tack, he and the Court could have avoided answering the question as to whether or not *Bowers* should be maintained. That clearly was of little interest to Justice Kennedy and the four justices who fully subscribed to his opinion: Justices Stevens, Souter, Ginsburg, and Breyer.

Kennedy presented the issue as one involving the Fourteenth Amendment's Due Process Clause, but unlike the *Bowers* Court, Kennedy did not see the case as turning on the question of whether or not there was a fundamental right to engage in homosexual sex. Instead, it was "whether the petitioners were free as adults to engage in the private [sexual] conduct in the exercise of their liberty." Examining the history of legislation, Kennedy found that, contrary to the *Bowers* majority, there was no clear historical record that supported the idea that the framers of the Constitution or the Fourteenth Amendment believed that government had the power to interfere with private, consensual sexual acts of adults. As a result, Kennedy concluded:

Bowers was not correct when it was decided, and it is not correct today. It ought not to remain binding precedent. *Bowers v. Hardwick* should be and is now overruled.

The present case does not involve minors. It does not involve persons who might be injured or coerced or who are situated in relationships where consent might not easily be refused. It does not involve public conduct or prostitution. It does not involve whether the government must give formal recognition to any relationship that homosexual persons seek to enter. The case does involve two adults who, with full and mutual consent from each other, engaged in sexual practices common to a homosexual lifestyle. The petitioners are entitled to respect for their private lives. The State cannot demean their existence or control their destiny by making their private sexual conduct a crime. . . . The Texas statute furthers no legitimate state interest which can justify its intrusion into the personal and private life of the individual.

Although it is unlikely that the U.S. Supreme Court as presently constituted would find a state's restriction of marriage to persons of the opposite sex unconstitutional, and Justice Kennedy certainly seeks to allay any such fears in the quotation above, still it is likely that in the not-too-distant future, federal courts will be presented with this issue. With *Bowers* gone, can advocates of same-sex marriage use *Lawrence* along with the *Loving* decision (finding a fundamental right to marry) as a basis to argue that denying marriage to same-sex partners was a denial of equal protection? Certainly, Justice Antonin Scalia feels that such a result is inevitable after *Lawrence.*

Today's opinion is the product of a Court, which is the product of a law-profession culture, that has largely signed on to the so-called homosexual agenda. . . . The Court today pretends that . . . we need not fear judicial imposition of homosexual marriage. . . . More illuminating than . . . [Kennedy's] disclaimer [of the possibility of homosexual

marriage] is the progression of thought . . . which notes the constitutional protections afforded to "personal decisions relating to *marriage,
procreation, contraception, family relationships, child rearing, and education,*" and then declares that "[p]ersons in a homosexual relationship may seek autonomy for these purposes, just as heterosexual persons do"(emphasis added). Today's opinion dismantles the structure
of constitutional law that has permitted a distinction to be made between heterosexual unions and homosexual unions, insofar as formal
recognition in marriage is concerned. If moral disapprobation of homosexual conduct is "no legitimate state interest," what justification
could there possibly be for denying the benefits of marriage to homosexual couples exercising "[t]he liberty protected by the Constitution"?

Certain members of Congress appear to agree with Scalia's
analysis, and talk about the need for a constitutional amendment
defining marriage as between a man and a woman was again heard
on Capitol Hill. Senate Republican leader Bill Frist of Tennessee
spoke in favor of such a measure only a few days after the Court's
decision.

CONCLUSION

Fans of the interpretist philosophy and of judicial self-restraint
obviously see any further expansion of rights under the Equal
Protection Clause as posing a danger both for the Court and the
future of democracy in the United States. They repeatedly point
out that the current politicization of the Court—exemplified both
by its being an issue in presidential and congressional campaigns
and in the now highly partisan tone that surrounds the process of
judicial selection at the federal level—is largely the result of the
Court's "invention" of a right of privacy and its action in *Roe* to
overturn state restrictions on abortions. Some on this side also
point out that had the Court exercised "self-restraint" in *Roe* and

deferred to legislatures on this issue, many of the same changes that came as a result of the *Roe* decision would likely have been adopted through the normal democratic processes with the judiciary being spared much of the criticism it has endured since 1973. In this vein, they argue that the Court by refusing in *Bowers* to invalidate the Georgia antisodomy statute was more prudent than the *Roe* Court. Far from solidifying antisodomy laws, the *Bowers* decision led in part to many states rethinking similar statutes and repealing them (since *Bowers,* thirteen states either repealed their antisodomy statutes or had them struck down by their state courts). By overturning *Bowers* in its *Lawrence v. Texas* (2003) decision, the Court will put to the test the claims of those who argue for judicial prudence. Already in response to *Lawrence,* Republican Senate Majority Leader Bill Frist has taken up the cudgels of those who want to amend the Constitution by defining marriage as a union only of a male and a female in a proposed Twenty-Eighth Amendment.

Those who champion judicial activism and noninterpretism would respond by noting that the decisions their opponents decry are decisions that have made both the judiciary and U.S. democracy stronger. The Court's finding that there was a fundamental right to vote in the reapportionment cases and its use of the same Equal Protection Clause to strike down legislation that treated women differently from men are shining examples to them of how a Court that is willing to challenge the political branches of government is able to move the nation closer to its democratic ideals. The fact that there is no historical basis for either of these actions is unimportant. The Court, according to advocates of an activist Court, should not hesitate to challenge legislation nor should it be limited to thinking within the "four corners" of the Constitution.

Like the right of privacy, the appeal to equality is a strong one, rooted in the very foundations of the American republic. This "First New Nation" was founded on the principle that "all men are created equal," a view to which President Abraham Lincoln in his brief remarks at the battlefield of Gettysburg called his fellow citizens to rededicate themselves. The opinions of Justices Brennan, Douglas, and Warren in the reapportionment cases clearly connect to these bedrock values. They served to persuade all but the most hard of heart. "One person, one vote" was a slogan that no appeal to the "intent of the framers" could stop. Would Thurgood Marshall's language in *San Antonio* been as effective in dealing with what seems to be the intractable problem of race in America? The fact that most state courts of last resort have reached results similar to what Marshall proposed in his *San Antonio* dissent may certainly be used to argue that the Court could have been more aggressive in that case. Marshall's language in the Court's affirmative action cases arguing that the legacy of slavery imposes a responsibility on white Americans to remedy the ills of that legacy may have been more persuasive than Powell's more cautious language in *Bakke.*

Abortion and homosexuality may, however, be different. They may call for more caution, more restraint on the part of the Court. Just as the Court probably was wise to take a more cautious route on issues involving welfare—polls show that no one likes welfare, even those who receive it—and laws affecting illegal aliens. Had the Court based its *Roe* opinion on the Equal Protection Clause rather than on a right of privacy derived from the Due Process Clause of the same amendment, such a decision might have received less criticism from scholars than the Blackmun opinion, but would it have triggered any less political opposition? The *Romer* decision did not trigger any long-lived debate, but that would not be the case for a decision that resulted in striking down sodomy statutes or allowing homosexuals to marry. The Court's *Lawrence* decisions will allow us to discover the answer to the former question.

The doctrine of "political questions," examined and limited by Justice Brennan in his *Baker* opinion, has continued to decline in significance in the succeeding years. As it had declined, more and more scholars have acknowledged that the differences between what were once referred to as the political branches, Congress and the president, and the nonpolitical judiciary, are more of degree and not of kind. The observation made long ago by the late Max Lerner that "constitutional decisions are not brought by constitutional storks," seems finally to have fully registered at least among students of the Court ranging from the once avant-garde critical legal studies types ("Crits") to more mainstream scholars (Fisher and Devins 2001; Peretti 1999).

Success in this political venture accordingly should be judged in terms of how the Court's decisions both strengthen U.S. democracy and the Court. Decisions that do neither or accomplish only one may prove to be additional examples of what Chief Justice Charles Evan Hughes labeled the Court's "self-inflicted wounds."

REFERENCES AND FURTHER READING

Brest, Paul. 1981. "The Fundamental Rights Controversy." *Yale Law Journal* 90: 1063–1105.

Ely, John Hart. 1980. *Democracy and Distrust: A Theory of Judicial Review.* Cambridge, MA: Harvard University Press.

Fairman, Charles. 1971. *Reconstruction and Reunion: History of the Supreme Court of the United States.* New York: MacMillan.

Fisher, Louis. 2002. *Religious Liberty in America: Political Safeguards.* Lawrence: University Press of Kansas.

Fisher, Louis, and Neal Devins. 2001. *Political Dynamics of Constitutional Law.* St. Paul, MN: West.

Greenhouse, Linda. 2003. "Supreme Court Takes Case on Black Voting Districts." *New York Times,* January 18, A12.

Gunther, Gerald. 1972. "The Supreme Court 1971 Term: Forward: In Search of Evolving Doctrine on a Changing Court: A Model for a Newer Equal Protection." *Harvard Law Review* 86: 1–48.

Gunther, Gerald, and Kathleen M. Sullivan. 1997. *Constitutional Law,* 13th ed. Westbury, NY: Foundation Press.

Hamilton, Charles V. 1973. *The Bench and the Ballot: Southern Federal Judges and Black Voters.* New York: Oxford University Press.

Jeffries, John C., Jr. 1994. *Justice Lewis F. Powell, Jr.: A Biography.* New York: Charles Scribner's Sons.

Lewis, Anthony. 1968. "Earl Warren." In Richard H. Sayler, Barry B. Boyer, and Robert E. Gooding Jr., eds., *The Warren Court: A Critical Analysis.* New York: Chelsea House.

McKay, Robert B. 1968. "Reapportionment: Success Story of the Warren Court." In Richard H. Sayler, Barry B. Boyer, and Robert E. Gooding Jr., eds., *The Warren Court: A Critical Analysis.* New York: Chelsea House.

Peretti, Terri Jennings. 1999. *In Defense of a Political Court.* Princeton, NJ: Princeton University Press.

Silverstein, Mark. 1994. *Judicious Choices: The New Politics of Supreme Court Confirmations.* New York: W. W. Norton.

Simon, James F. 1973. *In His Own Image: The Supreme Court in Richard Nixon's America.* New York: David McKay.

Vieira, Norman. 1998. *Constitutional Civil Rights in a Nutshell.* St. Paul, MN: West.

White, G. Edward. 1982. *Earl Warren: A Public Life.* New York: Oxford University Press.

Winter, Greg. 2003. "Schools Resegregate, Study Finds." *New York Times,* January 21, A14.

Yarbrough, Tinsley E. 2000. *The Rehnquist Court and the Constitution.* New York: Oxford University Press.

4

TWENTY-FIRST
CENTURY ISSUES

From the 1930s to the early 1990s, political scientist Max Lerner commented on the workings of the Supreme Court, both in the popular press and in academic journals. Few observers of the Court have equaled his acuity of vision of the workings of this branch of government. Shortly before his death, in an introduction to a collection of his articles, Lerner noted that "to a considerable extent the American people have turned the Constitution as covenant (with the justices as its keepers) into the stuff of myth." Lerner warned of the danger inherent in this transformation. "A crisis arises when this myth, which holds not only that America is the unique guarantor of equal justice under the text of the law, but that it can resolve its grand social conflicts by offering new perspectives on an old covenant, is put into question" (Lerner 1994, xii).

As the Supreme Court enters the twenty-first century, the Court seems to be entering a period that may be just as perilous for the Court as the situation an earlier Court faced in the mid-1930s, the era that spawned the court-packing crisis. Admittedly, such Cassandra-like predictions have been made many times since the 1930s, whether in the wake of the Court's *Brown* decision, after the Warren Court's decisions broadening First Amendment protections for members of the American Communist Party, in its rewriting the rules of criminal procedure such as in *Miranda v. Arizona* (1966), or after the Burger Court's decision on abortion in *Roe*. What seems to differentiate times such as those is the growing demystification of the Court. Although constitutional law scholars have long been disabused of the belief that it is "the Constitution that speaks and not the justices," the general public seems only recently to have realized, to use Justice James McReynolds's typically blunt characterization, that a judge was not "an amorphous dummy, unspotted by human emotions" (Abraham 1998, 352).

This demystification has been abetted by the growing politicization of the nomination and confirmation processes for federal judges. The aborted effort in 1968 of President Lyndon Johnson to promote his friend, close adviser, and former lawyer, Associate Justice Abe Fortas, to the Court's center chair as chief justice seems to have opened the current era of frequently bitter judicial confirmation battles. Although the degree of controversy has waxed and waned in the intervening years, the bottom line has been that the nomination of even federal district judges is no longer a matter of senatorial patronage. The shaping of the judicial branch of government has become one of the key battlegrounds in Washington politics, and one of the more important canvases on which a president can leave his image.

President Bill Clinton's two appointments, Ruth Bader Ginsburg (1993) and Stephen Breyer (1994), admittedly seem to have been exceptions to the rule that judicial nominations seem to produce high political theater. Yet they may be the veritable "exceptions that prove the rule." To what extent was the highly charged political climate a reason for an obvious judicial candidate such as New York Governor Mario Cuomo to take himself out of consideration or for Interior Secretary Bruce Babbitt, once considered another likely Clinton choice, never to have been nominated? The grilling that either would likely have been subjected to by the Republican minority on the Senate Judiciary Committee may have convinced the very political Clinton to decide not to use his political capital on their behalf.

Neither of Clinton's appointees was cut from the judicial cloth that most hard-core Democratic supporters would have desired in a nominee. "Thirteen years of judicial service . . . transformed the advocate of judicial activism [Ginsburg] into a proponent of judicial modesty" (Silverstein 1994, 168). Nor was either Ginsburg or Breyer the "homerun candidate" that Clinton had once promised for the high Court (Silverstein 1994, 175). Breyer, the eventual nominee to replace Harry Blackmun, seems to have been cut from the same modest judicial cloth as Ginsburg. His nomination also won plaudits from Senate Republican leader Bob Dole and the ranking Republican on the Judiciary Committee, Orrin Hatch, of Utah. Both of these highly talented jurists were confirmed with little fuss. The confirmation travails of Clinton's nominees for the lower federal courts, the courts of appeal and the federal district courts, was quite different. His nominees for the appeals courts and the federal district courts prompted a form of political trench warfare by Republicans that possibly exceeded in intensity the opposition Democrats had mounted to judicial nominees during the Reagan and Bush presidencies.

Despite the recapture of the Senate by Republicans in 2002, the judicial nomination process continues to be a prime political flash point. Democrats opposing the nominees of George W. Bush have vowed to expand their scrutiny of his nominees beyond issues of competence and proper judicial demeanor to questions about the nominees' ideology. They have also chosen to continue the battle on the floor of the Senate, using the filibuster to prevent the Senate from coming to a vote on confirmation.

Adding to the already high combustibility of the contemporary confirmation process are two other factors. The first arises from the role the Supreme Court played in deciding the presidential election of 2000. Bush lost the popular vote for president to Democratic candidate Vice President Al Gore. His victory in the electoral college was a result of the Supreme Court's decision in the case of *Bush v. Gore* (2000) that resulted in Bush's winning the key Florida electoral votes. The fact that the Court's decision was by what is now seen as a predictable 5–4 lineup—Rehnquist, O'Connor, Scalia, Kennedy, and Thomas for the majority and Stevens, Souter, Ginsburg, and Breyer in the minority—was probably not lost on an increasingly more sophisticated public. Many headline and editorial writers presented very much the same message: Bush was elected by the Supreme Court.

The second factor is the growing attention given to the next vacancy on the Supreme Court. On average, an opening occurs on the Court every twenty-two months (O'Brien 2003, 368). Not since the Marshall Court has there been as long a hiatus between vacancies on the Court as exists today. Stephen Breyer joined the Court on August 3, 1994. Clinton had no opportunity during his second term to make another appointment to the Court. Bush, now into his third year as president, has had no chance yet to affect the Court's composition. The longer the wait, the more attention will likely be focused on whoever is tapped to fill the next vacancy.

New York Democratic Senator Charles Schumer has made it clear that whoever is nominated will be grilled to determine what the nominee's judicial ideology actually is. No longer will senators who oppose a nominee be content to probe simply for flaws of judicial character or "smoking guns." A history of smoking marijuana, of inappropriate sexual advances, and the like will not be the only basis on which a senator will refuse to confirm a judicial nominee.

These factors have probably not been lost entirely on many average citizens, but what does this politicization mean for the Court? Can a Court that is more widely viewed as political be as effective in protecting rights, let alone as effective in expanding the scope of those rights? This may be the greatest challenge for the Court in the twenty-first century.

On the face of it, a Court that is seen as political would seem to lose the value of the so-called "cult of the robe." On the other hand, a "political court" that correctly adjusts its decisions to the aspirations of the American people, what one student of the Court has dubbed "value voting" (Peretti 1999, 102), might find that it can compete successfully in the political arena against the other two branches of government, particularly as they come increasingly to be perceived as puppets of particular "special interests." Value voting, according to Peretti, may prove more effective in serving "democratic political ends—political representation and responsiveness" than the more traditional appeals to activism or self-restraint, interpretism or noninterpretism (Peretti 1999, 131).

The Warren Court, in retrospect, seems to have succeeded in this regard. The Burger Court failed. The Rehnquist Court record is probably too recent to judge fairly and its most important decisions may not yet have been made. How future justices and how a future chief justice will use the power of the Court is even more difficult to predict.

Clearly, dramatic changes in the Supreme Court's makeup can be expected to occur during the next six years. Which president is making those nominations is as important as his or her willingness to expend political capital in securing their confirmation. No matter how much opposition such nominations trigger from the Senate, the lesson of recent history is clear: a president's power to nominate will trump the Senate's power to confirm. The Senate that rejected Richard Nixon's nominations of Clement Haynesworth and Harold Carswell confirmed the third nominee, Harry Blackmun—and, at least in 1970, no one would have predicted that Blackmun would become the disappointment to Nixon that he eventually became. Likewise, after rejecting Reagan's nomination of Robert Bork, the Senate confirmed Anthony

Kennedy. Kennedy, although clearly not as much to the liking of conservatives as Bork, was and has proved to be much more to their satisfaction than the man he replaced, Lewis Powell.

Whatever the composition of the future Court, issues of equality will surely continue to loom large on its docket. Equal protection will continue to be the primary prism through which the Court is likely to examine what Max Lerner called "the grand social conflicts" that will divide twenty-first century America.

REFERENCES AND FURTHER READING

Abraham, Henry J. 1998. *The Judicial Process: An Introductory Analysis of the Courts of the United States, England, and France.* New York: Oxford University Press.

Lerner, Max. 1994. *Nine Scorpions in a Bottle: Great Judges and Cases of the Supreme Court.* New York: Arcade Publishing.

O'Brien, David M. 2003. *Storm Center: The Supreme Court in American Politics.* New York: W. W. Norton.

Peretti, Terri Jennings. 1999. *In Defense of a Political Court.* Princeton, NJ: Princeton University Press.

Silverstein, Mark. 1994. *Judicious Choices: The New Politics of Supreme Court Confirmations.* New York: W. W. Norton.

5

KEY PEOPLE,
CASES, AND EVENTS

Adarand Constructors, Inc. v. Pena, **515 U.S. 200 (1995)**

Adarand Constructors challenged, under the Fifth Amendment's Due Process Clause, a federal program that provided financial incentives for contractors to subcontract parts of federal contracts to companies "controlled by 'socially and economically disadvantaged individuals,' and in particular, the Government's use of race-based presumptions in identifying such individuals." By a vote of 5–4, the Court sent the issue back to the lower federal court, requiring it to examine the program through the lens of "strict scrutiny," as Justice Sandra Day O'Connor wrote in the majority opinion. O'Connor also rejected the belief that the federal government had more leeway than the states in using race to enforce the provisions of the Fourteenth Amendment.

Although a majority of five had problems with the federal program, they could not agree on a common basis for their opinion. A subsequent decision is needed to clarify what the Court's standard is and whether, for instance, *Fullilove* (1980) is still good law.

Baker v. Carr, 369 U.S. 186 (1962)

The case arose as a result of the Tennessee legislature's failure to reapportion itself, a task it had last performed in 1901. Previous efforts to involve the federal courts in reapportionment had been turned aside on the grounds that they involved "political questions." In *Baker* the majority found that the issue was not a political question. The issue was framed as involving a denial of the fundamental right to vote in violation of the Fourteenth Amendment's guarantee of equal protection. Justice William Brennan wrote the Court's opinion. Justices Felix Frankfurter and John Marshall Harlan Jr. dissented, and Justice Charles Whittaker did not participate. Soon after the *Baker* decision, the Court formulated the now famous "one person, one vote" rule in *Gray v. Sanders* (1963).

Bowers v. Hardwick, 478 U.S. 186 (1986)

By a vote of 5–4, the Court upheld Georgia's power to punish homosexual sex. Hardwick had argued that the law violated the right to privacy that the Court had used earlier to strike down state laws prohibiting the use of contraceptives and laws prohibiting abortions. Bowers was overturned in the 2003 case *Lawrence v. Texas.*

Brown v. Board of Education of Topeka, Kansas, 347 U.S. 483 (1954)

Arguably the most important decision of the twentieth century, this unanimous decision, written by recently confirmed Chief Justice Earl Warren, held that segregation in public education violated the Fourteenth Amendment's guarantee of equal protection of the laws. Finding the historical record regarding the intent of the authors of the amendment "inconclusive" in the area of public school segregation, Warren proceeded to emphasize how discrimination made the segregated students feel inferior and that this feeling of inferiority denied them the guaranteed equal protection of the laws. Contrary to much of public opinion, Warren did not specifically overturn *Plessy* (1896), nor did he conclude that the Constitution required that government be "color-blind," the famous phrase from Justice John Marshall Harlan's dissent in *Plessy*.

Brown v. Board of Education of Topeka, Kansas, 349 U.S. 294 (1955)

Frequently referred to as *Brown II,* this case was the result of the Court's decision to ask the parties to the first case to return and argue as to how the mandate of *Brown I* should be implemented. Chief Justice Warren again wrote for a unanimous Court. The opinion held that federal district courts were to be in charge of seeing that the 1954 decision was complied with and that such action should be carried out "with all deliberate speed." The result was a decade of litigation in the lower courts that resulted in few African Americans setting foot into previously all-white schools.

Busing

In mandating that dual systems achieve racial balance or integration, *Green* (1968) set the stage for the busing controversies of the 1970s and 1980s. The Supreme Court, for the first time, upheld busing as a remedy for segregation in *Swann* (1971). The Court nationalized the busing issue in *Keyes* (1973) when it found that Denver, although never formally segregated, must bus in order to remedy the effects of policies and practices that the Court concluded were evidence of de jure segregation. *Milliken* (1974) limited the scope of busing when the Court refused to countenance cross-district busing unless there was proof of de jure segregation. Busing, however, remained a political flash point in many of the older cities of the North and the Midwest throughout the 1980s. Decisions in the

1990s, though, held that schools that had achieved racial balance could, if they so chose, end busing even if the result of doing so would be the establishment of one-race schools.

Civil Rights Act of 1964

Congress adopted no measures designed to protect the rights of African Americans from discrimination in the period from the Civil Rights Act of 1875, largely gutted by the Court's decisions in the *Civil Rights Cases* (1883), until 1964. The Civil Rights Act of 1957, adopted under the Eisenhower administration, although valuable symbolically, had little practical effect. Titles II and VII of the 1964 act prohibit discrimination in public accommodations and employment. Because of the Court's decision in the *Civil Rights Cases,* Congress opted to base the constitutionality of the 1964 act on its powers under Article I to regulate commerce among the states. The Court upheld this rationale in the 1964 case of *Katzenbach v. McClung.* Because of Court decisions that weakened the employment provision of the 1964 act, Congress adopted the Civil Rights Act of 1991, which clarified provisions of the 1964 act. Among other things, it provided for damages in cases involving employment discrimination and more clearly defined what is necessary for successful "disparate impact" actions.

Civil Rights Cases, 109 U.S. 3 (1883)

The Civil Rights Act of 1875 is frequently cited as the last gasp of the Radical Republicans aimed at reconstructing the South and guaranteeing the rights of the freedmen. Its major provisions banned discrimination on public conveyances, inns, and places of public amusement such as theaters. The act's authors believed that the Thirteenth and Fourteenth Amendments provided more than adequate basis upon which Congress could legislate. The Court disagreed, with only Justice John Marshall Harlan dissenting.

The seven-member majority (one justice did not participate) spoke through Justice Joseph Bradley. Bradley argued that in order for Congress to act, there had to be "state action." Private discrimination was beyond the scope of federal powers. Such discrimination could be remedied only by the states using their so-called police powers.

Cooper v. Aaron, 358 U.S. 1 (1958)

Implementation of *Brown* met with general resistance in most of the eleven states that had constituted the Confederate States of America. In contrast to most of the South, however, ending segregation in Little Rock, Arkansas, appeared to offer an exception to this rule. The intervention of Arkansas Governor Orval Faubus changed matters dramatically. His action to stop the admission of African Americans to the all-white Little Rock High School precipitated a showdown not only with the federal courts, but also with the Eisenhower administration, which was forced to send federal paratroopers and to federalize the Arkansas National Guard to maintain order. Faubus's defiance of a federal court order prompted the Supreme Court to issue this highly unusual opinion. The opinion in *Cooper* was signed by each of the nine justices. In it, they asserted that public officials in taking an oath to uphold the Constitution swore thereby to obey not only the Constitution but also the Court's decisions interpreting the Constitution. "No state legislative, executive, or judicial officer can war against the Constitution without violating his undertaking to support it."

Craig v. Boren, 429 U.S. 190 (1976)

Oklahoma had a law that allowed women to drink beer with an alcohol content of 3.2 percent (known as "near beer") at age eighteen but required men to be age twenty-one. By a vote of 7–2, the Court, in an opinion written by Justice William Brennan, held the statute unconstitutional. However, unlike its earlier decisions on gender discrimination in *Reed* and *Frontiero,* the Court did not claim that the statute was irrational. Instead, the Brennan opinion held that a higher standard must be applied to classifications based on gender. Such legislation "must serve important governmental objectives and must be substantially related to those objectives." Justice William Rehnquist and Chief Justice Warren Burger dissented. Rehnquist argued that because the discrimination was directed against males, it need not be as carefully scrutinized as legislation that adversely affected women. He also objected to the Court's creation of a midlevel test located somewhere between strict scrutiny and the deferential rationality test.

De Facto and De Jure Segregation

Literally translated from the Latin, these terms mean "by fact" and "by law." A majority of the Court has consistently held, following in the footsteps of the *Civil Rights Cases* (1883), that there must be evidence of government or state action for there to be a violation of the Fourteenth Amendment's guarantee of equal protection. In the early segregation cases arising in the southern states of the old Confederacy or in the border states, there was no argument as to the existence of state action that segregated on the basis of race. School ordinances and state laws clearly mandated a dual system, one for whites and one for blacks. When the issue of school segregation came north for the first time, in the case of *Keyes v. Denver School District 1* (1973), the situation was changed. Denver never had a formal system of segregation, as the Court had found in Topeka in *Brown.* Nevertheless, the Court found that the school board had engaged in practices that had the same effect, such as the way in which school boundary lines had been drawn. This, according to the Court, was *de jure* segregation.

In contrast, *de facto* segregation results from actions of private individuals. Housing in the United States is highly segregated, but this segregation has been held to be the result not of government action but rather of economics and personal choices. Using this distinction, a majority of the Court in *Milliken v. Bradley* (1974) refused to sustain a lower court ruling ordering the busing of African American children into suburban schools. For the majority, there was no evidence that the affected suburbs had ever taken any action that segregated students on the basis of race.

Deferential Review

Legislation, almost by its very nature, must discriminate. It establishes categories of behavior—those that are to be encouraged and those that are to be discouraged. Accordingly, although the Fourteenth Amendment's Equal Protection Clause provides that "No State shall . . . deny to any person within its jurisdiction the equal protection of the laws," this guarantee does not mean that a state cannot distinguish among persons. In situations that do not involve "suspect" categories, "semisuspect" categories, or "fundamental rights," the modern Court has adopted a test that is highly deferential to the wishes of legislatures.

An early expression of this position is found in the opinion of Justice William O. Douglas in *Railway Express Agency v. New York* (1949). A New York City ordinance prohibited advertising on trucks that was not related to the business of the trucks. Douglas upheld the ordinance, concluding that "if . . . the classification has [some] relation to the purpose for which it is made and does not contain the kind of discrimination against which [equal protection] affords protection"—classifications based on race, for example—it is constitutional. Legislation need not be wise or even just to be found rational. In contrast to the rationality required under the deferential standard, strict scrutiny puts the burden on government to justify classifications.

Dred Scott v. Sandford, 60 U.S. 393 (1857)

By a vote of 7–2, the Supreme Court struck down the Missouri Compromise as a violation of the Fifth Amendment's Due Process Clause. Although each of the nine justices wrote an opinion, the longest and most important was penned by Chief Justice Roger Taney. Taney, who is otherwise rated among the truly great justices of the Court, appears to have sought by this opinion to deal with the growing chasm between the North and the South that he and others saw as a threat to the Union. His opinion failed totally to heal the divide. Indeed, very likely it hastened the coming of the Civil War.

Taney's opinion would have been controversial enough if it had only voided the Missouri Compromise. Only one federal statute had been declared unconstitutional until then (in *Marbury v. Madison*, 1803). Not satisfied with doing only this, Taney proceeded to write an opinion that denied that any African American, whether slave or free, could ever be a citizen of the United States or of the states. Because African Americans had originally been brought to the colonies (and later to the states) as property, they were forever outside the political community established by the Constitution of 1787.

Equal Rights Amendment

The idea of an Equal Rights Amendment (ERA) that would provide women with the same protections the Fourteenth Amendment extended to African Americans has been introduced in every session of Congress since 1923. In 1972, Congress finally voted on an amendment that provided that "Equality of rights under the law shall not be denied or abridged by the United States or by any State on account of sex." Like the Fourteenth Amendment, it delegated power to the federal government to pass appropriate legislation necessary to enforce the amendment. At first it appeared that the amendment would be as quickly adopted as the Twenty-sixth Amendment, giving the right to vote to eighteen-year-olds, had been a year earlier.

Opponents of the ERA proved to be tenacious and skillful, however. They raised a variety of objections, ranging from the possibility that ratification of the ERA might deprive women of protection of laws passed for their benefit, to whether the ERA would make it impossible for the abortion rights decision of *Roe v. Wade* (1973) to be overturned, to whether the ERA would require single-sex rest rooms—the so-called "potty issue."

Congress extended the deadline for states to ratify the ERA, but even with the extension, the amendment failed to secure the necessary approval of three-quarters of the states. In addition to the arguments of the ERA's opponents, the Supreme Court's decisions interpreting the Fourteenth Amendment's Equal Protection Clause to strike down legislation that disadvantaged women may also have taken some of the steam out of the drive to ratify the ERA.

Fifteenth Amendment (1870)

Concern that the federal government lacked the constitutional power to protect the voting rights of the newly freed slaves, along with the realization that future Republican victories depended on the votes of African Americans, led to Congress's proposing the Fifteenth Amendment. The ratification votes in the states largely followed party lines, with Republicans voting in favor of the amendment and Democrats against it.

The Fifteenth Amendment had little effect, however, until the Supreme Court's decision in *Smith v. Allwright* (1944) outlawing the "white primary," the system that allowed the Democratic Party in the South to limit participation in its all-important primaries to whites only. The landmark Voting Rights Act of 1965 finally brought the full realization of the promise made by the adoption of the Fifteenth Amendment.

Fifth Amendment (1791)

The Fifth Amendment, one of the ten amendments that are referred to as the Bill of Rights, provides, among other things, that "No person shall . . . be deprived of life, liberty, or property, without due process of law. . . ." In challenging the forced movement of persons of Japanese ancestry to detention camps, Korematsu invoked this constitutional provision unsuccessfully in the case of *Korematsu v. United States* (1944). It was also the basis for the Court's 1954 decision in *Bolling v. Sharpe,* in which a unanimous Court held that the segregation of the public schools in the District of Columbia was unconstitutional. In that case, Chief Justice Earl Warren held that the Fifth Amendment's guarantee of due process implicitly contained a guarantee of equal protection. "[T]o impose a lesser duty" on the federal government than on the states was, according to Warren, "unthinkable."

Fourteenth Amendment (1868)

The most important of the three "Freedom Amendments," the Fourteenth Amendment was the handiwork of Senator Jacob Howard and Congressman John Bingham. Although the bulk of the amendment was designed to punish those who had rebelled against the Union, Section 1, which contains three important guarantees of individual rights, has become by far its most important part.

The Court has used the Fourteenth Amendment's Due Process Clause to carry over or incorporate to the states most of the guarantees of the Bill of Rights. As a result, these guarantees limit not only the power of the federal government but also that of the states. The Privileges or Immunities Clause plays little role in constitutional law, largely as a result of the 1873 *Slaughterhouse Cases.* In contrast, the Fourteenth Amendment's Equal Protection Clause provides the basis not only for its decisions on race and gender but also as the source of decisions involving fundamental rights.

Freeman v. Pitts, 503 U.S. 467 (1992)

In *Freeman* the Court upheld a lower court's decision to withdraw gradually from judicial supervision of the DeKalb County, Georgia, School District. According to Justice Anthony Kennedy, a system that had achieved "unitary status" was no longer required to take steps to guarantee racial balance. Although Kennedy did not win the support of all of his colleagues, several of whom concurred separately, none of them dissented.

Frontiero v. Richardson, 411 U.S. 677 (1973)

An Air Force regulation provided that male officers would automatically receive extra benefits on claiming a dependent spouse. In contrast, female officers were required to provide evidence that their spouse was dependent upon them for more than one-half of his support. With only Justice William Rehnquist in dissent, the Court voided the regulation as a violation of the Fifth Amendment's guarantee of due process. The majority was divided, however, between a four-member bloc that would have applied "strict scrutiny" and the remaining four justices. Three of the latter argued that were the Court to use "strict scrutiny" it would effectively short-circuit the then ongoing process of state ratification of the proposed Equal Rights Amendment.

Fullilove v. Klutznick, 448 U.S. 448 (1980)

Congress enacted the Public Works Employment Act in 1977, which created a "set-aside" providing that a set percentage of contracts would go to minority-controlled contractors. Although critics attacked the set-aside as a quota in disguise and hence a violation of the Court's opinion in *Bakke* (1978), a six-member majority, in an opinion written by Chief Justice Warren Burger, upheld the statute despite the claim that it violated the Fifth Amendment's guarantee of due process. The majority was split equally between those who argued that the federal government had more power in this area than the states and those who claimed that such a program was a form of benign—and therefore constitutional—classification.

Continued opposition to such programs and changes in the Court's makeup in the 1980s have called into question the continuing vitality of the *Fullilove* decision as precedent. The Court's subsequent decisions in *Richmond v. J. A. Croson Co.* (1989) and *Adarand Constructors v. Pena* (1995) are examples of this shift on the part of the Court.

Fundamental Rights

The Supreme Court's decision in *Baker v. Carr* (1962) to enter into the "political thicket" of legislative apportionment rested on the Court's conclusion that the Equal Protection Clause of the Fourteenth Amendment contained a fundamental right to vote. Subsequent decisions concluded that only the principle of "one person, one vote" could be used in drawing legislative lines. In *Reynolds v. Sims* (1964), the Court went considerably further, rejecting the "federal analogy" and requiring that both branches of a state legislature be based on population. Previously, many states had provided that each of a state's counties, regardless of population, have one state senator. Subsequently, in 1966, in the case of *Harper v. Virginia State Board of Elections,* the Court found, in an opinion penned by Justice William O. Douglas, that state poll taxes were unconstitutional. The Warren Court also found, in *Griffin v. Illinois* (1956), that "access to courts" was a fundamental right protected by the Equal Protection Clause.

The coming of the Burger Court (1969–1986) stemmed any further development of fundamental rights under the Equal Protection Clause. In *San Antonio Independent School District* (1973), for instance, in an opinion written by Justice Lewis Powell, the Court refused to find that education was a fundamental right.

The Court's controversial decision to locate a fundamental right to privacy (*Griswold v. Connecticut* [1965] and *Roe v. Wade* [1973]) in either the Ninth Amendment or in the Fourteenth Amendment's Due Process Clause has been labeled by some as a return to the days of "substantive due process." Some commentators, defenders of the results of the two decisions, have opined that the right to an abortion might have been more logically located in the Fourteenth Amendment's Equal Protection Clause instead of being posited as a liberty under the Due Process Clause.

Gender Discrimination

Despite the close relationship prior to the Civil War between the suffragette and abolitionist movements, this alliance broke down with the framing of the Fourteenth Amendment. Not only did it fail to extend rights to women, but it introduced into the Constitution for the first time what today would be called gender-specific language with Section 2's reference to "male inhabitants."

Subsequent decisions by the Court in the latter part of the nineteenth century and the early part of the twentieth century upheld legislation that stereotyped women as the "weaker" sex. Even the Warren Court upheld legislation that effectively resulted in the exclusion of women from jury service.

The Court's stance changed dramatically with the Burger Court. In *Reed v. Reed* (1971), the Court invalidated a statute that gave preference to men over women for the purposes of naming an executor in cases where the decedent had left no will. Two years later, the Court also struck down an Air Force regulation (*Frontiero v. Richardson*) that treated female officers differently from male officers in the allocation of benefits. In both of these cases, the majority of the justices purported to use the rationality standard. However, commentators argued that this was not the traditional deferential standard the Court had previously employed but rather was "rationality with bite."

In *Craig v. Boren* (1976), Justice William Brennan made explicit what many thought was implicit in the earlier *Reed* and *Frontiero* rulings: gender classifications were subject to more than the deferential standard of rationality. In order to be upheld, gender classifications "must serve important governmental objectives and must be substantially related to those objectives." With *Craig*, gender fell into a new category, dubbed "semisuspect." The more recent decision of *United States v. Virginia* (1996) witnessed the Court adjusting the standard closer to that of "strict scrutiny." Justice Ruth Bader Ginsburg's opinion calls for state action using gender to demonstrate "exceedingly persuasive justification."

Ginsburg, Ruth Bader

Ruth Bader Ginsburg was appointed to the U.S. Court of Appeals by President Jimmy Carter after a distinguished career as a law professor and a notable advocate of women's rights. In this advocacy role, Ginsburg has been hailed as the Thurgood Marshall of the women's movement. President Bill Clinton's nomination of Ginsburg in 1993 to replace retiring Justice Byron White was the first time a Democratic president was able to fill a vacancy on the Court since President Lyndon Johnson's nomination of Thurgood Marshall in 1967.

As a justice, Ginsburg has surprised many observers by generally hewing to a narrow view of the proper role for the Court. Her opinion in the case of *United States v. Virginia* (1996), however, allowed her to strengthen further the Court's intermediate standard for cases involving gender discrimination.

Gratz v. Bollinger (2003)

By a vote of 6–3, the Court, speaking through Chief Justice Rehnquist, struck down the University of Michigan's undergraduate affirmative action program. The fact that minority applicants automatically received a significant point advantage that appeared to preclude the individualized admissions decisions trumpeted by Justice Powell in the *Bakke* case appears to have enabled Rehnquist to garner the crucial vote of Justice O'Connor.

Green v. County School Board of New Kent County, 391 U.S. 430 (1968)

One of the most common responses to *Brown II* on the part of southern school districts was the implementation of "freedom-of-choice" plans. Under these plans, the parents of both white and black children were free to request the transfer of their children to what had previously been one-race schools. Generally, no whites opted to transfer to the formerly segregated black schools, and only a handful of parents of black schoolchildren requested admission to the formerly all-white schools.

A unanimous Court, in an opinion written by Justice William Brennan, rejected freedom-of-choice plans as an acceptable response to *Brown II*. Brennan's opinion went further. No longer was it enough for formerly segregated school systems to end practices that enforced segregation. Now it was necessary for such schools to achieve integration or racial balance.

Grutter v. Bollinger (2003)

With Justice O'Connor writing the Court's opinion, a five-member majority reaffirmed that *Bakke* was still good law. Specifically, the case involved a challenge to the University of Michigan Law School's use of race as one factor in making admissions decisions. In contrast to the situation in *Gratz*, O'Connor found that the procedure did guarantee individual attention to each applicant and that achieving diversity had a compelling state interest for both the university and for society.

Intermediate Scrutiny

Beginning with *Craig v. Boren* (1976), the Court has crafted a standard that, although not nearly as deferential to the legislature as the rationality standard, is not as demanding as strict scrutiny. In *Craig*, it was used in cases of gender discrimination, with gender being identified as a semisuspect category. Some of the justices who are more disposed to upholding affirmative action programs designed to help minorities have argued in dissents that the intermediate standard, and not compelling state interest, should be used in judging the constitutionality of such programs.

Keyes v. Denver School District 1, 413 U.S. 189 (1973)

Keyes involved a challenge to the practices of the Denver, Colorado, School District. Denver had never formally had a segregated or dual school system. Despite this, attorneys for the National Association for the Advancement of Colored People (NAACP) argued that a variety of district practices and policies resulted in the creation of a dual system in everything but name. The Court agreed. For the first time since *Brown* in a case involving race, the Court was not unanimous. Justice William Rehnquist dissented. Justice Lewis Powell, although concurring in the judgment, dissented on certain aspects of the decision. Justice William Brennan's opinion for the Court put northern and midwestern districts on notice that they might be future targets for desegregation suits. With *Keyes*, busing became a national political issue.

Lawrence v. Texas (2003)

Despite the fact that the appellants stressed the fact that Texas, by criminalizing same-sex sodomy and not sodomy involving heterosexuals, and that this was irrational and hence violated equal protection, the six-member majority chose to base its decision on the Due Process Clause. Justice Kennedy found that due process restricted states from criminalizing this particular form of private sexual activity. Kennedy was at pains to distinguish it from polygamy and incest and also sought to allay the fears of those who would see the decision as a first step toward allowing homosexual marriage. Chief Justice Rehnquist and Associate Justices Scalia and Thomas dissented.

Marshall, Thurgood

Thurgood Marshall was the primary strategist for the NAACP Legal Defense Fund's attack on segregation in education that eventually led to victory in *Brown v. Board of Education* (1954). The triumph in *Brown* was one of twenty-nine victories that Marshall won in Supreme Court cases. He was nominated by President John F. Kennedy and confirmed a judge of the U.S. Court of Appeals for the Second Circuit. In 1965, he became the first African American to be appointed solicitor general of the United States. In 1967, President Lyndon Johnson nominated him to succeed Justice Tom Clark on the Supreme Court.

Although Marshall wrote few Court opinions that are considered landmarks, his dissents on issues involving equal protection themselves constitute milestones in the Court's development. His dissents in *Regents of the University of California v. Bakke* (1978) and in *San Antonio Independent School District v. Rodriguez* (1973) offer a very different view of the Equal Protection Clause than the majority of the Court today accepts. In his dissent in *San Antonio*, Marshall argued that the Court should adopt a sliding scale for equal protection issues and not limit itself to the either-or stance argued for in Justice Powell's majority opinion. Powell held that distinctions based on "suspect categories" should be examined on the basis of "strict scrutiny" or "compelling state interest" and that other classifications need only to meet the low standard of "rationality."

Milliken v. Bradley, 418 U.S. 717 (1974)

A U.S. District Court had found that the Detroit public school system had engaged in practices similar to those found earlier in Denver in *Keyes* (1973). Given the overwhelming numbers of African Americans in the Detroit public schools, the judge concluded that there was no way for the Detroit system to be integrated as required by *Green* (1968). In order to achieve the status mandated by *Green,* the judge concluded that it would be necessary to involve Detroit's overwhelmingly white suburban public schools. By a vote of 5–4, with Chief Justice Warren Burger writing for the majority, the Court rejected cross-district busing unless there was evidence that the suburbs involved had also engaged, as Detroit had, in de jure segregation.

The dissenters, Justices William Brennan, Byron White, Thurgood Marshall, and William O. Douglas, disagreed, arguing among other things that by drawing the lines that divided city from suburb—municipal boundaries—the state had provided the means for de facto segregation to occur.

Nineteenth Amendment (1920)

The Nineteenth Amendment was modeled after the Fifteenth Amendment. Although some states had given women the right to vote, the Supreme Court had explicitly rejected the claim that women had a right to vote under the Privileges or Immunities Clause of the Fourteenth Amendment (*Minor v. Happersett,* 1875).

O'Connor, Sandra Day

During the presidential campaign of 1980, Republican candidate Ronald Reagan promised that, if elected, he would appoint a woman to the Court. Earlier, President Richard M. Nixon had almost submitted the name of a woman for the Court, but decided against it after charges were made that his candidate was unqualified. Shortly after taking office, Reagan had the opportunity to make good on his promise as a result of the retirement of Justice Potter Stewart. Although some opponents of the Court's abortion decision, *Roe v. Wade* (1973), expressed concern about her nomination, O'Connor was easily confirmed by the Senate. O'Connor is the only recent justice with experience both as a state court judge and as an elected public official. This experience may explain her willingness to join certain of her colleagues in voting to limit the power of the federal government and to hold that states are not subject to certain types of federal mandates.

Although O'Connor had been dubbed one of the "Stanford twins" early in her tenure on the Court because of her tendency to align herself closely with her Stanford Law School classmate, Associate Justice William H. Rehnquist, who would soon be elevated to chief justice, by the mid-1980s she had definitely established her independence. More often than not, hers has been the deciding vote in the Court's many 5–4 decisions, including the Court's decisions involving affirmative action. In this category O'Connor has taken the position that even when government uses race to improve the lot of minorities, it must show that the program serves a "compelling state interest." Unlike Justices such as Scalia, Rehnquist, and Thomas, however, O'Connor has allowed that she does not believe that this standard is necessarily fatal to any situation in which government is unable to establish past discrimination. This was evidenced most recently in her opinion in the case of *Grutter v. Bollinger* (2003), in which the Court by a vote of 5–4 upheld the University of Michigan Law School's affirmative action program.

Plessy v. Ferguson, 163 U.S. 537 (1896)

Louisiana had required that railroads provide "equal but separate accommodations for the white and colored races." Plessy, who was seven-eighths white and one-eighth black, challenged the statute as being in violation of the Thirteenth and Fifteenth Amendments. With only Justice John Marshall Harlan in dissent, the Court, in an opinion by Justice Henry Billings Brown, upheld the statute. In sustaining the statute, Brown reached back to a pre–Civil War precedent of the Supreme Judicial Court of Massachusetts upholding segregation of the public schools of Boston.

Supported by the Court's decision, southern and border states proceeded to segregate almost every aspect of public life, from parks to toilets to drinking fountains. In his dissent, Justice Harlan labeled segregation by law a "badge of servitude" for blacks and proclaimed that the Constitution was "color-blind."

Powell, Lewis F., Jr.

Justice Powell served on the Supreme Court from 1972 until his retirement in 1987. One of the four Nixon nominees who were confirmed, Powell often proved a disappointment to the man who appointed him. He frequently provided the crucial fifth vote for some of the most controversial decisions of the Burger Court. Perhaps more than any of his fellow justices of the 1970s and 1980s, Powell espoused and adhered to the judicial role of self-restraint.

Formulated by Harvard Law Professor James Bradley Thayer and practiced most notably by Justices Oliver Wendell Holmes Jr. and Felix Frankfurter, the self-restraint approach holds that the Court, as the least powerful and least democratic branch of government, generally should defer to the wishes of the other two branches of government and to the states and declare unconstitutional only laws that clearly and blatantly run afoul of the Constitution.

Accordingly, in *Frontiero v. Richardson* (1973), Powell, while voting to strike down the Air Force regulation as irrationally discriminating against female officers, refused to preempt the ongoing political process involving the then ongoing debate over ratifying the proposed Equal Rights Amendment. The same year, in *San Antonio v. Rodriguez,* Powell refused to find education to be a fundamental right or to rule that the economic distinctions among Texas school districts met the test for classification as a "suspect category." In *Bakke* (1978), Powell, while agreeing that quotas per se violated the Fourteenth Amendment, crafted an opinion that upheld a state university's right to consider race as one factor in making admissions decisions. In the busing cases, Powell argued that the distinction the Court made between de jure and de facto segregation was unworkable. At the same time, he cautioned against busing of younger children.

Regents of the University of California v. Bakke, 438 U.S. 265 (1978)

Four years before hearing *Bakke,* the Court had avoided addressing the issue of affirmative action by holding that the issue raised in *DeFunis v. Odegaard* (1974) was moot (DeFunis was in the last year of law studies by that time, and the law school he attended, which had been ordered by a lower court to admit him, indicated that regardless of how the Court ruled he would be allowed to complete his course of studies).

In *Bakke,* the facts established were that the University of California at Davis medical school had never discriminated on the basis of race, that it had two separate admissions committees, that a predetermined number of seats were reserved in the entering class for minorities, and that Bakke's score on the MCAT (Medical College Admission Test) and his grades were higher than those of any of the minority admissions.

On this basis, four of the justices found that the admissions policy violated the Civil Rights Act of 1964. Four other justices found that quotas could be justified to serve the compelling state interest of increasing the numbers of minorities practicing medicine. Justice Lewis Powell cast the deciding vote and wrote the Court's opinion. On the one hand, he found quotas unconstitutional; on the other hand, he argued that race could be used as one factor in achieving educational diversity.

Reynolds v. Sims, 377 U.S. 533 (1964)

By a vote of 8–1, the Court found in *Reynolds v. Sims* that representation in state legislatures must be based on population. Chief Justice Earl Warren declared, "Legislators represent people, not trees or acres. Legislators are elected by voters, not farms or cities or economic interests." The result was the end of a practice of basing representation in one branch of a state legislature on a basis other than population—the so-called "federal analogy."

Richmond v. J. A. Croson Co., 488 U.S. 469 (1989)

The City of Richmond believed that it was on sound constitutional ground when it adopted a set-aside plan for minority contractors that was modeled on the federal program upheld in *Fullilove* (1980). However, by a vote of 6–3, the Court found the program unconstitutional. Justice Sandra Day O'Connor wrote the judgment of the Court. Important for O'Connor in the decision was the fact that Richmond had shown no evidence that either the city or contractors working for the city had previously discriminated on the basis of race. O'Connor also seemed concerned that the city had not made any efforts to use race-neutral means to change the pattern of contracting in Richmond and that the program had no sunset provision or time when remedial action would end. As would be the case in the later decision of *Adarand* (1995), there was no single opinion that united the majority justices. The three dissenters argued that efforts to adopt legislation that was intended to benefit minorities need meet a much lower standard than "strict scrutiny."

Romer v. Evans, 517 U.S. 620 (1996)

The voters of Colorado had amended the state's constitution through a process referred to as initiative and referendum. Under this system, both laws and amendments can be enacted without action by elected officials. Amendment 2, as it was called, provided that no level of government in Colorado could adopt a measure that specifically gave protection to individuals on the basis of their "homosexual, lesbian, or bisexual orientation."

By a vote of 6–3, the Court, in an opinion written by Justice Anthony Kennedy, found the amendment to lack any rational relationship to any legitimate state interest. Instead, it demonstrated animus to a class of citizens. Justices Antonin Scalia, Clarence Thomas, and Chief Justice William Rehnquist dissented, arguing that the Court's opinion ignored the Court's earlier decision in *Bowers v. Hardwick* (1986), upholding the state's power to punish homosexual conduct.

Rostker v. Goldberg, 453 U.S. 57 (1981)

The Military Selective Service Act requires all males to register for the draft. Women do not register. By a vote of 6–3, the Court found, with Justice William Rehnquist writing the opinion, that the measure met the requirements of intermediate scrutiny necessary in cases of gender discrimination.

The dissenting justices pointed out that the case only involved registration and did not require the Court to address the related issue of whether women should serve in combat positions in the military.

Shaw v. Reno, 509 U.S. 630 (1993)

Shaw represents a new issue for the Court. In order to increase minority representation in legislatures, is it constitutional for those drawing legislative boundaries to use race as a major factor in drawing those lines. The creation of what are termed "max-black" districts has resulted in an increase in the numbers of African Americans in Congress and in state legislatures. In this case, by a 5–4 vote, the Court found that the program needed to be examined using strict scrutiny. Justice Sandra Day O'Connor wrote the opinion.

Strict Scrutiny

In contrast to the highly deferential standard of rationality that the Court applies to legislation that classifies persons on the basis of a factor such as age, strict scrutiny requires that government show a "compelling state interest" whenever it employs any "suspect" category as a basis for classification. Furthermore, the means used must be as "narrowly tailored" as possible to achieve the state's compelling interest.

Ironically, the Court's first use of the test came in the now highly criticized case of *Korematsu v. United States* (1944), in which a majority of the justices upheld President Franklin Roosevelt's executive order requiring persons of Japanese ancestry to report to detention camps.

Today, *Korematsu* seems the exception to the rule that legislation scrutinized for "compelling state interest" is struck down. In addition to "suspect categories," the test is also used when "fundamental rights" are involved.

Suspect Categories

Beginning with the Court's ruling in the *Slaughterhouse Cases* (1873), the Court has acknowledged that the guarantee of equal protection has a special relationship to blacks. As Justice Samuel Miller wrote in those cases, "The existence of laws in the States where the newly emancipated negroes resided, which discriminated with gross injustice and hardship against them as a class, was the evil to be remedied by this clause, and by it such laws are forbidden." Later, the Court held that discrimination based on nationality would also be struck down as violating equal protection (*Strauder v. West Virginia*, 1880).

Out of these and subsequent decisions, the concept of suspect categories developed. The famous footnote 4 of Justice Harlan Fiske Stone's opinion in *United States v. Carolene Products* (1938) referred to "discrete and insular minorities" of whom the Court must be particularly protective. Other cases have emphasized that these groups have been the victims of a long history of discrimination and that the characteristic that distinguishes them is immutable. Religion is sometimes listed as a suspect category despite the fact that religious discrimination seems more properly to be handled within the ambit of the First Amendment's guarantee of free exercise than of the Fourteenth Amendment's Equal Protection Clause.

Beginning with the Warren Court, a movement developed to increase the number of suspect categories. Poverty and illegitimacy, for a time, seemed to have been elevated to a status of suspect categories, but recent Court decisions seem to demonstrate that the Court is determined to limit suspect status to race, nationality, alienage, and religion.

In *Frontiero v. Richardson* (1973), the Court fell one vote short of defining gender as a suspect category. Had the Equal Rights Amendment been adopted, gender would definitely have enjoyed the same protection as race and the other accepted suspect categories. Legislation that uses a suspect category is subjected to "strict scrutiny" by the Court.

Swann v. Charlotte-Mecklenburg Board of Education, 402 U.S. 1 (1971)

In the wake of the Court's decision in *Green* (1968), busing became more and more a hot-button issue in American political life.

The Court was presented with it for the first time in *Swann*. A unanimous Court held, among other things, that busing might be used in order to remedy past state-mandated segregation. Chief Justice Warren Burger, although originally in the minority, wrote the opinion for a unanimous Court.

Thirteenth Amendment (1865)

Lincoln's Emancipation Proclamation had little effect on the conditions of those held in slavery. By its own terms, it freed only slaves who lived in areas in rebellion that were not under the control of federal authorities. Constitutionally it was also suspect, although the argument could be made that it was a legitimate use of the presidential power as commander in chief. Action on an amendment outlawing slavery was initiated in 1864. The Senate quickly approved, but supporters failed to get the necessary two-thirds vote in the House of Representatives. Only after the election of 1864 were its proponents able to muster the necessary votes in the House.

The 1883 decision in the *Civil Rights Cases* invoked for the first time the "badges of slavery" argument, but the phrase was interpreted narrowly by the majority. Justice John Marshall Harlan, however, in his dissent in these cases and in the later case of *Plessy v. Ferguson* (1896), gave a much broader reading to the concept. For Harlan, Congress had, as part of its enforcement power under the Thirteenth Amendment, the power to ban discrimination in public accommodations and hence the right to remove all "badges of slavery." In *Plessy*, Harlan continued sounding the same theme, arguing that segregation by states was a forbidden imposition of a "badge of slavery."

Unlike all the other guarantees of civil liberties and civil rights in the Constitution, the Thirteenth Amendment acts as a limit not only on government but also on the actions of private individuals.

Thomas, Clarence

Nominated by President George H. W. Bush in 1991 to succeed Thurgood Marshall on the Supreme Court, Thomas is the second African American to sit on the high court. More than any recent appointment to the Court, his appointment changed the Court's overall balance, since on almost every issue his stance represents the polar opposite of the person he replaced. On issues of equal protection, Thomas has consistently argued for a race-neutral or "color-blind" approach, and he has criticized affirmative action programs as taking an out-of-date and paternalistic approach to African Americans.

Before his appointment as an associate justice, Thomas served as a judge of the U.S. Court of Appeals for the District of Columbia and as chairman of the Equal Employment Opportunity Commission (EEOC). His confirmation to the Supreme Court was by a vote of 52–48, the smallest margin in modern Court history.

Twenty-fourth Amendment (1964)

One of the many tools used to disfranchise African Americans in the South was the poll tax. Although the idea of the poll tax predates the Constitution, many of the southern states added a twist to the old formula: The tax was cumulative. A person who had not been registered to vote until the person's fiftieth birthday, for example, owed a tax for every election that had occurred since the person had turned twenty-one. The Twenty-fourth Amendment abolished the poll tax for all federal elections.

In 1966, in the case of *Harper v. Virginia Board of Elections*, the Supreme Court declared that poll taxes for state and local elections were in violation of the Equal Protection Clause of the Fourteenth Amendment.

United States v. Virginia, 518 U.S. 515 (1996)

In 1990, the U.S. Department of Justice under the Bush administration instituted a suit challenging the refusal of Virginia authorities to admit women to the Virginia Military Institute (VMI). As a result, Virginia set up a parallel program at a private women's college. The Fourth Circuit Court of Appeals upheld the program, and the Justice Department under the Clinton administration appealed. The Supreme Court reversed the appeals court by a vote of 7–1 (with Justice Clarence Thomas not participating because of his son's attendance at the school).

The opinion of the Court was written by Justice Ruth Bader Ginsburg. In finding that Virginia's efforts fell short of the requirements of equal protection and ordering women admitted to VMI, Ginsburg proffered a new more demanding standard, which she termed an "exceedingly persuasive justification." Since the state failed to meet this standard, VMI was ordered to admit women. Chief Justice William Rehnquist, in his concurrence, argued that the Court should not abandon the test established in *Craig v. Boren* of an "important government objective." Scalia in his dissent concluded that Virginia had in fact met the standard required of it by *Craig.*

Voting Rights Act of 1965

Despite the adoption of the Fifteenth Amendment, the federal government, particularly after the end of Reconstruction that followed the disputed presidential election of 1876, did nothing to protect the voting rights of African Americans. Literacy tests, cumulative poll taxes, and the "white primary" all served to disfranchise almost all African Americans living in the South. As a result, in 1940, for instance, there were only about 150,000 African Americans registered to vote in the states of the old Confederacy. The Voting Rights Act shifted the burden of registration from blacks to the government. As a result of the act, federal registrars were dispatched to southern counties to register African American voters. The Court upheld the act as constitutional in *South Carolina v. Katzenbach* (1966).

Warren, Earl

Dwight Eisenhower's nomination of Earl Warren, a former governor of California and the unsuccessful Republican candidate for vice president in 1948, to succeed the late Chief Justice Fred Vinson demonstrates the vital importance for American politics and society of the president's role in shaping the federal judiciary. Warren assumed leadership of a Court that was still recovering from its clash in the 1930s with the Roosevelt administration and was further beset by sharp and bitter personal and ideological divisions.

Brown v. Board of Education had already been argued before the Vinson Court, which had ordered an unusual second round of briefs and arguments. Chief Justice Warren presided over this second round. With the help of Associate Justice Felix Frankfurter and by dint of his own personal and political skills, Warren succeeded in delivering a unanimous decision, something most scholars believe would have eluded his predecessor.

6

DOCUMENTS

THE DECLARATION OF INDEPENDENCE (1776)

Rutgers University political scientist Wilson Carey McWilliams has characterized the nation's two founding documents thusly: "The Declaration is poetry; the Constitution is prose." The writing of the Declaration of Independence was delegated to Thomas Jefferson and John Adams by the Continental Congress. Jefferson was clearly the dominant partner in the enterprise. His ideas borrowed heavily from the political writings of the English political philosopher John Locke. Jefferson's proclamation "that all men are created equal" continues to resonate in the politics not only of the United States, but in other nations as well. Much of the Declaration is taken up by specific indictments of "repeated injuries and usurpations" perpetrated on the colonists by "the present King of Great Britain." In his original draft, Jefferson proposed charging the king as well with the crime of introducing slaves to the colonies. Opposition from representatives of the southern colonies, however, resulted in the deletion of this charge.

July 4, 1776

In Congress, July 4, 1776,

THE UNANIMOUS DECLARATION OF THE THIRTEEN UNITED STATES OF AMERICA,

When in the Course of human events, it becomes necessary for one people to dissolve the political bands which have connected them with another, and to assume among the Powers of the earth, the separate and equal station to which the Laws of Nature and of Nature's God entitle them, a decent respect to the opinions of mankind requires that they should declare the causes which impel them to the separation.

We hold these truths to be self-evident, that all men are created equal, that they are endowed by their Creator with certain unalienable Rights, that among these are Life, Liberty and the pursuit of Happiness. That to secure these rights, Governments are instituted among men, deriving their just powers from the consent of the governed. That whenever any Form of Government becomes destructive of these ends, it is the Right of the People to alter or to abolish it, and to institute new Government, laying its foundation on such principles and organizing its powers in such form, as to them shall seem most likely to effect their Safety and Happiness. Prudence, indeed, will dictate that Governments long established should not be changed for light and transient causes; and accordingly all experience hath shown, that mankind are more disposed to suffer, while evils are sufferable, than to right themselves by abolishing the forms to which they are accustomed. But when a long train of abuses and usurpations, pursuing invariably the same Object evinces a design to reduce them under absolute Despotism, it is their right, it is their duty, to throw off such Government, and to provide new Guards for their future security. Such has been the patient sufferance of these Colonies; and such is now the necessity which constrains them to alter their former Systems of Government. The history of the present King of Great Britain is a history of repeated injuries and usurpations, all having in direct object the establishment of an absolute Tyranny over these States. . . .

We, therefore, the Representatives of the United States of America, in GENERAL CONGRESS, Assembled, appealing to the Supreme Judge of the World for the Rectitude of our Intentions, do, in the Name, and by Authority of the good People of these Colonies, solemnly Publish and Declare, That these United Colonies are, and of Right ought to be, FREE AND INDEPENDENT STATES; that they are absolved from all Allegiance to the British Crown, and that all political Connection between them and the State of Great Britain, is and ought to be totally dissolved; and that as FREE AND INDEPENDENT STATES, they have full Power to levy War, conclude Peace, contract Alliances, establish Commerce, and to do all other Acts and Things which INDEPENDENT STATES may of right do.

And for the support of this Declaration, with a firm Reliance on the Protection of divine Providence, we mutually pledge to each other our Lives, our Fortunes, and our sacred Honor.

Selections from
the U.S. Constitution (1787)

The Philadelphia Convention of 1787 was called by the Congress under the Articles of Confederation as a result of the growing realization on the part of much of the political leadership that significant changes needed to be made in the basic governing document so as to insure both the security of the United States and the preservation of individual rights. Although the Convention was supposedly limited to amending the Articles, it almost immediately proceeded to agree to take up James Madison's "Virginia Plan," thereby placing the Convention on a trajectory to replace the Articles with an entirely new constitution. Although overwhelmingly the delegates tended to agree with Madison's proposals, two issues threatened to derail the Convention. The first was the matter of representation. The delegates from the smaller states felt committed to preserving equal representation for each state in the legislature. The so-called "Great Compromise" resolved this controversy by providing that one branch of the legislature would be based on population and the other would represent the states. The second issue was slavery. The following selections represent the compromise the delegates reached on this issue.

Article. I.

Section. 1. All legislative Powers herein granted shall be vested in a Congress of the United States, which shall consist of a Senate and House of Representatives.

Section. 2. The House of Representatives shall be composed of Members chosen every second Year by the People of the several States, and the Electors in each State shall have the Qualifications requisite for Electors of the most numerous Branch of the State Legislature.

No Person shall be a Representative who shall not have attained to the Age of twenty five Years, and been seven Years a Citizen of the United States, and who shall not, when elected, be an Inhabitant of that State in which he shall be chosen.

[Representatives and direct Taxes shall be apportioned among the several States which may be included within this Union, according to their respective Numbers, which shall be determined by adding to the whole Number of free Persons, including those bound to Service for a Term of Years, and excluding Indians not taxed, three fifths of all other Persons.]*

* Changed by Section 2 of the Fourteenth Amendment.

. . .

Section. 9. The Migration or Importation of such Persons as any of the States now existing shall think proper to admit, shall not be prohibited by the Congress prior to the Year one thousand eight hundred and eight, but a Tax or duty may be imposed on such Importation, not exceeding ten dollars for each Person.

. . .

Article. IV.

. . .

Section. 2. The Citizens of each State shall be entitled to all Privileges and Immunities of Citizens in the several States.

A Person charged in any State with Treason, Felony, or other Crime, who shall flee from justice, and be found in another State, shall on Demand of the executive Authority of the State from which he fled, be delivered up, to be removed to the State having Jurisdiction of the Crime.

[No Person held to Service or Labour in one State, under the Laws thereof, escaping into another, shall, in Consequence of any Law or Regulation therein, be discharged from such Service or Labour, but shall be delivered up on Claim of the Party to whom such Service or Labour may be due.]*

* Changed by the Thirteenth Amendment

. . .

Article. V.

The Congress, whenever two thirds of both Houses shall deem it necessary, shall propose Amendments to this Constitution, or, on the Application of the Legislatures of two thirds of the several States, shall call a Convention for proposing Amendments, which, in either Case, shall be valid to all Intents and Purposes, as Part of this Constitution, when ratified by the Legislatures of three fourths of the several States, or by Conventions in three fourths thereof, as the one or the other Mode of Ratification may be proposed by the Congress; Provided that no

Amendment which may be made prior to the Year One thousand eight hundred and eight shall in any Manner affect the first and fourth Clauses in the Ninth Section of the first Article; and that no State, without its Consent, shall be deprived of its equal Suffrage in the Senate.

THE MISSOURI COMPROMISE (1820)

Although there was hope in the eighteenth century that slavery would gradually disappear as a result of economic forces and growing antipathy to the "peculiar institution," these hopes went by the boards with the invention of the cotton gin and the acquisition through the Louisiana Purchase of land that readily lent itself to the plantation system of agriculture. The possibility that slavery would expand into the new territory and that additional states would be created from this territory threatened to upset the balance between slave and free states in Congress. The application of Missouri to join the union in 1820 as a slave state brought the issue to a head. However, by pairing Missouri's admission with that of Maine (formerly as the Province of Maine, a part of Massachusetts), the crisis was again postponed. The Missouri Enabling Act, or as it is generally known, the Missouri Compromise, was part of this bargain.

An Act to authorize the people of the Missouri territory to form a constitution and state government, and for the admission of such state into the Union on an equal footing with the original states, and to prohibit slavery in certain territories.

Be it enacted That the inhabitants of that portion of the Missouri territory included within the boundaries hereinafter designated, be, and they are hereby, authorized to form for themselves a constitution and state government. . . .

SEC. 3. That all free white male citizens of the United States, who shall have arrived at the age of twenty-one years, and have resided in said territory three months previous to the day of election, and all other persons qualified to vote for representatives to the general assembly of the said territory, shall be qualified to be elected, and they are hereby qualified and authorized to vote, and choose representatives to form a convention. . . .

SEC. 8. That in all that territory ceded by France to the United States, under the name of Louisiana, which lies north of thirty-six degrees and thirty minutes north latitude, not included within the limits of the state, contemplated by this act, slavery and involuntary servitude, otherwise than in the punishment of crimes, whereof the parties shall have been duly convicted, shall be, and is hereby, forever prohibited: *Provided always,* That any person escaping into the same, from whom labour or service is lawfully claimed, in any state or territory of the United States, such fugitive may be lawfully reclaimed and conveyed to the person claiming his or her labour or service as aforesaid.

DRED SCOTT V. SANDFORD (1856)

No case is more often bracketed with the word infamous than that of Dred Scott. The case was initiated in 1846 by a slave, Dred Scott, and his wife, Harriet. They alleged that their owner Dr. John Emerson, an army surgeon, had in the course of his military duties taken them to places made free under the Missouri Compromise. Accordingly, they argued that they were now free and requested the state courts of Missouri to recognize this fact. The case dragged on and eventually became a lightning rod for the forces fighting over slavery. Despite precedents to the contrary, the Missouri Supreme Court ruled against Scott and in favor of Sandford, the brother of Emerson's widow who acted on her behalf to recover the escrowed wages of Scott.

Chief Justice Roger Taney's opinion was the longest opinion issued by the Court up to that time. Additionally, each of the nine justices wrote an opinion in the case, reverting to the practice of justices issuing decisions seriatim, *a practice that had ended with the Marshall Court. Only Justices Benjamin Curtis and John McLean dissented.*

Prior to the announcement of the decision, President James Buchanan was informed of what the Court would do and as a result included in his inaugural address an appeal to the American people to abide by whatever the Court decided.

This case was brought up, by writ of error, from the Circuit Court of the United States for the district of Missouri.

Mr. Chief Justice TANEY delivered the opinion of the court.

... There are two leading questions presented by the record: 1. Had the Circuit Court of the United States jurisdiction to hear and determine the case between these parties? And 2. If it had jurisdiction, is the judgment it has given erroneous or not? . . .

. . . Can a negro, whose ancestors were imported into this country, and sold as slaves, become a member of the political community . . . and as such become entitled to all the rights, and privileges, and immunities, guarantied . . . to the citizen? One of which rights is the privilege of suing in a court of the United States in the cases specified in the Constitution.

. . . [T]he plea applies to that class of persons only whose ancestors were negroes of the African race, and imported into this country, and sold and held as slaves. The only matter in issue before the court, therefore, is, whether the descendants of such slaves, when they shall be emancipated, or who are born of parents who had become free before their birth, are citizens of a State, in the sense in which the word citizen is used in the Constitution of the United States. . . .

The words "people of the United States" and "citizens" are synonymous terms. . . . The question before us is, whether [negroes] . . . compose a portion of this people . . . ? We think they are not, and that they are not included, and were not intended to be included, under the word "citizens" in the Constitution, and can therefore claim none of the rights and privileges which that instrument provides for and secures to citizens of the United States. On the contrary, they were at that time considered as a subordinate and inferior class of beings, who had been subjugated by the dominant race, and, whether emancipated or not, yet remained subject to their authority, and had no rights or privileges but such as those who held the power and the Government might choose to grant them.

It is not the province of the court to decide upon the justice or injustice . . . of these laws. The decision of that question belonged to the political or law-making power. . . . The duty of the court is, to interpret the instrument they have framed, with the best lights we can obtain on the subject, and to administer it as we find it, according to its true intent and meaning when it was adopted.

. . . [N]o State can, by any act or law of its own, passed since the adoption of the Constitution, introduce a new member into the political community created by the Constitution of the United States. It cannot make him a member of this community by making him a member of its own. . . .

The question then arises, whether the provisions of the Constitution ... embraced the negro African race, at that time in this country, and ... put it in the power of a single State to make him a citizen of the United States, and endue him with the full rights of citizenship in every other State without their consent? Does the Constitution ... act upon him whenever he shall be made free under the laws of a State, and raised there to the rank of a citizen, and immediately clothe him with all the privileges of a citizen in every other State, and in its own courts?

The court think the affirmative of these propositions cannot be maintained. And if it cannot, the plaintiff in error ... was not entitled to sue in its courts.

. . .

In the opinion of the court, the legislation and histories of the times, and the language used in the Declaration of Independence, show, that neither the class of persons who had been imported as slaves, nor their descendants, whether they had become free or not, were then acknowledged as a part of the people. . . .

They had for more than a century before been regarded as beings of an inferior order, and altogether unfit to associate with the white race, either in social or political relations; and so far inferior, that they had no rights which the white man was bound to respect; and that the negro might justly and lawfully be reduced to slavery for his benefit. He was bought and sold, and treated as an ordinary article of merchandise and traffic, whenever a profit could be made by it. This opinion was at that time fixed and universal in the civilized portion of the white race. . . .

The language of the Declaration of Independence is ... conclusive:

It begins by declaring that, "when in the course of human events it becomes necessary for one people to dissolve the political bands which have connected them with another, and to assume among the powers of the earth the separate and equal station to which the laws of nature and nature's God entitle them, a decent respect for the opinions of mankind requires that they should declare the causes which impel them to the separation."

It then proceeds to say: "We hold these truths to be self-evident: that all men are created equal; that they are endowed by their Creator with certain unalienable rights; that among them is life, liberty, and the pursuit of happiness; that to secure these rights, Governments are instituted, deriving their just powers from the consent of the governed."

The general words above quoted would seem to embrace the whole human family.... But it is too clear for dispute, that the enslaved African race were not intended to be included, and formed no part of the people who framed and adopted this declaration; for if the language, as understood in that day, would embrace them, the conduct of the distinguished men who framed the Declaration of Independence would have been utterly and flagrantly inconsistent with the principles they asserted; and instead of the sympathy of mankind, to which they so confidently appealed, they would have deserved and received universal rebuke and reprobation.

. . .

This state of public opinion had undergone no change when the Constitution was adopted, as is equally evident from its provisions and language.

. . .

To all this mass of proof we have still to add, that Congress has repeatedly legislated upon the same construction of the Constitution that we have given....

The first of these acts is the naturalization law, which was passed at the second session of the first Congress, March 26, 1790, and confines the right of becoming citizens "to aliens being free white persons."

. . .

No one, we presume, supposes that any change in public opinion or feeling, in relation to this unfortunate race, in the civilized nations of Europe or in this country, should induce the court to give to the words of the Constitution a more liberal construction in their favor than they were intended to bear when the instrument was framed and adopted.... What the construction was at that time, we think can hardly admit of doubt. We have the language of the Declaration of Independence and of the Articles of Confederation, in addition to the plain words of the Constitution itself ... all concurring together, and leading to the same result....

... [T]he court is of opinion, that ... Dred Scott was not a citizen of Missouri within the meaning of the Constitution ..., and not entitled as such to sue in its courts; and, consequently, that the Circuit Court had no jurisdiction of the case, and that the judgment on the plea in abatement is erroneous.

. . .

... [I]t has been said, that as this court has decided against the jurisdiction of the Circuit Court ..., it has no right to examine any question presented ...; and that anything it may say upon that part of the case will be extra-judicial, and mere *obiter dicta.*

This is a manifest mistake. ...

The correction of one error in the court below does not deprive the appellate court of the power of examining further into the record, and correcting any other material errors which may have been committed by the inferior court. ... [I]t is the daily practice of this court, and of all appellate courts where they reverse the judgment of an inferior court for error, to correct by its opinions whatever errors may appear on the record material to the case; and they have always held it to be their duty to do so where the silence of the court might lead to misconstruction or future controversy. ...

We proceed, therefore, to inquire whether the facts relied on by the plaintiff entitled him to his freedom. ...

The plaintiff was a negro slave, belonging to Dr. Emerson, who was a surgeon in the army. ... [H]e took the plaintiff from ... Missouri to the military post ... in ... Illinois, and held him there as a slave until ... 1836. At the time last mentioned, said Dr. Emerson removed the plaintiff from said military post ... to the military post at Fort Snelling, situate on the west bank of the Mississippi river, in the Territory known as Upper Louisiana, acquired by the United States of France, and situate north of the latitude of thirty-six degrees thirty minutes north, and north of the State of Missouri. Said Dr. Emerson held the plaintiff in slavery [there] ... from said last-mentioned date ... 1838.

...

Before the commencement of this suit, said Dr. Emerson sold ... the plaintiff, and Harriet, Eliza, and Lizzie, to the defendant, as slaves, and the defendant has ever since claimed ... each of them, as slaves.

In considering this ..., two questions arise: 1. Was he, together with his family, free in Missouri by reason of the stay in the territory of the United States hereinbefore mentioned? And 2. If they were not, is Scott himself free by reason of his removal to Rock Island, in the State of Illinois, as stated in the above admissions?

We proceed to examine the first question.

The act of Congress, upon which the plaintiff relies, declares that slavery and involuntary servitude, except as a punishment for crime, shall be forever prohibited in all that part of the territory ceded by France, under the name of Louisiana, which lies north of thirty-six degrees thirty minutes north latitude. . . . And the difficulty which meets us at the threshold of this part of the inquiry is, whether Congress was authorized to pass this law under . . . the Constitution; for if the authority is not given by that instrument, it is the duty of this court to declare it void and inoperative, and incapable of conferring freedom upon any one who is held as a slave. . . .

. . . [T]he power of Congress over the person or property of a citizen can never be a mere discretionary power under our Constitution. . . . The powers of the Government and the rights and privileges of the citizen are regulated and plainly defined by the Constitution. . . . It has no power of any kind beyond it; and it cannot, when it enters a Territory of the United States . . . assume discretionary or despotic powers which the Constitution has denied to it. . . . The Territory being a part of the United States, the Government and the citizen both enter it under the authority of the Constitution, with their respective rights defined and marked out; and the Federal Government can exercise no power over his person or property, beyond what that instrument confers, nor lawfully deny any right which it has reserved.

. . .

These powers, and others, in relation to rights of person . . . which are, in express and positive terms, denied to the General Government; and the rights of private property have been guarded with equal care. Thus the rights of property are united with the rights of person, and placed on the same ground by the fifth amendment to the Constitution, which provides that no person shall be deprived of life, liberty, and property, without due process of law. And an act of Congress which deprives a citizen of the United States of his liberty or property, merely because he came himself or brought his property into a particular Territory of the United States, and who had committed no offence against the laws, could hardly be dignified with the name of due process of law.

. . .

Upon these considerations, it is the opinion of the court that the act of Congress which prohibited a citizen from holding and owning property of this kind in the territory of the United States north of the line therein mentioned, is not warranted by the Constitution, and is therefore void; and that neither Dred Scott himself, nor any of his family, were made free by being carried into this territory. . . .

The Emancipation Proclamation (1863)

Although slavery was undoubtedly one of the issues that led to the secession of the southern states, northern attitudes on the issue of slavery were mixed at the outset of hostilities. Although abolitionists saw slavery as a stain that had to be removed by whatever means, others favored compensation to the slave owners, while others fought only to preserve the Union. Lincoln's attitudes on slavery appear to have reflected these differences and only gradually did he adopt the position that slavery should be ended. Acting under his power as commander-in-chief, Lincoln issued the Emancipation Proclamation. This act, in reality, was only symbolic. It applied only to those areas in rebellion. It did not alter the status of slaves in those states that had not seceded or in those areas of the South occupied by Union forces.

By the President of the United States of America:
A Proclamation.
Whereas on the 22d day of September, A.D. 1862, a proclamation was issued by the President of the United States, containing, among other things, the following, to wit:

"That on the 1st day of January, A.D. 1863, all persons held as slaves within any State or designated part of a State the people whereof shall then be in rebellion against the United States shall be then, thenceforward, and forever free. . . .

"That the executive will on the 1st day of January aforesaid, by proclamation, designate the States and parts of States, if any, in which the people thereof, respectively, shall then be in rebellion against the United States. . . ."

Now, therefore, I, Abraham Lincoln, President of the United States, by virtue of the power in me vested as Commander-in-Chief . . . , and as a fit and necessary war measure for suppressing said rebellion, do, on this 1st day of January, A.D. 1863 . . . designate as the States and parts of States wherein the people thereof, respectively, are this day in rebellion against the United States the following, to wit:

Arkansas, Texas, Louisiana (except the parishes of St. Bernard, Plaquemines, Jefferson, St. John, St. Charles, St. James, Ascension, Assumption, Terrebonne, Lafourche, St. Mary, St. Martin, and Orleans, including the city of New Orleans), Mississippi, Alabama, Florida, Georgia, South Carolina, North Carolina, and Virginia (except the forty-eight counties designated as West Virginia, and also the counties of Berkeley, Accomac, Northhampton, Elizabeth City, York, Princess Anne, and Norfolk, including the cities of Norfolk and Portsmouth), and which excepted parts are for the present left precisely as if this proclamation were not issued.

And by virtue of the power and for the purpose aforesaid, I do order and declare that all persons held as slaves within said designated States and parts of States are, and henceforward shall be, free; and that the Executive Government of the United States, including the military and naval authorities thereof, will recognize and maintain the freedom of said persons.

. . .

And upon this act, sincerely believed to be an act of justice, warranted by the Constitution upon military necessity, I invoke the considerate judgment of mankind and the gracious favor of Almighty God.

The "Freedom Amendments" (1865, 1868, 1870)

Democratic opponents of Republican President Abraham Lincoln, in criticizing the latter's policies expressed the wish for "the Union as it is, and the Constitution as it was." Their plaintive cry arose from the belief that under Lincoln the federal government had assumed until then unheard-of power and that within the federal government, the president had also exceeded the proper bounds of presidential power.

The adoption of the Thirteenth, Fourteenth, and Fifteenth Amendments both legitimized the growth of federal power that had occurred under Lincoln and pushed the boundaries of the federal government still further at the expense of state powers. The Thirteenth Amendment only was proposed by both houses of Congress after Lincoln's reelection in 1864. Many scholars argue that the Fourteenth and Fifteenth were adopted by Congress partly out of concern that certain pieces of Recon-

struction legislation might be held to be unconstitutional by the Supreme Court.

AMENDMENT XIII [Ratified December 6, 1865]

Section 1. Neither slavery nor involuntary servitude, except as a punishment for crime whereof the party shall have been duly convicted, shall exist within the United States, or any place subject to their jurisdiction.

Section 2. Congress shall have power to enforce this article by appropriate legislation.

AMENDMENT XIV [Ratified July 9, 1868]

Section 1. All persons born or naturalized in the United States, and subject to the jurisdiction thereof, are citizens of the United States and of the State wherein they reside. No State shall make or enforce any law which shall abridge the privileges or immunities of citizens of the United States; nor shall any State deprive any person of life, liberty, or property, without due process of law; nor deny to any person within its jurisdiction the equal protection of the laws.

Section 2. Representatives shall be apportioned among the several States according to their respective numbers, counting the whole number of persons in each State, excluding Indians not taxed. But when the right to vote at any election for the choice of electors for President and Vice President of the United States, Representatives in Congress, the Executive and Judicial officers of a State, or the members of the Legislature thereof, is denied to any of the male inhabitants of such State, being twenty-one years of age, and citizens of the United States, or in any way abridged, except for participation in rebellion, or other crime, the basis of representation therein shall be reduced in the proportion which the number of such male citizens shall bear to the whole number of male citizens twenty-one years of age in such State.

Section 3. No person shall be a Senator or Representative in Congress, or elector of President and Vice President, or hold any office, civil or military, under the United States, or under any State, who having previously taken an oath, as a member of Congress, or as an officer of the United States, or as a member of any State legislature, or as an executive or judicial officer of any State, to support the Constitution of the United States, shall have engaged in insurrection or rebellion against the same, or given aid or comfort to the enemies thereof. But Congress may by a vote of two-thirds of each House, remove such disability.

Section 4. The validity of the public debt of the United States, authorized by law, including debts incurred for payment of pensions and bounties for services in suppressing insurrection or rebellion, shall not be questioned. But neither the United States nor any State shall assume or pay any debt or obligation incurred in aid of insurrection or rebellion against the United States, or any claim for the loss or emancipation of any slave; but all such debts, obligations and claims shall be held illegal and void.

Section 5. The Congress shall have power to enforce, by appropriate legislation, the provisions of this article.

AMENDMENT XV [Ratified February 3, 1870]

Section 1. The right of citizens of the United States to vote shall not be denied or abridged by the United States or by any State on account of race, color, or previous condition of servitude.

Section 2. The Congress shall have power to enforce this article by appropriate legislation.

THE CIVIL RIGHTS CASES (1883)

The adoption of the Civil Rights Act of 1875 is generally seen as representing the last gasp of those who sought to use the power of the federal government to improve the lot of the recently emancipated slaves. The disputed presidential election of 1876 led to the decision to withdraw federal troops from the south and for all meaningful purposes ended Reconstruction. That year also marked the end of the ascendancy of the so-called Radical Republicans, men such as Pennsylvania's Representative Thaddeus Stevens and Massachusetts Senator Charles Sumner.

Although the Court in The Slaughterhouse Cases *(1873) had asserted that even "[t]he most cursory glance at [the Thirteenth, Fourteenth, and Fifteenth Amendments] discloses a unity of purpose ... the freedom of the slave race, the security and firm establishment of that freedom, and the protection of the newly-made freeman and citizen from the oppressions of those who had formerly exercised unlimited dominion over him," the Court's language in* The Civil Rights Cases *sounded a very different tone. Only the lone dissenter, the former Kentucky slave-holder, John*

Marshall Harlan, saw the power of the federal government to protect the freed slaves in such broad terms.

The Civil Rights Cases *established the principle that for there to be a violation of the Equal Protection Clause there needed to be evidence of "state action." This requirement continues to be followed today and is evidenced in the current Court's distinction between de jure segregation, segregation that results from action by law, by government, and de facto, segregation that results from factors over which government has no control, e.g., residential segregation, segregation that results from the choice of individuals as to where they wish to live.*

Justice Joseph BRADLEY delivered the opinion of the Court:

It is obvious that the primary and important question in all the cases is the constitutionality of the law; for if the law is unconstitutional none of the prosecutions can stand.

The sections of the law referred to provide as follows:

"Section 1. That all persons . . . shall be entitled to the full and equal enjoyment of the accommodations, advantages, facilities, and privileges of inns, public conveyances on land or water, theaters, and other places of public amusement; subject only to the conditions and limitations established by law, and applicable alike to citizens of every race and color, regardless of any previous condition of servitude.

Sec. 2. That any person who shall violate the foregoing section by denying to any citizen . . . the full enjoyment of any of the accomodations, advantages, facilities, or privileges . . . shall be fined not less than $500 nor more than $1,000, or shall be imprisoned not less than 30 days nor more than one year." . . .

Has congress constitutional power to make such a law? Of course, no one will contend that the power to pass it was contained in the constitution before the adoption of the last three amendments. The power is sought, first, in the fourteenth amendment. . . .

The first section of the fourteenth amendment . . . , after declaring who shall be citizens of the United States, and of the several states, is prohibitory in its character, and prohibitory upon the states. It declares that "[n]o state shall make or enforce any law which shall abridge the privileges or immunities of citizens of the United States; nor shall any state deprive any person of life, liberty, or property without due process of law; nor deny to any person within its jurisdiction the equal protection of the laws." It is state action of a particular character that is prohibited. Individual invasion of individual rights is not the subject matter of the amendment. . . .

. . . [U]ntil some state law has been passed, or some state action through its officers or agents has been taken, adverse to the rights of citizens sought to be protected by the fourteenth amendment, no legislation of the United States under said amendment . . . can be called into activity, for the prohibitions of the amendment are against state laws and acts done under state authority. . . .

It is absurd to affirm that, because the rights of life, liberty, and property (which include all civil rights that men have) are by the amendment sought to be protected against invasion on the part of the state without due process of law, congress may, therefore, provide due process of law for their vindication in every case; and that, because the denial by a state to any persons of the equal protection of the laws is prohibited by the amendment, therefore congress may establish laws for their equal protection. In fine, the legislation which congress is authorized to adopt in this behalf is not general legislation upon the rights of the citizen, but corrective legislation; that is, such as may be necessary and proper for counteracting such laws. . . .

An inspection of the law shows that it makes no reference whatever to any supposed or apprehended violation of the fourteenth amendment on the part of the states. . . . It proceeds *ex directo* to declare that certain acts committed by individuals shall be deemed offenses, and shall be prosecuted and punished by proceedings in the courts of the United States. It does not profess to be corrective of any constitutional wrong committed by the states. . . . It applies equally to cases arising in states which have the justest laws respecting the personal rights of citizens . . . as to those which arise in states that may have violated the prohibition of the amendment. In other words, it steps into the domain of local jurisprudence, and lays down rules for the conduct of individuals in society towards each other. . . . If this legislation is appropriate . . . , it is difficult to see where it is to stop. Why may not congress, with equal show of authority, enact a code of laws for the enforcement and vindication of all rights of life, liberty, and property? . . .

... [T]he power of congress to adopt direct and primary, as distinguished from corrective, legislation ... is sought, in the second place, from the thirteenth amendment, which abolishes slavery. ...

... Conceding the major proposition to be true, that congress has a right to enact all necessary and proper laws for the obliteration and prevention of slavery, with all its badges and incidents, is the minor proposition also true, that the denial to any person of admission to the accommodations and privileges of an inn, a public conveyance, or a theater, does subject that person to any form of servitude, or tend to fasten upon him any badge of slavery? If it does not, then power to pass the law is not found in the thirteenth amendment.

...

The long existence of African slavery in this country gave us very distinct notions of what it was, and what were its necessary incidents. Compulsory service of the slave for the benefit of the master, restraint of his movements except by the master's will, disability to hold property, to make contracts, to have a standing in court, to be a witness against a white person, and such like burdens and incapacities were the inseparable incidents of the institution. Severer punishments for crimes were imposed on the slave than on free persons guilty of the same offenses. Congress, as we have seen, by the civil rights bill of 1866, passed in view of the thirteenth amendment, before the fourteenth was adopted, undertook to wipe out these burdens and disabilities, the necessary incidents of slavery ... and to secure to all citizens of every race and color, and without regard to previous servitude, those fundamental rights which are the essence of civil freedom, namely, the same right to make and enforce contracts, to sue, be parties, give evidence, and to inherit, purchase, lease, sell, and convey property, as is enjoyed by white citizens. Whether this legislation was fully authorized by the thirteenth amendment alone, without the support which it afterwards received from the fourteenth amendment, after the adoption of which it was reenacted with some additions, it is not necessary to inquire. It is referred to for the purpose of showing that at that time (in 1866) congress did not assume, under the authority given by the thirteenth amendment, to adjust what may be called the social rights of men and races in the community; but only to declare and vindicate those fundamental rights which appertain to the essence of citizenship, and the enjoyment or deprivation of which constitutes the essential distinction between freedom and slavery. ... The only question under the present head, therefore, is, whether the refusal to any persons of the accommodations of an inn, or a public conveyance, or a place of public amusement, by an individual, and without any sanction or support from any state law or regulation, does inflict upon such persons any manner of servitude, or form of slavery, as those terms are understood in this country? . . .

. . . [W]e are forced to the conclusion that such an act of refusal has nothing to do with slavery or involuntary servitude, and that if it is violative of any right of the party, his redress is to be sought under the laws of the state; or, if those laws are adverse to his rights and do not protect him, his remedy will be found in the corrective legislation which congress has adopted, or may adopt. . . . It would be running the slavery argument into the ground to make it apply to every act of discrimination which a person may see fit to make as to the guests he will entertain, or as to the people he will take into his coach or cab or car, or admit to his concert or theater, or deal with in other matters of intercourse or business. Innkeepers and public carriers, by the laws of all the states, so far as we are aware, are bound, to the extent of their facilities, to furnish proper accommodation to all unobjectionable persons who in good faith apply for them. If the laws themselves make any unjust discrimination, amenable to the prohibitions of the fourteenth amendment, congress has full power to afford a remedy under that amendment and in accordance with it.

When a man has emerged from slavery, and by the aid of beneficent legislation has shaken off the inseparable concomitants of that state, there must be some stage in the progress of his elevation when he takes the rank of a mere citizen, and ceases to be the special favorite of the laws, and when his rights as a citizen, or a man, are to be protected in the ordinary modes by which other men's rights are protected. There were thousands of free colored people in this country before the abolition of slavery. . . . Mere discriminations on account of race or color were not regarded as badges of slavery. . . .

. . . [W]e are of opinion that no . . . authority for . . . the law in question can be found in either the thirteenth or fourteenth amendment of the constitution; and . . . it must necessarily be declared void . . .

Justice John HARLAN, dissenting.

The opinion in these cases proceeds . . . upon grounds entirely too narrow and artificial. The substance and spirit of the recent amendments of the constitution have been sacrificed by a subtle and ingenious verbal criticism. "It is not the words of the law but the internal sense of it that makes the law. The letter of the law is the body; the sense and reason of the law is the soul." Constitutional provisions, adopted in the interest of liberty, and for the purpose of securing, through national legislation, if need be, rights inhering in a state of freedom, and belonging to American citizenship, have been so construed as to defeat the ends the people desired to accomplish, which they attempted to accomplish, and which they supposed they had accomplished by changes in their fundamental law. . . .

The thirteenth amendment, my brethren concede, did something more than to prohibit slavery. . . . They admit that it established and decreed universal civil freedom throughout the United States. But did the freedom thus established involve nothing more than exemption from actual slavery? Was nothing more intended than to forbid one man from owning another as property? Was it the purpose of the nation simply to destroy the institution, and then remit the race, theretofore held in bondage, to the several states for such protection, in their civil rights, necessarily growing out of freedom, as those states, in their discretion, choose to provide? Were the states, against whose solemn protest the institution was destroyed, to be left perfectly free, so far as national interference was concerned, to make or allow discriminations against that race, as such, in the enjoyment of those fundamental rights that inhere in a state of freedom? . . .

That there are burdens and disabilities which constitute badges of slavery and servitude, and that the express power delegated to congress to enforce, by appropriate legislation, the thirteenth amendment, may be exerted by legislation of a direct and primary character . . . are propositions which ought to be deemed indisputable. They lie at the very foundation of the civil rights act of 1866. Whether that act was fully authorized by the thirteenth amendment alone, without the support which it afterwards received from the fourteenth amendment, after the adoption of which it was reenacted with some additions, the court, in its opinion, says it is unnecessary to inquire. . . .

Congress has not . . . entered the domain of state control and supervision. It does not assume to prescribe the general conditions and limitations under which inns, public conveyances, and places of public amusement shall be conducted or managed. It simply declares in effect that since the nation has established universal freedom in this country for all time, there shall be no discrimination, based merely upon race or color, in respect of the legal rights in the accommodations and advantages of public conveyances, inns, and places of public amusement.

I am of opinion that such discrimination is a badge of servitude, the imposition of which congress may prevent under its power, through appropriate legislation, to enforce the thirteenth amendment; and consequently, without reference to its enlarged power under the fourteenth amendment, the act of March 1, 1875, is not, in my judgment, repugnant to the constitution.

It remains now to consider these cases with reference to the power congress has possessed since the adoption of the fourteenth amendment.

Before the adoption of the recent amendments it had become . . . the established doctrine of this court that negroes, whose ancestors had been imported and sold as slaves, could not become citizens of a state, or even of the United States, with the rights and privileges guarantied to citizens by the national constitution; further, that one might have all the rights and privileges of a citizen of a state without being a citizen in the sense in which that word was used in the national constitution, and without being entitled to the privileges and immunities of citizens of the several states. Still further, between the adoption of the thirteenth amendment and the proposal by congress of the fourteenth amendment, on June 16, 1866, the statute-books of several of the states, as we have seen, had become loaded down with enactments which, under the guise of apprentice, vagrant, and contract regulations, sought to keep the colored race in a condition, practically, of servitude. It was openly announced that whatever rights persons of that race might have as freemen, under the guaranties of the national constitution, they could not become citizens of a state, with the rights belonging to citizens, except by the consent of such state; consequently, that their civil rights, as citizens of the state, depended entirely upon state legislation. To meet this new peril to the black race, that the purposes of the nation might not be doubted or defeated, and by way of further enlargement of the power of congress, the fourteenth amendment was proposed for adoption.

Remembering that this court, in the *Slaughterhouse Cases,* declared that the one pervading purpose found in all the recent amendments, lying at the foundation of each, and without which none of them would have been suggested, was "the freedom of the slave race, the security and firm establishment of that freedom, and the protection of the newly-made freeman and citizen from the oppression of those who had formerly exercised unlimited dominion over him;" that each amendment was addressed primarily to the grievances of that race. . . .

This court has always given a broad and liberal construction to the constitution, so as to enable congress, by legislation, to enforce rights secured by that instrument. . . . Under given circumstances, that which the court characterizes as corrective legislation might be sufficient. Under other circumstances primary direct legislation may be required. But it is for congress, not the judiciary, to say which is best adapted to the end to be attained. . . .

My brethren say that when a man has emerged from slavery, and by the aid of beneficient legislation has shaken off the inseparable concomitants of that state, there must be some stage in the progress of his elevation when he takes the rank of a mere citizen, and ceases to be the special favorite of the laws, and when his rights as a citizen, or a man, are to be protected in the ordinary modes by which other men's rights are protected. It is, I submit, scarcely just to say that the colored race has been the special favorite of the laws. What the nation, through congress, has sought to accomplish in reference to that race is, what had already been done in every state in the Union for the white race, to secure and protect rights belonging to them as freemen and citizens; nothing more. The one underlying purpose of congressional legislation has been to enable the black race to take the rank of mere citizens. The difficulty has been to compel a recognition of their legal right to take that rank, and to secure the enjoyment of privileges belonging, under the law, to them as a component part of the people for whose welfare and happiness government is ordained. At every step in this direction the nation has been confronted with class tyranny, which a contemporary English historian says is, of all tyrannies, the most intolerable. . . . Today it is the colored race which is denied, by corporations and individuals wielding public authority, rights fundamental in their freedom and citizenship. At some future time it may be some other race that will fall under the ban. If the constitutional amendments be enforced, according to the intent with which, as I conceive, they were adopted, there cannot be, in this republic, any class of human beings in practical subjection to another class, with power in the latter to dole out to the former just such privileges as they may choose to grant. . . .

For the reasons stated I feel constrained to withhold my assent to the opinion of the court.

PLESSY V. FERGUSON (1896)

Justice Joseph Bradley found in The Civil Rights Cases *that the Civil Rights Act of 1875 went beyond the powers granted to the federal government in that the activities prohibited were not the result of state action, but rather represented the choices of private individuals.* Plessy *stemmed from a situation that clearly involved state action. Louisiana adopted legislation that required the separation of the two races on railroad cars. Homer Plessy, seven-eighths white and one eighth black, took a seat in the "whites-only" carriage, but was requested to move. He sued. Again only Justice Harlan dissented. The opinion of the Court was written by Harvard-educated Justice Henry Brown. His opinion sanctioned the concept of "separate but equal."*

Mr. Justice BROWN delivered the opinion of the Court.

This case turns upon the constitutionality of an act . . . of Louisiana, passed in 1890, providing for separate railway carriages for the white and colored races.

The first section of the statute enacts "that all railway companies carrying passengers in their coaches in this state, shall provide equal but separate accommodations for the white, and colored races, providing two or more passenger coaches for each passenger train, or by dividing the passenger coaches by a partition so as to secure separate accommodations. . . . No person or persons shall be permitted to occupy seats in coaches, other than the ones assigned to them, on account of the race they belong to."

. . .

The information . . . charged . . . that Plessy . . . was assigned . . . to the coach used for the race to which he belonged, but he insisted upon going into a coach used by the race to which he did not belong. . . .

. . .

The constitutionality of this act is attacked upon the ground that it conflicts both with the thirteenth amendment of the constitution, abolishing slavery, and the fourteenth amendment, which prohibits certain restrictive legislation on the part of the states.

1. That it does not conflict with the thirteenth amendment . . . is too clear for argument. Slavery implies involuntary servitude,—a state of bondage; the ownership of mankind as a chattel, or, at least, the control of the labor and services of one man for the benefit of another. . . .

. . . [I]n the *Civil Rights Cases,* it was said that the act of a mere individual . . . refusing accommodations to colored people, cannot be justly regarded as imposing any badge of slavery or servitude upon the applicant, but only as involving an ordinary civil injury, properly cognizable by the laws of the state, and presumably subject to redress by those laws. . . .

A statute which implies merely a legal distinction between the white and colored races—a distinction which is founded in the color of the two races, and which must always exist so long as white men are distinguished from the other race by color—has no tendency to destroy the legal equality of the two races, or re-establish a state of involuntary servitude. . . .

2. By the fourteenth amendment, all persons born or naturalized in the United States, and subject to the jurisdiction thereof, are made citizens of the United States and of the state wherein they reside; and the states are forbidden from making or enforcing any law which shall abridge the privileges or immunities of citizens of the United States, or shall deprive any person of life, liberty, or property without due process of law, or deny to any person within their jurisdiction the equal protection of the laws.

. . . The object of the amendment was undoubtedly to enforce the absolute equality of the two races before the law, but, in the nature of things, it could not have been intended to abolish distinctions based upon color, or to enforce social, as distinguished from political, equality, or a commingling of the two races upon terms unsatisfactory to either. Laws permitting, and even requiring, their separation, in places where they are liable to be brought into contact, do not necessarily imply the inferiority of either race to the other, and have been generally, if not universally, recognized as within the competency of the state legislatures in the exercise of their police power. The most common instance of this is connected with the establishment of separate schools for white and colored children, which have been held to be a valid exercise of the legislative power even by courts of states where the political rights of the colored race have been longest and most earnestly enforced.

One of the earliest of these cases is that of *Roberts v. City of Boston*, in which the supreme judicial court of Massachusetts held that the general school committee of Boston had power to make provision for the instruction of colored children in separate schools established exclusively for them, and to prohibit their attendance upon the other schools. "The great principle," said Chief Justice Shaw, "advanced by the learned and eloquent advocate for the plaintiff [Mr. Charles Sumner], is that, by the constitution and laws of Massachusetts, all persons, without distinction of age or sex, birth or color, origin or condition, are equal before the law. . . . But, when this great principle comes to be applied to the actual and various conditions of persons in society, it will not warrant the assertion that men and women are legally clothed with the same civil and political powers, and that children and adults are legally to have the same functions and be subject to the same treatment; but only that the rights of all, as they are settled and regulated by law, are equally entitled to the paternal consideration and protection of the law for their maintenance and security." It was held that the powers of the committee extended to the establishment of separate schools for children of different ages, sexes and colors, and that they might also establish special schools for poor and neglected children, who have become too old to attend the primary school. . . . Similar laws have been enacted by congress under its general power of legislation over the District of Columbia. . . .

The distinction between laws interfering with the political equality of the negro and those requiring the separation of the two races in schools, theaters, and railway carriages has been frequently drawn by this court. Thus, in *Strauder v. West Virginia*, it was held that a law . . . limiting to white male persons 21 years of age, and citizens of the state, the right to sit upon juries, was a discrimination which implied a legal inferiority in civil society, which lessened the security of the right of the colored race, and was a step towards reducing them to a condition of servility. . . .

. . . [I]t is also suggested by the learned counsel for the plaintiff in error that the same argument that will justify the state legislature in requiring railways to provide separate accommodations for the two races will also authorize them to require separate cars to be provided for people whose hair is of a certain color, or who are aliens, or who belong to certain nationalities, or to enact laws requiring colored people to walk upon one side of the street, and white people upon the other, or requiring white men's houses to be painted white, and colored men's black, or their vehicles or business signs to be of different colors, upon the theory that one side of the street is as good as the other, or that a house or vehicle of one color is as good as one of another color. The reply to all this is that every exercise of the police power must be reasonable, and extend only to such laws as are enacted in good faith for the promotion of the public good, and not for the annoyance or oppression of a particular class. Thus, in *Yick Wo v. Hopkins,* it was held by this court that a municipal ordinance ... regulat[ing] the carrying on of public laundries ... violated ... the constitution ... , if it conferred upon the municipal authorities arbitrary power ... It was held to be a covert attempt ... to make an arbitrary and unjust discrimination against the Chinese race. ...

We consider the underlying fallacy of the plaintiff's argument to consist in the assumption that the enforced separation of the two races stamps the colored race with a badge of inferiority. If this be so, it is not by reason of anything found in the act, but solely because the colored race chooses to put that construction upon it. The argument necessarily assumes that if, as has been more than once the case, and is not unlikely to be so again, the colored race should become the dominant power in the state legislature, and should enact a law in precisely similar terms, it would thereby relegate the white race to an inferior position. We imagine that the white race; at least, would not acquiesce in this assumption. The argument also assumes that social prejudices may be overcome by legislation, and that equal rights cannot be secured to the negro except by an enforced commingling of the two races. We cannot accept this proposition. If the two races are to meet upon terms of social equality, it must be the result of natural affinities, a mutual appreciation of each other's merits, and a voluntary consent of individuals. ... Legislation is powerless to eradicate racial instincts, or to abolish distinctions based upon physical differences, and the attempt to do so can only result in accentuating the difficulties of the present situation. If the civil and political rights of both races be equal, one cannot be inferior to the other civilly or politically. If one race be inferior to the other socially, the constitution of the United States cannot put them upon the same plane.

. . .

The judgment of the court below is therefore affirmed.

Mr. Justice BREWER did not hear the argument or participate in the decision of this case.

Mr. Justice HARLAN dissenting.

 . . .The thirteenth amendment does not permit the withholding or the deprivation of any right necessarily inhering in freedom. It not only struck down the institution of slavery as previously existing in the United States, but it prevents the imposition of any burdens or disabilities that constitute badges of slavery or servitude. . . . But, that amendment having been found inadequate to the protection of the rights of those who had been in slavery, it was followed by the fourteenth amendment, which added greatly to the dignity and glory of American citizenship, and to the security of personal liberty. . . . These two amendments, if enforced according to their true intent and meaning, will protect all the civil rights that pertain to freedom and citizenship. . . .

These notable additions to the fundamental law were welcomed by the friends of liberty throughout the world. They removed the race line from our governmental systems. They had, as this court has said, a common purpose, namely, to secure "to a race recently emancipated, a race that through many generations have been held in slavery, all the civil rights that the superior race enjoy." They declared, in legal effect, this court has further said, "that the law in the states shall be the same for the black as for the white; that all persons, whether colored or white, shall stand equal before the laws of the states; and in regard to the colored race, for whose protection the amendment was primarily designed, that no discrimination shall be made against them by law because of their color. . . ."

It was said . . . that . . . Louisiana does not discriminate against either race, but prescribes a rule applicable alike to white and colored citizens. But this argument does not meet the difficulty. Every one knows that the statute in question had its origin in the purpose, not so much to exclude white persons from railroad cars occupied by blacks, as to exclude colored people from coaches occupied by or assigned to white persons. . . . No one would be so wanting in candor as to assert the contrary. . . .

The white race deems itself to be the dominant race in this country. And so it is, in prestige, in achievements, in education, in wealth, and in power. So, I doubt not, it will continue to be for all time, if it remains true to its great heritage, and holds fast to the principles of constitutional liberty. But in view of the constitution, in the eye of the law, there is in this country no superior, dominant, ruling class of citizens. There is no caste here. Our constitution is color-blind, and neither knows nor tolerates classes among citizens. In respect of civil rights, all citizens are equal before the law. The humblest is the peer of the most powerful. The law regards man as man, and takes no account of his surroundings or of his color. . . .

In my opinion, the judgment this day rendered will, in time, prove to be quite as pernicious as the decision made by this tribunal in the *Dred Scott* case.

BROWN V. BOARD OF EDUCATION (1954)

Beginning in 1939, the Legal Defense Fund of the National Association for the Advancement of Colored People (NAACP) had mapped a careful strategy aimed at bringing about the end of segregation in education through litigation. The Vinson Court accepted the Brown suit against the Board of Education of Topeka along with challenges to public schools located in Virginia, South Carolina, Delaware, and the District of Columbia. The Court's decision in the latter case, based on the argument that segregation of the district's schools by Congress violated the Fifth Amendment's due process guarantee, was decided separately from Brown and is known as Bolling v. Sharpe.

Brown was first argued in December of 1952. Most scholars agree that the Court was divided after the first argument. The Court took the unusual step of requesting a second round of arguments. This took place a year later with a new chief justice, Earl Warren. Warren, with the help of Justice Felix Frankfurter, was able to unify all nine justices behind his relatively brief opinion. The Court found "separate but equal" had no place in public education in the 1950s. Having reached that conclusion, the Court called for further argument as to how its decision would be implemented. This was handed down a year later in Brown II.

Mr. Chief Justice WARREN delivered the opinion of the Court.

These cases come to us from the States of Kansas, South Carolina, Virginia, and Delaware. . . .

The plaintiffs contend that segregated public schools are not "equal" and cannot be made "equal," and that hence they are deprived of the equal protection of the laws. . . . Argument was heard in the 1952 Term, and re-argument was heard this Term. . . .

Reargument was largely devoted to the circumstances surrounding the adoption of the Fourteenth Amendment in 1868. It covered exhaustively consideration of the Amendment in Congress, ratification by the states, then existing practices in racial segregation, and the views of proponents and opponents of the Amendment. This discussion and our own investigation convince us that, although these sources cast some light, it is not enough to resolve the problem with which we are faced. At best, they are inconclusive. The most avid proponents of the post-War Amendments undoubtedly intended them to remove all legal distinctions among "all persons born or naturalized in the United States." Their opponents, just as certainly, were antagonistic to both the letter and the spirit of the Amendments and wished them to have the most limited effect. What others in Congress and the state legislatures had in mind cannot be determined with any degree of certainty.

. . .

In the first cases in this Court construing the Fourteenth Amendment, decided shortly after its adoption, the Court interpreted it as proscribing all state-imposed discriminations against the Negro race. The doctrine of "separate but equal" did not make its appearance in this Court until 1896 in the case of *Plessy v. Ferguson,* involving not education but transportation. American courts have since labored with the doctrine for over half a century. . . .

We come then to the question presented: Does segregation of children in public schools solely on the basis of race, even though the physical facilities and other "tangible" factors may be equal, deprive the children of the minority group of equal educational opportunities? We believe that it does.

In *Sweatt v. Painter,* in finding that a segregated law school for Negroes could not provide them equal educational opportunities, this Court relied in large part on "those qualities which are incapable of objective measurement but which make for greatness in a law school." In *McLaurin v. Oklahoma State Regents,* the Court, in requiring that a Negro admitted to a white graduate school be treated like all other students, again resorted to intangible considerations: " . . . his ability to study, to engage in discussions and exchange views with other students, and, in general, to learn his profession."

Such considerations apply with added force to children in grade and high schools. To separate them from others of similar age and qualifications solely because of their race generates a feeling of inferiority as to their status in the community that may affect their hearts and minds in a way unlikely ever to be undone. The effect of this separation on their educational opportunities was well stated by a finding in the Kansas case by a court which nevertheless felt compelled to rule against the Negro plaintiffs:

> Segregation of white and colored children in public schools has a detrimental effect upon the colored children. The impact is greater when it has the sanction of the law; for the policy of separating the races is usually interpreted as denoting the inferiority of the negro group. A sense of inferiority affects the motivation of a child to learn. Segregation with the sanction of law, therefore, has a tendency to [retard] the educational and mental development of negro children and to deprive them of some of the benefits they would receive in a racial[ly] integrated school system.

Whatever may have been the extent of psychological knowledge at the time of *Plessy v. Ferguson*, this finding is amply supported by modern authority. Any language in *Plessy v. Ferguson* contrary to this finding is rejected.

We conclude that in the field of public education the doctrine of "separate but equal" has no place. Separate educational facilities are inherently unequal. Therefore, we hold that the plaintiffs and others similarly situated for whom the actions have been brought are, by reason of the segregation complained of, deprived of the equal protection of the laws guaranteed by the Fourteenth Amendment. . . .

BROWN V. BOARD OF EDUCATION II (1955)

The Court's decision in 1955 is generally referred to as Brown II. *In it, the Court's left it to federal district courts to supervise the desegregation process. Warren's opinion ended with a phrase taken from an earlier decision by legendary Justice Oliver Wendell Holmes, Jr.: "with all deliber-*

ate speed." Later critics of the decision would observe that although there was much deliberation by southern school boards as to how they should comply with Brown, there was no speed. Few African American students from segregated or dual school systems would find their situation at all changed by the end of the 1950s.

Mr. Chief Justice WARREN delivered the opinion of the Court.

These cases were decided on May 17, 1954. The opinions of that date, declaring the fundamental principle that racial discrimination in public education is unconstitutional, are incorporated herein by reference. All provisions of federal, state, or local law requiring or permitting such discrimination must yield to this principle. There remains for consideration the manner in which relief is to be accorded.

. . .

Full implementation of these constitutional principles may require solution of varied local school problems. School authorities have the primary responsibility for elucidating, assessing, and solving these problems; courts will have to consider whether the action of school authorities constitutes good faith implementation of the governing constitutional principles. Because of their proximity to local conditions and the possible need for further hearings, the courts which originally heard these cases can best perform this judicial appraisal. Accordingly, we believe it appropriate to remand the cases to those courts.

. . . [T]he courts will require that the defendants make a prompt and reasonable start toward full compliance with our May 17, 1954, ruling. Once such a start has been made, the courts may find that additional time is necessary to carry out the ruling in an effective manner. The burden rests upon the defendants to establish that such time is necessary in the public interest and is consistent with good faith compliance at the earliest practicable date. To that end, the courts may consider problems related to administration, arising from the physical condition of the school plant, the school transportation system, personnel, revision of school districts and attendance areas into compact units to achieve a system of determining admission to the public schools on a nonracial basis, and revision of local laws and regulations which may be necessary in solving the foregoing problems. They will also consider the adequacy of any plans the defendants may propose to meet these problems and to effectuate a transition to a racially nondiscriminatory school system. During this period of transition, the courts will retain jurisdiction of these cases.

The judgments below, except that in the Delaware case, are accordingly reversed and the cases are remanded to the District Courts to take such proceedings and enter such orders and decrees consistent with this opinion as are necessary and proper to admit to public schools on a racially nondiscriminatory basis with all deliberate speed the parties to these cases. . . .

COOPER V. AARON (1958)

In the oral argument that preceded the first Brown *decision, South Carolina's distinguished attorney, John W. Davis, had warned the Court that South Carolina had no intention of coming before the Court in "sackcloth and ashes as Thad Stevens would have wished." Davis's warning was to prove accurate. The defenders of school segregation and the South's vast panoply of Jim Crow legislation would not give way easily.*

Arkansas and its capital, Little Rock, seemed different. Given its topography, the plantation system had never really been established in Arkansas as it had been in the more fertile coastal states of the south. The Little Rock School Board seemed ready to take steps to begin to end segregation. The state's governor, Orville Faubus, had different ideas. Faubus's defiance led to the Court's issuing an opinion signed by all nine justices. The opinion asserted that not only was the Constitution the supreme law of the land, but decisions of the Court were also the supreme law of the land.

Opinion of the Court by the Chief Justice, Mr. Justice BLACK, Mr. Justice FRANKFURTER, Mr. Justice DOUGLAS, Mr. Justice BURTON, Mr. Justice CLARK, Mr. Justice HARLAN, Mr. Justice BRENNAN, and Mr. Justice WHITTAKER announced September 29, 1958.

As this case reaches us it raises questions of the highest importance to the maintenance of our federal system of government. It necessarily involves a claim by the Governor and Legislature of a State that there is no duty on state officials to obey federal court orders resting on this Court's considered interpretation of the United States Constitution. Specifically it involves actions by the Governor and Legislature of

Arkansas upon the premise that they are not bound by our holding in *Brown v. Board of Education. . . .* We reject these contentions.

. . .

The controlling legal principles are plain. The command of the Fourteenth Amendment is that no "State" shall deny to any person within its jurisdiction the equal protection of the laws. . . ." The constitutional provision, therefore, must mean that no agency of the State, or of the officers or agents by whom its powers are exerted, shall deny to any person within its jurisdiction the equal protection of the laws. Whoever, by virtue of public position under a State government, . . . denies or takes away the equal protection of the laws, violates the constitutional inhibition; and as he acts in the name and for the State, and is clothed with the State's power, his act is that of the State. . . . In short, the constitutional rights of children not to be discriminated against in school admission on grounds of race or color declared by this Court in the *Brown* case can neither be nullified openly and directly by state legislators or state executive or judicial officers, nor nullified indirectly by them through evasive schemes for segregation whether attempted "ingeniously or ingenuously."

What has been said, in the light of the facts developed, is enough to dispose of the case. However, we should answer the premise of the actions of the Governor and Legislature that they are not bound by our holding in the *Brown* case. It is necessary only to recall some basic constitutional propositions which are settled doctrine.

Article VI . . . makes the Constitution the "supreme Law of the Land." In 1803, Chief Justice Marshall, speaking for a unanimous Court, referring to the Constitution as "the fundamental and paramount law of the nation," declared in the notable case of *Marbury v. Madison* that "It is emphatically the province and duty of the judicial department to say what the law is." This decision declared the basic principle that the federal judiciary is supreme in the exposition of the law of the Constitution, and that principle has ever since been respected by this Court and the Country as a permanent and indispensable feature of our constitutional system. It follows that the interpretation of the Fourteenth Amendment enunciated by this Court in the *Brown* case is the supreme law of the land, and Art. VI of the Constitution makes it of binding effect on the States "any Thing in the Constitution or Laws of any State to the Contrary notwithstanding." Every state legislator and executive and judicial officer is solemnly committed by oath taken pursuant to Art. VI, cl. 3, "to support this Constitution." Chief Justice Taney, speaking for a unanimous Court in 1859, said that this requirement reflected the framers' "anxiety to preserve it [the Constitution] in full force, in all its powers, and to guard against resistance to or evasion of its authority, on the part of a State. . . ."

No state legislator or executive or judicial officer can war against the Constitution without violating his undertaking to support it. Chief Justice Marshall spoke for a unanimous Court in saying that: "If the legislatures of the several states may, at will, annul the judgments of the courts of the United States, and destroy the rights acquired under those judgments, the constitution itself becomes a solemn mockery . . ." (*United States v. Peters*). . . .

Concurring opinion of Mr. Justice FRANKFURTER.
While unreservedly participating with my brethren in our joint opinion, I deem it appropriate also to deal individually with the great issue here at stake.

. . .

We are now asked to hold that the illegal, forcible interference by the State of Arkansas with the continuance of what the Constitution commands, and the consequences in disorder that it entrained, should be recognized as justification for undoing what the School Board had formulated, what the District Court in 1955 had directed to be carried out, and what was in process of obedience. No explanation that may be offered in support of such a request can obscure the inescapable meaning that law should bow to force. To yield to such a claim would be to enthrone official lawlessness, and lawlessness if not checked is the precursor of anarchy. On the few tragic occasions in the history of the Nation, North and South, when law was forcibly resisted or systematically evaded, it has signalled the breakdown of constitutional processes of government on which ultimately rest the liberties of all. Violent resistance to law cannot be made a legal reason for its suspension without loosening the fabric of our society. What could this mean but to acknowledge that disorder under the aegis of a State has moral superiority over the law of the Constitution? For those in authority thus to defy the law of the land is profoundly subversive not only of our constitutional system but of the presuppositions of a democratic society. The State "must . . . yield to an authority that is paramount to the State." This language of command to a State is Mr. Justice Holmes'....

The duty to abstain from resistance to "the supreme Law of the Land," U.S. Const., Art. VI 12, as declared by the organ of our Government for ascertaining it, does not require immediate approval of it nor does it deny the right of dissent. Criticism need not be stilled. Active obstruction or defiance is barred.... The Constitution is not the formulation of the merely personal views of the members of this Court, nor can its authority be reduced to the claim that state officials are its controlling interpreters. Local customs, however hardened by time, are not decreed in heaven....

REYNOLDS V. SIMS (1964)

In 1962 in the case of Baker v. Carr, the Court finally agreed that the issue of legislative apportionment was justiciable and not a "political question," a matter to be left to the sole discretion of the two political branches of government, the legislature and the executive. Reynolds found that the right to vote was a fundamental right and that as a result any system of apportionment that was not based on population was a violation of the Fourteenth Amendment. With this opinion, the Court rejected the so-called "federal analogy." On this basis, many states had provided that while one branch of the legislature would be based on population the other branch would be based on some other method of representation, for example, equal representation for each of a state's counties regardless of population.

Mr. Chief Justice WARREN delivered the opinion of the Court.

...The right to vote freely for the candidate of one's choice is of the essence of a democratic society, and any restrictions on that right strike at the heart of representative government. And the right of suffrage can be denied by a debasement or dilution of the weight of a citizen's vote just as effectively as by wholly prohibiting the free exercise of the franchise.

... [S]ince the right to exercise the franchise in a free and unimpaired manner is preservative of other basic civil and political rights, any alleged infringement of the right of citizens to vote must be carefully and meticulously scrutinized. Almost a century ago, in *Yick Wo v. Hopkins*, the Court referred to "the political franchise of voting" as "a fundamental political right, because preservative of all rights."

Legislators represent people, not trees or acres. Legislators are elected by voters, not farms or cities or economic interests. As long as ours is a representative form of government, and our legislatures are those instruments of government elected directly by and directly representative of the people, the right to elect legislators in a free and unimpaired fashion is a bedrock of our political system. It could hardly be gainsaid that a constitutional claim had been asserted by an allegation that certain otherwise qualified voters had been entirely prohibited from voting for members of their state legislature. And, if a State should provide that the votes of citizens in one part of the State should be given two times, or five times, or 10 times the weight of votes of citizens in another part of the State, it could hardly be contended that the right to vote of those residing in the disfavored areas had not been effectively diluted. . . .

Logically, in a society ostensibly grounded on representative government, it would seem reasonable that a majority of the people of a State could elect a majority of that State's legislators. To conclude differently, and to sanction minority control of state legislative bodies, would appear to deny majority rights in a way that far surpasses any possible denial of minority rights that might otherwise be thought to result. . . . Since the achieving of fair and effective representation for all citizens is concededly the basic aim of legislative apportionment, we conclude that the Equal Protection Clause guarantees the opportunity for equal participation by all voters in the election of state legislators. Diluting the weight of votes because of place of residence impairs basic constitutional rights under the Fourteenth Amendment just as much as invidious discriminations based upon factors such as race (*Brown v. Board of Education*). . . . Our constitutional system amply provides for the protection of minorities by means other than giving them majority control of state legislatures. And the democratic ideals of equality and majority rule, which have served this Nation so well in the past, are hardly of any less significance for the present and the future.

We are told that the matter of apportioning representation in a state legislature is a complex and many-faceted one. We are advised that States can rationally consider factors other than population in apportioning legislative representation. We are admonished not to restrict the power of the States to impose differing views as to political philosophy on their citizens. We are cautioned about the dangers of entering into political thickets and mathematical quagmires. Our answer is this: a denial of constitutionally protected rights demands judicial protection; our oath and our office require no less of us. . . .

We hold that, as a basic constitutional standard, the Equal Protection Clause requires that the seats in both houses of a bicameral state legislature must be apportioned on a population basis. Simply stated, an individual's right to vote for state legislators is unconstitutionally impaired when its weight is in a substantial fashion diluted when compared with votes of citizens living in other parts of the state. . . .

By holding that as a federal constitutional requisite both houses of a state legislature must be apportioned on a population basis, we mean that the Equal Protection Clause requires that a State make an honest and good faith effort to construct districts, in both houses of its legislature, as nearly of equal population as is practicable. We realize that it is a practical impossibility to arrange legislative districts so that each one has an identical number of residents, or citizens, or voters. Mathematical exactness or precision is hardly a workable constitutional requirement.

Mr. Justice HARLAN, dissenting.

. . .The Court's constitutional discussion . . . is remarkable . . . for its failure to address itself at all to the Fourteenth Amendment as a whole or to the legislative history of the Amendment pertinent to the matter at hand. Stripped of aphorisms, the Court's argument boils down to the assertion that appellees' right to vote has been invidiously "debased" or "diluted" by systems of apportionment which entitle them to vote for fewer legislators than other voters, an assertion which is tied to the Equal Protection Clause only by the constitutionally frail tautology that "equal" means "equal."

Had the Court paused to probe more deeply into the matter, it would have found that the Equal Protection Clause was never intended to inhibit the States in choosing any democratic method they pleased for the apportionment of their legislatures. This is shown by the language of the Fourteenth Amendment taken as a whole, by the understanding of those who proposed and ratified it, and by the political practices of the States at the time the Amendment was adopted. It is confirmed by numerous state and congressional actions since the adoption of the Fourteenth Amendment, and by the common understanding of the Amendment as evidenced by subsequent constitutional amendments and decisions of this Court before *Baker v. Carr* made an abrupt break with the past in 1962.

The failure of the Court to consider any of these matters cannot be excused or explained by any concept of "developing" constitutionalism. It is meaningless to speak of constitutional "development" when both the language and history of the controlling provisions of the Constitution are wholly ignored. . . .

The Court's elaboration of its new "constitutional" doctrine indicates how far—and how unwisely—it has strayed from the appropriate bounds of its authority. The consequence of today's decision is that in all but the handful of States which may already satisfy the new requirements the local District Court or, it may be, the state courts, are given blanket authority and the constitutional duty to supervise apportionment of the State Legislatures. It is difficult to imagine a more intolerable and inappropriate interference by the judiciary with the independent legislatures of the States.

. . .

These decisions also cut deeply into the fabric of our federalism. What must follow from them may eventually appear to be the product of state legislatures. Nevertheless, no thinking person can fail to recognize that the aftermath of these cases, however desirable it may be thought in itself, will have been achieved at the cost of a radical alteration in the relationship between the States and the Federal Government, more particularly the Federal Judiciary. Only one who has an overbearing impatience with the federal system and its political processes will believe that that cost was not too high or was inevitable.

Finally, these decisions give support to a current mistaken view of the Constitution and the constitutional function of this Court. This view, in a nutshell, is that every major social ill in this country can find its cure in some constitutional "principle," and that this Court should "take the lead" in promoting reform when other branches of government fail to act. The Constitution is not a panacea for every blot upon the public welfare, nor should this Court, ordained as a judicial body, be thought of as a general haven for reform movements. The Constitution is an instrument of government, fundamental to which is the premise that in a diffusion of governmental authority lies the greatest promise that this Nation will realize liberty for all its citizens. This Court, limited in function in accordance with that premise, does not serve its high purpose when it exceeds its authority, even to satisfy justified impatience with the slow workings of the political process. For when, in the name of constitutional interpretation, the Court adds something to the Constitution that was deliberately excluded from it, the Court in reality substitutes its view of what should be so for the amending process.

GREEN V. COUNTY SCHOOL BOARD (1968)

Contrary to much of public opinion, the end of segregation did not automatically result in integration. Green *represented the Court's final frustration with the lack of "all deliberate speed." More than that, however, the Brennan opinion found that so-called "freedom of choice" plans would not suffice. Systems that had operated as "dual systems" were now put on notice that they must take steps to transform themselves into unitary, that is, integrated systems.*

Mr. Justice BRENNAN delivered the opinion of the Court.

The question for decision is whether . . . respondent School Board's . . . "freedom-of-choice" plan . . . constitutes adequate compliance with the Board's responsibility "to achieve a system of determining admission to the public schools on a nonracial basis (*Brown v. Board of Education II*). . . .

Petitioners brought this action . . . seeking injunctive relief against respondent's continued maintenance of an alleged racially segregated school system. New Kent County is a rural county in Eastern Virginia. About one-half of its population of some 4,500 are Negroes. There is no residential segregation in the county; persons of both races reside throughout. The school system has only two schools, the New Kent school on the east side of the county and the George W. Watkins school on the west side. . . . [T]he District Court found that the "school system serves approximately 1,300 pupils, of which 740 are Negro and 550 are White. The School Board operates one white combined elementary and high school [New Kent], and one Negro combined elementary and high school [George W. Watkins]. There are no attendance zones. Each school serves the entire county." The record indicates that 21 school buses—11 serving the Watkins school and 10 serving the New Kent school—travel overlapping routes throughout the county to transport pupils to and from the two schools.

The segregated system was initially established and maintained under the compulsion of Virginia constitutional and statutory provisions mandating racial segregation in public education. . . .

The pattern of separate "white" and "Negro" schools . . . established under compulsion of state laws is precisely the pattern of segregation to which *Brown I* and *Brown II* were particularly addressed, and which *Brown I* declared unconstitutionally denied Negro school children equal protection of the laws. Racial identification of the system's schools was complete, extending not just to the composition of student bodies at the two schools but to every facet of school operations—faculty, staff, transportation, extracurricular activities and facilities. In short, the State, acting through the local school board and school officials, organized and operated a dual system, part "white" and part "Negro."

It was such dual systems that 14 years ago *Brown I* held unconstitutional and a year later *Brown II* held must be abolished; school boards operating such school systems were required by *Brown II* "to effectuate a transition to a racially nondiscriminatory school system." It is of course true that for the time immediately after *Brown II* the concern was with making an initial break in a long-established pattern of excluding Negro children from schools attended by white children. The principal focus was on obtaining for those Negro children courageous enough to break with tradition a place in the "white" schools. . . .

It is against this background that 13 years after *Brown II* commanded the abolition of dual systems we must measure the effectiveness of respondent School Board's "freedom-of-choice" plan to achieve that end. The School Board contends that it has fully discharged its obligation by adopting a plan by which every student, regardless of race, may "freely" choose the school he will attend. The Board attempts to cast the issue in its broadest form by arguing that its "freedom-of-choice" plan may be faulted only by reading the Fourteenth Amendment as universally requiring "compulsory integration," a reading it insists the wording of the Amendment will not support. But that argument ignores the thrust of *Brown II.* . . . *Brown II* was a call for the dismantling of well-entrenched dual systems tempered by an awareness that complex and multifaceted problems would arise which would require time and flexibility for a successful resolution. School boards such as the respondent then operating state-compelled dual systems were nevertheless clearly charged with the affirmative duty to take whatever steps might be necessary to convert to a unitary system in which racial discrimination would be eliminated root and branch. . . .

The New Kent School Board's "freedom-of-choice" plan cannot be accepted as a sufficient step to "effectuate a transition" to a unitary system. In three years of operation not a single white child has chosen to attend Watkins school and although 115 Negro children enrolled in New Kent school in 1967 (up from 35 in 1965 and 111 in 1966) 85% of the Negro children in the system still attend the all-Negro Watkins school. In other words, the school system remains a dual system. . . .

SWANN V. CHARLOTTE-MECKLENBURG SCHOOL DISTRICT (1971)

The Charlotte-Mecklenburg School District had maintained a segregated system prior to Brown. *In order to conform to the Court's mandate in* Green, *the federal district court ordered, among other things, the busing of students in order to achieve a unitary system. Busing was already on the political radar screen and both Congress and President Richard Nixon had declared their opposition to it. Defense of the "neighborhood" school became popular for many politicians courting white voters.*

Mr. Chief Justice BURGER delivered the opinion of the Court.

. . .This case and those argued with it arose in States having a long history of maintaining two sets of schools in a single school system deliberately operated to carry out a governmental policy to separate pupils in schools solely on the basis of race. That was what *Brown v. Board of Education* was all about. These cases present us with the problem of defining in more precise terms than heretofore the scope of the duty of school authorities and district courts in implementing *Brown I* and the mandate to eliminate dual systems and establish unitary systems at once. . . .

Over the 16 years since *Brown II*, many difficulties were encountered in implementation of the basic constitutional requirement that the State not discriminate between public school children on the basis of their race. Nothing in our national experience prior to 1955 prepared anyone for dealing with changes and adjustments of the magnitude and complexity encountered since then. Deliberate resistance of some to the Court's mandates has impeded the good-faith efforts of others to bring school systems into compliance. . . .

By the time the Court considered *Green v. County School Board,* very little progress had been made in many areas where dual school systems had historically been maintained by operation of state laws. In *Green,* the Court required that:

The burden on a school board today is to come forward with a plan that promises realistically to work . . . now . . . until it is clear that state-imposed segregation has been completely removed.

This was plain language, yet the 1969 Term of Court brought fresh evidence of the dilatory tactics of many school authorities. . . .

The problems encountered by the . . . courts . . . make plain that we should now try to amplify guidelines. . . . The failure of local authorities to meet their constitutional obligations aggravated the massive problem of converting from the state-enforced discrimination of racially separate school systems. This process has been rendered more difficult by changes since 1954 in the structure and patterns of communities, the growth of student population, movement of families, and other changes, some of which had marked impact on school planning, sometimes neutralizing or negating remedial action before it was fully implemented. Rural areas accustomed for half a century to the consolidated school systems implemented by bus transportation could make adjustments more readily than metropolitan areas with dense and shifting population, numerous schools, congested and complex traffic patterns.

The objective today remains to eliminate from the public schools all vestiges of state-imposed segregation. Segregation was the evil struck down by *Brown I* as contrary to the equal protection guarantees of the Constitution. That was the violation sought to be corrected by the remedial measures of *Brown II.* That was the basis for the holding in *Green* that school authorities are "clearly charged with the affirmative duty to take whatever steps might be necessary to convert to a unitary system in which racial discrimination would be eliminated root and branch."

If school authorities fail in their affirmative obligations under these holdings, judicial authority may be invoked. Once a right and a violation have been shown, the scope of a district court's equitable powers to remedy past wrongs is broad, for breadth and flexibility are inherent in equitable remedies.

. . .

School authorities are traditionally charged with broad power to formulate and implement educational policy and might well conclude, for example, that in order to prepare students to live in a pluralistic society each school should have a prescribed ratio of Negro to white students reflecting the proportion for the district as a whole. To do this as an educational policy is within the broad discretionary powers of school authorities; absent a finding of a constitutional violation, however, that would not be within the authority of a federal court. As with any equity case, the nature of the violation determines the scope of the remedy. In default by the school authorities of their obligation to proffer acceptable remedies, a district court has broad power to fashion a remedy that will assure a unitary school system.

The school authorities argue that the equity powers of federal district courts have been limited by Title IV of the Civil Rights Act of 1964, 42 U.S.C. 2000c. The language and the history of Title IV show that it was enacted not to limit but to define the role of the Federal Government in the implementation of the *Brown I* decision. . . . Section 2000c (b) defines "desegregation" as it is used in Title IV:

"Desegregation" means the assignment of students to public schools and within such schools without regard to their race, color, religion, or national origin, but "desegregation" shall not mean the assignment of students to public schools in order to overcome racial imbalance.

Section 2000c–6, authorizing the Attorney General to institute federal suits, contains the following proviso:

Nothing herein shall empower any official or court of the United States to issue any order seeking to achieve a racial balance in any school by requiring the transportation of pupils or students from one school to another or one school district to another in order to achieve such racial balance, or otherwise enlarge the existing power of the court to insure compliance with constitutional standards.

On their face, the sections quoted purport only to insure that the provisions of Title IV of the Civil Rights Act of 1964 will not be read as granting new powers.... There is no suggestion of an intention to restrict those powers or withdraw from courts their historic equitable remedial powers. The legislative history of Title IV indicates that Congress was concerned that the Act might be read as creating a right of action under the Fourteenth Amendment in the situation of so-called "*de facto* segregation," where racial imbalance exists in the schools but with no showing that this was brought about by discriminatory action of state authorities....

When a system has been dual in these respects, the first remedial responsibility of school authorities is to eliminate invidious racial distinctions. With respect to such matters as transportation, supporting personnel, and extracurricular activities, no more than this may be necessary. Similar corrective action must be taken with regard to the maintenance of buildings and the distribution of equipment. In these areas, normal administrative practice should produce schools of like quality, facilities, and staffs....

The construction of new schools and the closing of old ones are two of the most important functions of local school authorities and also two of the most complex. They must decide questions of location and capacity in light of population growth, finances, land values, site availability, through an almost endless list of factors to be considered....

In the past, choices in this respect have been used as a potent weapon for creating or maintaining a state-segregated school system. In addition to the classic pattern of building schools specifically intended for Negro or white students, school authorities have sometimes, since *Brown,* closed schools which appeared likely to become racially mixed through changes in neighborhood residential patterns. This was sometimes accompanied by building new schools in the areas of white suburban expansion farthest from Negro population centers in order to maintain the separation of the races with a minimum departure from the formal principles of "neighborhood zoning." Such a policy does more than simply influence the short-run composition of the student body of a new school. It may well promote segregated residential patterns which, when combined with "neighborhood zoning," further lock the school system into the mold of separation of the races. Upon a proper showing a district court may consider this in fashioning a remedy.

...The central issue in this case is that of student assignment, and there are essentially four problem areas:

. . .

(1) Racial Balances or Racial Quotas.

The constant theme and thrust of every holding from *Brown I* to date is that state-enforced separation of races in public schools is discrimination that violates the Equal Protection Clause. The remedy commanded was to dismantle dual school systems.

We are concerned in these cases with the elimination of the discrimination inherent in the dual school systems, not with myriad factors of human existence which can cause discrimination in a multitude of ways on racial, religious, or ethnic grounds. The target of the cases from *Brown I* to the present was the dual school system. The elimination of racial discrimination in public schools is a large task and one that should not be retarded by efforts to achieve broader purposes lying beyond the jurisdiction of school authorities. One vehicle can carry only a limited amount of baggage. It would not serve the important objective of *Brown I* to seek to use school desegregation cases for purposes beyond their scope, although desegregation of schools ultimately will have impact on other forms of discrimination. . . .

In this case it is urged that the District Court has imposed a racial balance requirement of 71%–29% on individual schools. The fact that no such objective was actually achieved—and would appear to be impossible—tends to blunt that claim, yet in the opinion and order of the District Court . . . , we find that court directing that efforts should be made to reach a 71–29 ratio in the various schools so that there will be no basis for contending that one school is racially different from the others. . . .

We see therefore that the use made of mathematical ratios was no more than a starting point in the process of shaping a remedy, rather than an inflexible requirement. From that starting point the District Court proceeded to frame a decree that was within its discretionary powers, as an equitable remedy for the particular circumstances. . . .

(2) One-race Schools.

The record in this case reveals the familiar phenomenon that . . . minority groups are often found concentrated in one part of the city. In some circumstances certain schools may remain all or largely of one race until new schools can be provided or neighborhood patterns change. Schools all or predominately of one race in a district of mixed population will require close scrutiny to determine that school assignments are not part of state-enforced segregation. . . .

(3) Remedial Altering of Attendance Zones.

The maps submitted in these cases graphically demonstrate that one of the principal tools employed by school planners and by courts to break up the dual school system has been a frank—and sometimes drastic—gerrymandering of school districts. . . . More often than not, these zones are neither compact nor contiguous; indeed they may be on opposite ends of the city. As an interim corrective measure, this cannot be said to be beyond the broad remedial powers of a court.

(4) Transportation of Students.

The scope of permissible transportation of students as an implement of a remedial decree has never been defined by this Court and by the very nature of the problem it cannot be defined with precision. No rigid guidelines . . . can be given for application to the infinite variety of problems presented in thousands of situations. Bus transportation has been an integral part of the public education system for years, and was perhaps the single most important factor in the transition from the one-room schoolhouse to the consolidated school. Eighteen million of the Nation's public school children, approximately 39%, were transported to their schools by bus in 1969–1970 in all parts of the country. . . . The Charlotte school authorities did not purport to assign students on the basis of geographically drawn zones until 1965 and then they allowed almost unlimited transfer privileges. The District Court's conclusion that assignment of children to the school nearest their home serving their grade would not produce an effective dismantling of the dual system is supported by the record.

Thus the remedial techniques used in the District Court's order were within that court's power to provide equitable relief; implementation of the decree is well within the capacity of the school authority.

The decree provided that the buses used to implement the plan would operate on direct routes. Students would be picked up at schools near their homes and transported to the schools they were to attend. The trips for elementary school pupils average about seven miles and the District Court found that they would take "not over 35 minutes at the most." This system compares favorably with the transportation plan previously operated in Charlotte under which each day 23,600 students on all grade levels were transported an average of 15 miles one way for an average trip requiring over an hour. In these circumstances, we find no basis for holding that the local school authorities may not be required to employ bus transportation as one tool of school desegregation. Desegregation plans cannot be limited to the walk-in school.

. . .

At some point, these school authorities and others like them should have achieved full compliance with this Court's decision in *Brown I.* The systems would then be "unitary" in the sense required by our decisions in *Green* and *Alexander.*

It does not follow that the communities served by such systems will remain demographically stable, for in a growing, mobile society, few will do so. Neither school authorities nor district courts are constitutionally required to make year-by-year adjustments of the racial composition of student bodies once the affirmative duty to desegregate has been accomplished and racial discrimination through official action is eliminated from the system. . . .

. . . [T]he judgment of the Court of Appeals is affirmed. . . .

FRONTIERO V. RICHARDSON (1973)

The civil rights movement of the 1950s and the 1960s affected not only race relations, but triggered other groups to question the equality of treatment they received at the hands of the law. The women's movement was the first such group to use arguments similar to those earlier raised by the NAACP. Unlike African Americans, women did not limit their efforts only to the courts. Turning their efforts to Congress, they persuaded Congress by lopsided votes to submit an Equal Rights Amendment to the states for their ratification. A year earlier year, in the case of Reed v. Reed *(1971), the Court had declared a state law that preferred the appointment of a male as an executor of an estate to a female "irrational."*

Frontiero *found a Court that, although more than sympathetic to the claims advanced by advocates of women's rights, was divided on how active a role it should take in view of Congress's action regarding ERA.*

Mr. Justice BRENNAN announced the judgment of the Court and an opinion in which Mr. Justice DOUGLAS, Mr. Justice WHITE, and Mr. Justice MARSHALL join.

The question before us concerns the right of a female member of the uniformed services to claim her spouse as a "dependent" for the purposes of obtaining increased quarters allowances and medical and dental benefits . . . on an equal footing with male members. . . . [A] serviceman may claim his wife as a "dependent" without regard to whether she is in fact dependent upon him for any part of her support. A servicewoman, on the other hand, may not claim her husband as a "dependent" . . . unless he is in fact dependent upon her for over one-half of his support. Thus, the question for decision is whether this difference in treatment constitutes an unconstitutional discrimination against servicewomen in violation of the Due Process Clause of the Fifth Amendment. A three-judge District Court . . . , one judge dissenting, rejected this contention and sustained the constitutionality of the provisions of the statutes making this distinction. . . . We reverse.

I

. . .Although the legislative history of these statutes sheds virtually no light on the purposes underlying the differential treatment accorded male and female members, a majority of the three-judge District Court surmised that Congress might reasonably have concluded that, since the husband in our society is generally the "bread-winner" in the family— and the wife typically the "dependent" partner it would be more economical to require married female members claiming husbands to prove actual dependency than to extend the presumption of dependency to such members." Indeed, given the fact that approximately 99% of all members of the uniformed services are male, the District Court speculated that such differential treatment might conceivably lead to a "considerable saving of administrative expense and manpower."

II

At the outset, appellants contend that classifications based upon sex, like classifications based upon race, alienage, and national origin, are inherently suspect and must therefore be subjected to close judicial scrutiny. We agree and, indeed, find at least implicit support for such an approach in our unanimous decision only last Term in *Reed v. Reed.*

. . .[In *Reed,* the state] . . . contended that the statutory scheme was a reasonable measure designed to reduce the workload on probate courts by eliminating one class of contests. Moreover, appellee argued that the mandatory preference for male applicants was in itself reasonable since "men [are] as a rule more conversant with business affairs than . . . women." Indeed, appellee maintained that "it is a matter of common knowledge, that women still are not engaged in politics, the professions, business or industry to the extent that men are." . . .

Despite these contentions, however, the Court held the statutory preference for male applicants unconstitutional. In reaching this result, the Court implicitly rejected appellee's apparently rational explanation of the statutory scheme. . . . This departure from "traditional" rational-basis analysis with respect to sex-based classifications is clearly justified.

There can be no doubt that our Nation has had a long and unfortunate history of sex discrimination. Traditionally, such discrimination was rationalized by an attitude of "romantic paternalism" which, in practical effect, put women, not on a pedestal, but in a cage. Indeed, this paternalistic attitude became so firmly rooted in our national consciousness that, 100 years ago, a distinguished Member of this Court [Justice Bradley] was able to proclaim:

> Man is, or should be, woman's protector and defender. The natural and proper timidity and delicacy which belongs to the female sex evidently unfits it for many of the occupations of civil life. . . . The paramount destiny and mission of woman are to fulfill the noble and benign offices of wife and mother. This is the law of the Creator" (*Bradwell v. State* 1873).

. . . [S]ince sex, like race and national origin, is an immutable characteristic determined solely by the accident of birth, the imposition of special disabilities upon the members of a particular sex because of their sex would seem to violate "the basic concept of our system that legal burdens should bear some relationship to individual responsibility. . . ." And what differentiates sex from such nonsuspect statuses as intelligence or physical disability, and aligns it with the recognized suspect criteria, is that the sex characteristic frequently bears no relation to ability to perform or contribute to society. . . . As a result, statutory distinctions between the sexes often have the effect of invidiously relegating the entire class of females to inferior legal status without regard to the actual capabilities of its individual members.

We might also note that, over the past decade, Congress has itself manifested an increasing sensitivity to sex-based classifications. In Tit[le] VII of the Civil Rights Act of 1964, for example, Congress expressly declared that no employer, labor union, or other organization subject to the provisions of the Act shall discriminate against any individual on the basis of "race, color, religion, sex, or national origin."

With these considerations in mind, we can only conclude that classifications based upon sex, like classifications based upon race, alienage, or national origin, are inherently suspect, and must therefore be subjected to strict judicial scrutiny. Applying the analysis mandated by that stricter standard of review, it is clear that the statutory scheme now before us is constitutionally invalid. . . .

Reversed.

Mr. Justice STEWART concurs in the judgment, agreeing that the statutes before us work an invidious discrimination in violation of the Constitution (*Reed v. Reed*).

Mr. Justice REHNQUIST dissents for the reasons stated by Judge Rives in his opinion for the District Court, *Frontiero v. Laird,* 341 F. Supp. 201 (1972).

Mr. Justice POWELL, with whom the Chief Justice and Mr. Justice BLACKMUN join, concurring in the judgment.

I agree that the challenged statutes constitute an unconstitutional discrimination . . . , but I cannot join the opinion of Mr. Justice BRENNAN, which would hold that all classifications based upon sex, "like classifications based upon race, alienage, and national origin," are "inherently suspect and must therefore be subjected to close judicial scrutiny." It is unnecessary for the Court in this case to characterize sex as a suspect classification, with all of the far-reaching implications of such a holding. *Reed,* which abundantly supports our decision today, did not add sex to the narrowly limited group of classifications which are inherently suspect. . . .

There is another, and I find compelling, reason for deferring a general categorizing of sex classifications as invoking the strictest test of judicial scrutiny. The Equal Rights Amendment, which if adopted will resolve the substance of this precise question, has been approved by the Congress and submitted for ratification by the States. If this Amendment is duly adopted, it will represent the will of the people accomplished in the manner prescribed by the Constitution. By acting prematurely and unnecessarily, as I view it, the Court has assumed a decisional responsibility at the very time when state legislatures, functioning within the traditional democratic process, are debating the proposed Amendment. It seems to me that this reaching out to pre-empt by judicial action a major political decision which is currently in process of resolution does not reflect appropriate respect for duly prescribed legislative processes.

There are times when this Court, under our system, cannot avoid a constitutional decision on issues which normally should be resolved by the elected representatives of the people. But democratic institutions are weakened, and confidence in the restraint of the Court is impaired, when we appear unnecessarily to decide sensitive issues of broad social and political importance at the very time they are under consideration within the prescribed constitutional processes.

KEYES V. SCHOOL DISTRICT NO. 1, DENVER (1973)

Until the Keyes *decision involving the schools of Denver, Colorado, the battles over school segregation had been waged in the states of the old Confederacy or in the border states, areas where segregation had been the law of the land prior to* Brown. *Denver had never had a formal system of school segregation. It never had a system that designated certain schools for "whites only" and others "blacks only." Still, the plaintiffs alleged that the school board had engaged in a pattern of activities that produced very much the same result.*

Justice William Brennan found that such a pattern constituted evidence of de jure segregation. For the first time since Brown *in a case involving race, the Court's decision was not unanimous.*

Mr. Justice BRENNAN delivered the opinion of the Court.

This school desegregation case concerns the Denver . . . school system. That system has never been operated under a constitutional or statutory provision that mandated or permitted racial segregation in public education. Rather, the gravamen of this action . . . is that respondent School Board alone by use of various techniques such as the manipulation of student attendance zones, school site selection and a neighborhood school policy, created or maintained racially or ethnically . . . segregated schools throughout the school district, entitling petitioners to a decree directing desegregation of the entire school district.

. . . The District Court found that by the construction of a new, relatively small elementary school, Barrett, in the middle of the Negro community west of Park Hill, by the gerrymandering of student attendance zones, by the use of so-called "optional zones," and by the excessive use of mobile classroom units, among other things, the respondent School Board had engaged over almost a decade after 1960 in an unconstitutional policy of deliberate racial segregation with respect to the Park Hill schools. . . .

. . . [W]here plaintiffs prove that the school authorities have carried out a systematic program of segregation affecting a substantial portion of the students, schools, teachers, and facilities within the school system, it is only common sense to conclude that there exists a predicate for a finding of the existence of a dual school system. Several considerations support this conclusion. First, it is obvious that a practice of concentrating Negroes in certain schools by structuring attendance zones or designating "feeder" schools on the basis of race has the reciprocal effect of keeping other nearby schools predominantly white. Similarly, the practice of building a school . . . to a certain size and in a certain location, "with conscious knowledge that it would be a segregated school," has a substantial reciprocal effect on the racial composition of other nearby schools. So also, the use of mobile classrooms, the drafting of student transfer policies, the transportation of students, and the assignment of faculty and staff, on racially identifiable bases, have the clear effect of earmarking schools according to their racial composition, and this, in turn, together with the elements of student assignment and school construction, may have a profound reciprocal effect on the racial composition of residential neighborhoods within a metropolitan area, thereby causing further racial concentration within the schools. . . .

This is merely an application of the well-settled evidentiary principle that "the prior doing of other similar acts, whether clearly a part of a scheme or not, is useful as reducing the possibility that the act in question was done with innocent intent." 2 J. Wigmore, Evidence 200 (3d ed. 1940). . . .

Applying these principles . . . , we hold that a finding of intentionally segregative school board actions in a meaningful portion of a school system . . . creates a presumption that other segregated schooling within the system is not adventitious. It establishes, in other words, a *prima facie* case of unlawful segregative design on the part of school authorities, and shifts to those authorities the burden of proving that other segregated schools within the system are not also the result of intentionally segregative actions.

. . .

The respondent School Board invoked at trial its "neighborhood school policy" as explaining racial and ethnic concentrations within the core city schools, arguing that since the core city area population had long been Negro and Hispano [sic], the concentrations were necessarily the result of residential patterns and not of purposefully segregative policies. We have no occasion to consider in this case whether a "neighborhood school policy" of itself will justify racial or ethnic concentrations in the absence of a finding that school authorities have committed acts constituting *de jure* segregation.

. . .

In summary, the District Court on remand, first, will afford . . . [the] School Board the opportunity to prove its contention that the Park Hill area is a separate . . . section of the school district that should be treated as isolated from the rest of the district. If respondent School Board fails to prove that contention, the District Court, second, will determine whether respondent School Board's conduct over almost a decade after 1960 in carrying out a policy of deliberate racial segregation in the Park Hill schools constitutes the entire school system a dual school system. If the District Court determines that the Denver school system is a dual school system, respondent School Board has the affirmative duty to desegregate the entire system "root and branch" (*Green v. County School*). . . .

Mr. Justice DOUGLAS.

While I join the opinion of the Court, I agree with my Brother POWELL that there is, for the purposes of the Equal Protection Clause of the Fourteenth Amendment as applied to the school cases, no difference between *de facto* and *de jure* segregation. The school board is a state agency and the lines that it draws, the locations it selects for school sites, the allocation it makes of students, the budgets it prepares are state action for Fourteenth Amendment purposes.

Mr. Justice POWELL concurring in part and dissenting in part.

. . . This is the first school desegregation case to reach this Court which involves a major city outside the South. It comes from Denver, Colorado, a city and a State which have not operated public schools under constitutional or statutory provisions which mandated or permitted racial segregation. . . .

The situation in Denver is generally comparable to that in other large cities across the country in which there is a substantial minority population and where desegregation has not been ordered by the federal courts. There is segregation in the schools of many of these cities fully as pervasive as that in southern cities prior to the desegregation decrees of the past decade and a half. The focus of the school desegregation problem has now shifted from the South to the country as a whole. Unwilling and foot-dragging as the process was in most places, substantial progress toward achieving integration has been made in Southern States. No comparable progress has been made in many nonsouthern cities with large minority populations primarily because of the *de facto / de jure* distinction nurtured by the courts and accepted complacently by many of the same voices which denounced the evils of segregated schools in the South. . . .

The Court's decision today, while adhering to the *de jure / de facto* distinction, will require the application of the *Green/Swann* doctrine of "affirmative duty" to the Denver School Board despite the absence of any history of state-mandated school segregation. The only evidence of a constitutional violation was found in various decisions of the School Board. I concur in the Court's position that the public school authorities are the responsible agency of the State, and that if the affirmative-duty doctrine is sound constitutional law for Charlotte, it is equally so for Denver. I would not, however, perpetuate the *de jure / de facto* distinction nor would I leave to petitioners the initial tortuous effort of identifying "segregative acts" and deducing "segregative intent." I would hold, quite simply, that where segregated public schools exist within a school district to a substantial degree, there is a *prima facie* case that the duly constituted public authorities . . . are sufficiently responsible to warrant imposing upon them a nationally applicable burden to demonstrate they nevertheless are operating a genuinely integrated school system.

. . .

Public schools are creatures of the State, and whether the segregation is state-created or state-assisted or merely state-perpetuated should be irrelevant to constitutional principle. . . . Where state action and supervision are so pervasive and where, after years of such action, segregated schools continue to exist within the district to a substantial degree, this Court is justified in finding a *prima facie* case of a constitutional violation. The burden then must fall on the school board to demonstrate it is operating an "integrated school system."

. . .

The controlling case is *Swann,* and the question which will confront and confound the District Court . . . is what, indeed, does *Swann* require? . . . To the extent that *Swann* may be thought to require large-scale or long-distance transportation of students in our metropolitan school districts, I record my profound misgivings. Nothing in our Constitution commands or encourages any such court-compelled disruption of public education. . . .

The Equal Protection Clause does, indeed, command that racial discrimination not be tolerated in the decisions of public school authorities. But it does not require that school authorities undertake widespread student transportation solely for the sake of maximizing integration.

. . . There is nothing in the Constitution, its history, or—until recently—in the jurisprudence of this Court that mandates the employment of forced transportation of young and teenage children to achieve a single interest, as important as that interest may be. We have strayed, quite far as I view it, from the rationale . . . that courts in fashioning remedies must be "guided by equitable principles" which include the "adjusting and reconciling [of] public and private needs."

I urge a return to this rationale. This would result . . . in no prohibition on court-ordered student transportation in furtherance of desegregation. But it would require that the legitimate community interests in neighborhood school systems be accorded far greater respect. In the balancing of interests so appropriate to a fair and just equitable decree, transportation orders should be applied with special caution to any proposal as disruptive of family life and interests—and ultimately of education itself—as extensive transportation of elementary-age children solely for desegregation purposes. As a minimum, this Court should not require school boards to engage in the unnecessary transportation away from their neighborhoods of elementary-age children. It is at this age level that neighborhood education performs its most vital role. It is with respect to children of tender years that the greatest concern exists for their physical and psychological health. It is also here, at the elementary school, that the rights of parents and children are most sharply implicated.

Mr. Justice REHNQUIST, dissenting.

. . . The Court's opinion obscures . . . factual differences between the situation shown by the record to have existed in Denver and the situations dealt with in earlier school desegregation opinions of the Court. . . .

. . . [I]t is quite conceivable that the School Board might have engaged in the racial gerrymandering of the attendance boundary between two particular schools in order to keep one largely Negro and Hispano, and the other largely Anglo. . . . Such action would have deprived affected minority students who were the victims of such gerrymandering of their constitutional right to equal protection of the laws. But if the school board had been evenhanded in its drawing of the attendance lines for other schools in the district, minority students required to attend other schools within the district would have suffered no such deprivation. It certainly would not reflect normal English usage to describe the entire district as "segregated" on such a state of facts, and it would be a quite unprecedented application of principles of equitable relief to determine that if the gerrymandering of one attendance zone were proved, particular racial mixtures could be required by a federal district court for every school in the district.

. . .

Underlying the Court's entire opinion is its apparent thesis . . . that if a single attendance zone between two individual schools in the large metropolitan district is found by him to have been "gerrymandered," the school district is guilty of operating a "dual" school system, and is apparently a candidate for what is in practice a federal receivership. . . . Yet, unless the Equal Protection Clause of the Fourteenth Amendment now be held to embody a principle of "taint," found in some primitive legal systems but discarded centuries ago in ours, such a result can only be described as the product of judicial fiat.

. . .

The drastic extension of *Brown* which Green represented was barely, if at all, explicated in the latter opinion. To require that a genuinely "dual" system be disestablished, in the sense that the assignment of a child to a particular school is not made to depend on his race, is one thing. To require that school boards affirmatively undertake to achieve racial mixing in schools where such mixing is not achieved in sufficient degree by neutrally drawn boundary lines is quite obviously something else.

The Court's own language in *Green* makes it unmistakably clear that this significant extension of *Brown*'s prohibition against discrimination, and the conversion of that prohibition into an affirmative duty to integrate, was made in the context of a school system which had for a number of years rigidly excluded Negroes from attending the same schools as were attended by whites. Whatever may be the soundness of that decision in the context of a genuinely "dual" school system, where segregation of the races had once been mandated by law, I can see no constitutional justification for it in a situation such as that which the record shows to have obtained in Denver.

SAN ANTONIO SCHOOL DISTRICT V. RODRIGUEZ (1973)

The Court's announcement of a fundamental right to vote in Reynolds v. Sims *(1964) opened up the possibility that there were other "fundamental rights" that could be used to challenge state legislation that made distinctions among people as to the enjoyment of such rights. Opponents of school funding programs that were based solely on the property tax saw* Reynolds *as providing a means to bring about a thorough-going reform of education funding. Many state supreme courts agreed with this argument and found that the use of the property tax to fund public education was unconstitutional. When* San Antonio v. Rodriguez *was argued before the Supreme Court, many Court-watchers predicted that the High Court would follow the lead of these state courts. The* San Antonio *decision, accordingly, proved to be quite a surprise to them.*

Mr. Justice POWELL delivered the opinion of the Court.

This suit attacking the Texas system of financing public education was initiated by Mexican-American parents whose children attend the elementary and secondary schools in the Edgewood Independent School District . . . in San Antonio. . . . They brought a class action on behalf of schoolchildren throughout the State who are members of minority groups or who are poor and reside in school districts having a low property tax base. . . . [A] three-judge court . . . rendered its judgment . . . holding the Texas school finance system unconstitutional under the Equal Protection Clause. . . . The State appealed, and we noted probable jurisdiction. . . . For the reasons stated in this opinion, we reverse the decision of the District Court.

... [T]he Edgewood Independent School District, has been compared throughout this litigation with the Alamo Heights Independent School District. This comparison between the least and most affluent districts in the San Antonio area serves to illustrate the manner in which the dual system of finance operates and to indicate the extent to which substantial disparities exist despite the State's impressive progress in recent years. Edgewood is one of seven public school districts in the metropolitan area.... The district is situated in the core-city sector of San Antonio in a residential neighborhood that has little commercial or industrial property. The residents are predominantly of Mexican-American descent: approximately 90% of the student population is Mexican-American and over 6% is Negro. The average assessed property value per pupil is $5,960—the lowest in the metropolitan area—and the median family income ($4,686) is also the lowest. At an equalized tax rate of $1.05 per $100 of assessed property—the highest in the metropolitan area—the district contributed $26 to the education of each child.... The Foundation Program contributed $222 per pupil for a state-local total of $248. Federal funds added another $108 for a total of $356 per pupil.

Alamo Heights is the most affluent school district in San Antonio.... The school population is predominantly "Anglo," having only 18% Mexican-Americans and less than 1% Negroes. The assessed property value per pupil exceeds $49,000, and the median family income is $8,001.... [T]he local tax rate of $.85 per $100 of valuation yielded $333 per pupil over and above its contribution to the Foundation Program. Coupled with the $225 provided from that Program, the district was able to supply $558 per student. Supplemented by a $36 per-pupil grant from federal sources, Alamo Heights spent $594 per pupil.

. . .

Texas virtually concedes that its historically rooted dual system of financing education could not withstand the strict judicial scrutiny that this Court has found appropriate in reviewing legislative judgments that interfere with fundamental constitutional rights or that involve suspect classifications. If, as previous decisions have indicated, strict scrutiny means that the State's system is not entitled to the usual presumption of validity ..., the Texas financing system and its counterpart in virtually every other State will not pass muster.... Apart from its concession that educational financing in Texas has "defects" and "imperfections," the

State defends the system's rationality with vigor and disputes the District Court's finding that it lacks a "reasonable basis."

This, then, establishes the framework for our analysis. We must decide, first, whether the Texas system of financing public education operates to the disadvantage of some suspect class or impinges upon a fundamental right explicitly or implicitly protected by the Constitution, thereby requiring strict judicial scrutiny. If so, the judgment of the District Court should be affirmed. If not, the Texas scheme must still be examined to determine whether it rationally furthers some legitimate, articulated state purpose and therefore does not constitute an invidious discrimination in violation of the Equal Protection Clause of the Fourteenth Amendment.

. . .

The wealth discrimination discovered by the District Court in this case, and by several other courts that have recently struck down school-financing laws in other States, is quite unlike any of the forms of wealth discrimination heretofore reviewed by this Court. Rather than focusing on the unique features of the alleged discrimination, the courts in these cases have virtually assumed their findings of a suspect classification through a simplistic process of analysis: since, under the traditional systems of financing public schools, some poorer people receive less expensive educations than other more affluent people, these systems discriminate on the basis of wealth. This approach largely ignores the hard threshold questions, including whether it makes a difference for purposes of consideration under the Constitution that the class of disadvantaged "poor" cannot be identified or defined in customary equal protection terms, and whether the relative—rather than absolute—nature of the asserted deprivation is of significant consequence. Before a State's laws and the justifications for the classifications they create are subjected to strict judicial scrutiny, we think these threshold considerations must be analyzed more closely than they were in the court below.

. . .

For these two reasons—the absence of any evidence that the financing system discriminates against any definable category of "poor" people or that it results in the absolute deprivation of education—the disadvantaged class is not susceptible of identification in traditional terms.

. . . It is not the province of this Court to create substantive constitutional rights in the name of guaranteeing equal protection of the laws. Thus, the key to discovering whether education is "fundamental" is not

to be found in comparisons of the relative societal significance of education as opposed to subsistence or housing. Nor is it to be found by
weighing whether education is as important as the right to travel. Rather,
the answer lies in assessing whether there is a right to education explicitly or implicitly guaranteed by the Constitution.

Education, of course, is not among the rights afforded explicit protection under our Federal Constitution. Nor do we find any basis for saying it is implicitly so protected. As we have said, the undisputed importance of education will not alone cause this Court to depart from the
usual standard for reviewing a State's social and economic legislation. It
is appellees' contention, however, that education is distinguishable from
other services and benefits provided by the State because it bears a pecu-
liarly close relationship to other rights and liberties accorded protection
under the Constitution. Specifically, they insist that education is itself a
fundamental personal right because it is essential to the effective exercise
of First Amendment freedoms and to intelligent utilization of the right
to vote.... The "marketplace of ideas" is an empty forum for those
lacking basic communicative tools....

A similar line of reasoning is pursued with respect to the right to
vote....

We need not dispute any of these propositions. The Court has long
afforded zealous protection against unjustifiable governmental interference with the individual's rights to speak and to vote. Yet we have never
presumed to possess either the ability or the authority to guarantee to
the citizenry the most effective speech or the most informed electoral
choice. That these may be desirable goals of a system of freedom of expression and of a representative form of government is not to be
doubted.... But they are not values to be pursued by or implemented
by judicial intrusion into otherwise legitimate state activities.

. . .

In light of the considerable attention that has focused on the District
Court opinion in this case and on its California predecessor, *Serrano v.
Priest* (1971), a cautionary postscript seems appropriate. It cannot be
questioned that the constitutional judgment reached by the District
Court and approved by our dissenting Brothers today would occasion
in Texas and elsewhere an unprecedented upheaval in public education.
Some commentators have concluded that, whatever the contours of the
alternative financing programs that might be devised and approved, the

result could not avoid being a beneficial one. But, just as there is nothing simple about the constitutional issues involved in these cases, there is nothing simple or certain about predicting the consequences of massive change in the financing and control of public education. . . .

These practical considerations, of course, play no role in the adjudication of the constitutional issues presented here. But they serve to highlight the wisdom of the traditional limitations on this Court's function. The consideration and initiation of fundamental reforms with respect to state taxation and education are matters reserved for the legislative processes of the various States, and we do no violence to the values of federalism and separation of powers by staying our hand. We hardly need add that this Court's action today is not to be viewed as placing its judicial imprimatur on the status quo. . . . But the ultimate solutions must come from the lawmakers and from the democratic pressures of those who elect them.

Reversed.

Mr. Justice MARSHALL, with whom Mr. Justice DOUGLAS concurs, dissenting.

. . .In my judgment, the right of every American to an equal start in life, so far as the provision of a state service as important as education is concerned, is far too vital to permit state discrimination on grounds as tenuous as those presented by this record. Nor can I accept the notion that it is sufficient to remit these appellees to the vagaries of the political process which, contrary to the majority's suggestion, has proved singularly unsuited to the task of providing a remedy for this discrimination. I, for one, am unsatisfied with the hope of an ultimate "political" solution sometime in the indefinite future while, in the meantime, countless children unjustifiably receive inferior educations that "may affect their hearts and minds in a way unlikely ever to be undone" (*Brown v. Board of Education*). I must therefore respectfully dissent.

. . .

I cannot accept the majority's labored efforts to demonstrate that fundamental interests, which call for strict scrutiny of the challenged classification, encompass only established rights which we are somehow bound to recognize from the text of the Constitution itself. To be sure, some interests which the Court has deemed to be fundamental for purposes of equal protection analysis are themselves constitutionally protected rights. . . . But it will not do to suggest that the "answer" to whether an interest is fundamental for purposes of equal protection analysis is always determined by whether that interest "is a right . . . explicitly or implicitly guaranteed by the Constitution."

I would like to know where the Constitution guarantees the right to procreate, *Skinner v. Oklahoma* (1942), or the right to vote in state elections, e. g., *Reynolds v. Sims*. . . . These are instances in which, due to the importance of the interests at stake, the Court has displayed a strong concern with the existence of discriminatory state treatment. But the Court has never said or indicated that these are interests which independently enjoy full-blown constitutional protection.

. . . [I]t seems to me inescapably clear that this Court has consistently adjusted the care with which it will review state discrimination in light of the constitutional significance of the interests affected and the invidiousness of the particular classification. In the context of economic interests, we find that discriminatory state action is almost always sustained, for such interests are generally far removed from constitutional guarantees. . . . But the situation differs markedly when discrimination against important individual interests with constitutional implications and against particularly disadvantaged or powerless classes is involved. The majority suggests, however, that a variable standard of review would give this Court the appearance of a "superlegislature." I cannot agree. Such an approach seems to me a part of the guarantees of our Constitution and of the historic experiences with oppression of and discrimination against discrete, powerless minorities which underlie that document. In truth, the Court itself will be open to the criticism raised by the majority so long as it continues on its present course of effectively selecting in private which cases will be afforded special consideration without acknowledging the true basis of its action. Opinions such as . . . *Reed* seem drawn more as efforts to shield rather than to reveal the true basis of the Court's decisions. Such obfuscated action may be appropriate to a political body such as a legislature, but it is not appropriate to this Court. Open debate of the bases for the Court's action is essential to the rationality and consistency of our decisionmaking process. Only in this way can we avoid the label of legislature and ensure the integrity of the judicial process.

Nevertheless, the majority today attempts to force this case into the same category for purposes of equal protection analysis as decisions involving discrimination affecting commercial interests. By so doing, the majority singles this case out for analytic treatment at odds with what seems to me to be the clear trend of recent decisions in this Court, and thereby ignores the constitutional importance of the interest at stake and the invidiousness of the particular classification, factors that call for far more than the lenient scrutiny of the Texas financing scheme which the majority pursues. Yet if the discrimination inherent in the Texas scheme is scrutinized with the care demanded by the interest and classification present in this case, the unconstitutionality of that scheme is unmistakable.

MILLIKEN V. BRADLEY (1974)

Keyes made the issue of busing a political issue not just in the states of the old Confederacy, but an issue in almost all of the old cities of the north and midwest. By the 1970s, suburbanization and white flight from city schools made it difficult to achieve any real degree of true integration in these old core cities. One solution was to order busing of city students into the suburbs. By a vote of 5–4, Chief Justice Warren Burger reversed the lower court's order mandating busing into the suburbs. With this decision, the busing issue would be limited to the increasingly minority-dominated cities. Suburban schools, where there were few blacks, would not be affected.

Mr. Chief Justice BURGER delivered the opinion of the Court.

We granted certiorari . . . to determine whether a federal court may impose a multidistrict, areawide remedy to a single-district *de jure* segregation problem absent any finding that the other included school districts have failed to operate unitary school systems within their districts, absent any claim or finding that the boundary lines of any affected school district were established with the purpose of fostering racial segregation in public schools, [and] absent any finding that the included districts committed acts which effected segregation within the other districts. . . .

The District Court found that the Detroit Board of Education created and maintained optional attendance zones. . . . These zones, the court found, had the "natural, probable, foreseeable and actual effect" of allowing white pupils to escape identifiably Negro schools. . . . [T]he District Court concluded, the natural and actual effect of these acts was the creation and perpetuation of school segregation within Detroit. [It also found certain actions by the State of Michigan] to have . . . "acted to impede, delay and minimize racial integration in Detroit schools."

. . . [T]he District Court proceeded to order the Detroit Board . . . to submit desegregation plans limited to the segregation problems found to be existing within the city. . . . At the same time, however, the state defendants were directed to submit desegregation plans encompassing the three-county metropolitan area despite the fact that the 85 outlying school districts of these three counties were not parties to the action and despite the fact that there had been no claim that these outlying districts had committed constitutional violations. . . .

The controlling principle consistently expounded in our holdings is that the scope of the remedy is determined by the nature and extent of the constitutional violation. Before the boundaries of separate and autonomous school districts may be set aside by consolidating the separate units for remedial purposes or by imposing a cross-district remedy, it must first be shown that there has been a constitutional violation within one district that produces a significant segregative effect in another district. . . .

The record before us, voluminous as it is, contains evidence of de jure segregated conditions only in the Detroit schools. . . . With no showing of significant violation by the 53 outlying school districts and no evidence of any interdistrict violation or effect, the court went beyond the original theory of the case . . . and mandated a metropolitan area remedy. To approve the remedy ordered by the court would impose on the outlying districts, not shown to have committed any constitutional violation, [is] . . . wholly impermissible. . . .

Mr. Justice DOUGLAS, dissenting.
. . .As I indicated in *Keyes*, there is so far as the school cases go no constitutional difference between *de facto* and *de jure* segregation. . . . The creation of the school districts in Metropolitan Detroit either maintained existing segregation or caused additional segregation. Restrictive covenants maintained by state action or inaction build black ghettos. . . .

Mr. Justice WHITE, with whom Mr. Justice DOUGLAS, Mr. Justice BRENNAN, and Mr. Justice MARSHALL join, dissenting.

...Until today, the permissible contours of the equitable authority of the district courts to remedy the unlawful establishment of a dual school system have been extensive, adaptable, and fully responsive to the ultimate goal of achieving "the greatest possible degree of actual desegregation." ... [U]ntil now the Court has not accepted the proposition that effective enforcement of the Fourteenth Amendment could be limited by political or administrative boundary lines demarcated by the very State responsible for the constitutional violation.... Until now the Court has instead looked to practical considerations in effectuating a desegregation decree such as excessive distance, transportation time, and hazards to the safety of the schoolchildren involved in a proposed plan....

Nor does the Court's conclusion follow from the talismanic invocation of the desirability of local control over education. Local autonomy over school affairs, in the sense of the community's participation in the decisions affecting the education of its children, is, of course, an important interest. But presently constituted school district lines do not delimit fixed and unchangeable areas of a local educational community....

Finally, I remain wholly unpersuaded by the Court's assertion that "the remedy is necessarily designed, as all remedies are, to restore the victims of discriminatory conduct to the position they would have occupied in the absence of such conduct." In the first place, under this premise the Court's judgment is itself infirm; for had the Detroit school system not followed an official policy of segregation throughout the 1950's and 1960's, Negroes and whites would have been going to school together. There would have been no, or at least not as many, recognizable Negro schools and none, or at least not as many, white schools, but "just schools," and neither Negroes nor whites would have suffered from the effects of segregated education, with all its shortcomings. Surely the Court's remedy will not restore to the Negro community, stigmatized as it was by the dual school system, what it would have enjoyed over all or most of this period if the remedy is confined to present-day Detroit; for the maximum remedy available within that area will leave many of the schools almost totally black, and the system itself will be predominantly black and will become increasingly so....

Mr. Justice MARSHALL, with whom Mr. Justice DOUGLAS, Mr. Justice BRENNAN, and Mr. Justice WHITE join, dissenting.

In *Brown* this Court held that segregation of children in public schools on the basis of race deprives minority group children of equal educational opportunities and therefore denies them the equal protection of the laws under the Fourteenth Amendment. This Court recognized then that remedying decades of segregation in public education would not be an easy task. Subsequent events, unfortunately, have seen that prediction bear bitter fruit. But however imbedded old ways, however ingrained old prejudices, this Court has not been diverted from its appointed task of making "a living truth" of our constitutional ideal of equal justice under law.

After 20 years of small, often difficult steps toward that great end, the Court today takes a giant step backwards. . . .

Desegregation is not and was never expected to be an easy task. Racial attitudes ingrained in our Nation's childhood and adolescence are not quickly thrown aside in its middle years. But just as the inconvenience of some cannot be allowed to stand in the way of the rights of others, so public opposition, no matter how strident, cannot be permitted to divert this Court from the enforcement of the constitutional principles at issue in this case. Today's holding, I fear, is more a reflection of a perceived public mood that we have gone far enough in enforcing the Constitution's guarantee of equal justice than it is the product of neutral principles of law. In the short run, it may seem to be the easier course to allow our great metropolitan areas to be divided up each into two cities—one white, the other black—but it is a course, I predict, our people will ultimately regret. I dissent.

CRAIG V. BOREN (1976)

An Oklahoma law that allowed women over eighteen to consume 3.2% or "near" beer while requiring males to be twenty-one in order to consume the beverage allowed the Court to fashion a new standard to use in determining whether legislation that classified on the basis of gender was constitutional.

Mr. Justice BRENNAN delivered the opinion of the Court.

. . . Oklahoma statute prohibits the sale of "nonintoxicating" 3.2% beer to males under the age of 21 and to females under the age of 18. The question to be decided is whether such a gender-based differential constitutes a denial to males 18–20 years of age of the equal protection of the laws in violation of the Fourteenth Amendment.

This action was brought ... by appellant Craig, a male then between 18 and 21 years of age. ... on the ground that it constituted invidious discrimination against males 18–20 years of age. A three judge court ... sustained the constitutionality of the statutory differential. ...

... *Reed* emphasized that statutory classifications that distinguish between males and females are "subject to scrutiny under the Equal Protection Clause." To withstand constitutional challenge, previous cases establish that classifications by gender must serve important governmental objectives and must be substantially related to achievement of those objectives. Thus, in *Reed,* the objectives of "reducing the workload on probate courts," and "avoiding intrafamily controversy," were deemed of insufficient importance to sustain use of an overt gender criterion in the appointment of administrators of intestate decedents' estates. Decisions following *Reed* similarly have rejected administrative ease and convenience as sufficiently important objectives to justify gender-based classifications. ...

The District Court recognized that *Reed v. Reed* was controlling. In applying the teachings of that case, the court found the requisite important governmental objective in the traffic-safety goal proffered by the Oklahoma Attorney General. It then concluded that the statistics introduced by the appellees established that the gender-based distinction was substantially related to achievement of that goal.

. . .

Even were this statistical evidence accepted as accurate, it nevertheless offers only a weak answer to the equal protection question presented here. The most focused and relevant of the statistical surveys, arrests of 18–20-year-olds for alcohol-related driving offenses, exemplifies the ultimate unpersuasiveness of this evidentiary record. Viewed in terms of the correlation between sex and the actual activity that Oklahoma seeks to regulate—driving while under the influence of alcohol—the statistics broadly establish that .18% of females and 2% of males in that age group were arrested for that offense. While such a disparity is not trivial in a statistical sense, it hardly can form the basis for employment of a gender line as a classifying device. Certainly if maleness is to serve as a proxy for drinking and driving, a correlation of 2% must be considered an unduly tenuous "fit." ...

There is no reason to belabor this line of analysis. It is unrealistic to expect either members of the judiciary or state officials to be well versed in the rigors of experimental or statistical technique. But this merely illustrates that proving broad sociological propositions by statistics is a dubious business, and one that inevitably is in tension with the normative philosophy that underlies the Equal Protection Clause. Suffice to say that the showing offered by the appellees does not satisfy us that sex represents a legitimate, accurate proxy for the regulation of drinking and driving. . . .

We hold, therefore, that under *Reed*, Oklahoma's 3.2% beer statute invidiously discriminates against males 18–20 years of age.

Mr. Justice STEVENS, concurring.

There is only one Equal Protection Clause. It requires every State to govern impartially. It does not direct the courts to apply one standard of review in some cases and a different standard in other cases. . . .

I am inclined to believe that what has become known as the two-tiered analysis of equal protection claims does not describe a completely logical method of deciding cases, but rather is a method the Court has employed to explain decisions that actually apply a single standard in a reasonably consistent fashion. . . .

Mr. Justice STEWART, concurring in the judgment.

. . .The disparity created by these Oklahoma statutes amounts to total irrationality. For the statistics upon which the State now relies, whatever their other shortcomings, wholly fail to prove or even suggest that 3.2% beer is somehow more deleterious when it comes into the hands of a male aged 18–20 than of a female of like age. The disparate statutory treatment of the sexes here, without even a colorably valid justification or explanation, thus amounts to invidious discrimination.

Mr. Chief Justice BURGER, dissenting.

. . .The means employed by the Oklahoma Legislature to achieve the objectives sought may not be agreeable to some judges, but since eight Members of the Court think the means not irrational, I see no basis for striking down the statute as violative of the Constitution simply because we find it unwise, unneeded, or possibly even a bit foolish.

With Mr. Justice REHNQUIST, I would affirm the judgment of the District Court.

Mr. Justice REHNQUIST, dissenting.

The Court's disposition of this case is objectionable on two grounds. First is its conclusion that men challenging a gender-based statute which treats them less favorably than women may invoke a more stringent standard of judicial review than pertains to most other types of classifications. Second is the Court's enunciation of this standard, without citation to any source, as being that "classifications by gender must serve important governmental objectives and must be substantially related to achievement of those objectives." The only redeeming feature of the Court's opinion, to my mind, is that it apparently signals a retreat by those who joined the plurality opinion in *Frontiero v. Richardson,* from their view that sex is a "suspect" classification for purposes of equal protection analysis. I think the Oklahoma statute challenged here need pass only the "rational basis" equal protection analysis expounded in cases such as ... *Williamson v. Lee Optical Co.* (1955). ...

REGENTS OF THE UNIVERSITY OF CALIFORNIA V. BAKKE (1978)

Few issues have so persistently divided Americans as that of affirmative action or, as its opponents labeled it, racial quotas. The Burger Court reflected these divisions every bit as much as did the American public. Justice Lewis Powell held the key vote and straddled the fissure that divided the other eight justices into two four-judge blocs. For his part, Powell rejected quotas as violating equal protection, but went on to argue that the goal of achieving a "diverse student body" allowed universities to use race as one factor, among others, in making admissions decisions.

Mr. Justice POWELL announced the judgment of the Court.

This case presents a challenge to the special admissions program of ... the Medical School of the University of California at Davis, which is designed to assure the admission of a specified number of students from certain minority groups. ...

For the reasons stated in the following opinion, I believe that so much of the judgment of the California court as holds petitioner's special admissions program unlawful and directs that respondent be admitted to the Medical School must be affirmed. For the reasons expressed in a separate opinion, my Brothers the Chief Justice, Mr. Justice STEWART, Mr. Justice REHNQUIST, and Mr. Justice STEVENS concur in this judgment.

I also conclude for the reasons stated in the following opinion that the portion of the court's judgment enjoining petitioner from according any consideration to race in its admissions process must be reversed. For reasons expressed in separate opinions, my Brothers Mr. Justice BRENNAN, Mr. Justice WHITE, Mr. Justice MARSHALL, and Mr. Justice BLACKMUN concur in this judgment.

Affirmed in part and reversed in part.

I

The Medical School of the University of California at Davis opened in 1968. . . . In 1971, the size of the entering class was increased to 100 students, a level at which it remains. No admissions program for disadvantaged or minority students existed when the school opened, and the first class contained three Asians but no blacks, no Mexican-Americans, and no American Indians. Over the next two years, the faculty devised a special admissions program to increase the representation of "disadvantaged" students in each Medical School class. The special program consisted of a separate admissions system operating in coordination with the regular admissions process.

. . .

The special admissions program operated with a separate committee, a majority of whom were members of minority groups. On the 1973 application form, candidates were asked to indicate whether they wished to be considered as "economically and/or educationally disadvantaged" applicants; on the 1974 form the question was whether they wished to be considered as members of a "minority group," which the Medical School apparently viewed as "Blacks," "Chicanos," "Asians," and "American Indians." . . . If these questions were answered affirmatively, the application was forwarded to the special admissions committee. No formal definition of "disadvantaged" was ever produced, but the chairman of the special committee screened each application to see whether it reflected economic or educational deprivation. . . .

Allan Bakke is a white male who applied to the Davis Medical School. . . .

Bakke's 1974 application was completed early in the year. His student interviewer gave him an overall rating of 94, finding him "friendly, well tempered, conscientious and delightful to speak with." His faculty interviewer was, by coincidence, the same Dr. Lowrey to whom he had written in protest of the special admissions program. Dr. Lowrey found Bakke "rather limited in his approach" to the problems of the medical profession and found disturbing Bakke's "very definite opinions which were based more on his personal viewpoints than upon a study of the total problem." Dr. Lowrey gave Bakke the lowest of his six ratings, an 86; his total was 549 out of 600. Again, Bakke's application was rejected. . . . In both years, applicants were admitted under the special program with grade point averages, MCAT scores, and benchmark scores significantly lower than Bakke's.

After the second rejection, Bakke filed the instant suit in the Superior Court of California. . . . He alleged that the Medical School's special admissions program operated to exclude him from the school on the basis of his race. . . . The trial court found that the special program operated as a racial quota, because minority applicants in the special program were rated only against one another and 16 places in the class of 100 were reserved for them. Declaring that the University could not take race into account in making admissions decisions, the trial court held the challenged program violative of the Federal Constitution, the State Constitution, and Title VI. . . .

B

The language of [Title VI], like that of the Equal Protection Clause, is majestic in its sweep:

No person in the United States shall, on the ground of race, color, or national origin, be excluded from participation in, be denied the benefits of, or be subjected to discrimination under any program or activity receiving Federal financial assistance.

The concept of "discrimination," like the phrase "equal protection of the laws," is susceptible of varying interpretations. . . .

. . . [T]he legislation's supporters [refused] precisely to define the term "discrimination." Opponents sharply criticized this failure, but proponents of the bill merely replied that the meaning of "discrimination" would be made clear by reference to the Constitution or other existing law. For example, Senator Humphrey noted the relevance of the Constitution:

As I have said, the bill has a simple purpose. That purpose is to give fellow citizens—Negroes—the same rights and opportunities that white people take for granted. This is no more than what was preached by the prophets, and by Christ Himself. It is no more than what our Constitution guarantees.

In view of the clear legislative intent, Title VI must be held to proscribe only those racial classifications that would violate the Equal Protection Clause or the Fifth Amendment. . . .

IV

We have held that in "order to justify the use of a suspect classification, a State must show that its purpose or interest is both constitutionally permissible and substantial, and that its use of the classification is "necessary . . . to the accomplishment of its purpose or the safeguarding of its interest." . . . The special admissions program purports to serve the purposes of: (i) "reducing the historic deficit of traditionally disfavored minorities in medical schools and in the medical profession," (ii) countering the effects of societal discrimination; (iii) increasing the number of physicians who will practice in communities currently underserved; and (iv) obtaining the educational benefits that flow from an ethnically diverse student body. It is necessary to decide which, if any, of these purposes is substantial enough to support the use of a suspect classification.

A

. . .The fourth goal asserted by petitioner is the attainment of a diverse student body. This clearly is a constitutionally permissible goal for an institution of higher education. Academic freedom, though not a specifically enumerated constitutional right, long has been viewed as a special concern of the First Amendment. The freedom of a university to make its own judgments as to education includes the selection of its student body. . . .

Ethnic diversity, however, is only one element in a range of factors a university properly may consider in attaining the goal of a heterogeneous student body. Although a university must have wide discretion in making the sensitive judgments as to who should be admitted, constitutional limitations protecting individual rights may not be disregarded. Respondent urges—and the courts below have held—that petitioner's dual admissions program is a racial classification that impermissibly infringes his rights under the Fourteenth Amendment. As the interest of diversity is compelling in the context of a university's admissions program, the question remains whether the program's racial classification is necessary to promote this interest.

V

A

It may be assumed that the reservation of a specified number of seats in each class for individuals from the preferred ethnic groups would contribute to the attainment of considerable ethnic diversity in the student body. But petitioner's argument that this is the only effective means of serving the interest of diversity is seriously flawed. . . .

The experience of other university admissions programs, which take race into account in achieving the educational diversity valued by the First Amendment, demonstrates that the assignment of a fixed number of places to a minority group is not a necessary means toward that end. An illuminating example is found in the Harvard College program:

In recent years Harvard College has expanded the concept of diversity to include students from disadvantaged economic, racial and ethnic groups. Harvard College now recruits not only Californians or Louisianans but also blacks and Chicanos and other minority students. . . .

In practice, this new definition of diversity has meant that race has been a factor in some admission decisions. When the Committee on Admissions reviews the large middle group of applicants who are "admissible" and deemed capable of doing good work in their courses, the race of an applicant may tip the balance in his favor just as geographic origin or a life spent on a farm may tip the balance in other candidates' cases. A farm boy from Idaho can bring something to Harvard College that a Bostonian cannot offer. Similarly, a black student can usually bring something that a white person cannot offer. . . .

In such an admissions program, race or ethnic background may be deemed a "plus" in a particular applicant's file, yet it does not insulate the individual from comparison with all other candidates for the available seats. . . .

This kind of program treats each applicant as an individual in the admissions process. The applicant who loses out on the last available seat to another candidate receiving a "plus" on the basis of ethnic background will not have been foreclosed from all consideration for that seat simply because he was not the right color or had the wrong surname. It would mean only that his combined qualifications, which may have included similar nonobjective factors, did not outweigh those of the other applicant. His qualifications would have been weighed fairly and competitively, and he would have no basis to complain of unequal treatment under the Fourteenth Amendment.

In summary, it is evident that the Davis special admissions program involves the use of an explicit racial classification never before countenanced by this Court. It tells applicants who are not Negro, Asian, or Chicano that they are totally excluded from a specific percentage of the seats in an entering class. No matter how strong their qualifications, quantitative and extracurricular, including their own potential for contribution to educational diversity, they are never afforded the chance to compete with applicants from the preferred groups for the special admissions seats. At the same time, the preferred applicants have the opportunity to compete for every seat in the class.

The fatal flaw in petitioner's preferential program is its disregard of individual rights as guaranteed by the Fourteenth Amendment. Such rights are not absolute. But when a State's distribution of benefits or imposition of burdens hinges on ancestry or the color of a person's skin, that individual is entitled to a demonstration that the challenged classification is necessary to promote a substantial state interest. Petitioner has failed to carry this burden. For this reason, that portion of the California court's judgment holding petitioner's special admissions program invalid under the Fourteenth Amendment must be affirmed.

Opinion of Mr. Justice BRENNAN, Mr. Justice WHITE, Mr. Justice MARSHALL, and Mr. Justice BLACKMUN, concurring in the judgment in part and dissenting in part.

The Court today . . . affirms the constitutional power of Federal and State Governments to act affirmatively to achieve equal opportunity for all. The difficulty of the issue presented—whether government may use race-conscious programs to redress the continuing effects of past discrimination and the mature consideration which each of our Brethren has brought to it have resulted in many opinions, no single one speaking for the Court. But this should not and must not mask the central meaning of today's opinions: Government may take race into account when it acts not to demean or insult any racial group, but to remedy disadvantages cast on minorities by past racial prejudice, at least when appropriate findings have been made by judicial, legislative, or administrative bodies with competence to act in this area.

The Chief Justice and our Brothers STEWART, REHNQUIST, and STEVENS, have concluded that Title VI of the Civil Rights Act of 1964, prohibits programs such as that at the Davis Medical School. On this statutory theory alone, they would hold that respondent Allan Bakke's rights have been violated and that he must, therefore, be admitted to the Medical School. Our Brother POWELL, reaching the Constitution, concludes that, although race may be taken into account in university admissions, the particular special admissions program used by petitioner, which resulted in the exclusion of respondent Bakke, was not shown to be necessary to achieve petitioner's stated goals. Accordingly, these Members of the Court form a majority of five affirming the judgment of the Supreme Court of California insofar as it holds that respondent Bakke "is entitled to an order that he be admitted to the University." ...

I

Our Nation was founded on the principle that "all Men are created equal." Yet candor requires acknowledgment that the Framers of our Constitution, to forge the 13 Colonies into one Nation, openly compromised this principle of equality with its antithesis: slavery. The consequences of this compromise are well known and have aptly been called our "American Dilemma." Still, it is well to recount how recent the time has been, if it has yet come, when the promise of our principles has flowered into the actuality of equal opportunity for all regardless of race or color.

The Fourteenth Amendment, the embodiment in the Constitution of our abiding belief in human equality, has been the law of our land for only slightly more than half its 200 years. And for half of that half, the Equal Protection Clause of the Amendment was largely moribund. ...

Against this background, claims that law must be "color-blind" or that the datum of race is no longer relevant to public policy must be seen as aspiration rather than as description of reality. This is not to denigrate aspiration; for reality rebukes us that race has too often been used by those who would stigmatize and oppress minorities. Yet we cannot ... let color blindness become myopia which masks the reality that many "created equal" have been treated within our lifetimes as inferior both by the law and by their fellow citizens.

. . .

Unquestionably, we have held that a government practice or statute which restricts "fundamental rights" or which contains "suspect classifications" is to be subjected to "strict scrutiny" and can be justified only if it furthers a compelling government purpose and, even then, only if no less restrictive alternative is available. But no fundamental right is involved here. Nor do whites as a class have any of the "traditional indicia of suspectness: the class is not saddled with such disabilities, or subjected to such a history of purposeful unequal treatment, or relegated to such a position of political powerlessness as to command extraordinary protection from the majoritarian political process" (see *United States v. Carolene Products Co.*).

. . .

On the other hand, the fact that this case does not fit neatly into our prior analytic framework for race cases does not mean that it should be analyzed by applying the very loose rational-basis standard of review that is the very least that is always applied in equal protection cases. . . . Instead, a number of considerations—developed in gender-discrimination cases but which carry even more force when applied to racial classifications—lead us to conclude that racial classifications designed to further remedial purposes "must serve important governmental objectives and must be substantially related to achievement of those objectives."

. . .

Davis' articulated purpose of remedying the effects of past societal discrimination is, under our cases, sufficiently important to justify the use of race-conscious admissions programs where there is a sound basis for concluding that minority underrepresentation is substantial and chronic, and that the handicap of past discrimination is impeding access of minorities to the Medical School.

. . .

The "Harvard" program, as those employing it readily concede, openly and successfully employs a racial criterion for the purpose of ensuring that some of the scarce places in institutions of higher education are allocated to disadvantaged minority students. That the Harvard approach does not also make public the extent of the preference and the precise workings of the system while the Davis program employs a specific, openly stated number, does not condemn the latter plan for purposes of Fourteenth Amendment adjudication. It may be that the Harvard plan is more acceptable to the public than is the Davis "quota." If it is, any State, including California, is free to adopt it in preference to a less acceptable alternative, just as it is generally free, as far as the Constitution is concerned, to abjure granting any racial preferences in its admissions program. But there is no basis for preferring a particular preference program simply because in achieving the same goals that the Davis Medical School is pursuing, it proceeds in a manner that is not immediately apparent to the public.

Mr. Justice MARSHALL:

I agree with the judgment of the Court only insofar as it permits a university to consider the race of an applicant in making admissions decisions. I do not agree that petitioner's admissions program violates the Constitution. For it must be remembered that, during most of the past 200 years, the Constitution as interpreted by this Court did not prohibit the most ingenious and pervasive forms of discrimination against the Negro. Now, when a state acts to remedy the effects of that legacy of discrimination, I cannot believe that this same Constitution stands as a barrier.

I

A

Three hundred and fifty years ago, the Negro was dragged to this country in chains to be sold into slavery. Uprooted from his homeland and thrust into bondage for forced labor, the slave was deprived of all legal rights. It was unlawful to teach him to read; he could be sold away from his family and friends at the whim of his master; and killing or maiming him was not a crime. The system of slavery brutalized and dehumanized both master and slave.

. . .

The status of the Negro as property was officially erased by his emancipation at the end of the Civil War. But the long-awaited emancipation, while freeing the Negro from slavery, did not bring him citizenship or equality in any meaningful way. Slavery was replaced by a system of "laws which imposed upon the colored race onerous disabilities and burdens, and curtailed their rights in the pursuit of life, liberty, and property to such an extent that their freedom was of little value" (*Slaughter-House Cases*). Despite the passage of the Thirteenth, Fourteenth, and Fifteenth Amendments, the Negro was systematically denied the rights those Amendments were supposed to secure. The combined actions and inactions of the State and Federal Governments maintained Negroes in a position of legal inferiority for another century after the Civil War.

. . .

The position of the Negro today in America is the tragic but inevitable consequence of centuries of unequal treatment. Measured by any benchmark of comfort or achievement, meaningful equality remains a distant dream for the Negro.

A Negro child today has a life expectancy which is shorter by more than five years than that of a white child. The Negro child's mother is over three times more likely to die of complications in childbirth, and the infant mortality rate for Negroes is nearly twice that for whites. The median income of the Negro family is only 60% that of the median of a white family, and the percentage of Negroes who live in families with incomes below the poverty line is nearly four times greater than that of whites.

When the Negro child reaches working age, he finds that America offers him significantly less than it offers his white counterpart. For Negro adults, the unemployment rate is twice that of whites, and the unemployment rate for Negro teenagers is nearly three times that of white teenagers. A Negro male who completes four years of college can expect a median annual income of merely $110 more than a white male who has only a high school diploma. Although Negroes represent 11.5% of the population, they are only 1.2% of the lawyers and judges, 2% of the physicians, 2.3% of the dentists, 1.1 % of the engineers and 2.6% of the college and university professors.

The relationship between those figures and the history of unequal treatment afforded to the Negro cannot be denied. At every point from birth to death the impact of the past is reflected in the still disfavored position of the Negro.

In light of the sorry history of discrimination and its devastating impact on the lives of Negroes, bringing the Negro into the mainstream of American life should be a state interest of the highest order. To fail to do so is to ensure that America will forever remain a divided society.

. . .

It is plain that the Fourteenth Amendment was not intended to prohibit measures designed to remedy the effects of the Nation's past treatment of Negroes. The Congress that passed the Fourteenth Amendment is the same Congress that passed the 1866 Freedmen's Bureau Act, an Act that provided many of its benefits only to Negroes (Act of July 16, 1866). Although the Freedmen's Bureau legislation provided aid for refugees, thereby including white persons within some of the relief measures, the bill was regarded, to the dismay of many Congressmen, as "solely and entirely for the freedmen, and to the exclusion of all other persons. . . ." Indeed, the bill was bitterly opposed on the ground that it "undertakes to make the negro in some respects . . . superior . . . and gives them favors that the poor white boy in the North cannot get." The bill's supporters defended it—not by rebutting the claim of special treatment—but by pointing to the need for such treatment. . . .

Since the Congress that considered and rejected the objections to the 1866 Freedmen's Bureau Act concerning special relief to Negroes also proposed the Fourteenth Amendment, it is inconceivable that the Fourteenth Amendment was intended to prohibit all race-conscious relief measures. . . .

While I applaud the judgment of the Court that a university may consider race in its admissions process, it is more than a little ironic that, after several hundred years of class-based discrimination against Negroes, the Court is unwilling to hold that a class-based remedy for that discrimination is permissible. In declining to so hold, today's judgment ignores the fact that for several hundred years Negroes have been discriminated against, not as individuals, but rather solely because of the color of their skins. It is unnecessary in 20th-century America to have individual Negroes demonstrate that they have been victims of racial discrimination; the racism of our society has been so pervasive that none, regardless of wealth or position, has managed to escape its impact. The experience of Negroes in America has been different in kind, not just in degree, from that of other ethnic groups. It is not merely the history of slavery alone but also that a whole people were marked as inferior by the law. And that mark has endured. The dream of America as the great melting pot has not been realized for the Negro; because of his skin color he never even made it into the pot.

. . .

I fear that we have come full circle. After the Civil War our Government started several "affirmative action" programs. This Court in the *Civil Rights Cases* and *Plessy v. Ferguson* destroyed the movement toward complete equality. For almost a century no action was taken, and this nonaction was with the tacit approval of the courts. Then we had *Brown v. Board of Education* and the Civil Rights Acts of Congress, followed by numerous affirmative-action programs. Now, we have this

Court again stepping in, this time to stop affirmative-action programs of the type used by the University of California.

R OSTKER V. GOLDBERG (1 9 8 1)

Although the Equal Rights Amendment failed to gain ratification from the required three-quarters of the states and, as a result, died, suits by women challenging allegedly discriminatory legislation before the Supreme Court were routinely successful. Indeed, some wondered whether the adoption of ERA would have had any but symbolic effect. Justice William Rehnquist's opinion upholding the Military Selective Service Act's refusal to require women to register for the draft may be an example of how the ERA may have triggered a different result had ERA been adopted.

Justice REHNQUIST delivered the opinion of the Court.

The question presented is whether the Military Selective Service Act . . . violates the Fifth Amendment to the United States Constitution in authorizing the President to require the registration of males and not females.

I

. . . [T]he District Court issued an opinion finding that the Act violated the Due Process Clause of the Fifth Amendment and permanently enjoined the Government from requiring registration under the Act. . . . [T]he court rejected plaintiffs' suggestions that the equal protection claim should be tested under "strict scrutiny," and also rejected defendants' argument that the deference due Congress in the area of military affairs required application of the traditional "minimum scrutiny" test. Applying the "important government interest" test articulated in *Craig,* the court struck down the MSSA. . . .

No one could deny that under the test of *Craig v. Boren,* the Government's interest in raising and supporting armies is an "important governmental interest." . . . Nor can it be denied that the imposing number of cases from this Court previously cited suggest that judicial deference to such congressional exercise of authority is at its apogee when legislative action under the congressional authority to raise and support armies and make rules and regulations for their governance is challenged. . . .

III

This case is quite different from several of the gender-based discrimination cases we have considered in that, despite appellees' assertions, Congress did not act "unthinkingly" or "reflexively and not for any considered reason." The question of registering women for the draft not only received considerable national attention and was the subject of wide-ranging public debate, but also was extensively considered by Congress in hearings, floor debate, and in committee. . . .

Congress' decision to authorize the registration of only men, therefore, does not violate the Due Process Clause. The exemption of women from registration is not only sufficiently but also closely related to Congress' purpose in authorizing registration. The fact that Congress and the Executive have decided that women should not serve in combat fully justifies Congress in not authorizing their registration, since the purpose of registration is to develop a pool of potential combat troops. . . .

In light of the foregoing, we conclude that Congress acted well within its constitutional authority when it authorized the registration of men, and not women, under the Military Selective Service Act. . . .

Reversed.

Justice MARSHALL, with whom Justice BRENNAN joins, dissenting.

. . .By now it should be clear that statutes like the MSSA, which discriminate on the basis of gender, must be examined under the "heightened" scrutiny mandated by *Craig*. Under this test, a gender-based classification cannot withstand constitutional challenge unless the classification is substantially related to the achievement of an important governmental objective. . . .

The MSSA states that "an adequate armed strength must be achieved and maintained to insure the security of this Nation." I agree with the majority, that "[n]o one could deny that . . . the Government's interest in raising and supporting armies is an 'important governmental interest.'" Consequently, the first part of the *Craig* test is satisfied. But the question remains whether the discriminatory means employed itself substantially serves the statutory end. . . .

According to the Senate Report, "[t]he policy precluding the use of women in combat is . . . the most important reason for not including women in a registration system." . . .

Had appellees raised a constitutional challenge to the prohibition against assignment of women to combat, this discussion in the Senate Report might well provide persuasive reasons for upholding the restrictions. But the validity of the combat restrictions is not an issue we need decide in this case. Moreover, since the combat restrictions on women have already been accomplished through statutes and policies that remain in force whether or not women are required to register or to be drafted, including women in registration and draft plans will not result in their being assigned to combat roles. Thus, even assuming that precluding the use of women in combat is an important governmental interest in its own right, there can be no suggestion that the exclusion of women from registration and a draft is substantially related to the achievement of this goal.

BOWERS V. HARDWICK (1986)

The Court's decisions in Griswold v. Connecticut *(1965) and* Roe v. Wade *(1973), decisions based on the right of privacy found in the Fourteenth Amendment's guarantee of due process, gave hope to opponents of state legislation criminalizing acts of sodomy that such statutes were equally defective as earlier laws that had prohibited the use of contraceptives and that had prohibited or limited abortion. With Justice Lewis Powell providing the key vote, the Supreme Court rejected the analogy and upheld the Georgia statute.*

Justice WHITE delivered the opinion of the Court.

. . . Hardwick (hereafter respondent) was charged with violating the Georgia statute criminalizing sodomy by committing that act with another adult male in the bedroom of respondent's home. . . .

This case does not require a judgment on whether laws against sodomy between consenting adults in general, or between homosexuals in particular, are wise or desirable. It raises no question about the right or propriety of state legislative decisions to repeal their laws that criminalize homosexual sodomy, or of state-court decisions invalidating those laws on state constitutional grounds. The issue presented is whether the Federal Constitution confers a fundamental right upon homosexuals to engage in sodomy and hence invalidates the laws of the many States that still make such conduct illegal and have done so for a very long time. . . .

We first register our disagreement with the Court of Appeals and with respondent that the Court's prior cases have construed the Constitution to confer a right of privacy that extends to homosexual sodomy and for all intents and purposes have decided this case....

... No connection between family, marriage, or procreation on the one hand and homosexual activity on the other has been demonstrated.... Moreover, any claim that these cases nevertheless stand for the proposition that any kind of private sexual conduct between consenting adults is constitutionally insulated from state proscription is unsupportable....

Precedent aside, however, respondent would have us announce, as the Court of Appeals did, a fundamental right to engage in homosexual sodomy. This we are quite unwilling to do. It is true that despite the language of the Due Process Clauses of the Fifth and Fourteenth Amendments, which appears to focus only on the processes by which life, liberty, or property is taken, the cases are legion in which those Clauses have been interpreted to have substantive content, subsuming rights that to a great extent are immune from federal or state regulation or proscription. Among such cases are those recognizing rights that have little or no textual support in the constitutional language. *Meyer, Prince,* and *Pierce* fall in this category, as do the privacy cases from *Griswold* to *Carey.*

Striving to assure itself and the public that announcing rights not readily identifiable in the Constitution's text involves much more than the imposition of the Justices' own choice of values on the States and the Federal Government, the Court has sought to identify the nature of the rights qualifying for heightened judicial protection. In *Palko v. Connecticut* (1937), it was said that this category includes those fundamental liberties that are "implicit in the concept of ordered liberty," such that "neither liberty nor justice would exist if [they] were sacrificed." A different description of fundamental liberties appeared in *Moore v. East Cleveland* (1977) where they are characterized as those liberties that are "deeply rooted in this Nation's history and tradition."

It is obvious to us that neither of these formulations would extend a fundamental right to homosexuals to engage in acts of consensual sodomy. Proscriptions against that conduct have ancient roots....

Even if the conduct at issue here is not a fundamental right, respondent asserts that there must be a rational basis for the law and that there is none in this case other than the presumed belief of a majority of the electorate in Georgia that homosexual sodomy is immoral and unacceptable. This is said to be an inadequate rationale to support the law. The law, however, is constantly based on notions of morality, and if all laws representing essentially moral choices are to be invalidated under the Due Process Clause, the courts will be very busy indeed. Even respondent makes no such claim, but insists that majority sentiments about the morality of homosexuality should be declared inadequate. We do not agree, and are unpersuaded that the sodomy laws of some 25 States should be invalidated on this basis.

Accordingly, the judgment of the Court of Appeals is reversed.

Justice POWELL, concurring.

I join the opinion of the Court. I agree with the Court that there is no fundamental right—*i.e.*, no substantive right under the Due Process Clause.... This is not to suggest, however, that respondent may not be protected by the Eighth Amendment of the Constitution. The Georgia statute at issue in this case authorizes a court to imprison a person for up to 20 years for a single private, consensual act of sodomy. In my view, a prison sentence for such conduct—certainly a sentence of long duration—would create a serious Eighth Amendment issue....

Justice BLACKMUN, with whom Justice BRENNAN, Justice MARSHALL, and Justice STEVENS join, dissenting.

This case is no more about "a fundamental right to engage in homosexual sodomy," as the Court purports to declare than *Stanley v. Georgia* (1969), was about a fundamental right to watch obscene movies, or *Katz v. United States* (1967), was about a fundamental right to place interstate bets from a telephone booth. Rather, this case is about "the most comprehensive of rights and the right most valued by civilized men," namely, "the right to be let alone" (*Olmstead v. United States* (1928) [Brandeis, J., dissenting]).

. . .

The Court's failure to comprehend the magnitude of the liberty interests at stake in this case leads it to slight the question whether petitioner, on behalf of the State, has justified Georgia's infringement on these interests....

First, petitioner asserts that the acts made criminal by the statute may have serious adverse consequences for "the general public health and welfare," such as spreading communicable diseases or fostering other criminal activity. . . . Nothing in the record before the Court provides any justification for finding the activity forbidden . . . to be physically dangerous, either to the persons engaged in it or to others.

. . . Essentially, petitioner argues, and the Court agrees, that the fact that the acts . . . "for hundreds of years, if not thousands, have been uniformly condemned as immoral" is a sufficient reason to permit a State to ban them today.

I cannot agree that either the length of time a majority has held its convictions or the passions with which it defends them can withdraw legislation from this Court's security (see, *e.g.*, *Roe v. Wade*).

The assertion that "traditional Judeo-Christian values proscribe" the conduct involved cannot provide an adequate justification. . . . That certain, but by no means all, religious groups condemn the behavior at issue gives the State no license to impose their judgments on the entire citizenry. The legitimacy of secular legislation depends instead on whether the State can advance some justification for its law beyond its conformity to religious doctrine. . . .

This case involves no real interference with the rights of others, for the mere knowledge that other individuals do not adhere to one's value system cannot be a legally cognizable interest, let alone an interest that can justify invading the houses, hearts, and minds of citizens who choose to live their lives differently.

It took but three years for the Court to see the error in its analysis in *Minersville School District v. Gobitis* (1940), and to recognize that the threat to national cohesion posed by a refusal to salute the flag was vastly outweighed by the threat to those same values posed by compelling such a salute (see *West Virginia Board of Education v. Barnette* [1943]). I can only hope that here, too, the Court soon will reconsider its analysis and conclude that depriving individuals of the right to choose for themselves how to conduct their intimate relationships poses a far greater threat to the values most deeply rooted in our Nation's history than tolerance of nonconformity could ever do. Because I think the Court today betrays those values, I dissent.

Justice STEVENS, with whom Justice BRENNAN and Justice
MARSHALL join, dissenting.

...Society has every right to encourage its individual members to follow particular traditions in expressing affection for one another and in
gratifying their personal desires. It, of course, may prohibit an individual from imposing his will on another to satisfy his own selfish interests.
It also may prevent an individual from interfering with, or violating, a
legally sanctioned and protected relationship, such as marriage. And it
may explain the relative advantages and disadvantages of different forms
of intimate expression. But when individual married couples are isolated
from observation by others, the way in which they voluntarily choose to
conduct their intimate relations is a matter for them—not the State—to
decide. The essential "liberty" that animated the development of the law
in cases like *Griswold* [and] *Eisenstadt* ... surely embraces the right to
engage in nonreproductive, sexual conduct that others may consider of-
fensive or immoral.

Richmond v. J. A. Croson Co. (1989)

Bakke *did not settle the issue of affirmative action. Although the Burger
Court sustained a federal program in* Fullilove v. Klutznick *(1980), the
Reagan appointments to the Court produced a Court whose interpretation
of the Equal Protection Clause differed dramatically from the views
prevalent a decade earlier. Although the dissenters in* Croson *saw the case
as identical to* Fullilove, *the majority took a very different viewpoint.*

Justice O'CONNOR announced the judgment of the Court and delivered the opinion of the Court with respect to Parts I, III-B, and IV, an
opinion with respect to Part II, in which the Chief Justice and Justice
WHITE join, and an opinion with respect to Parts III-A and V, in which
the Chief Justice, Justice WHITE, and Justice KENNEDY join.

In this case, we confront once again the tension between the Fourteenth Amendment's guarantee of equal treatment to all citizens, and the
use of race-based measures to ameliorate the effects of past discrimination on the opportunities enjoyed by members of minority groups in
our society. In *Fullilove v. Klutznick* (1980), we held that a congressional
program requiring that 10% of certain federal construction grants be
awarded to minority contractors did not violate the equal protection

principles embodied in the Due Process Clause of the Fifth Amendment. . . .

I

On April 11, 1983, the Richmond City Council adopted the Minority Business Utilization Plan. . . . The Plan required prime contractors to whom the city awarded construction contracts to subcontract at least 30% of the dollar amount of the contract to one or more Minority Business Enterprises. . . .

There was no direct evidence of race discrimination on the part of the city in letting contracts or any evidence that the city's prime contractors had discriminated against minority-owned subcontractors. . . .

II

. . . . [A]ppellee argues that the city must limit any race-based remedial efforts to eradicating the effects of its own prior discrimination. This is essentially the position taken by the Court of Appeals below. Appellant argues that our decision in *Fullilove* is controlling, and that as a result the city of Richmond enjoys sweeping legislative power to define and attack the effects of prior discrimination in its local construction industry. We find that neither of these two rather stark alternatives can withstand analysis.

. . .

That Congress may identify and redress the effects of society-wide discrimination does not mean that, *a fortiori,* the States and their political subdivisions are free to decide that such remedies are appropriate. Section 1 of the Fourteenth Amendment is an explicit constraint on state power and the States must undertake any remedial efforts in accordance with that provision. To hold otherwise would be to cede control over the content of the Equal Protection Clause to the 50 state legislatures and their myriad political subdivisions. . . . We believe that such a result would be contrary to the intentions of the Framers of the Fourteenth Amendment, who desired to place clear limits on the States' use of race as a criterion for legislative action, and to have the federal courts enforce those limitations. . . .

[However], . . . if the city could show that it had essentially become a "passive participant" in a system of racial exclusion practiced by elements of the local construction industry, we think it clear that the city could take affirmative steps to dismantle such a system. It is beyond dispute that any public entity, state or federal, has a compelling interest in assuring that public dollars, drawn from the tax contributions of all citizens, do not serve to finance the evil of private prejudice. . . .

III

A

. . . [T]he "rights created by the first section of the Fourteenth Amendment are, by its terms, guaranteed to the individual. The rights established are personal rights." The Richmond Plan denies certain citizens the opportunity to compete for a fixed percentage of public contracts based solely upon their race. To whatever racial group these citizens belong, their "personal rights" to be treated with equal dignity and respect are implicated by a rigid rule erecting race as the sole criterion in an aspect of public decisionmaking.

Absent searching judicial inquiry into the justification for such race-based measures, there is simply no way of determining what classifications are "benign" or "remedial" and what classifications are in fact motivated by illegitimate notions of racial inferiority or simple racial politics. Indeed, the purpose of strict scrutiny is to "smoke out" illegitimate uses of race by assuring that the legislative body is pursuing a goal important enough to warrant use of a highly suspect tool. The test also ensures that the means chosen "fit" this compelling goal so closely that there is little or no possibility that the motive for the classification was illegitimate racial prejudice or stereotype.

Classifications based on race carry a danger of stigmatic harm. Unless they are strictly reserved for remedial settings, they may in fact promote notions of racial inferiority and lead to a politics of racial hostility. . . .

Under the standard proposed by Justice MARSHALL'S dissent, "race-conscious classifications designed to further remedial goals," are forthwith subject to a relaxed standard of review. . . .

Even were we to accept a reading of the guarantee of equal protection under which the level of scrutiny varies according to the ability of different groups to defend their interests in the representative process, heightened scrutiny would still be appropriate in the circumstances of this case. One of the central arguments for applying a less exacting standard to "benign" racial classifications is that such measures essentially involve a choice made by dominant racial groups to disadvantage themselves. If one aspect of the judiciary's role under the Equal Protection Clause is to protect "discrete and insular minorities" from majoritarian prejudice or indifference, some maintain that these concerns are not implicated when the "white majority" places burdens upon itself.

In this case, blacks constitute approximately 50% of the population of the city of Richmond. Five of the nine seats on the city council are held by blacks. The concern that a political majority will more easily act to the disadvantage of a minority based on unwarranted assumptions or incomplete facts would seem to militate for, not against, the application of heightened judicial scrutiny in this case.

. . .

In sum, none of the evidence presented by the city points to any identified discrimination in the Richmond construction industry. We, therefore, hold that the city has failed to demonstrate a compelling interest in apportioning public contracting opportunities on the basis of race. To accept Richmond's claim that past societal discrimination alone can serve as the basis for rigid racial preferences would be to open the door to competing claims for "remedial relief" for every disadvantaged group. The dream of a Nation of equal citizens in a society where race is irrelevant to personal opportunity and achievement would be lost in a mosaic of shifting preferences based on inherently unmeasurable claims of past wrongs. . . .

The foregoing analysis applies only to the inclusion of blacks within the Richmond set-aside program. There is absolutely no evidence of past discrimination against Spanish-speaking, Oriental, Indian, Eskimo, or Aleut persons in any aspect of the Richmond construction industry. . . . It may well be that Richmond has never had an Aleut or Eskimo citizen. The random inclusion of racial groups that, as a practical matter, may never have suffered from discrimination in the construction industry in Richmond suggests that perhaps the city's purpose was not in fact to remedy past discrimination.

If a 30% set-aside was "narrowly tailored" to compensate black contractors for past discrimination, one may legitimately ask why they are forced to share this "remedial relief" with an Aleut citizen who moves to Richmond tomorrow? The gross overinclusiveness of Richmond's racial preference strongly impugns the city's claim of remedial motivation. . . .

IV

. . . Because the city of Richmond has failed to identify the need for remedial action in the awarding of its public construction contracts, its treatment of its citizens on a racial basis violates the dictates of the Equal Protection Clause. Accordingly, the judgment of the Court of Appeals for the Fourth Circuit is affirmed.

Justice STEVENS, concurring in part and concurring in the judgment.

A central purpose of the Fourteenth Amendment is to further the national goal of equal opportunity for all our citizens. In order to achieve that goal we must learn from our past mistakes, but I believe the Constitution requires us to evaluate our policy decisions—including those that govern the relationships among different racial and ethnic groups—primarily by studying their probable impact on the future. I therefore do not agree with the premise that seems to underlie today's decision . . . that a governmental decision that rests on a racial classification is never permissible except as a remedy for a past wrong.

Justice SCALIA, concurring in the judgment.

I agree with much of the Court's opinion, and, in particular, with JUSTICE O'CONNOR'S conclusion that strict scrutiny must be applied to all governmental classification by race, whether or not its asserted purpose is "remedial" or "benign." I do not agree, however, with JUSTICE O'CONNOR'S dictum suggesting that, despite the Fourteenth Amendment, state and local governments may in some circumstances discriminate on the basis of race in order (in a broad sense) "to ameliorate the effects of past discrimination." . . .

It is plainly true that in our society blacks have suffered discrimination immeasurably greater than any directed at other racial groups. But those who believe that racial preferences can help to "even the score" display, and reinforce, a manner of thinking by race that was the source of the injustice and that will, if it endures within our society, be the source of more injustice still. The relevant proposition is not that it was blacks, or Jews, or Irish who were discriminated against, but that it was individual men and women, "created equal," who were discriminated against. And the relevant resolve is that that should never happen again. Racial preferences appear to "even the score" (in some small degree) only if one embraces the proposition that our society is appropriately viewed as divided into races, making it right that an injustice rendered in the past to a black man should be compensated for by discriminating against a white. Nothing is worth that embrace. Since blacks have been disproportionately disadvantaged by racial discrimination, any race-neutral remedial program aimed at the disadvantaged as such will have a disproportionately beneficial impact on blacks. Only such a program, and not one that operates on the basis of race, is in accord with the letter and the spirit of our Constitution.

Justice MARSHALL, with whom Justice BRENNAN and Justice BLACKMUN join, dissenting.

. . .

A

Today, for the first time, a majority of this Court has adopted strict scrutiny as its standard of Equal Protection Clause review of race-conscious remedial measures. This is an unwelcome development. A profound difference separates governmental actions that themselves are racist, and governmental actions that seek to remedy the effects of prior racism or to prevent neutral governmental activity from perpetuating the effects of such racism.

Racial classifications "drawn on the presumption that one race is inferior to another or because they put the weight of government behind racial hatred and separatism" warrant the strictest judicial scrutiny because of the very irrelevance of these rationales. By contrast, racial classifications drawn for the purpose of remedying the effects of discrimination that itself was race based have a highly pertinent basis: the tragic and indelible fact that discrimination against blacks and other racial minorities in this Nation has pervaded our Nation's history and continues to scar our society. . . .

In concluding that remedial classifications warrant no different standard of review under the Constitution than the most brutal and repugnant forms of state-sponsored racism, a majority of this Court signals that it regards racial discrimination as largely a phenomenon of the past, and that government bodies need no longer preoccupy themselves with rectifying racial injustice. I, however, do not believe this Nation is anywhere close to eradicating racial discrimination or its vestiges. In constitutionalizing its wishful thinking,the majority today does a grave disservice not only to those victims of past and present racial discrimination in this Nation whom government has sought to assist, but also to this Court's long tradition of approaching issues of race with the utmost sensitivity.

B

I am also troubled by the majority's assertion that, even if it did not believe generally in strict scrutiny of race-based remedial measures, "the circumstances of this case" require this Court to look upon the Richmond City Council's measure with the strictest scrutiny. The sole such circumstance which the majority cites, however, is the fact that blacks in Richmond are a "dominant racial group" in the city. In support of this characterization of dominance, the majority observes that "blacks constitute approximately 50% of the population of the city of Richmond" and that "five of the nine seats on the City Council are held by blacks."

While I agree that the numerical and political supremacy of a given racial group is a factor bearing upon the level of scrutiny to be applied, this Court has never held that numerical inferiority, standing alone, makes a racial group "suspect" and thus entitled to strict scrutiny review. Rather, we have identified other "traditional indicia of suspectness": whether a group has been "saddled with such disabilities, or subjected to such a history of purposeful unequal treatment, or relegated to such a position of political powerlessness as to command extraordinary protection from the majoritarian political process."

It cannot seriously be suggested that nonminorities in Richmond have any "history of purposeful unequal treatment." . . .

Justice BLACKMUN, with whom Justice BRENNAN joins, dissenting.

I join Justice MARSHALL'S perceptive and incisive opinion revealing great sensitivity toward those who have suffered the pains of economic discrimination in the construction trades for so long.

I never thought that I would live to see the day when the city of Richmond, Virginia, the cradle of the old Confederacy, sought on its own, within a narrow confine, to lessen the stark impact of persistent discrimination. But Richmond, to its great credit, acted. Yet this Court, the supposed bastion of equality, strikes down Richmond's efforts as though discrimination had never existed or was not demonstrated in this particular litigation.

FREEMAN V. PITTS (1992)

The Green *decision clearly mandated that formerly segregated systems must achieve "unitary" status. It did not say what would happen when this was achieved or whether all aspects of a system had to be changed before a district court could release a school system from its supervision. Although the Court's opinion in* Freeman *was unanimous, the separate opinions reflect very different attitudes about the role of courts in supervising public school systems.*

Justice KENNEDY delivered the opinion of the Court.

... This case involves a court-ordered desegregation decree for the DeKalb County School System (DCSS). DCSS now serves some 73,000 students ... , and is the 32d largest elementary and secondary school system in the Nation.

DCSS has been subject to the supervision ... of the United States District Court ... since 1969, when it was ordered to dismantle its dual school system. In 1986, petitioners filed a motion for final dismissal. The District Court ruled that DCSS had not achieved unitary status in all respects, but had done so in student attendance and three other categories. In its order, the District Court relinquished remedial control as to those aspects of the system in which unitary status had been achieved, and retained supervisory authority only for those aspects of the school system in which the district was not in full compliance. The Court of Appeals for the Eleventh Circuit reversed holding that a district court should retain full remedial authority over a school system until it achieves unitary status in six categories at the same time for several years. We now reverse the judgment of the Court of Appeals ... , holding that a district court is permitted to withdraw judicial supervision with respect to discrete categories in which the school district has achieved compliance with a court-ordered desegregation plan. ...

The District Court found DCSS to be "an innovative school system that has traveled the often long road to unitary status almost to its end," noting that the court has continually been impressed by the successes of the DCSS and its dedication to providing a quality education for all students within that system. ...

A

The duty and responsibility of a school district once segregated by law is to take all steps necessary to eliminate the vestiges of the unconstitutional *de jure* system. This is required in order to ensure that the principal wrong of the *de jure* system, the injuries and stigma inflicted upon the race disfavored by the violation, is no longer present. This was the rationale and the objective of *Brown I* and *Brown II.*

. . .

That the term "unitary" does not have fixed meaning or content is not inconsistent with the principles that control the exercise of equitable power. The essence of a court's equity power lies in its inherent capacity to adjust remedies in a feasible and practical way to eliminate the conditions or redress the injuries caused by unlawful action. Equitable remedies must be flexible if these underlying principles are to be enforced with fairness and precision. . . .

. . . A federal court in a school desegregation case has the discretion to order an incremental or partial withdrawal of its supervision and control. This discretion derives both from the constitutional authority which justified its intervention in the first instance and its ultimate objectives in formulating the decree. . . . In construing the remedial authority of the district courts, we have been guided by the principles that "judicial powers may be exercised only on the basis of a constitutional violation," and that "the nature of the violation determines the scope of the remedy" (Swann). . . .

We have said that the court's end purpose must be to remedy the violation and, in addition, to restore state and local authorities to the control of a school system that is operating in compliance with the Constitution. . . .

We hold that, in the course of supervising desegregation plans, federal courts have the authority to relinquish supervision and control of school districts in incremental stages, before full compliance has been achieved in every area of school operations. . . . In considering these factors, a court should give particular attention to the school system's record of compliance. A school system is better positioned to demonstrate its good faith commitment to a constitutional course of action when its policies form a consistent pattern of lawful conduct directed to eliminating earlier violations. And with the passage of time, the degree to which racial imbalances continue to represent vestiges of a constitutional violation may diminish, and the practicability and efficacy of various remedies ran be evaluated with more precision.

JUSTICE SCALIA, concurring.

. . .At some time, we must acknowledge that it has become absurd to assume, without any further proof, that violations of the Constitution dating from the days when Lyndon Johnson was President, or earlier, continue to have an appreciable effect upon current operation of schools. We are close to that time. While we must continue to prohibit, without qualification, all racial discrimination in the operation of public schools, and to afford remedies that eliminate not only the discrimination but its identified consequences, we should consider laying aside the extraordinary, and increasingly counterfactual, presumption of *Green*. We must soon revert to the ordinary principles of our law, of our democratic heritage, and of our educational tradition: that plaintiffs alleging equal protection violations must prove intent and causation, and not merely the existence of racial disparity.

Justice BLACKMUN, with whom Justice STEVENS and Justice O'CONNOR join, concurring in the judgment.

. . .DCSS has undertaken only limited remedial actions since the 1976 court order. The number of students participating in the M-to-M program has expanded somewhat, composing about 6% of the current student population. The district also has adopted magnet programs, but they involve fewer than 1% of the system's students. Doubtless DCSS could have started and expanded its magnet and M-to-M programs more promptly; it could have built and closed schools with a view toward promoting integration of both schools and neighborhoods; redrawn attendance zones; integrated its faculty and administrators; and spent its funds equally. But it did not. DCSS must prove that the measures it actually implemented satisfy its obligation to eliminate the vestiges of *de jure* segregation originally discovered in 1969, and still found to exist in 1976.

The District Court apparently has concluded that DCSS should be relieved of the responsibility to desegregate because such responsibility would be burdensome. To be sure, changes in demographic patterns aggravated the vestiges of segregation and made it more difficult for DCSS to desegregate. But an integrated school system is no less desirable because it is difficult to achieve, and it is no less a constitutional imperative because that imperative has gone unmet for 38 years.

Although respondents challenged the District Court's causation conclusions in the Court of Appeals, that court did not reach the issue. Accordingly, in addition to the issues the Court suggests be considered in further proceedings, I would remand for the Court of Appeals to review, under the foregoing principles, the District Court's finding that DCSS has met its burden of proving the racially identifiable schools are in no way the result of past segregative action.

SHAW V. RENO (1993)

Gerrymandering has a long history in U.S. politics. Generally, it has been used by the majority party to increase its majority in the legislature. This is accomplished by concentrating members of the minority party into certain districts while creating a greater number of districts in which it has a solid majority. Attempts to increase the number of African Americans in legislatures led certain states to create districts that would be most likely to elect African Americans. This was attacked as a form of racial gerrymandering. The resulting cases raise issues similar to those raised in affirmative action cases and pose the question of whether race should be used to advantage a formerly disadvantaged group.

Justice O'CONNOR delivered the opinion of the Court.

This case involves two of the most complex and sensitive issues this Court has faced in recent years: the meaning of the constitutional "right" to vote, and the propriety of race-based state legislation designed to benefit members of historically disadvantaged racial minority groups. As a result of the 1990 census, North Carolina became entitled to a 12th seat in the United States House of Representatives. The General Assembly enacted a reapportionment plan that included one majority-black congressional district. After the Attorney General of the United States objected to the plan pursuant to . . . the Voting Rights Act of 1965, the General Assembly passed new legislation creating a second majority-black district. Appellants allege that the revised plan, which contains district boundary lines of dramatically irregular shape, constitutes an unconstitutional racial gerrymander. . . .

The voting age population of North Carolina is approximately 78% white, 20% black, and 1% Native American; the remaining 1% is predominantly Asian. . . .

The first of the two majority-black districts contained in the revised plan, District 1, is somewhat hook shaped. . . . District 1 has been compared to a "Rorschach inkblot test," a "bug splattered on a windshield."

The second majority-black district, District 12, is even more unusually shaped. It is approximately 160 miles long and, for much of its length, no wider than the I-85 corridor. It winds in snake like fashion through tobacco country, financial centers, and manufacturing areas "until it gobbles in enough enclaves of black neighborhoods Northbound and southbound drivers on I-85 sometimes find themselves in separate districts in one county, only to trade districts when they enter the next county." Of the 10 counties through which District 12 passes, 5 are cut into 3 different districts; even towns are divided. At one point, the district remains contiguous only because it intersects at a single point with two other districts before crossing over them. One state legislator has remarked that "[i]f you drove down the interstate with both car doors open, you'd kill most of the people in the district." The district even has inspired poetry: "Ask not for whom the line is drawn; it is drawn to avoid thee."

. . .

Our focus is on appellants' claim that the State engaged in unconstitutional racial gerrymandering. That argument strikes a powerful historical chord: it is unsettling how closely the North Carolina plan resembles the most egregious racial gerrymanders of the past.

An understanding of the nature of appellants' claim is critical to our resolution of the case. In their complaint, appellants did not claim that the General Assembly's reapportionment plan unconstitutionally "diluted" white voting strength. They did not even claim to be white. Rather, appellants' complaint alleged that the deliberate segregation of voters into separate districts on the basis of race violated their constitutional right to participate in a "color-blind" electoral process.

Despite their invocation of the ideal of a "color-blind" Constitution, appellants appear to concede that race-conscious redistricting is not always unconstitutional.

. . .

Put differently, we believe that reapportionment is one area in which appearances do matter. A reapportionment plan that includes in one district individuals who belong to the same race, but who are otherwise widely separated by geographical and political boundaries, and who may have little in common with one another but the color of their skin, bears an uncomfortable resemblance to political apartheid. . . .

Racial classifications of any sort pose the risk of lasting harm to our society. They reinforce the belief, held by too many for too much of our history, that individuals should be judged by the color of their skin. Racial classifications with respect to voting carry particular dangers. Racial gerrymandering, even for remedial purposes, may balkanize us into competing racial factions; it threatens to carry us further from the goal of a political system in which race no longer matters—a goal that the Fourteenth and Fifteenth Amendments embody, and to which the Nation continues to aspire. It is for these reasons that race-based districting by our state legislatures demands close judicial scrutiny.

... [W]e hold only that appellants have stated a claim under the Equal Protection Clause by alleging that the North Carolina General Assembly adopted a reapportionment scheme so irrational on its face that it can be understood only as an effort to segregate voters into separate voting districts because of their race, and that the separation lacks sufficient justification. If the allegation of racial gerrymandering remains uncontradicted, the District Court further must determine whether the North Carolina plan is narrowly tailored to further a compelling governmental interest. Accordingly, we reverse the judgment of the District Court and remand the case for further proceedings consistent with this opinion.

It is so ordered.

Justice WHITE, with whom Justice BLACKMUN and Justice STEVENS join, dissenting.

The facts of this case mirror those presented in *United Jewish Organizations of Williamsburgh, Inc. v. Carey* (1977) (*UJO*), where the Court rejected a claim that creation of a majority-minority district violated the Constitution.... Of particular relevance, five of the Justices reasoned that members of the white majority could not plausibly argue that their influence over the political process had been unfairly canceled.... [T]hey held that plaintiffs were not entitled to relief under the Constitution's Equal Protection Clause. On the same reasoning, I would affirm the District Court's dismissal of appellants' claim in this instance.

The Court today chooses not to overrule, but rather to sidestep, *UJO*. It does so by glossing over the striking similarities, focusing on surface differences, most notably the (admittedly unusual) shape of the newly created district and imagining an entirely new cause of action. Because the holding is limited to such anomalous circumstances, it perhaps will not substantially hamper a State's legitimate efforts to redistrict in favor of racial minorities. Nonetheless, the notion that North Carolina's plan, under which whites remain a voting majority in a disproportionate number of congressional districts, and pursuant to which the State has sent its first black representatives since Reconstruction to the United States Congress, might have violated appellants' constitutional rights is both a fiction and a departure from settled equal protection principles. Seeing no good reason to engage in either, I dissent.

. . .

Although I disagree with the holding that appellants' claim is cognizable, the Court's discussion of the level of scrutiny it requires warrants a few comments. I have no doubt that a State's compliance with the Voting Rights Act clearly constitutes a compelling interest. . . .

The Court, while seemingly agreeing with this position, warns that the State's redistricting effort must be "narrowly tailored" to further its interest in complying with the law. It is evident to me, however, that what North Carolina did was precisely tailored to meet the objection of the Attorney General to its prior plan. Hence, I see no need for a remand at all, even accepting the majority's basic approach to this case.

Furthermore, how it intends to manage this standard, I do not know. Is it more "narrowly tailored" to create an irregular majority-minority district, as opposed to one that is compact but harms other state interests such as incumbency protection or the representation of rural interests? Of the following two options—creation of two minority influence districts or of a single majority-minority district—is one "narrowly tailored" and the other not? . . .

Justice SOUTER, dissenting.

Today, the Court recognizes a new cause of action under which a State's electoral redistricting plan that includes a configuration "so bizarre," that it "rationally cannot be understood as anything other than an effort to separate voters into different districts on the basis of race [without] sufficient justification," will be subjected to strict scrutiny. In my view, there is no justification for the Court's determination to depart from our prior decisions by carving out this narrow group of cases for strict scrutiny in place of the review customarily applied in cases dealing with discrimination in electoral districting on the basis of race.

Until today, the Court has analyzed equal protection claims involving race in electoral districting differently from equal protection claims involving other forms of governmental conduct. . . . Unlike other contexts in which we have addressed the State's conscious use of race, see, *e.g.*, *Richmond v. J.A. Croson Co.*, electoral districting calls for decisions that nearly always require some consideration of race for legitimate reasons where there is a racially mixed population. As long as members of racial groups have the commonality of interest implicit in our ability to talk about concepts like "minority voting strength," and "dilution of minority votes," and as long as racial bloc voting takes place, legislators will have to take race into account in order to avoid dilution of minority voting strength in the districting plans they adopt. One need look no further than the Voting Rights Act to understand that this may be required, and we have held that race may constitutionally be taken into account in order to comply with that Act.

ADARAND CONSTRUCTORS, INC., PETITIONER V. FEDERICO PEÑA, SECRETARY OF TRANSPORTATION, ET AL. (1995)

The gradual transformation of the Court on the issue of affirmative action came into even clearer focus with its decision in Adarand. *Justice Sandra Day O'Connor's decision signaled to many opposed to the use of race in making university admissions decisions to mount a new series of challenges to university affirmative action programs. Lower federal courts struck down admissions programs both at the University of Georgia and at the University of Texas School of Law. In the latter case, a majority of the judges of the Appeals Court panel even went so far as to opine as a result of the Supreme Court's recent decisions that* Bakke *was no longer "good law."*

Justice O'CONNOR announced the judgment of the Court and delivered an opinion with respect to Parts I, II, III-A, III-B, III-D, and IV, which is for the Court except insofar as it might be inconsistent with the views expressed in Justice SCALIA'S concurrence, and an opinion with respect to Part III-C in which Justice KENNEDY joins.

Petitioner Adarand Constructors, Inc., claims that the Federal Government's practice of giving general contractors on government projects a financial incentive to hire subcontractors controlled by "socially and economically disadvantaged individuals," and in particular, the Government's use of race-based presumptions in identifying such individuals, violates the equal protection component of the Fifth Amendment's Due Process Clause. The Court of Appeals rejected Adarand's claim. We conclude, however, that courts should analyze cases of this kind under a different standard of review than the one the Court of Appeals applied. We therefore vacate the Court of Appeals' judgment and remand the case for further proceedings. . . .

To benefit from this clause, Mountain Gravel had to hire a subcontractor who had been certified as a small disadvantaged business. . . . After losing the guardrail subcontract to Gonzales, Adarand filed suit against various federal officials in the United States District Court . . . , claiming that the race-based presumptions involved in the use of subcontracting . . . violate Adarand's right to equal protection.

. . .

Adarand's claim arises under the Fifth Amendment to the Constitution, which provides that "No person shall . . . be deprived of life, liberty, or property, without due process of law." Although this Court has always understood that clause to provide some measure of protection against arbitrary treatment by the Federal Government, it is not as explicit a guarantee of equal treatment as the Fourteenth Amendment. . . .

A

. . . In *Bolling v. Sharpe,* the Court for the first time explicitly questioned the existence of any difference between the obligations of the Federal Government and the States to avoid racial classifications. *Bolling* did note that "[t]he 'equal protection of the laws' is a more explicit safeguard of prohibited unfairness than 'due process of law.'" But *Bolling* then concluded that, "[i]n view of [the] decision that the Constitution prohibits the states from maintaining racially segregated public schools, it would be unthinkable that the same Constitution would impose a lesser duty on the Federal Government." . . .

B

. . . In *Fullilove v. Klutznick,* the Court upheld Congress' inclusion of a 10% set-aside for minority-owned businesses. . . . As in *Bakke,* there was no opinion for the Court. Chief Justice Burger, in an opin-

ion joined by Justices White and Powell, observed that "[a]ny preference based on racial or ethnic criteria must necessarily receive a most
searching examination to make sure that it does not conflict with constitutional guarantees.... It employed instead a two-part test which
asked, first, "whether the objectives of th[e] legislation are within the
power of Congress," and second, "whether the limited use of racial
and ethnic criteria, in the context presented, is a constitutionally permissible means for achieving the congressional objectives." It then upheld the program under that test, adding at the end of the opinion that
the program also "would survive judicial review under either 'test' articulated in the several *Bakke* opinions, and that the program before
the Court could not be characterized "as a 'narrowly tailored' remedial
measure."

. . .

The Court's failure to produce a majority opinion in *Bakke* [and]
Fullilove . . . left unresolved the proper analysis for remedial race-based
governmental action....

The Court resolved the issue, at least in part, in *Croson* . . . [holding]
that "the standard of review under the Equal Protection Clause is not
dependent on the race of those burdened or benefited by a particular
classification," and that the single standard of review for racial classifications should be "strict scrutiny." . . .

A year later, however, the Court took a surprising turn....

By adopting intermediate scrutiny as the standard of review for congressionally mandated "benign" racial classifications, *Metro Broadcasting* departed from prior cases in two significant respects. First, it turned
its back on *Croson*'s explanation of why strict scrutiny of all governmental racial classifications is essential....

    C

. . . *Metro Broadcasting* undermined important principles of this
Court's equal protection jurisprudence, established in a line of cases
stretching back over fifty years. Those principles together stood for an
"embracing" and "intrinsically sound" understanding of equal protection "verified by experience," namely, that the Constitution imposes
upon federal, state, and local governmental actors the same obligation to
respect the personal right to equal protection of the laws. This case
therefore presents precisely the situation described by Justice Frankfurter in *Helvering:* we cannot adhere to our most recent decision with-

out colliding with an accepted and established doctrine. We also note that *Metro Broadcasting's* application of different standards of review to federal and state racial classifications has been consistently criticized by commentators.

. . .

It is worth pointing out the difference between the applications of *stare decisis* in this case and in *Planned Parenthood of Southeastern Pa. v. Casey. Casey* explained how considerations of *stare decisis* inform the decision whether to overrule a long-established precedent that has become integrated into the fabric of the law. Overruling precedent of that kind naturally may have consequences for "the ideal of the rule of law." In addition, such precedent is likely to have engendered substantial reliance, as was true in *Casey* itself. . . . But in this case, as we have explained, we do not face a precedent of that kind, because *Metro Broadcasting* itself departed from our prior cases—and did so quite recently. By refusing to follow *Metro Broadcasting*, then, we do not depart from the fabric of the law; we restore it. . . .

Our action today makes explicit what Justice Powell thought implicit in the *Fullilove* lead opinion: federal racial classifications, like those of a State, must serve a compelling governmental interest, and must be narrowly tailored to further that interest. . . .

Finally, we wish to dispel the notion that strict scrutiny is "strict in theory, but fatal in fact." . . . When race-based action is necessary to further a compelling interest, such action is within constitutional constraints if it satisfies the "narrow tailoring" test this Court has set out in previous cases.

IV

Because our decision today alters the playing field in some important respects, we think it best to remand the case to the lower courts for further consideration in light of the principles we have announced. . . .

Justice SCALIA, concurring in part and concurring in the judgment.

I join the opinion of the Court . . . except insofar as it may be inconsistent with the following: In my view, government can never have a "compelling interest" in discriminating on the basis of race in order to "make up" for past racial discrimination in the opposite direction. Individuals who have been wronged by unlawful racial discrimination should be made whole; but under our Constitution there can be no such thing as either a creditor or a debtor race. That concept is alien to the Constitution's focus upon the individual. . . . To pursue the concept of racial entitlement—even for the most admirable and benign of purposes—is to reinforce and preserve for future mischief the way of thinking that produced race slavery, race privilege and race hatred. In the eyes of government, we are just one race here. It is American.

Justice THOMAS, concurring in part and concurring in the judgment.

I agree with the majority's conclusion that strict scrutiny applies to all government classifications based on race. I write separately, however, to express my disagreement with the premise underlying Justice STEVENS' and Justice GINSBURG's dissents: that there is a racial paternalism exception to the principle of equal protection. I believe that there is a "moral [and] constitutional equivalence," between laws designed to subjugate a race and those that distribute benefits on the basis of race in order to foster some current notion of equality. Government cannot make us equal; it can only recognize, respect, and protect us as equal before the law.

. . .

In my mind, government-sponsored racial discrimination based on benign prejudice is just as noxious as discrimination inspired by malicious prejudice. In each instance, it is racial discrimination, plain and simple.

Justice STEVENS, with whom Justice GINSBURG joins, dissenting.

. . .The consistency that the Court espouses would disregard the difference between a "No Trespassing" sign and a welcome mat. It would treat a Dixiecrat Senator's decision to vote against Thurgood Marshall's confirmation in order to keep African Americans off the Supreme Court as on a par with President Johnson's evaluation of his nominee's race as a positive factor. . . .

The Court's explanation for treating dissimilar race-based decisions as though they were equally objectionable is a supposed inability to differentiate between "invidious" and "benign" discrimination. But the term "affirmative action" is common and well understood. Its presence in everyday parlance shows that people understand the difference between good intentions and bad. As with any legal concept, some cases may be difficult to classify, but our equal protection jurisprudence has identified a critical difference between state action that imposes burdens on a disfavored few and state action that benefits the few "in spite of" its adverse effects on the many.

. . .

The Court's concept of "congruence" assumes that there is no significant difference between a decision by the Congress of the United States to adopt an affirmative-action program and such a decision by a State or a municipality. In my opinion that assumption is untenable. It ignores important practical and legal differences between federal and state or local decisionmakers.

These differences have been identified repeatedly and consistently both in opinions of the Court and in separate opinions authored by members of today's majority. Thus, in *Metro Broadcasting, Inc. v. FCC,* (1990), in which we upheld a federal program designed to foster racial diversity in broadcasting, we identified the special "institutional competence" of our National Legislature. . . . *Fullilove* . . . admonished this Court to "'approach our task with appropriate deference to the Congress,' a co-equal branch charged by the Constitution with the power to "provide for the . . . general Welfare of the United States" and "to enforce, by appropriate legislation," the equal protection guarantees of the Fourteenth Amendment." . . .

An additional reason for giving greater deference to the National Legislature than to a local law-making body is that federal affirmative-action programs represent the will of our entire Nation's elected representatives, whereas a state or local program may have an impact on nonresident entities who played no part in the decision to enact it. . . .

The divisions in this difficult case should not obscure the Court's recognition of the persistence of racial inequality and a majority's acknowledgement of Congress' authority to act affirmatively, not only to end discrimination, but also to counteract discrimination's lingering effects.

Given this history and its practical consequences, Congress surely can conclude that a carefully designed affirmative action program may help to realize, finally, the "equal protection of the laws" the Fourteenth Amendment has promised since 1868.

ROMER V. EVANS (1996)

By a vote of 5–4, the Supreme Court found in the case of Bowers v.
Hardwick (1986) that the right of privacy did not prohibit a state from
criminalizing sodomy. Ten years later, the Court found itself again con-
fronted with the issue of homosexuality. This time the issue was whether
a Colorado amendment adopted by the process of initiative and referen-
dum violated the Equal Protection Clause. The 6–3 decision prompted
the dissenters to predict that the decision, based on the equal protection
guarantee, would inevitably lead to a further challenge to an issue they
believed settled by Bowers.

Justice KENNEDY delivered the opinion of the Court.

One century ago, the first Justice Harlan admonished this Court that
the Constitution "neither knows nor tolerates classes among citizens."
Unheeded then, those words now are understood to state a commitment
to the law's neutrality where the rights of persons are at stake. The Equal
Protection Clause enforces this principle and today requires us to hold
invalid a provision of Colorado's Constitution.

I

The enactment challenged in this case is an amendment to the Constitution of the State of Colorado, adopted in a 1992 statewide referendum.... The impetus for the amendment and the contentious campaign
that preceded its adoption came in large part from ordinances that had
been passed in various Colorado municipalities....

Amendment 2, in explicit terms, does more than repeal or rescind
these provisions. It prohibits all legislative, executive or judicial action at
any level of state or local government designed to protect the named
class, a class we shall refer to as homosexual persons or gays and lesbians. The amendment reads:

No Protected Status Based on Homosexual, Lesbian, or Bisexual Orientation. Neither the State of Colorado ... nor any of its ... political
subdivisions, municipalities or school districts, shall enact ... any
statute ... whereby homosexual, lesbian or bisexual orientation, conduct, practices or relationships shall constitute or otherwise be the basis
of or entitle any person or class of persons to have or claim any minority status, quota preferences, protected status or claim of discrimination....

II

The State's principal argument in defense of Amendment 2 is that it puts gays and lesbians in the same position as all other persons. So, the State says, the measure does no more than deny homosexuals special rights. This reading of the amendment's language is implausible. . . .

Amendment 2 bars homosexuals from securing protection against the injuries that . . . public-accommodations laws address. That in itself is a severe consequence, but there is more. Amendment 2, in addition, nullifies specific legal protections for this targeted class in all transactions in housing, sale of real estate, insurance, health and welfare services, private education, and employment.

Not confined to the private sphere, Amendment 2 also operates to repeal and forbid all laws or policies providing specific protection for gays or lesbians from discrimination by every level of Colorado government. . . .

Amendment 2's reach may not be limited to specific laws passed for the benefit of gays and lesbians. It is a fair, if not necessary, inference from the broad language of the amendment that it deprives gays and lesbians even of the protection of general laws and policies that prohibit arbitrary discrimination in governmental and private settings. . . .

III

The Fourteenth Amendment's promise that no person shall be denied the equal protection of the laws must co-exist with the practical necessity that most legislation classifies for one purpose or another, with resulting disadvantage to various groups or persons. We have attempted to reconcile the principle with the reality by stating that, if a law neither burdens a fundamental right nor targets a suspect class, we will uphold the legislative classification so long as it bears a rational relation to some legitimate end.

Amendment 2 fails, indeed defies, even this conventional inquiry. First, the amendment has the peculiar property of imposing a broad and undifferentiated disability on a single named group, an exceptional and, as we shall explain, invalid form of legislation. Second, its sheer breadth is so discontinuous with the reasons offered for it that the amendment seems inexplicable by anything but animus toward the class that it affects; it lacks a rational relationship to legitimate state interests.

. . .

It is not within our constitutional tradition to enact laws of this sort. Central both to the idea of the rule of law and to our own Constitution's guarantee of equal protection is the principle that government and each of its parts remain open on impartial terms to all who seek its assistance. "Equal protection of the laws is not achieved through indiscriminate imposition of inequalities." . . .

A second and related point is that laws of the kind now before us raise the inevitable inference that the disadvantage imposed is born of animosity toward the class of persons affected. "[I]f the constitutional conception of 'equal protection of the laws' means anything, it must at the very least mean that a bare . . . desire to harm a politically unpopular group cannot constitute a legitimate governmental interest." . . . Amendment 2, however, in making a general announcement that gays and lesbians shall not have any particular protections from the law, inflicts on them immediate, continuing, and real injuries that outrun and belie any legitimate justifications that may be claimed for it. We conclude that, in addition to the far-reaching deficiencies of Amendment 2 that we have noted, the principles it offends, in another sense, are conventional and venerable; a law must bear a rational relationship to a legitimate governmental purpose, and Amendment 2 does not.

Justice SCALIA, with whom the Chief Justice and Justice THOMAS join, dissenting.

The Court has mistaken a *Kulturkampf* for a fit of spite. The constitutional amendment before us here is not the manifestation of a "bare . . . desire to harm" homosexuals, but is rather a modest attempt by seemingly tolerant Coloradans to preserve traditional sexual mores against the efforts of a politically powerful minority to revise those mores through use of the laws. That objective, and the means chosen to achieve it, are not only unimpeachable under any constitutional doctrine hitherto pronounced (hence the opinion's heavy reliance upon principles of righteousness rather than judicial holdings); they have been specifically approved by the Congress of the United States and by this Court.

In holding that homosexuality cannot be singled out for disfavorable treatment, the Court contradicts a decision, unchallenged here, pronounced only 10 years ago (see *Bowers v. Hardwick*), and places the prestige of this institution behind the proposition that opposition to homosexuality is as reprehensible as racial or religious bias.

. . .

Despite all of its hand-wringing about the potential effect of Amendment 2 on general antidiscrimination laws, the Court's opinion ultimately does not dispute all this, but assumes it to be true. The only denial of equal treatment it contends homosexuals have suffered is this: They may not obtain preferential treatment without amending the state constitution. That is to say, the principle underlying the Court's opinion is that one who is accorded equal treatment under the laws, but cannot as readily as others obtain preferential treatment under the laws, has been denied equal protection of the laws. If merely stating this alleged "equal protection" violation does not suffice to refute it, our constitutional jurisprudence has achieved terminal silliness.

The central thesis of the Court's reasoning is that any group is denied equal protection when, to obtain advantage (or, presumably, to avoid disadvantage), it must have recourse to a more general and hence more difficult level of political decisionmaking than others. The world has never heard of such a principle, which is why the Court's opinion is so long on emotive utterance and so short on relevant legal citation. And it seems to me most unlikely that any multilevel democracy can function under such a principle. For whenever a disadvantage is imposed, or conferral of a benefit is prohibited, at one of the higher levels of democratic decisionmaking (i.e., by the state legislature rather than local government, or by the people at large in the state constitution rather than the legislature), the affected group has (under this theory) been denied equal protection. To take the simplest of examples, consider a state law prohibiting the award of municipal contracts to relatives of mayors or city councilmen. Once such a law is passed, the group composed of such relatives must, in order to get the benefit of city contracts, persuade the state legislature—unlike all other citizens, who need only persuade the municipality. It is ridiculous to consider this a denial of equal protection, which is why the Court's theory is unheard-of.

I turn next to whether there was a legitimate rational basis for the substance of the constitutional amendment—for the prohibition of special protection for homosexuals. It is unsurprising that the Court avoids discussion of this question, since the answer is so obviously yes, The case most relevant to the issue before us today is not even mentioned in the Court's opinion: In *Bowers v. Hardwick,* we held that the

Constitution does not prohibit what virtually all States had done from the founding of the Republic until very recent years—making homosexual conduct a crime. That holding is unassailable, except by those who think that the Constitution changes to suit current fashions. . . .

If it is constitutionally permissible for a State to make homosexual conduct criminal, surely it is constitutionally permissible for a State to enact other laws merely disfavoring homosexual conduct. . . .

The foregoing suffices to establish what the Court's failure to cite any case remotely in point would lead one to suspect: No principle set forth in the Constitution, nor even any imagined by this Court in the past 200 years, prohibits what Colorado has done here. But the case for Colorado is much stronger than that. What it has done is not only unprohibited, but eminently reasonable, with close, congressionally approved precedent in earlier constitutional practice.

First, as to its eminent reasonableness. The Court's opinion contains grim, disapproving hints that Coloradans have been guilty of "animus" or "animosity" toward homosexuality, as though that has been established as un-American. Of course it is our moral heritage that one should not hate any human being or class of human beings. But I had thought that one could consider certain conduct reprehensible—murder, for example, or polygamy, or cruelty to animals—and could exhibit even "animus" toward such conduct. Surely that is the only sort of "animus" at issue here: moral disapproval of homosexual conduct, the same sort of moral disapproval that produced the centuries-old criminal laws that we held constitutional in *Bowers*. . . .

. . . The constitutions of the States of Arizona, Idaho, New Mexico, Oklahoma, and Utah to this day contain provisions stating that polygamy is "forever prohibited." Polygamists, and those who have a polygamous "orientation," have been "singled out" by these provisions for much more severe treatment than merely denial of favored status; and that treatment can only be changed by achieving amendment of the state constitutions. The Court's disposition today suggests that these provisions are unconstitutional, and that polygamy must be permitted in these States on a state-legislated, or perhaps even local-option, basis—unless, of course, polygamists for some reason have fewer constitutional rights than homosexuals.

The United States Congress, by the way, required the inclusion of these antipolygamy provisions in the constitutions . . . as a condition of their admission to statehood. . . . Thus, this "singling out" of the sexual practices of a single group for statewide, democratic vote—so utterly alien to our constitutional system, the Court would have us believe—has not only happened but has received the explicit approval of the United States Congress.

. . .

Today's opinion has no foundation in American constitutional law, and barely pretends to. The people of Colorado have adopted an entirely reasonable provision which does not even disfavor homosexuals in any substantive sense, but merely denies them preferential treatment. Amendment 2 is designed to prevent piecemeal deterioration of the sexual morality favored by a majority of Coloradans, and is not only an appropriate means to that legitimate end, but a means that Americans have employed before. Striking it down is an act, not of judicial judgment, but of political will. I dissent.

UNITED STATES V. VIRGINIA (1996)

Prior to her appointment to the U.S. Court of Appeals by President Jimmy Carter, Ruth Bader Ginsburg had played a role in developing the Supreme Court's jurisprudence on gender discrimination that was similar to the role Thurgood Marshall had played earlier for the rights of African Americans. Appointed to the Court by President William Clinton in 1993, Justice Ginsburg was able in United States v. Virginia *to move the Court several steps closer to the strict scrutiny test for gender discrimination the Court uses in cases involving race.*

Justice GINSBURG delivered the opinion of the Court.

Virginia's public institutions of higher learning include an incomparable military college, Virginia Military Institute (VMI). The United States maintains that the Constitution's equal protection guarantee precludes Virginia from reserving exclusively to men the unique educational opportunities VMI affords. We agree.

I.

Founded in 1839, VMI is today the sole single-sex school among Virginia's 15 public institutions of higher learning. VMI's distinctive mission is to produce "citizen-soldiers," men prepared for leadership in civilian life and in military service. VMI pursues this mission through pervasive training of a kind not available anywhere else in Virginia. Assigning prime place to character development, VMI uses an "adversative method" modeled on English public schools and once characteristic of military instruction. . . .

VMI has notably succeeded in its mission to produce leaders; among its alumni are military generals, Members of Congress, and business executives. The school's alumni overwhelmingly perceive that their VMI training helped them to realize their personal goals. VMI's endowment reflects the loyalty of its graduates; VMI has the largest per-student endowment of all undergraduate institutions in the Nation.

Neither the goal of producing citizen-soldiers nor VMI's implementing methodology is inherently unsuitable to women. And the school's impressive record in producing leaders has made admission desirable to some women. Nevertheless, Virginia has elected to preserve exclusively for men the advantages and opportunities a VMI education affords.

II.

. . .In 1990, prompted by a complaint filed with the Attorney General by a female high-school student seeking admission to VMI, the United States sued the Commonwealth of Virginia and VMI, alleging that VMI's exclusively male admission policy violated the Equal Protection Clause of the Fourteenth Amendment. . . .

The District Court ruled in favor of VMI, however, and rejected the equal protection challenge pressed by the United States. . . . The District Court reasoned that education in "a single-gender environment, be it male or female," yields substantial benefits. VMI's school for men brought diversity to an otherwise coeducational Virginia system, and that diversity was "enhanced by VMI's unique method of instruction." If single-gender education for males ranks as an important governmental objective, it becomes obvious, the District Court concluded, that the only means of achieving the objective "is to exclude women from the all-male institution—VMI."

. . .

The Court of Appeals for the Fourth Circuit disagreed and vacated the District Court's judgment. The appellate court held: "The Commonwealth of Virginia has not . . . advanced any state policy by which it can justify its determination, under an announced policy of diversity, to afford VMI's unique type of program to men and not to women."

. . .

In response to the Fourth Circuit's ruling, Virginia proposed a parallel program for women: Virginia Women's Institute for Leadership (VWIL). The 4-year, state-sponsored undergraduate program would be located at Mary Baldwin College, a private liberal arts school for women, and would be open, initially, to about 25 to 30 students. Although VWIL would share VMI's mission—to produce "citizen-soldiers"—the VWIL program would differ, as does Mary Baldwin College, from VMI in academic offerings, methods of education, and financial resources.

. . .

Virginia returned to the District Court seeking approval of its proposed remedial plan, and the court decided the plan met the requirements of the Equal Protection Clause. . . . A divided Court of Appeals affirmed the District Court's judgment. This time, the appellate court determined to give "greater scrutiny to the selection of means than to the [State's] proffered objective." The official objective or purpose, the court said, should be reviewed deferentially. Respect for the "legislative will," the court reasoned, meant that the judiciary should take a "cautious approach," inquiring into the "legitima[cy]" of the governmental objective and refusing approval for any purpose revealed to be "pernicious." . . .

IV.

We note . . . the core instruction of this Court's pathmarking decisions . . . [that p]arties who seek to defend gender-based government action must demonstrate an "exceedingly persuasive justification" for that action.

Today's skeptical scrutiny of official action denying rights or opportunities based on sex responds to volumes of history. As a plurality of this Court acknowledged a generation ago, "our Nation has had a long and unfortunate history of sex discrimination." Through a century plus three decades and more of that history, women did not count among voters composing "We the People"; not until 1920 did women gain a constitutional right to the franchise. And for a half century thereafter, it remained the prevailing doctrine that government, both federal and state, could withhold from women opportunities accorded men so long as any "basis in reason" could be conceived for the discrimination. . . .

In 1971, for the first time in our Nation's history, this Court ruled in favor of a woman who complained that her State had denied her the equal protection of its laws. . . . Since *Reed,* the Court has repeatedly recognized that neither federal nor state government acts compatibly with the equal protection principle when a law or official policy denies to women, simply because they are women, full citizenship stature— equal opportunity to aspire, achieve, participate in and contribute to society based on their individual talents and capacities. . . .

Without equating gender classifications, for all purposes, to classifications based on race or national origin, the Court, in post-*Reed* decisions, has carefully inspected official action that closes a door or denies opportunity to women (or to men). . . .

The heightened review standard our precedent establishes does not make sex a proscribed classification.

. . . [W]e find no persuasive evidence in this record that VMI's male-only admission policy "is in furtherance of a state policy of 'diversity.'" . . . Virginia next argues that VMI's adversative method of training provides educational benefits that cannot be made available, unmodified, to women. . . .

It may be assumed, for purposes of this decision, that most women would not choose VMI's adversative method. As Fourth Circuit Judge Motz observed, however, in her dissent from the Court of Appeals' denial of rehearing en banc, it is also probable that "many men would not want to be educated in such an environment." (On that point, even our dissenting colleague might agree.) Education, to be sure, is not a "one size fits all" business. The issue, however, is not whether "women—or men—should be forced to attend VMI"; rather, the question is whether the State can constitutionally deny to women who have the will and capacity, the training and attendant opportunities that VMI uniquely affords.

. . .

Women's successful entry into the federal military academies, and their participation in the Nation's military forces, indicate that Virginia's fears for the future of VMI may not be solidly grounded. The State's justification for excluding all women from "citizen-soldier" training for which some are qualified, in any event, cannot rank as "exceedingly persuasive," as we have explained and applied that standard. . . .

VI.

In the second phase of the litigation, Virginia presented its remedial plan—maintain VMI as a male-only college and create VWIL as a separate program for women. . . .

VIII

...VMI, too, offers an educational opportunity no other Virginia institution provides, and the school's "prestige"—associated with its success in developing "citizen-soldiers"—is unequaled. Virginia has closed this facility to its daughters and, instead, has devised for them a "parallel program," with a faculty less impressively credentialed and less well paid, more limited course offerings, fewer opportunities for military training and for scientific specialization (cf. *Sweatt*). VMI, beyond question, "possesses to a far greater degree" than the VWIL program "those qualities which are incapable of objective measurement but which make for greatness in a... school," including "position and influence of the alumni, standing in the community, traditions and prestige." Women seeking and fit for a VMI-quality education cannot be offered anything less, under the State's obligation to afford them genuinely equal protection.

Justice THOMAS took no part in the consideration or decision of this case.

Chief Justice REHNQUIST, concurring in judgment.
... While I agree with [the Court's] conclusions, I disagree with the Court's analysis and so I write separately.
. . .
While terms like "important governmental objective" and "substantially related" are hardly models of precision, they have more content and specificity than does the phrase "exceedingly persuasive justification." That phrase is best confined, as it was first used, as an observation on the difficulty of meeting the applicable test, not as a formulation of the test itself....

I do not think, however, that the State's options were as limited as the majority may imply ... Had Virginia made a genuine effort to devote comparable public resources to a facility for women, and followed through on such a plan, it might well have avoided an equal protection violation. I do not believe the State was faced with the stark choice of either admitting women to VMI, on the one hand, or abandoning VMI and starting from scratch for both men and women, on the other.

But, as I have noted, neither the governing board of VMI nor the State took any action after 1982. If diversity in the form of single-sex, as well as coeducational, institutions of higher learning were to be available to Virginians, that diversity had to be available to women as well as to men.

Justice SCALIA, dissenting.

Today the Court shuts down an institution that has served the people of the Commonwealth of Virginia with pride and distinction for over a century and a half. To achieve that desired result, it rejects (contrary to our established practice) the factual findings of two courts below, sweeps aside the precedents of this Court, and ignores the history of our people. As to facts: it explicitly rejects the finding that there exist "gender-based developmental differences" supporting Virginia's restriction of the "adversative" method to only a men's institution, and the finding that the all-male composition of the Virginia Military Institute (VMI) is essential to that institution's character. As to precedent: it drastically revises our established standards for reviewing sex-based classifications. And as to history: it counts for nothing the long tradition, enduring down to the present, of men's military colleges supported by both States and the Federal Government.

Much of the Court's opinion is devoted to deprecating the closed-mindedness of our forebears with regard to women's education, and even with regard to the treatment of women in areas that have nothing to do with education. Closed-minded they were—as every age is, including our own, with regard to matters it cannot guess, because it simply does not consider them debatable. The virtue of a democratic system with a First Amendment is that it readily enables the people, over time, to be persuaded that what they took for granted is not so, and to change their laws accordingly. That system is destroyed if the smug assurances of each age are removed from the democratic process and written into the Constitution. So to counterbalance the Court's criticism of our ancestors, let me say a word in their praise: they left us free to change. The same cannot be said of this most illiberal Court, which has embarked on a course of inscribing one after another of the current preferences of the society (and in some cases only the counter-majoritarian preferences of the society's law-trained elite) into our Basic Law. Today it enshrines the notion that no substantial educational value is to be served by an all-men's military academy—so that the decision by the people of Virginia to maintain such an institution denies equal protection to women who cannot attend that institution but can attend others. Since it is entirely clear that the Constitution of the United States—the old one—takes no sides in this educational debate, I dissent.

GRATZ AND HAMACHER V.
BOLLINGER (2003)

The undergraduate admissions program at the University of Michigan provided an automatic twenty point award toward the admissions index to any underrepresented minority. Gratz and Hamacher were refused admission and subsequently sued. The Court, speaking through Chief Justice Rehnquist, found that "the manner in which the University considers the race of applicants in its undergraduate admissions guidelines" violated both the Equal Protection Clause and Title VI of the Civil Rights Act of 1964. Rehnquist contrasted the "holistic" approach in Grutter *with the very mechanical approach in* Gratz *and argued that the undergraduate program had made race "decisive" in the decision-making process and that this was constitutionally defective.*

Chief Justice REHNQUIST delivered the opinion of the Court.

We granted certiorari in this case to decide whether "the University of Michigan's use of racial preferences in undergraduate admissions violate[s] the Equal Protection Clause of the Fourteenth Amendment [or] Title VI of the Civil Rights Act of 1964." . . . Because we find that the manner in which the University considers the race of applicants in its undergraduate admissions guidelines violates these constitutional and statutory provisions, we reverse that portion of the District Court's decision upholding the guidelines.

. . .

Petitioners argue . . . that the University's use of race in undergraduate admissions violates the Fourteenth Amendment. Specifically, they contend that this Court has only sanctioned the use of racial classifications to remedy identified discrimination, a justification on which respondents have never relied. Petitioners further argue that "diversity as a basis for employing racial preferences is simply too open-ended, ill-defined, and indefinite to constitute a compelling interest capable of supporting narrowly-tailored means." But for the reasons set forth today in *Grutter* v. *Bollinger* the Court has rejected these arguments of petitioners.

Petitioners alternatively argue that even if the University's interest in
diversity can constitute a compelling state interest, the District Court er-
roneously concluded that the University's use of race in its current
freshman admissions policy is narrowly tailored to achieve such an interest. Petitioners argue that the guidelines the University began using in
1999 do not "remotely resemble the kind of consideration of race and
ethnicity that Justice Powell endorsed in *Bakke.*"

. . .

Justice Powell's opinion in *Bakke* emphasized the importance of considering each particular applicant as an individual, assessing all of the
qualities that individual possesses, and in turn, evaluating that individual's ability to contribute to the unique setting of higher education. The
admissions program Justice Powell described, however, did not contem-
plate that any single characteristic automatically ensured a specific and
identifiable contribution to a university's diversity. . . .

The current LSA policy does not provide such individualized consideration. The . . . [Michigan] policy automatically distributes 20 points to
every single applicant from an "underrepresented minority" group. . . .
Moreover, unlike Justice Powell's example, where the race of a "particular black applicant" could be considered without being decisive, [Michi-
gan's] automatic distribution of 20 points has the effect of making "the
factor of race . . . decisive" for virtually every minimally qualified underrepresented minority applicant.

. . .

Respondents contend that "[t]he volume of applications and the pre-
sentation of applicant information make it impractical for [them] to use
the . . . admissions system" upheld by the Court today in *Grutter.* But
the fact that the implementation of a program capable of providing individualized consideration might present administrative challenges does
not render constitutional an otherwise problematic system. . . .

We conclude, therefore, that because the University's use of race in its
current freshman admissions policy is not narrowly tailored to achieve
respondents' asserted compelling interest in diversity, the admissions
policy violates the Equal Protection Clause of the Fourteenth Amendment. We further find that the admissions policy also violates Title VI
and 42 U. S. C. § 1981. Accordingly, we reverse . . . the District Court's
decision. . . .

Justice SOUTER, with whom Justice GINSBURG joins as to Part II, dissenting.

...The very nature of a college's permissible practice of awarding value to racial diversity means that race must be considered in a way that increases some applicants' chances for admission. Since college admission is not left entirely to inarticulate intuition, it is hard to see what is inappropriate in assigning some stated value to a relevant characteristic, whether it be reasoning ability, writing style, running speed, or minority race. Justice Powell's plus factors necessarily are assigned some values. The college simply does by a numbered scale what the law school accomplishes in its "holistic review." [T]he distinction does not imply that applicants to the undergraduate college are denied individualized consideration or a fair chance to compete on the basis of all the various merits their applications may disclose.

Nor is it possible to say that the 20 points convert race into a decisive factor comparable to reserving minority places as in *Bakke.* Of course we can conceive of a point system in which the "plus" factor given to minority applicants would be so extreme as to guarantee every minority applicant a higher rank than every nonminority applicant in the university's admissions system. But petitioners do not have a convincing argument that the freshman admissions system operates this way. The present record obviously shows that nonminority applicants may achieve higher selection point totals than minority applicants owing to characteristics other than race, and the fact that the university admits "virtually every qualified under-represented minority applicant," may reflect nothing more than the likelihood that very few qualified minority applicants apply. . . .

Justice GINSBURG, with whom Justice SOUTER joins, dissenting. Justice BREYER joins Part I of this opinion.

I

Educational institutions, the Court acknowledges, are not barred from any and all consideration of race when making admissions decisions. But the Court once again maintains that the same standard of review controls judicial inspection of all official race classifications. This insistence on "consistency" would be fitting were our Nation free of the vestiges of rank discrimination long reinforced by law. But we are not far distant from an overtly discriminatory past, and the effects of centuries of law-sanctioned inequality remain painfully evident in our communities and schools.

In the wake "of a system of racial caste only recently ended," large disparities endure. Unemployment, poverty, and access to health care vary disproportionately by race. Neighborhoods and schools remain racially divided. African American and Hispanic children are all too often educated in poverty-stricken and underperforming institutions. Adult African Americans and Hispanics generally earn less than whites with equivalent levels of education. Equally credentialed job applicants receive different receptions depending on their race. Irrational prejudice is still encountered in real estate markets and consumer transactions. . . .

The Constitution instructs all who act for the government that they may not "deny to any person . . . the equal protection of the laws." In implementing this equality instruction, as I see it, government decision-makers may properly distinguish between policies of exclusion and inclusion. Actions designed to burden groups long denied full citizenship stature are not sensibly ranked with measures taken to hasten the day when entrenched discrimination and its aftereffects have been extirpated. . . .

Our jurisprudence ranks race a "suspect" category, "not because [race] is inevitably an impermissible classification, but because it is one which usually, to our national shame, has been drawn for the purpose of maintaining racial inequality." But where race is considered "for the purpose of achieving equality," no automatic proscription is in order. For, as insightfully explained, "[t]he Constitution is both color blind and color conscious." . . .

II

Examining in this light the admissions policy employed by the University of Michigan's College of Literature, Science, and the Arts (College), and for the reasons well stated by Justice SOUTER, I see no constitutional infirmity. . . .

The stain of generations of racial oppression is still visible in our society and the determination to hasten its removal remains vital. One can reasonably anticipate, therefore, that colleges and universities will seek to maintain their minority enrollment—and the networks and opportunities thereby opened to minority graduates—whether or not they can do so in full candor through adoption of affirmative action plans of the kind here at issue. Without recourse to such plans, institutions of higher education may resort to camouflage. . . . If honesty is the best policy, surely Michigan's accurately described, fully disclosed College affirmative action program is preferable to achieving similar numbers through winks, nods, and disguises.

GRUTTER V. BOLLINGER (2003)

Decided on the same day as Gratz v. Bollinger, Grutter *is probably the more important of the two cases. Justice Sandra Day O'Connor, writing for a bare majority of five justices, rejected Grutter's challenge to the admissions practices of the University of Michigan Law School, finding that diversity was a "compelling state interest" in the context of education and that race could be used even in situations where there was no prior evidence of discrimination. O'Connor's opinion firmly endorsed Powell's* Bakke *opinion as the touchstone for all affirmative action cases. She praised the Michigan program for giving the individualized attention to applicants upon which Justice Powell had commented favorably in using Harvard as an example of what a constitutionally valid admissions program should look like.*

O'Connor also advanced the concept that all affirmative action programs should have a sunset provision, suggesting that after another twenty-five years, courts should be ready to invalidate any programs that still operated.

Justice O'CONNOR delivered the opinion of the Court. This case requires us to decide whether the use of race as a factor in student admissions by the University of Michigan Law School . . . is unlawful.

I

A

The Law School ranks among the Nation's top law schools. It receives more than 3,500 applications each year for a class of around 350 students. Seeking to "admit a group of students who individually and collectively are among the most capable," the Law School looks for individuals with "substantial promise for success in law school" and "a strong likelihood of succeeding in the practice of law and contributing in diverse ways to the well-being of others." More broadly, the Law School seeks "a mix of students with varying backgrounds and experiences who will respect and learn from each other." In 1992 . . . the Law School sought to ensure that its efforts to achieve student body diversity complied with this Court's most recent ruling on the use of race in university admissions (see *Regents of Univ. of Cal. v. Bakke*). . . .

In reviewing an applicant's file, admissions officials must consider the applicant's undergraduate grade point average (GPA) and Law School Admissions Test (LSAT) score because they are important (if imperfect) predictors of academic success in law school. . . . The policy makes clear, however, that even the highest possible score does not guarantee admission to the Law School. . . . Rather, the policy requires admissions officials to look beyond grades and test scores to other criteria that are important to the Law School's educational objectives. So-called "soft variables" such as "the enthusiasm of recommenders, the quality of the undergraduate institution, the quality of the applicant's essay, and the areas and difficulty of undergraduate course selection" are all brought to bear in assessing an "applicant's likely contributions to the intellectual and social life of the institution."

The policy aspires to "achieve that diversity which has the potential to enrich everyone's education and thus make a law school class stronger than the sum of its parts." . . . The policy . . . reaffirm[s] the Law School's long-standing commitment to "one particular type of diversity," that is, "racial and ethnic diversity with special reference to the inclusion of students from groups which have been historically discriminated against, like African Americans, Hispanics, and Native Americans, who without this commitment might not be represented in our student body in meaningful numbers." By enrolling a " 'critical mass' of [underrepresented] minority students," the Law School seeks to "ensur[e] their ability to make unique contributions to the character of the Law School." . . .

B

Petitioner Barbara Grutter is a white Michigan resident who applied to the Law School in 1996 with a 3.8 grade point average and 161 LSAT score. The Law School initially placed petitioner on a waiting list, but subsequently rejected her application. . . .

Petitioner alleged that respondents discriminated against her on the basis of race in violation of the Fourteenth Amendment; Title VI of the Civil Rights Act of 1964, 78 Stat. 252, 42 U.S.C. §2000d; and Rev. Stat. § 1977, as amended, 42 U.S.C. §1981.

Petitioner further alleged that her application was rejected because the Law School uses race as a "predominant" factor, giving applicants who belong to certain minority groups "a significantly greater chance of admission than students with similar credentials from disfavored racial groups." . . .

In an attempt to quantify the extent to which the Law School actually considers race in making admissions decisions, the parties introduced voluminous evidence at trial. Relying on data obtained from the Law School, petitioner's expert, Dr. Kinley Larntz, generated and analyzed "admissions grids" for the years in question. . . . He concluded that membership in certain minority groups "is an extremely strong factor in the decision for acceptance," and that applicants from these minority groups "are given an extremely large allowance for admission" as compared to applicants who are members of nonfavored groups. Dr. Larntz conceded, however, that race is not the predominant factor in the Law School's admissions calculus.

. . .

We granted certiorari to resolve the disagreement among the Courts of Appeals on a question of national importance: Whether diversity is a compelling interest that can justify the narrowly tailored use of race in selecting applicants for admission to public universities. Compare *Hopwood* v. *Texas* (1996) (holding that diversity is not a compelling state interest), with *Smith* v. *University of Wash. Law School* (2000) (holding that it is).

II

A

We last addressed the use of race in public higher education over 25 years ago [i]n the landmark *Bakke* case. . . .

Since this Court's splintered decision in *Bakke*, Justice Powell's opinion announcing the judgment of the Court has served as the touchstone for constitutional analysis of race-conscious admissions policies. Public and private universities across the Nation have modeled their own admissions programs on Justice Powell's views on permissible race-conscious policies. . . .

B

The Equal Protection Clause provides that no State shall "deny to any person within its jurisdiction the equal protection of the laws." Because the Fourteenth Amendment "protect[s] *persons,* not *groups,*" all "governmental action based on race—a *group* classification long recognized as in most circumstances irrelevant and therefore prohibited—should be subjected to detailed judicial inquiry to ensure that the *personal* right to equal protection of the laws has not been infringed" (*Adarand*).

It follows from that principle that "government may treat people differently because of their race only for the most compelling reasons."

We have held that all racial classifications imposed by government "must be analyzed by a reviewing court under strict scrutiny." This means that such classifications are constitutional only if they are narrowly tailored to further compelling governmental interests. . . .

III

A

With these principles in mind, we turn to the question whether the Law School's use of race is justified by a compelling state interest. Before this Court, as they have throughout this litigation, respondents assert only one justification for their use of race in the admissions process: obtaining "the educational benefits that flow from a diverse student body." In other words, the Law School asks us to recognize, in the context of higher education, a compelling state interest in student body diversity.

We first wish to dispel the notion that the Law School's argument has been foreclosed, either expressly or implicitly, by our affirmative-action cases decided since *Bakke*. It is true that some language in those opinions might be read to suggest that remedying past discrimination is the only permissible justification for race-based governmental action. . . . But we have never held that the only governmental use of race that can survive strict scrutiny is remedying past discrimination. Nor, since *Bakke*, have we directly addressed the use of race in the context of public higher education. Today, we hold that the Law School has a compelling interest in attaining a diverse student body.

The Law School's educational judgment that such diversity is essential to its educational mission is one to which we defer. The Law School's assessment that diversity will, in fact, yield educational benefits is substantiated by respondents and their *amici*. . . . These benefits are not theoretical, but real, as major American businesses have made clear [in their briefs]. . . .

These benefits are substantial. . . . [T]he Law School's admissions policy promotes "cross-racial understanding," helps to break down racial stereotypes, and "enables [students] to better understand persons of different races." These benefits are "important and laudable," because "classroom discussion is livelier, more spirited, and simply more enlightening and interesting" when the students have "the greatest possible variety of backgrounds." . . .

B

Even in the limited circumstance when drawing racial distinctions is permissible to further a compelling state interest, government is still "constrained in how it may pursue that end: [T]he means chosen to accomplish the [government's] asserted purpose must be specifically and narrowly framed to accomplish that purpose." . . .

To be narrowly tailored, a race-conscious admissions program cannot use a quota system—it cannot "insulat[e] each category of applicants with certain desired qualifications from competition with all other applicants." Instead, a university may consider race or ethnicity only as a "'plus' in a particular applicant's file," without "insulat[ing] the individual from comparison with all other candidates for the available seats."

We find that the Law School's admissions program bears the hallmarks of a narrowly tailored plan. As Justice Powell made clear in *Bakke*, truly individualized consideration demands that race be used in a flexible, nonmechanical way. . . .

We are satisfied that the Law School's admissions program, like the Harvard plan described by Justice Powell, does not operate as a quota. . . .

Here, the Law School engages in a highly individualized, holistic review of each applicant's file, giving serious consideration to all the ways an applicant might contribute to a diverse educational environment. The Law School affords this individualized consideration to applicants of all races. There is no policy, either *de jure* or *de facto*, of automatic acceptance or rejection based on any single "soft" variable. Unlike the program at issue in *Gratz v. Bollinger*, the Law School awards no mechanical, predetermined diversity "bonuses" based on race or ethnicity. . . .

We are mindful, however, that "[a] core purpose of the Fourteenth Amendment was to do away with all governmentally imposed discrimination based on race." Accordingly, race-conscious admissions policies must be limited in time. This requirement reflects that racial classifications, however compelling their goals, are potentially so dangerous that they may be employed no more broadly than the interest demands. Enshrining a permanent justification for racial preferences would offend this fundamental equal protection principle. We see no reason to exempt race-conscious admissions programs from the requirement that all governmental use of race must have a logical end point. The Law School, too, concedes that all "race-conscious programs must have reasonable durational limits."

In the context of higher education, the durational requirement can be met by sunset provisions in race-conscious admissions policies and periodic reviews to determine whether racial preferences are still necessary to achieve student body diversity. Universities in California, Florida, and Washington State, where racial preferences in admissions are prohibited by state law, are currently engaged in experimenting with a wide variety of alternative approaches.... ("[T]he States may perform their role as laboratories for experimentation to devise various solutions where the best solution is far from clear.")

The requirement that all race-conscious admissions programs have a termination point "assure[s] all citizens that the deviation from the norm of equal treatment of all racial and ethnic groups is a temporary matter, a measure taken in the service of the goal of equality itself." ...

... It has been 25 years since Justice Powell first approved the use of race to further an interest in student body diversity.... We expect that 25 years from now, the use of racial preferences will no longer be necessary to further the interest approved today.

Justice SCALIA, with whom Justice THOMAS joins, concurring in part and dissenting in part.

...Unlike a clear constitutional holding that racial preferences in state educational institutions are impermissible, or even a clear anti-constitutional holding that racial preferences in state educational institutions are OK, today's *Grutter-Gratz* split double header seems perversely designed to prolong the controversy and the litigation. Some future lawsuits will presumably focus on whether the discriminatory scheme in question contains enough evaluation of the applicant "as an individual," and sufficiently avoids "separate admissions tracks" to fall under *Grutter* rather than *Gratz*. Some will focus on whether a university has gone beyond the bounds of a "good faith effort" and has so zealously pursued its "critical mass" as to make it an unconstitutional *de facto* quota system, rather than merely "a permissible goal."

Justice THOMAS, with whom Justice SCALIA joins as to Parts I-VII, concurring in part and dissenting in part.

Frederick Douglass, speaking to a group of abolitionists almost 140 years ago, delivered a message lost on today's majority:

> [I]n regard to the colored people, there is always more that is benevolent, I perceive, than just, manifested towards us. What I ask for the negro is not benevolence, not pity, not sympathy, but simply *justice*. The American people have always been anxious to know what they shall do with us.... I have had but one answer from the beginning. Do nothing with us! Your doing with us has already played the mischief with us. Do nothing with us! If the apples will not remain on the tree of their own strength, if they are worm-eaten at the core, if they are early ripe and disposed to fall, let them fall! ... And if the negro cannot stand on his own legs, let him fall also. All I ask is, give him a chance to stand on his own legs! Let him alone! ... [Y]our interference is doing him positive injury.

Like Douglass, I believe blacks can achieve in every avenue of American life without the meddling of university administrators. Because I wish to see all students succeed whatever their color, I share, in some respect, the sympathies of those who sponsor the type of discrimination advanced by the University of Michigan Law School. The Constitution does not, however, tolerate institutional devotion to the status quo in admissions policies when such devotion ripens into racial discrimination. Nor does the Constitution countenance the unprecedented deference the Court gives to the Law School, an approach inconsistent with the very concept of "strict scrutiny."

No one would argue that a university could set up a lower general admission standard and then impose heightened requirements only on black applicants. Similarly, a university may not maintain a high admission standard and grant exemptions to favored races. The Law School, of its own choosing, and for its own purposes, maintains an exclusionary admissions system that it knows produces racially disproportionate results. Racial discrimination is not a permissible solution to the self-inflicted wounds of this elitist admissions policy.

The majority upholds the Law School's racial discrimination not by interpreting the people's Constitution, but by responding to a faddish slogan of the cognoscenti. Nevertheless, I concur in part in the Court's opinion. First, I agree with the Court insofar as its decision, which approves of only one racial classification, confirms that further use of race in admissions remains unlawful. Second, I agree with the Court's holding that racial discrimination in higher education admissions will be illegal in 25 years. I respectfully dissent from the remainder of the Court's opinion and the judgment, however, because I believe that the Law School's current use of race violates the Equal Protection Clause and that the Constitution means the same thing today as it will in 300 months.

I

The majority agrees that the Law School's racial discrimination should be subjected to strict scrutiny. . . .

A majority of the Court has validated only two circumstances where "pressing public necessity" or a "compelling state interest" can possibly justify racial discrimination by state actors. First, the lesson of *Korematsu* is that national security constitutes a "pressing public necessity," though the government's use of race to advance that objective must be narrowly tailored. Second, the Court has recognized as a compelling state interest a government's effort to remedy past discrimination for which it is responsible. . . .

II

Unlike the majority, I seek to define with precision the interest being asserted by the Law School before determining whether that interest is so compelling as to justify racial discrimination. . . .

One must consider the Law School's refusal to entertain changes to its current admissions system that might produce the same educational benefits. . . .

With the adoption of different admissions methods, such as accepting all students who meet minimum qualifications, the Law School could achieve its vision of the racially aesthetic student body without the use of racial discrimination. The Law School concedes this, but the Court holds, implicitly and under the guise of narrow tailoring, that the Law School has a compelling state interest in doing what it wants to do. I cannot agree. First, under strict scrutiny, the Law School's assessment of the benefits of racial discrimination and devotion to the admissions status quo are not entitled to any sort of deference, grounded in the First Amendment or anywhere else. Second, even if its "academic selectivity" must be maintained at all costs along with racial discrimination, the Court ignores the fact that other top law schools have succeeded in meeting their aesthetic demands without racial discrimination.

... [N]o modern law school can claim ignorance of the poor performance of blacks, relatively speaking, on the Law School Admissions Test (LSAT). Nevertheless, law schools continue to use the test and then attempt to "correct" for black underperformance by using racial discrimination in admissions so as to obtain their aesthetic student body. The Law School's continued adherence to measures it knows produce racially skewed results is not entitled to deference by this Court. The Law School itself admits that the test is imperfect, as it must, given that it regularly admits students who score at or below 150 (the national median) on the test (showing that, between 1995 and 2000, the Law School admitted 37 students—27 of whom were black; 31 of whom were "underrepresented minorities"—with LSAT scores of 150 or lower). And the Law School's *amici* cannot seem to agree on the fundamental question whether the test itself is useful. . . .

Having decided to use the LSAT, the Law School must accept the constitutional burdens that come with this decision. The Law School may freely continue to employ the LSAT and other allegedly merit-based standards in whatever fashion it likes. What the Equal Protection Clause forbids, but the Court today allows, is the use of these standards hand-in-hand with racial discrimination. An infinite variety of admissions methods are available to the Law School. Considering all of the radical thinking that has historically occurred at this country's universities, the Law School's intractable approach toward admissions is striking.

. . .

Beyond the harm the Law School's racial discrimination visits upon its test subjects, no social science has disproved the notion that this discrimination "engender[s] attitudes of superiority or, alternatively, provoke[s] resentment among those who believe that they have been wronged by the government's use of race" (*Adarand*, THOMAS concurring in part and concurring in judgment). "These programs stamp minorities with a badge of inferiority and may cause them to develop dependencies or to adopt an attitude that they are 'entitled' to preferences."

It is uncontested that each year, the Law School admits a handful of blacks who would be admitted in the absence of racial discrimination. Who can differentiate between those who belong and those who do not? The majority of blacks are admitted to the Law School because of discrimination, and because of this policy all are tarred as undeserving. This problem of stigma does not depend on determinacy as to whether those stigmatized are actually the "beneficiaries" of racial discrimination. When blacks take positions in the highest places of government, industry, or academia, it is an open question today whether their skin color played a part in their advancement. The question itself is the stigma. . . .

B

. . . In recent years there has been virtually no change . . . in the proportion of law school applicants with LSAT scores of 165 and higher who are black. In 1993 blacks constituted 1.1% of law school applicants in that score range, though they represented 11.1% of all applicants. In 2000 the comparable numbers were 1.0% and 11.3%. No one can seriously contend, and the Court does not, that the racial gap in academic credentials will disappear in 25 years. Nor is the Court's holding that racial discrimination will be unconstitutional in 25 years made contingent on the gap closing in that time.

Indeed, the very existence of racial discrimination of the type practiced by the Law School may impede the narrowing of the LSAT testing gap. An applicant's LSAT score can improve dramatically with preparation, but such preparation is a cost, and there must be sufficient benefits attached to an improved score to justify additional study. Whites scoring between 163 and 167 on the LSAT are routinely rejected by the Law School, and thus whites aspiring to admission at the Law School have every incentive to improve their score to levels above that range. See App. 199 (showing that in 2000, 209 out of 422 white applicants [to Michigan] were rejected in this scoring range). Blacks, on the other hand, are nearly guaranteed admission if they score above 155 (*Id.*, at 198, showing that 63 out of 77 black applicants are accepted with LSAT scores above 155). As admission prospects approach certainty, there is no incentive for the black applicant to continue to prepare for the LSAT once he is reasonably assured of achieving the requisite score. It is far from certain that the LSAT test-taker's behavior is responsive to the Law School's admissions policies. Nevertheless, the possibility remains that this racial discrimination will help fulfill the bigot's prophecy about black underperformance just as it confirms the conspiracy theorist's belief that "institutional racism" is at fault for every racial disparity in our society.

. . .

For the immediate future, however, the majority has placed its *imprimatur* on a practice that can only weaken the principle of equality embodied in the Declaration of Independence and the Equal Protection Clause. "Our Constitution is color-blind, and neither knows nor tolerates classes among citizens" (*Plessy*). It has been nearly 140 years since Frederick Douglass asked the intellectual ancestors of the Law School to "[d]o nothing with us!" and the Nation adopted the Fourteenth Amendment. Now we must wait another 25 years to see this principle of equality vindicated. I therefore respectfully dissent. . . .

LAWRENCE AND GARNER V. TEXAS (2003)

Lawrence and Garner were arrested for engaging in homosexual sex in their own home. The police had entered the house with a valid search warrant. The Texas statute, unlike the Georgia statute that was the basis for the prosecution in Bowers v. Hardwick *(1986), criminalized sodomy only for persons of the same sex. As a result, attorneys for Lawrence and Garner based their argument largely on the claim that the statute violated the Equal Protection Clause. Of the six justices who voted to strike down the statute, only Justice O'Connor based her decision on the Equal Protection Clause. The other five justices in the majority invoked Fourteenth Amendment due process as the basis for their opinion. Chief Justice Rehnquist and Associate Justices Scalia and Thomas dissented.*

Justice KENNEDY delivered the opinion of the Court.

Liberty protects the person from unwarranted government intrusions into a dwelling or other private places. In our tradition the State is not omnipresent in the home. And there are other spheres of our lives and existence, outside the home, where the State should not be a dominant presence. Freedom extends beyond spatial bounds. Liberty presumes an autonomy of self that includes freedom of thought, belief, expression, and certain intimate conduct. The instant case involves liberty of the person both in its spatial and more transcendent dimensions.

I

The question before the Court is the validity of a Texas statute making it a crime for two persons of the same sex to engage in certain intimate sexual conduct.

. . .

We granted *certiorari* . . . to consider three questions:

1. Whether Petitioners' criminal convictions under the Texas "Homosexual Conduct" law—which criminalizes sexual intimacy by same-sex couples, but not identical behavior by different-sex couples—violate the Fourteenth Amendment guarantee of equal protection of laws?

2. Whether Petitioners' criminal convictions for adult consensual sexual intimacy in the home violate their vital interests in liberty and privacy protected by the Due Process Clause of the Fourteenth Amendment?

3. Whether *Bowers v. Hardwick* (1986), should be overruled?'

The petitioners were adults at the time of the alleged offense. Their conduct was in private and consensual.

II

We conclude the case should be resolved by determining whether the petitioners were free as adults to engage in the private conduct in the exercise of their liberty under the Due Process Clause of the Fourteenth Amendment to the Constitution. For this inquiry we deem it necessary to reconsider the Court's holding in *Bowers.*

. . .

The facts in *Bowers* had some similarities to the instant case. A police officer, whose right to enter seems not to have been in question, observed Hardwick, in his own bedroom, engaging in intimate sexual conduct with another adult male. The conduct was in violation of a Georgia statute making it a criminal offense to engage in sodomy. One difference between the two cases is that the Georgia statute prohibited the conduct whether or not the participants were of the same sex, while the Texas statute, as we have seen, applies only to participants of the same sex. . . .

The Court began its substantive discussion in *Bowers* as follows: "The issue presented is whether the Federal Constitution confers a fundamental right upon homosexuals to engage in sodomy and hence invalidates the laws of the many States that still make such conduct illegal and have done so for a very long time." That statement, we now conclude, discloses the Court's own failure to appreciate the extent of the liberty at stake. To say that the issue in *Bowers* was simply the right to engage in certain sexual conduct demeans the claim the individual put forward, just as it would demean a married couple were it to be said marriage is simply about the right to have sexual intercourse. The laws involved in *Bowers* and here are, to be sure, statutes that purport to do no more than prohibit a particular sexual act. Their penalties and purposes, though, have more far-reaching consequences, touching upon the most private human conduct, sexual behavior, and in the most private of places, the home. The statutes do seek to control a personal relationship that, whether or not entitled to formal recognition in the law, is within the liberty of persons to choose without being punished as criminals.

. . .

Having misapprehended the claim of liberty there presented to it, and thus stating the claim to be whether there is a fundamental right to engage in consensual sodomy, the *Bowers* Court said: "Proscriptions against that conduct have ancient roots." In academic writings, and in many of the scholarly *amicus* briefs filed to assist the Court in this case, there are fundamental criticisms of the historical premises relied upon by the majority and concurring opinions in *Bowers*. . . .

At the outset it should be noted that there is no long-standing history in this country of laws directed at homosexual conduct as a distinct matter. . . .

Laws prohibiting sodomy do not seem to have been enforced against consenting adults acting in private. A substantial number of sodomy prosecutions and convictions for which there are surviving records were for predatory acts against those who could not or did not consent, as in the case of a minor or the victim of an assault. . . .

In summary, the historical grounds relied upon in *Bowers* are more complex than the majority opinion and the concurring opinion by Chief Justice Burger indicate. Their historical premises are not without doubt and, at the very least, are overstated.

It must be acknowledged, of course, that the Court in *Bowers* was making the broader point that for centuries there have been powerful voices to condemn homosexual conduct as immoral. The condemnation has been shaped by religious beliefs, conceptions of right and acceptable behavior, and respect for the traditional family. For many persons these are not trivial concerns but profound and deep convictions accepted as ethical and moral principles to which they aspire and which thus determine the course of their lives. These considerations do not answer the question before us, however. The issue is whether the majority may use the power of the State to enforce these views on the whole society through operation of the criminal law. . . .

In *Bowers* the Court referred to the fact that before 1961 all 50 States had outlawed sodomy, and that at the time of the Court's decision 24 States and the District of Columbia had sodomy laws. . . .

The sweeping references by Chief Justice Burger to the history of Western civilization and to Judeo-Christian moral and ethical standards did not take account of other authorities pointing in an opposite direction. A committee advising the British Parliament recommended in 1957 repeal of laws punishing homosexual conduct. . . . Parliament enacted the substance of those recommendations 10 years later.

Of even more importance, almost five years before *Bowers* was decided the European Court of Human Rights considered a case with parallels to *Bowers* and to today's case. . . . The court held that the laws proscribing the conduct were invalid under the European Convention on Human Rights. . . . [This] decision is at odds with the premise in *Bowers* that the claim put forward was insubstantial in our Western civilization.

In our own constitutional system the deficiencies in *Bowers* became even more apparent in the years following its announcement. The 25 States with laws prohibiting the relevant conduct referenced in the *Bowers* decision are reduced now to 13, of which 4 enforce their laws only against homosexual conduct. In those States where sodomy is still proscribed, whether for same-sex or heterosexual conduct, there is a pattern of non-enforcement with respect to consenting adults acting in private. . . .

Two principal cases decided after *Bowers* cast its holding into even more doubt. In *Planned Parenthood of Southeastern Pa. v. Casey* (1992), the Court reaffirmed the substantive force of the liberty protected by the Due Process Clause. The *Casey* decision again confirmed that our laws and tradition afford constitutional protection to personal decisions relating to marriage, procreation, contraception, family relationships, child rearing, and education. . . .

Persons in a homosexual relationship may seek autonomy for these purposes, just as heterosexual persons do. The decision in *Bowers* would deny them this right.

The second post-*Bowers* case of principal relevance is *Romer v. Evans* (1996). There the Court struck down class-based legislation directed at homosexuals as a violation of the Equal Protection Clause. . . .

As an alternative argument in this case, counsel for the petitioners and some *amici* contend that *Romer* provides the basis for declaring the Texas statute invalid under the Equal Protection Clause. That is a tenable argument, but we conclude the instant case requires us to address whether *Bowers* itself has continuing validity. Were we to hold the statute invalid under the Equal Protection Clause some might question whether a prohibition would be valid if drawn differently, say, to prohibit the conduct both between same-sex and different-sex participants.

. . .

The foundations of *Bowers* have sustained serious erosion from our recent decisions in *Casey* and *Romer*. When our precedent has been thus weakened, criticism from other sources is of greater significance. In the United States criticism of *Bowers* has been substantial and continuing, disapproving of its reasoning in all respects, not just as to its historical assumptions. . . .

Bowers was not correct when it was decided, and it is not correct today. It ought not to remain binding precedent. *Bowers v. Hardwick* should be and now is overruled.

The present case does not involve minors. It does not involve persons who might be injured or coerced or who are situated in relationships where consent might not easily be refused. It does not involve public conduct or prostitution. It does not involve whether the government must give formal recognition to any relationship that homosexual persons seek to enter. The case does involve two adults who, with full and mutual consent from each other, engaged in sexual practices common to a homosexual lifestyle. The petitioners are entitled to respect for their private lives. The State cannot demean their existence or control their destiny by making their private sexual conduct a crime. Their right to liberty under the Due Process Clause gives them the full right to engage in their conduct without intervention of the government. "It is a promise of the Constitution that there is a realm of personal liberty which the government may not enter" (*Casey*). The Texas statute furthers no legitimate state interest which can justify its intrusion into the personal and private life of the individual.

Had those who drew and ratified the Due Process Clauses of the Fifth Amendment or the Fourteenth Amendment known the components of liberty in its manifold possibilities, they might have been more specific. They did not presume to have this insight. They knew times can blind us to certain truths and later generations can see that laws once thought necessary and proper in fact serve only to oppress. As the Constitution endures, persons in every generation can invoke its principles in their own search for greater freedom.

The judgment of the Court of Appeals for the Texas Fourteenth District is reversed. . . .

Justice O'CONNOR, concurring in the judgment.

The Court today overrules *Bowers v. Hardwick* (1986). I joined *Bowers,* and do not join the Court in overruling it. Nevertheless, I agree with the Court that Texas' statute banning same-sex sodomy is unconstitutional. Rather than relying on the substantive component of the Fourteenth Amendment's Due Process Clause, as the Court does, I base my conclusion on the Fourteenth Amendment's Equal Protection Clause.

The Equal Protection Clause of the Fourteenth Amendment "is essentially a direction that all persons similarly situated should be treated alike." . . . Under our rational basis standard of review, "legislation is presumed to be valid and will be sustained if the classification drawn by the statute is rationally related to a legitimate state interest." . . .

The statute at issue here makes sodomy a crime only if a person "engages in deviate sexual intercourse with another individual of the same sex." Sodomy between opposite-sex partners, however, is not a crime in Texas. That is, Texas treats the same conduct differently based solely on the participants. . . .

The Texas statute makes homosexuals unequal in the eyes of the law by making particular conduct—and only that conduct—subject to criminal sanction. . . .

Texas attempts to justify its law, and the effects of the law, by arguing that the statute satisfies rational basis review because it furthers the legitimate governmental interest of the promotion of morality. In *Bowers,* we held that a state law criminalizing sodomy as applied to homosexual couples did not violate substantive due process. We rejected the argument that no rational basis existed to justify the law, pointing to the government's interest in promoting morality. The only question in front of the Court in *Bowers* was whether the substantive component of the Due Process Clause protected a right to engage in homosexual sodomy. *Bowers* did not hold that moral disapproval of a group is a rational basis under the Equal Protection Clause to criminalize homosexual sodomy when heterosexual sodomy is not punished.

This case raises a different issue than *Bowers:* whether, under the Equal Protection Clause, moral disapproval is a legitimate state interest to justify by itself a statute that bans homosexual sodomy, but not heterosexual sodomy. It is not. Moral disapproval of this group, like a bare desire to harm the group, is an interest that is insufficient to satisfy rational basis review under the Equal Protection Clause. . . .

Justice SCALIA, with whom the Chief Justice and Justice THOMAS join, dissenting.

. . .

I

I begin with the Court's surprising readiness to reconsider a decision rendered a mere 17 years ago in *Bowers v. Hardwick.* I do not myself believe in rigid adherence to *stare decisis* in constitutional cases; but I do believe that we should be consistent rather than manipulative in invoking the doctrine. Today's opinions in support of reversal do not bother to distinguish—or indeed, even bother to mention—the paean to *stare decisis* co-authored by three Members of today's majority in *Planned Parenthood v. Casey.* There, when *stare decisis* meant preservation of judicially invented abortion rights, the widespread criticism of *Roe* was strong reason to *reaffirm* it. . . .

Today, however, the widespread opposition to *Bowers,* a decision resolving an issue as "intensely divisive" as the issue in *Roe,* is offered as a reason in favor of overruling it.

. . .

To tell the truth, it does not surprise me, and should surprise no one, that the Court has chosen today to revise the standards of *stare decisis* set forth in *Casey.* It has thereby exposed *Casey's* extraordinary deference to precedent for the result-oriented expedient that it is.

II

Having decided that it need not adhere to *stare decisis,* the Court still must establish that *Bowers* was wrongly decided and that the Texas statute, as applied to petitioners, is unconstitutional.

. . .

Our opinions applying the doctrine known as "substantive due process" hold that the Due Process Clause prohibits States from infringing fundamental liberty interests, unless the infringement is narrowly tailored to serve a compelling state interest. We have held repeatedly, in cases the Court today does not overrule, that *only* fundamental rights qualify for this so-called "heightened scrutiny" protection—that is, rights which are "deeply rooted in this Nation's history and tradition." . . .

Bowers held, first, that criminal prohibitions of homosexual sodomy are not subject to heightened scrutiny because they do not implicate a "fundamental right" under the Due Process Clause. . . . *Bowers* concluded that a right to engage in homosexual sodomy was not "deeply rooted in this Nation's history and tradition."

The Court today does not overrule this holding. Not once does it describe homosexual sodomy as a "fundamental right" or a "fundamental liberty interest," nor does it subject the Texas statute to strict scrutiny. Instead, having failed to establish that the right to homosexual sodomy is "deeply rooted in this Nation's history and tradition," the Court concludes that the application of Texas's statute to petitioners' conduct fails the rational-basis test, and overrules *Bowers'* holding to the contrary. . . .

IV

. . .The Texas statute undeniably seeks to further the belief of its citizens that certain forms of sexual behavior are "immoral and unacceptable" (*Bowers*—the same interest furthered by criminal laws against fornication, bigamy, adultery, adult incest, bestiality, and obscenity). *Bowers* held that this *was* a legitimate state interest. The Court today reaches the opposite conclusion. The Texas statute, it says, "furthers *no legitimate state interest* which can justify its intrusion into the personal and private life of the individual" (emphasis added). The Court embraces instead Justice STEVENS' declaration in his *Bowers* dissent that "the fact that the governing majority in a State has traditionally viewed a particular practice as immoral is not a sufficient reason for upholding a law prohibiting the practice." This effectively decrees the end of all morals legislation. If, as the Court asserts, the promotion of majoritarian sexual morality is not even a *legitimate* state interest, none of the above-mentioned laws can survive rational-basis review.

V

Finally, I turn to petitioners' equal-protection challenge, which no Member of the Court save Justice O'CONNOR embraces: On its face §21.06(a) applies equally to all persons. Men and women, heterosexuals and homosexuals, are all subject to its prohibition of deviate sexual intercourse with someone of the same sex. To be sure, §21.06 does distinguish between the sexes insofar as concerns the partner with whom the sexual acts are performed: men can violate the law only with other men, and women only with other women. But this cannot itself be a denial of equal protection, since it is precisely the same distinction regarding partner that is drawn in state laws prohibiting marriage with someone of the same sex while permitting marriage with someone of the opposite sex.

. . .

Today's opinion is the product of a Court, which is the product of a law-profession culture, that has largely signed on to the so-called homosexual agenda, by which I mean the agenda promoted by some homosexual activists directed at eliminating the moral opprobrium that has traditionally attached to homosexual conduct. . . .

One of the most revealing statements in today's opinion is the Court's grim warning that the criminalization of homosexual conduct is "an invitation to subject homosexual persons to discrimination both in the public and in the private spheres." It is clear from this that the Court has taken sides in the culture war, departing from its role of assuring, as neutral observer, that the democratic rules of engagement are observed. Many Americans do not want persons who openly engage in homosexual conduct as partners in their business, as scoutmasters for their children, as teachers in their children's schools, or as boarders in their home. They view this as protecting themselves and their families from a lifestyle that they believe to be immoral and destructive. The Court views it as "discrimination" which it is the function of our judgments to deter. So imbued is the Court with the law profession's anti-anti-homosexual culture, that it is seemingly unaware that the attitudes of that culture are not obviously "mainstream"; that in most States what the Court calls "discrimination" against those who engage in homosexual acts is perfectly legal; that proposals to ban such "discrimination" under Title VII have repeatedly been rejected by Congress; that in some cases such "discrimination" *is mandated* by federal statute (mandating discharge from the armed forces of any service member who engages in or intends to engage in homosexual acts); and that in some cases such "discrimination" is a constitutional right, see *Boy Scouts of America v. Dale* (2000).

Let me be clear that I have nothing against homosexuals, or any other group, promoting their agenda through normal democratic means. Social perceptions of sexual and other morality change over time, and every group has the right to persuade its fellow citizens that its view of such matters is the best. That homosexuals have achieved some success in that enterprise is attested to by the fact that Texas is one of the few remaining States that criminalize private, consensual homosexual acts. But persuading one's fellow citizens is one thing, and imposing one's views in absence of democratic majority will is something else. I would no more *require* a State to criminalize homosexual acts—or, for that matter, display *any* moral disapprobation of them—than I would *forbid* it to do so. What Texas has chosen to do is well within the range of traditional democratic action, and its hand should not be stayed through the invention of a brand-new "constitutional right" by a Court that is impatient of democratic change. It is indeed true that "later generations can see that laws once thought necessary and proper in fact serve only to oppress," and when that happens, later generations can repeal those laws. But it is the premise of our system that those judgments are to be made by the people, and not imposed by a governing caste that knows best.

One of the benefits of leaving regulation of this matter to the people rather than to the courts is that the people, unlike judges, need not carry things to their logical conclusion. The people may feel that their disapprobation of homosexual conduct is strong enough to disallow homosexual marriage, but not strong enough to criminalize private homosexual acts—and may legislate accordingly. The Court today pretends that it possesses a similar freedom of action, so that that we need not fear judicial imposition of homosexual marriage, as has recently occurred in Canada (in a decision that the Canadian Government has chosen not to appeal; see *Halpern* v. *Toronto* [2003]). At the end of its opinion—after having laid waste the foundations of our rational-basis jurisprudence—the Court says that the present case "does not involve whether the government must give formal recognition to any relationship that homosexual persons seek to enter." Do not believe it. More illuminating than this bald, unreasoned disclaimer is the progression of thought displayed by an earlier passage in the Court's opinion, which notes the constitutional protections afforded to "personal decisions relating to *marriage*, procreation, contraception, family relationships, child rearing, and education," and then declares that "[p]ersons in a homosexual relationship may seek autonomy for these purposes, just as heterosexual persons do." Today's opinion dismantles the structure of constitutional law that has permitted a distinction to be made between heterosexual and homosexual unions, insofar as formal recognition in marriage is concerned. If moral disapprobation of homosexual conduct is "no legitimate state interest" for purposes of proscribing that conduct . . . , what justification could there possibly be for denying the benefits of marriage to homosexual couples exercising "[t]he liberty protected by the Constitution"? . . . This case "does not involve" the issue of homosexual marriage only if one entertains the belief that principle and logic have nothing to do with the decisions of this Court. Many will hope that, as the Court comfortingly assures us, this is so.

The matters appropriate for this Court's resolution are only three: Texas's prohibition of sodomy neither infringes a "fundamental right" (which the Court does not dispute), nor is unsupported by a rational relation to what the Constitution considers a legitimate state interest, nor denies the equal protection of the laws. I dissent.

Justice THOMAS, dissenting.

I join Justice SCALIA's dissenting opinion. I write separately to note that the law before the Court today "is . . . uncommonly silly" (*Griswold v. Connecticut* [1965; Stewart, dissenting]). If I were a member of the Texas Legislature, I would vote to repeal it. Punishing someone for expressing his sexual preference through noncommercial consensual conduct with another adult does not appear to be a worthy way to expend valuable law enforcement resources.

Notwithstanding this, I recognize that as a member of this Court I am not empowered to help petitioners and others similarly situated. My duty, rather, is to "decide cases 'agreeably to the Constitution and laws of the United States.'" And, just like Justice Stewart, I "can find [neither in the Bill of Rights nor any other part of the Constitution a] general right of privacy," or as the Court terms it today, the "liberty of the person both in its spatial and more transcendent dimensions."

CHRONOLOGY

1619	First black slaves arrive in Virginia colony.
1662	Virginia law establishes that the children of slaves will also be slaves.
1680s–1700s	Development of plantation system in the upper South.
1776	Declaration of Independence.
1781	Articles of Confederation ratified.
1787	Northwest Ordinance adopted; included in it is a prohibition of slavery in the territory.
1789	Constitution ratified. Five provisions in it explicitly refer to slavery, although the term itself is never employed.
1790	Slavery permitted in the Southwest Territory.
1807	Congress passes legislation outlawing the slave trade beginning in 1808.
1820	Missouri Compromise adopted, outlawing slavery north of latitude 36'30".
1820	Missouri admitted to the Union as a slave state.
1825	Chief Justice John Marshall, writing in the case of *The Antelope* (1825), holds that the slave trade is "contrary to the law of nature" but "consistent with the law of nations."
1841	In the case of *United States v. Amistad,* the Court rules that because the slave trade is illegal, all the slaves on the Spanish slave ship *Amistad* are free.

1842	In *Prigg v. Pennsylvania,* the Court holds that Pennsylvania's "personal liberty" law prohibiting the extradition of fugitive slaves is unconstitutional.
1848	Seneca Falls Women's Rights Convention issues the Declaration of Sentiments, modeled on the Declaration of Independence.
1850	Fugitive Slave Act of 1793 amended to make it easier for slave owners to reclaim their slaves, part of the so-called Compromise of 1850.
1857	In *Dred Scott v. Sandford,* the Court holds in a 7–2 decision that both the Missouri Compromise is unconstitutional and that blacks could never be citizens.
1862	President Abraham Lincoln issues Emancipation Proclamation declaring that as of January 1, 1863, all slaves in areas in rebellion are free.
1865	Thirteenth Amendment, abolishing slavery, ratified.
1866	Freedmen's Bureau Bill adopted over the veto of President Andrew Johnson. Congress also adopts Civil Rights Act seeking to overturn Chief Justice Taney's definition of citizenship in *Dred Scott.* Fourteenth Amendment proposed.
1867	Military Reconstruction Acts adopted.
1868	Fourteenth Amendment ratified.
1869	In *Ex parte McCardle,* the Court accepts congressional power to restrict its jurisdiction over certain Reconstruction legislation.
1870	Fifteenth Amendment guaranteeing the voting rights of ex-slaves ratified.
1873	*Slaughterhouse Cases* is decided by a vote of 5–4, giving a narrow view of the terms of the Fourteenth Amendment.

1875	Sometimes seen as the last gasp of Reconstruction, the Civil Rights Act prohibits discrimination based on race in inns, theaters, and public transportation. A section prohibiting school segregation is stripped from the bill before the vote.
1877	President Rutherford B. Hayes withdraws federal troops from the South.
1883	By a vote of 8–1, the Court overturns the Civil Rights Act of 1875 (*Civil Rights Cases*).
1890	Force Bill introduced by Representative Henry Cabot Lodge. The bill would have reduced representation from states that denied blacks suffrage and would have enabled the federal government to supervise voting places.
1896	*Plessy v. Ferguson*, by a vote of 8–1, establishes that "separate but equal" does not violate the Fourteenth Amendment's Equal Protection Clause.
1908	In *Muller v. Oregon*, the Court upholds the power of state governments to regulate working conditions for women. Similar legislation affecting men during this period was routinely struck down as unconstitutional.
1909	National Association for the Advancement of Colored People established.
1917	In *Buchanan v. Warley*, the Court strikes down government-enforced residential segregation.
1920	Nineteenth Amendment, enfranchising women, adopted.
1938	Court requires Missouri to admit a black applicant to law school in *Missouri ex re. Gaines v. Canada*.
1939	NAACP Legal Defense Fund established to coordinate attack on segregation.

1948	A unanimous Court finds in *Shelly v. Kraemer* that restrictive housing covenants cannot be enforced by government.
	Democratic Convention adopts civil rights plank, leading to a walkout of many southern delegates.
1954	Supreme Court unanimously finds school segregation unconstitutional in *Brown v. Board of Education of Topeka, Kansas.*
1955	In subsequent enforcement decision, the Court provides that federal district courts will supervise the desegregation process, which will occur "with all deliberate speed."
1956	Congress passes first Civil Rights Act since Reconstruction.
1961	President John Kennedy creates President's Commission on the Status of Women.
1962	Court enters "political thicket" and finds malapportionment a violation of a fundamental right guaranteed by the Equal Protection Clause.
1964	Congress adopts a significant Civil Rights Act based on the federal government's power over interstate commerce, prohibiting among other things discrimination in public accommodations and establishing the Equal Employment Opportunity Commission. The act also prohibits discrimination against women.
	Chief Justice Earl Warren writes opinion in the case of *Reynolds v. Sims* requiring that all legislatures be apportioned on the basis of population.
1965	Voting Rights Act authorizes federal government to register voters in areas where there had been discrimination or low rates of voter participation.

1966	National Organization for Women (NOW) established, with Betty Friedan as first president.

1967 President Lyndon Johnson nominates Thurgood Marshall, the first African American to sit on the Supreme Court.

1968 Court's decision in *Green v. County School Board* calls for integration and not simply the end of segregation in formerly segregated schools.

1971 In *Swann v. Charlotte-Mecklenburg Board of Education,* the Court upholds use of busing to end segregation and achieve racially balanced schools.

In *Reed v. Reed,* the Burger Court stakes a new stance on laws that treat men and women differently.

1972 Congress proposes ill-fated Equal Rights Amendment.

1976 Court announces in *Craig v. Boren* intermediate standard of review for government actions that employ gender as a classification.

1978 In *Regents of the University of California v. Bakke,* the Court holds that the use of quotas violates the Equal Protection Clause but upholds the use of race as one factor among others in fostering diversity.

1981 Sandra Day O'Connor confirmed as first woman to sit on Supreme Court. President Ronald Reagan had promised during the campaign of 1980 to nominate a woman.

1986 A 5–4 majority of the Court upholds Georgia's antisodomy statute in *Bowers v. Hardwick.*

1991 President George H. W. Bush's nominee, Clarence Thomas, is confirmed by Senate to replace retiring Justice Thurgood Marshall.

1993   Ruth Bader Ginsburg, nominated by President Bill Clinton, becomes second woman to serve on the Supreme Court.

1995   By a vote of 5–4, the Court appears to signal in *Adarand Constructors, Inc. v. Pena* its intention to require that government affirmative action policies meet test of "compelling state interest."

1996   Justice Ginsburg, in the case of *United States v. Virginia,* introduces a new test for cases involving gender discrimination. Such classifications must meet the standard of representing an "exceedingly persuasive justification."

2003   A majority of the Court in *Grutter v. Bollinger* upholds affirmative action in education, endorsing Justice Powell's opinion in *Bakke* that diversity is a "compelling state interest."

The Court also overturns *Bowers,* finding that state sodomy statutes are unconstitutional, in *Lawrence v. Texas.*

TABLE OF CASES

Please note that 2003 cases have not yet been assigned locator numbers.

ANNOTATED BIBLIOGRAPHY

GENERAL WORKS

Now in its seventh edition, Alfred H. Kelly, Winfred Harbison, and Herman Belz, 1991, *The American Constitution: Its Origins and Development*, 2 volumes (New York: W.W. Norton) remains the definitive study of constitutional history. "Slavery and the Constitution" (chapter 14), "Reconstruction: The Nationalization of Civil Rights" (chapter 17), "Congressional Reconstruction" (chapter 18), and "Civil Rights and the Constitution" (chapter 29) provide a broad overview of the subject, along with a wealth of detail and sources for the student who wants to pursue specific paths of research. Now in its eighth edition, Henry J. Abraham and Barbara A. Perry, 1998, *Freedom and the Court: Civil Rights and Liberties in the United States* (Lawrence: University Press of Kansas) provides a broad survey from the very first cases to the most recent dealing with race and gender in "Race: The American Dilemma: The Evolving Equal Protection of the Laws" (chapter 7), and "Gender and Race under the New Equal Protection" (chapter 8). Gerald Gunther is generally recognized as the preeminent scholarly interpreter of the Fourteenth Amendment's Equal Protection Clause, and Kathleen Sullivan and Gerald Gunther, 2001, *Constitutional Law*, 14th ed. (New York: Foundation Press), is probably the best casebook to use for purposes of studying the Equal Protection Clause. Gerald Gunther's classic article on the subject was published in 1972: "The Supreme Court 1971 Term: Forward: In Search of Evolving Doctrine on a Changing Court; A Model for a Newer Equal Protection," *Harvard Law Review* 86: 1–48. Kermit Hall, ed., 1992, *The Oxford Companion to the Supreme Court of the United States* (New York: Oxford University Press) is an invaluable resource for any student of the Court and constitutional law. Each selection contains helpful citations to further sources. Finally, J. W. Peltason, 1997, *Corwin and Peltason's Understanding the Constitution,* 14th ed. (Fort Worth: Harcourt Brace College Publishers) provides a carefully crafted analysis of how the Court has interpreted the various sections of the Constitution.

The late U.S. Appeals Court Judge A. Leon Higginbotham Jr., 1978, *In the Matter of Color: Race and The American Legal Process: The Colonial Period* (New York: Oxford University Press) provides an in-depth examination of the development of slavery from the first settlement in Virginia until the American Revolution. C. Vann Woodward's classic text, 1966, *The Strange Career of Jim Crow,* 2nd rev. ed. (New York: Oxford University Press) documents how the South came to be segregated in the period after the end of Reconstruction.

The Constitution and Nineteenth-Century Cases

Slavery was an issue that threatened the Constitutional Convention of 1787. William M. Wiecek, 1977, *The Sources of Antislavery Constitutionalism in America, 1760–1848* (Ithaca, NY: Cornell University Press) traces its development. Paul Finkelman, ed., 1981, *An Imperfect Union: Slavery, Federalism, and Comity* (Chapel Hill: University of North Carolina Press) and Mark V. Tushnet, 1981, *The American Law of Slavery, 1810–1860: Considerations of Humanity and Interest* (Princeton, NJ: Princeton University Press) trace the effects of slavery on the development of American law in the nineteenth century. The enforcement of the Fugitive Slave Laws and the ways in which the northern states sought to counter their application is the subject of Thomas D. Morris, 1974, *Free Men All: The Personal Liberty Laws of the North: 1780–1861* (Baltimore: Johns Hopkins University Press). Don E. Fehrenbacker, 1978, *The Dred Scott Case: Its Significance in American Law and Politics* (New York: Oxford University Press) provides easily the best discussion of this momentous decision of the Taney Court. Walter Ehrlich, 1979, *They Have No Rights: Dred Scott's Struggle for Freedom* (Westport, CT: Greenwood Press) offers a shorter work than Fehrenbacker's on the case. John R. Howard, 1999, *The Shifting Wind: The Supreme Court and Civil Rights from Reconstruction to Brown* (Albany: State University of New York Press) examines how the Court gutted congressional efforts to enforce equal rights and led to the establishment in

Plessy of "separate but equal." Howard also examines the twentieth-century cases leading up to *Brown.* Lois B. Moreland, 1970, *White Racism and the Law* (Columbus, OH: Charles E. Merrill) examines the consequences of the distinction the Court made in the *Civil Rights Cases* between state action and private action.

THE "FREEDOM AMENDMENTS" AND RECONSTRUCTION

Although some have seen the Civil War as the true American revolution, Herman Belz, 1998, *Abraham Lincoln, Constitutionalism, and Equal Protection* (New York: Fordham University Press) argues that the Constitution of 1787 survived and that the process by which it was changed was evolutionary and not revolutionary. Phillip S. Paludan, 1975, *A Covenant with Death: The Constitution, Law, and Equality in the Civil War Era* (Urbana: University of Illinois Press) offers another perspective. The definitive study of the period is undoubtedly Charles Fairman, 1971, *Reconstruction and Reunion,* 2 volumes (New York: Macmillan). Fairman provides a highly detailed account of the drafting of the amendments and of other Reconstruction-era legislation. Another source for students interested in the background of the Fourteenth Amendment is Joseph B. James, 1956, *The Framing of the Fourteenth Amendment* (Urbana: University of Illinois Press). James is also the author of the 1984 work, *The Ratification of the Fourteenth Amendment* (Macon, GA: Mercer University Press). Raoul Berger, 1997, *Government by Judiciary: The Transformation of the Fourteenth Amendment,* 2nd ed. (Indianapolis: Liberty Fund) presents a very different view of the motives behind the framing of the Fourteenth Amendment. Two chapters in particular, "Negro Suffrage Was Excluded," and "Segregated Schools," should be of most interest to those interested in civil rights. William E. Nelson, 1988, *The Fourteenth Amendment: From Political Principle to Judicial Doctrine* (Cambridge, MA: Harvard University Press) offers both a description of the drafting of the amendment and how it was interpreted by the Court up to *Lochner.* The failure of the post–Civil War amendments to address the issue of women's rights and the fact that they introduced, for the first time in the Constitution, gender-specific language, is addressed by Suzanne M. Marilley, 1996, *Woman Suffrage and the Origins of Liberal Feminism in the United States: 1820–1920* (Cambridge, MA: Harvard University Press); Stanley I. Kutler, 1968, *Judicial Power and Reconstruction Politics* (Chicago: University of Chicago Press) examines the struggle for power between Congress and the courts during the post–Civil War period.

BROWN V. BOARD OF EDUCATION

Rarely does a book succeed in satisfying both scholar and general reader as much as Richard Kluger, 1975, *Simple Justice* (New York: Alfred Knopf). Kluger surveys the development of Jim Crow laws, the NAACP attack on segregation, the genesis and disposition of the *Brown* case, and how that decision continues to affect American society. For those who seek a brief description of *Brown*, Daniel M. Berman, 1966, *It Is So Ordered: The Supreme Court Rules on School Segregation* (New York: W. W. Norton) is more than satisfying at 161 pages including appendices. William H. Harbaugh, 1973, *Lawyer's Lawyer: The Life of John W. Davis* (New York: Oxford University Press) details the lengthy career of the attorney chosen by former Supreme Court justice and South Carolina governor James F. Byrnes to defend that state's commitment to segregated education. Among those opposing Davis's efforts was Constance Baker Motley, 1998, *Equal Justice under Law: An Autobiography of Constance Baker Motley* (New York: Farrar, Straus, and Giroux). Baker joined the Legal Defense Fund in 1945 and later became the first African American woman on the federal bench. J. Harvie Wilkinson, 1979, *From Brown to Bakke: The Supreme Court and School Integration, 1954–1978* (New York: Oxford University Press) provides a careful critique of how the Burger Court failed to follow in the footsteps of its predecessor and how the focus of the debate has switched from ending segregation to achieving integration. James T. Patterson, 2001, *Brown v. Board of Education: A Civil Rights Milestone and Its Troubled Legacy* (New York: Oxford University Press) takes the legacy of *Brown* up to the current controversies involving race in the United States. Leon Friedman, 1969, *Argument: The Oral Argument before the Supreme Court in Brown v. Board of Education of Topeka, 1952–55* (New York: Chelsea House) provides the full arguments before the Court. Mark Whitman, ed., *Removing a Badge of Slavery: The Record of Brown v. Board of Education* (Princeton, NJ: Markus Wiener), provides some of the briefs filed in the case as well as commentary by distinguished scholars. Bernard D. Reams Jr. and Paul E. Wilson, 1975, *Segregation and the Fourteenth Amendment in the States* (Buffalo: William S. Hein) contains an excellent collection of the arguments made by the defenders of segregation with regard to the "original intent" of the framers of the Fourteenth Amendment. William Gillette, 1965, *The*

Right to Vote: Politics and the Passage of the Fifteenth Amendment (Baltimore: Johns Hopkins University Press) provides a detailed description of the process by which the Fifteenth Amendment guaranteeing the right of the newly freed slaves to vote was framed, proposed, and adopted. Gillette makes heavy use of the records of the debates as well as contemporary articles from newspapers. J. W. Peltason, 1971, *Fifty-eight Lonely Men: Southern Federal Judges and School Desegregation* (Urbana: University of Illinois Press) tells the story of how federal district court judges, charged by *Brown II* with the implementation of desegregation, tackled this thankless task. John H. McCord, ed., 1969, *With All Deliberate Speed: Civil Rights Theory and Reality* (Urbana: University of Illinois Press) offers a collection of articles devoted to a description of how civil rights was or was not being achieved. Stephen L. Wasby et al., 1977, *Desegregation from Brown to Alexander* (Carbondale: Southern Illinois University Press) examine the efforts to achieve the promise of *Brown* up through 1969 and the advent of the Burger Court.

CIVIL RIGHTS

Mark Tushnet, 1987, *The NAACP's Legal Strategy against Segregated Education, 1925–1950* (Chapel Hill: University of North Carolina Press) examines the NAACP and later the Legal Defense Fund's efforts to use the courts to reverse *Plessy* in the realm of education. *Brown II* entrusted the enforcement of the Court's decisions to the federal district courts. Charles V. Hamilton, 1973, *The Bench and the Ballot: Southern Federal Judges and Black Voters* (New York: Oxford University Press) focuses on the Voting Rights Act of 1965 and the efforts of federal judges to carry it out. A 1976 book by Steven F. Lawson, *Black Ballots: Voting Rights in the South: 1944–1969* (New York: Columbia University Press) details the struggle for voting rights by Blacks beginning with challenges to the poll tax and the white primary and progressing through the adoption of the Civil Rights Act of 1964 and the Voting Rights Act of 1965 and their consequences. Alexander M. Bickel, 1967, "The Voting Rights Cases," in *The Supreme Court Review, 1966* (Chicago: University of Chicago Press), 79–102, looks at the case of *Katzenbach v. Morgan* and the Court's expansive reading of the Fifteenth Amendment's enforcement power. Although the Court generally receives the most attention in talking about civil rights, the other two branches in many ways have played a more important role. Certainly, this is true in terms of enforcement. Brian K. Landsberg, 1997, *Enforcing Civil Rights:*

Race Discrimination and the Department of Justice (Lawrence: University Press of Kansas) examines the justices' role from the 1960s to the present. Robert D. Loevy, ed., 1997, *The Civil Rights Act of 1964: The Passage of the Law That Ended Racial Segregation* (Albany: State University of New York Press) provides a collection of articles dealing with the passage of the landmark legislation, including one authored by one of the act's chief advocates, Senator Hubert H. Humphrey. A more detailed analysis of the passage of the bill can be found in Daniel M. Berman, 1966, *A Bill Becomes a Law: Congress Enacts Civil Rights Legislation* (New York: Macmillan). Richard Bardolph and Bernard Grofman, ed., 2000, *Legacies of the 1964 Civil Rights Act* (Charlottesville: University Press of Virginia) examines the social and political effects of this major landmark in civil rights legislation. Hugh Davis Graham, 1990, *The Civil Rights Era: Origins and Development of National Policy, 1960–1972* (New York: Oxford University Press) offers a broad overview of the social and political changes that occurred in these tumultuous years.

AFFIRMATIVE ACTION

The first challenge to affirmative action policies was brought by Marco De-Funis. DeFunis challenged the admission practices of the University of Washington Law School. The Supreme Court refused to take the case, declaring it moot. An excellent account of DeFunis's case is provided in Robert M. O'Neil, 1975, *Discriminating against Discrimination: Preferential Admissions and the DeFunis Case* (Bloomington: Indiana University Press). Richard A. Posner, 1975, "The DeFunis Case and the Constitutionality of Preferential Treatment of Racial Minorities" in *The Supreme Court Review, 1974* (Chicago: University of Chicago Press), 1–32; Allan P. Sindler, 1978, *Bakke, DeFunis, and Minority Admissions* (New York: Longman), although written a quarter of a century ago, still provide an excellent starting point for students of affirmative action. Timothy J. O'Neill, 1985, *Bakke and the Politics of Equality: Friends and Foes in the Classroom of Litigation* (Middletown, CT: Wesleyan University Press) reviews the motivations of the various parties involved in bringing the case to the Supreme Court. Jo Ann Ooiman Robinson, ed., 2002, *Affirmative Action: A Documentary History* (Westport, CT: Greenwood Press) provides an excellent compendium of legislation, executive orders, and commentary on affirmative action from the beginning to the present. Henry J. Abraham is one of academe's leading critics of affirmative action. An excellent representation of Abraham's views is found in Gary L. McDowell, ed., 1981, *Taking the Constitution Seriously: Essays on the Constitution and Constitutional Law* (Dubuque, IA: Kendall-Hunt), specifically in the selection "Some Post-*Bakke*-and-*Weber* Reflections on 'Reverse Discrimination.'" A contrast to Abraham's viewpoint is provided by Charles R. Lawrence III and Mari J. Matsuda, 1997, *We Won't Go Back: Making a Case for Affirmative Action* (Boston: Houghton Mifflin). A philosophic argument concerning affirmative action is made by Ronald J. Fiscus, 1992, *The Constitutional Logic of Affirmative Action* (Durham, NC: Duke University Press). David A. Strauss, 1987, "The Myth of Colorblindness," in *The Supreme Court Review, 1986* (Chicago: University of Chicago Press), 90–134, argues that the famous phrase from the elder Justice Harlan's dissent in *Plessy* is unhelpful in solving current issues of affirmative action. Gabriel J. Chin, 1998, *Affirmative Action and the Constitution,* 3 volumes (New York: Garland Publishing Company) provides the most complete collection of articles, cases, and legislation available on the subject, beginning in 1964 and ending in 1997. Venturing into the matter of prediction is Mary Anne Case, 2001, "Lessons for the Future of Affirmative Action from the Past of the Religion Clauses," in *The Supreme Court Review, 2000* (Chicago: University of Chicago Press), 325–356. Case sees "colorblindness" as analogous to the position of those who argue for absolute and total separation between church and state. Neither, according to Case, is acceptable.

Busing

Outspoken conservative University of Texas law professor Lino Graglia found his nomination to the U.S. Court of Appeals blocked by the Senate. In part, his 1976 book *Disaster by Decree: The Supreme Court Decisions on Race and the Schools* (Ithaca, NY: Cornell University Press) helped opponents of his nomination win. Eleanor P. Wolf, 1978, "Northern School Desegregation and Residential Choice," in *The Supreme Court Review, 1977* (Chicago: University of Chicago Press), 63–86, looks at the effect of de facto segregation on the problem of busing.

Fundamental Rights

The fact that the Court did not posit a fundamental right to education in the Texas school funding case surprised many. Judith Areen and Leonard Ross, 1974, "The Rodriguez Case: Judicial Oversight of School Finance" in *The*

Supreme Court Review, 1973 (Chicago: University of Chicago Press), 33–56, relate how the case came about and how the Court reacted. Dennis J. Hutchinson, 1983, "More Substantive Equal Protection? A Note on *Plyer v. Doe*," in *The Supreme Court Review, 1982* (Chicago: University of Chicago Press), 167–194, looked at the Court's decision requiring Texas to allow the children of illegal immigrants to attend public schools. John Pincus, ed., 1974, *School Finance in Transition* (Cambridge, MA: Ballinger Publishing Company) looks at the California case of *Serrano v. Priest,* which many thought would influence the Supreme Court's subsequent ruling in *Rodriguez,* and the developments that immediately followed that decision.

GENDER

Claire Sherman Thomas, 1991, *Sex Discrimination in a Nutshell* (St. Paul, MN: West Publishing Co.) provides a good start for those studying the evolution of the Court's current position on women's rights. Dorothy L. Rhode, 1989, *Justice and Gender: Sex Discrimination and the Law* (Cambridge, MA: Harvard University Press) offers analysis of the claims for equal rights by women and current matters of contention. Leslie Goldstein, 1979, *The Constitutional Rights of Women: Cases in Law and Social Change* (New York: Longman) remains valuable today because it places the issue of sex discrimination in the broader context of constitutional law development. A more recent work edited by Goldstein, 1992, *The Difference Debate: Feminist Jurisprudence* (Lanham, MD: Rowman and Littlefield) brings together the views of various scholars on issues involving women's rights and equality. Sometimes referred to as the Thurgood Marshall of the women's movement, Ruth Bader Ginsburg, 1976, *The Supreme Court Review, 1975* (Chicago: University of Chicago Press), 1–24, examines the Court's decisions on gender during the 1973 and 1974 terms, including the landmark ruling in *Frontiero*. Marlene Stein Wortman has edited a two-volume collection of materials, 1985, *Women in American Law* (New York: Holmes and Meier) that include laws, cases, and readings dealing with the issue from colonial times until the 1980s.

RIGHT TO VOTE

Written in the wake of the Supreme Court's decision in *Reynolds v. Sims,* Carl A. Auerbach, 1964, "The Reapportionment Cases: One Person, One Vote: One Vote, One Value," in *The Supreme Court Review,* 1965 (Chicago: University of Chicago Press), 1–87, reviews how the Court ventured into Felix Frankfurter's "political thicket" and the results. Robert B. McKay, 1965, *Reapportionment: The Law and Politics of Equal Representation* (New York: Twentieth Century Fund) examines both the *Baker* and *Reynolds* decisions and provides highly detailed state-by-state descriptions of apportionment practices. Richard C. Cortner, 1970, *The Reapportionment Cases* (Knoxville: University of Tennessee Press) also covers both major reapportionment cases and provides selections from the oral arguments as well as careful analysis of the Court's rulings. Robert C. Dixon Jr., 1968, *Democratic Representation: Reapportionment in Law and Politics* (New York: Oxford University Press) provides valuable insight into the efforts of Congress to overturn *Reynolds.* Alexander Keyssar, 2000, *The Right to Vote: The Contested History of Democracy in the United States* (New York: Basic Books) traces the growth of the franchise from the adoption of the Constitution until today. Chandler Davidson, ed., 1984, *Minority Vote Dilution* (Washington, DC: Howard University Press) provides a collection of articles that look at the many ways by which black voting strength is minimized by political stratagems of the majority.

The issue of gerrymandering is examined by Dean Alfange Jr., 1987, "Gerrymandering and the Constitution: Into the Thorns of the Thicket at Last," in *The Supreme Court Review, 1986* (Chicago: University of Chicago Press), 176–258. Pamela S. Karlan, 1994, "All over the Map: The Supreme Court's Voting Rights Trilogy," in *The Supreme Court Review, 1993* (Chicago: University of Chicago Press), 245–288, looks at the current state of confusion resulting from the Court's often apparently contradictory decisions concerning legislative apportionment and race. Samuel Issacharoff, 1995, "The Constitutional Contours of Race and Politics, in *The Supreme Court Review, 1995* (Chicago: University of Chicago Press), 45–70, focuses on the "max-black" districting case of *Reno v. Shaw.*

SUPREME COURT JUSTICES

Despite the opinion he wrote in *Dred Scott*, Chief Justice Roger Brooke Taney is still considered one of the "great" justices of the Supreme Court. Among the biographies of Taney are Walker Lewis, 1965, *Without Fear or Favor: A Biography of Roger Brooke Taney* (Boston: Houghton Mifflin) and Carl B. Swisher, 1935, *Roger Taney* (New York: Macmillan). Tinsley E. Yarbrough, 1995, *Judicial Enigma: The First Justice Harlan* (New York: Oxford University Press) puts Harlan's famous dissents in the *Civil Rights Cases* and *Plessy v. Ferguson* in perspective.

To understand the change that took place on the Court as a result of the so-called "judicial revolution of 1937," Alpheus Thomas Mason, 1956, *Harlan Fiske Stone: Pillar of the Law* (New York: Viking Press) offers the definitive study of the justice whose famous footnote 4 set the tone for the Court in the years to come. Hugo L. Black's appointment to the Supreme Court by President Franklin D. Roosevelt ushered in the dawn of the "Modern Court." Gerald T. Dunne, 1977, *Hugo Black and the Judicial Revolution* (New York: Simon and Schuster) provides a detailed study of Black's rise to the Court and devotes a chapter to the *Brown* decision and Black's role in the result. Roger K. Newman, 1994, *Hugo Black: A Biography* (New York: Fordham University Press) provides a biography that surveys Black's thirty-four years on the high bench. James F. Simon, 1989, *The Antagonists: Hugo Black, Felix Frankfurter, and Civil Liberties in Modern America* (New York: Simon and Schuster), apart from outlining what divided these two Roosevelt appointees, deals with their work together in ensuring unanimity in *Brown.* Also useful in this regard is Melvin I. Urofsky, 1991, *Felix Frankfurter: Judicial Restraint and Individual Liberties* (Boston: Twayne), which devotes a full chapter to the topic "Civil Rights and the Super Chief." G. Edward White, 1982, *Earl Warren: A Public Life* (New York: Oxford University Press) focuses more on Warren as an individual and how he saw his role on the Court than the cases he decided. An exception is *Brown,* a case White sees as shaping the chief justice. Bernard Schwartz, 1983, *Super Chief: Earl Warren and his Supreme Court: A Judicial Biography* (New York: New York University Press) provides a highly detailed review of the Warren Court and its decisions. Chapter 3, "Warren and the *Brown* Case," offers insight into the Court's reaction to the issues presented by *Brown* and its companion cases. Jack Harrison Pollack, 1979, *Earl Warren: The Judge Who Changed America* (Englewood Cliffs, NJ: Prentice-Hall) is a more popularly oriented biography. Justice William J. Brennan is seen more and more as possibly the most influential justice of the twentieth century. His long tenure and prolific output of opinions will keep biographers busy for much of the twenty-first century. Journalist Kim Isaac Eisler presents a highly readable study of Brennan in his 1993 book, *A Justice for All: William J. Brennan, Jr., and the Decisions that Transformed America* (New York: Simon and Schuster). E. Joshua Rosenkranz and Bernard Schwartz, eds., 1997, *Justice Brennan's Enduring Influence: Reason and Passion* (New York: W. W. Norton) offer the reader a variety of articles by practitioners, scholars, and reporters. The section on "Equality" is helpful on issues of gender, race, and voting rights. Earl M. Maltz, 2000, *The Chief*

Justiceship of Warren Burger, 1969–1986 (Columbia: University of South Carolina Press) is part of a series published by University of South Carolina Press on the chief justices. In addition to a chapter on race, there is also a valuable chapter on nonracial classifications and the Burger Court. Vincent Blasi is the editor of a 1983 work, *The Burger Court: The Counter-Revolution that Wasn't* (New Haven: Yale University Press) that includes an article by Paul Brest on race and one by future Justice Ruth Bader Ginsburg on gender discrimination. No justice exercised more power in terms of casting the decisive fifth vote on the Burger Court than Justice Lewis F. Powell. Major examples include *Bakke* and *Bowers v. Hardwick*. John C. Jeffries Jr., a former clerk for Powell and now professor at the University of Virginia School of Law, is the author of the 1994 biography, *Justice Lewis F. Powell, Jr.: A Biography* (New York: Charles Scribner's Sons). Jeffries's biography contains informative chapters on "Race and the Public School," "*Bakke* and Beyond," and "Changing Times *(Bowers)*." Randall W. Bland, 1973, *Private Pressure on Public Law: The Legal Career of Justice Thurgood Marshall* (Port Washington, NY: Kennikat Press) provides a thorough review of Marshall's career prior to his confirmation in 1967 as an associate justice. Mark V. Tushnet, 1994, *Making Civil Rights Law: Thurgood Marshall and the Supreme Court, 1936–1961* (New York: Oxford University Press) offers a fuller description of Marshall's work as the NAACP's lead attorney. His 1997 book, *Making Constitutional Law: Thurgood Marshall and the Supreme Court, 1961–1991* (New York: Oxford University Press), however, provides the best review of Marshall and his work on the Court. Juan Williams, author of *Eyes on the Prize,* provides a very readable study of Marshall both as lawyer and justice in his 1998 book, *Thurgood Marshall: American Revolutionary* (New York: Times Books). An earlier study of Chief Justice William Rehnquist is Sue Davis, 1989, *Justice Rehnquist and the Constitution* (Princeton, NJ: Princeton University Press). Davis demonstrates how early in his judicial career Rehnquist had developed his own philosophy on the Equal Protection Clause. The ability of Chief Justice Rehnquist to marshal the Court hangs frequently on the vote of Justice Sandra Day O'Connor, who, according to Nancy Maveety, 1996, is *The Strategist on the Supreme Court: Justice Sandra Day O'Connor* (Lanham, MD: Rowman and Littlefield). Occupying the conservative wing of the current Court are Justices Antonin Scalia and Clarence Thomas. Scott Douglas Gerber, 1999, *First Principles: The Jurisprudence of Clarence Thomas* (New York: New York University Press) presents a clear picture of the second African American to sit on the Court and puts particular emphasis on

Thomas's role in issues involving civil rights. Howard A. Brisbin Jr., 1997, *Justice Antonin Scalia and the Conservative Revival* (Baltimore: Johns Hopkins University Press) and David A. Schultz and Christopher E. Smith, 1996, *The Jurisprudential Vision of Justice Antonin Scalia* (Lanham, MD: Rowman and Littlefield) provide a good basis for understanding the Court's most eloquent if also most conservative spokesperson and his drive for a "color-blind" Constitution.

THE U.S. SUPREME COURT

Two excellent introductions to how the Court operates are among the classics in the discipline. The seventh edition (1998) of Henry J. Abraham's *The Judicial Process: An Introductory Analysis of the Courts of the United States, England, and France* (New York: Oxford University Press), provides an in-depth look at how the judiciary operates and the how judges make their decisions. Walter F. Murphy, C. Herman Pritchett, and Lee Epstein have kept up to date the finest collection of articles about the workings of the judiciary in the fifth edition (2002) of *Courts, Judges, and Politics* (Boston: McGraw-Hill). C. Herman Pritchett, one of the most distinguished writers on the Supreme Court, provides a carefully reasoned analysis of the record of the Vinson Court in his 1954 book, *Civil Liberties and the Vinson Court* (Chicago: University of Chicago Press). Although the Court under Chief Justice Fred Vinson tended to hew to a conservative, self-restraint-oriented position, its decisions on race were cut from quite a different bolt of cloth. Melvin L. Urofsky, 1997, *Division and Discord: The Supreme Court under Stone and Vinson, 1941–1953* (Columbia: University of South Carolina Press) details the tensions that dominated the Court prior to the appointment of Earl Warren in 1953. Richard H. Sayler et al.'s 1969 edited work, *The Warren Court: A Critical Analysis* (New York: Chelsea House) provides a valuable portrait of Chief Justice Earl Warren by Anthony Lewis, then the *New York Times*'s reporter on the Court, as well as chapters on the reapportionment decisions and desegregation. James F. Simon, in his 1973 work *In His Own Image: The Supreme Court in Richard Nixon's America* (New York: Donald McKay) paints a picture of the Burger Court as one that would dramatically reverse the civil liberties and civil rights advances of the Warren Court, which never occurred. Bob Woodward and Scott Armstrong, 1979, relying on the tales and tricks of the justices' own clerks, provided an unsettling (for some) study of how the Burger Court operated in *The Brethren: Inside the Supreme Court* (New York: Simon and Schuster).

Tinsley E. Yarbrough, 2002, *The Rehnquist Court and the Constitution* (New York: Oxford University Press) analyzes the changes brought by the ascendancy of Chief Justice Rehnquist and his conservative allies on the Court in the realm of civil liberties and civil rights. Yarbrough provides careful and detailed analysis of all the major cases. Louis Fisher and Neal Devins, 2001, *Political Dynamics of Constitutional Law* (St. Paul, MN: West Group) and Terri Jennings Peretti, 1999, *In Defense of a Political Court* (Princeton, NJ: Princeton University Press) are major forces within the study of constitutional law bent on emphasizing the highly political nature of what the Supreme Court does.

INTERNET SOURCES

Internet sources pop up as often as mushrooms after the rain; some also disappear as quickly. Web addresses also seem to change for no apparent reason.

Supreme Court Opinions

There are a variety of sites on which Supreme Court opinions can be found. Each site has its own advantages and fans. The brief comments below should not be read as cataloging everything that can be found at a particular site, but only a few highlights.

Cornell Law School (http://www.law.cornell.edu). Maintained by the Legal Information Institute, the Cornell Law School site gives access both to state constitutions and to state and federal laws.

Findlaw (http://www.findlaw.com). Arguably the best law-related site, Findlaw has Supreme Court decisions going back to 1893. It also allows access to decisions of the U.S. Courts of Appeals and many state courts as well as law-related news stories.

Oyez Project (http://www.oyez.nwu.org). The invention of Professor Jerry Goldman, the Oyez site has all oral arguments before the Court since 1995 and seeks eventually to provide access back to 1955, when arguments were first taped. Also located at the site is a "virtual tour" of the Supreme Court Building and information on the justices.

Supreme Court of the United States (http://supremecourtus.gov). The official site of the U.S. Supreme Court. Among the many features of this site is access to the Court's docket and schedule for oral argument. It also provides access to related Web sites, including the Department of Justice and the Solicitor General's Office.

Organizations

American Bar Association (http://www.abanet.org/home.html). The ABA has a section on its home page highlighting its diversity initiatives.

American Civil Liberties Union (http://www.aclu.org). The ACLU has sections on its home page devoted to the subjects of racial equality, women's rights, and lesbian and gay rights.

Center for Individual Rights (http://www.cir-usa.org). A conservative organization that is much involved in challenging the use of race in admissions practices in colleges and universities.

Eagle Forum (http://www.eagleforum.org). Founded by Phyllis Schlafly to oppose the Equal Rights Amendment, Eagle Forum continues to monitor what it sees as the excesses of feminist drives for gender neutrality.

Equal Employment Opportunity Commission (www.eeoc.gov). In addition to providing updates on the current activity of the EEOC, this site allows the student quick access to federal antidiscrimination legislation.

Leadership Conference on Civil Rights (http://civilrights.org). The site of an umbrella organization of groups supporting civil rights.

National Association for the Advancement of Colored People (www.naacp.org). This site provides a history of the NAACP and information on its current activities.

NAACP Legal Defense Fund (http://wwwnaacpldf.org). Founded in 1939, the Legal Defense Fund bore the brunt of litigation aimed at ending school segregation. Its Web site gives information on current litigation that it has undertaken.

National Organization for Women (http://www.now.org). NOW keeps abreast of legal developments, court decisions, and the judicial selection process in order to advance its goals of ending gender and other forms of alleged discrimination.

General Information

Affirmative Action and Diversity Project (http://aad.english.ucsb.edu/aa.html). Maintained at the University of California at Santa Barbara, the site has a great deal of material on affirmative action questions in California. It also has an excellent collection of articles on the subject.

"Color-Blind" Sites

Adversity.net links page (http://www.adversity.net/topten.htm). This Web page provides links to a vast array of organizations, groups, and foundations opposed to use of race in making decisions.

University of Colorado Libraries Affirmative Action Page (http://www-libraries.colorado.edu/ps/gov/us/affact.htm). This page provides a quick entrance to government sites dealing with affirmative action.

University of Wisconsin–Stout Gender Discrimination Site (http://www.uwstout.edu/affirm/women/links.htm). This page provides links to a host of organizations championing women's and gay and lesbian rights.

INDEX

About the Author

Francis Graham Lee is professor of political science at St. Joseph's University in Philadelphia, Pennsylvania.